Denny Colt, a young criminologist,
believed to have lost his life in a fight against crime,
was buried in a state of suspended animation.

He awoke one day in Wildwood Cemetery,
determined to carry on his struggle...
his true identity known only to Police Commissioner Dolan.

He is feared by criminals of all stripes as the SPIRIT!

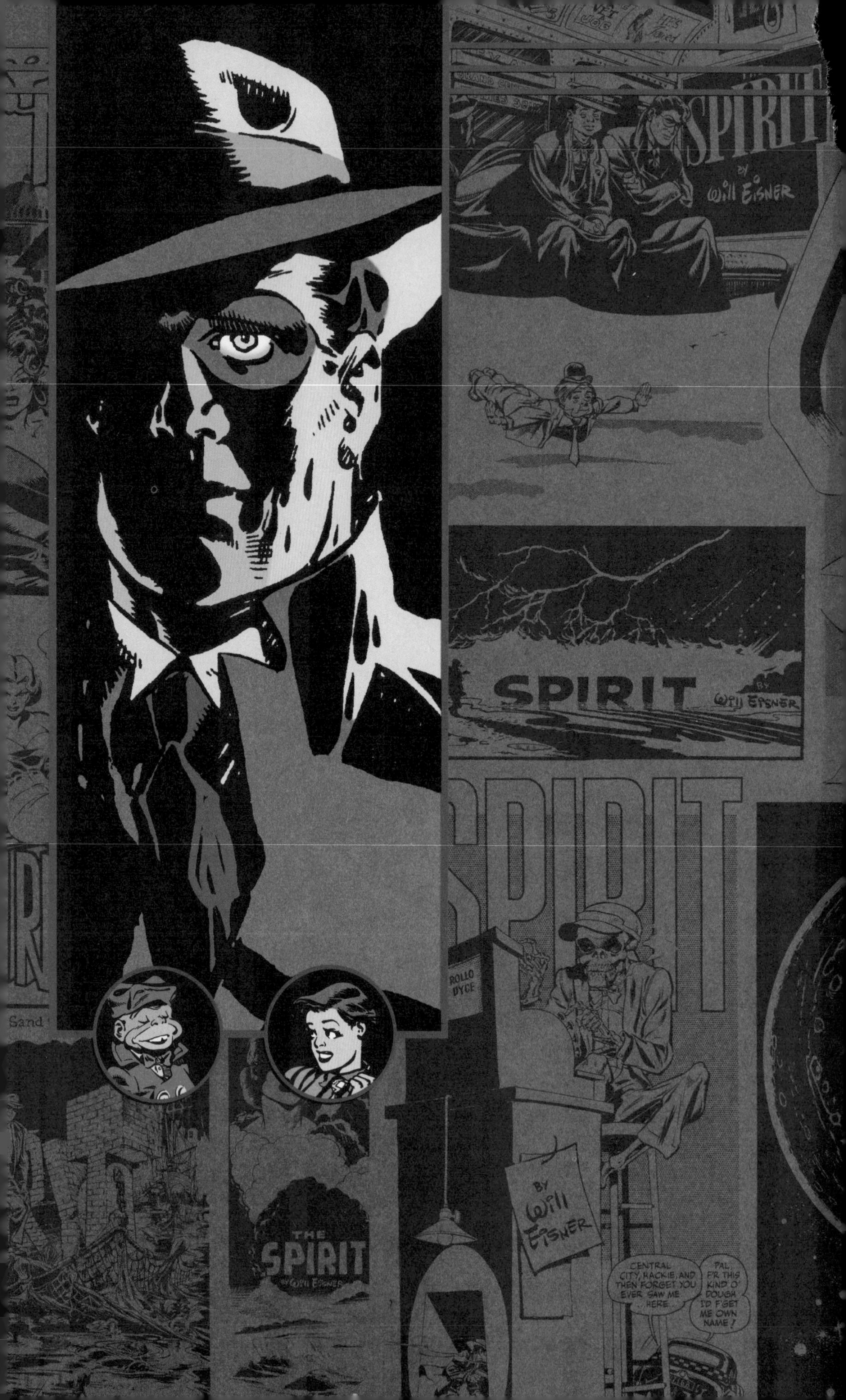
SPIRIT
BY
WILL EISNER
SPIRIT
BY
WILL EISNER
SPIRIT
ROLLO DYCE
Sand
THE
SPIRIT
BY WILL EISNER
BY
WILL EISNER
CENTRAL CITY, HACKIE, AND THEN FORGET YOU EVER SAW ME HERE.
PAL, F'R THIS KIND O' DOUGH I'D F'GET ME OWN NAME!

THE BEST OF THE SPIRIT

BY WILL EISNER

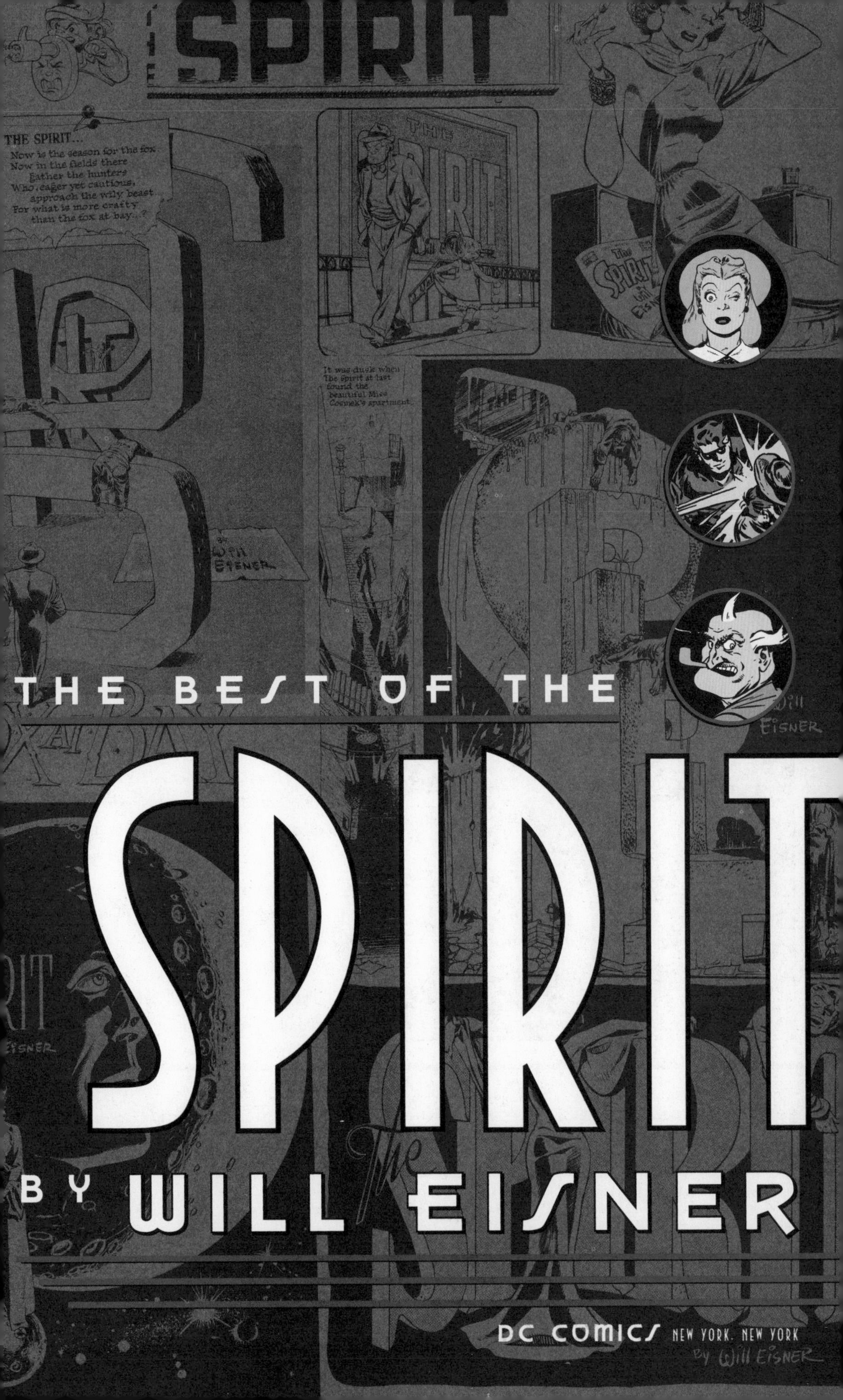

SPIRIT
THE SPIRIT...
Now is the season for the fox.
Now in the fields there
gather the hunters
Who, eager yet cautious,
approach the wily beast.
For what is more crafty
than the fox at bay..?
It was dusk when
The Spirit at last
found the
beautiful Miss
Connek's apartment.
BY WILL EISNER
WILL EISNER

DC COMICS NEW YORK, NEW YORK

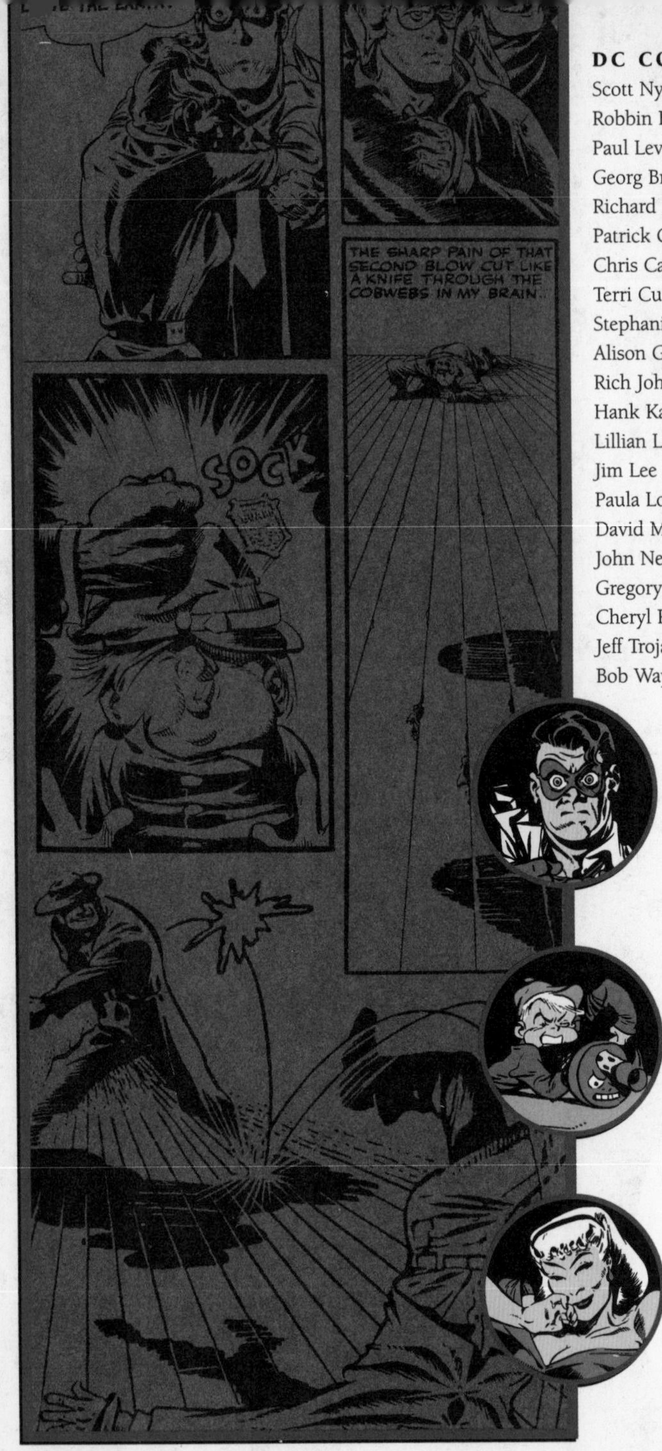
THE SHARP PAIN OF THAT SECOND BLOW CUT LIKE A KNIFE THROUGH THE COBWEBS IN MY BRAIN...
SOCK

Throughout the run of The Spirit, *Will Eisner was assisted by many talented individuals, among them John Belfi, Phillip (Tex) Blaisdell, Chris Christiansen, Jack Cole, Martin DeMuth, Jim Dixon, Jules Feiffer, Lou Fine, Dick French, Jerry Grandenetti, Abe Kaenegson, Jack Keller, Robin King, Alex Kotzky, Joe Kubert, Andre LeBlanc, Marilyn Mercer, Klaus Nordling, Ben Oda, Bob Palmer, Don Perlin, Bob Powell, Sam Rosen, Aldo Rubano, Sam Schwartz, John Spranger, Manny Stallman, Manly Wade Wellman, Al Wenzel, Wallace Wood, and Bill Woolfolk.*

The Author and publisher wish to thank them for their vital contributions.

DC Comics, 1700 Broadway, New York, NY 10019. A Warner Bros. Entertainment Company
Printed in Canada. Third Printing. ISBN: 978-1-4012-0755-7.

Cover illustrations by Will Eisner.
Cover color and interior color reconstruction by Jamison.
Special thanks to Bill Blackbeard, Director of the San Francisco Academy of Comic Art, and Diamond International Galleries for loan of source material, and to Denis Kitchen.
Publication design by Amie Brockway-Metcalf.

TABLE OF CONTENTS

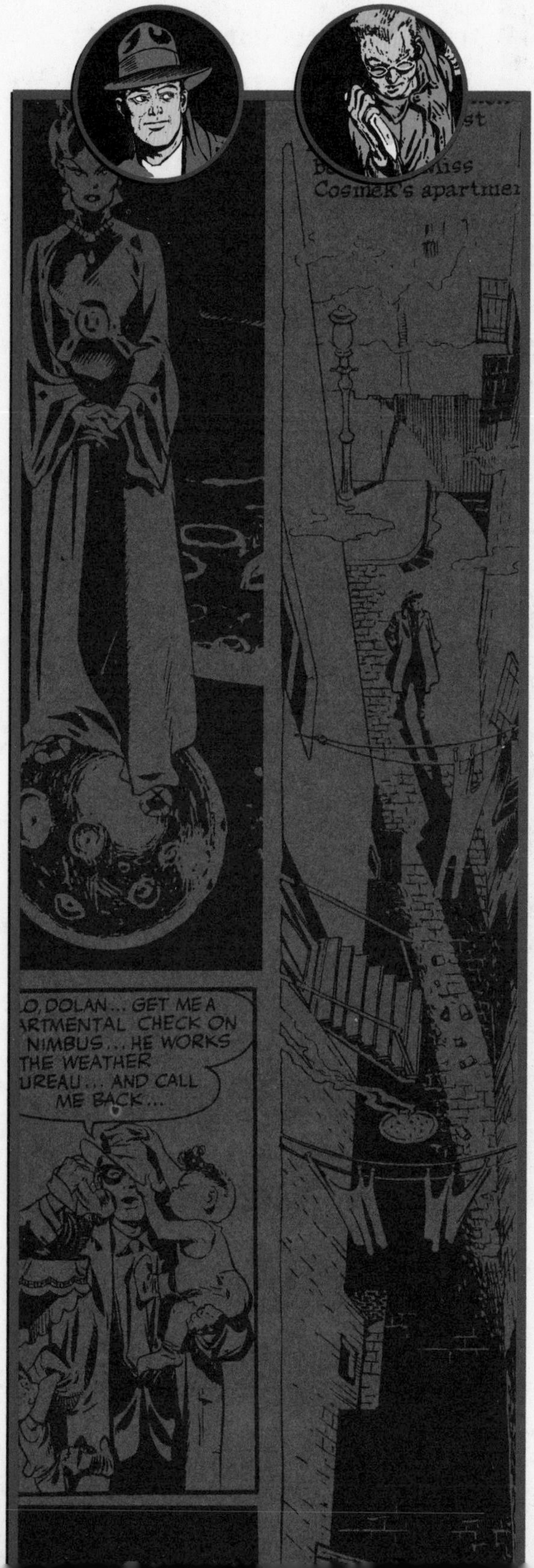

O, DOLAN... GET ME A
ARTMENTAL CHECK ON
NIMBUS... HE WORKS
THE WEATHER
UREAU... AND CALL
ME BACK...

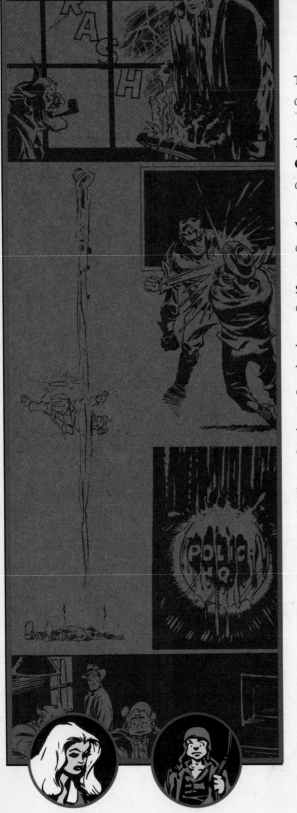

THE SPIRIT: AN INTRODUCTION

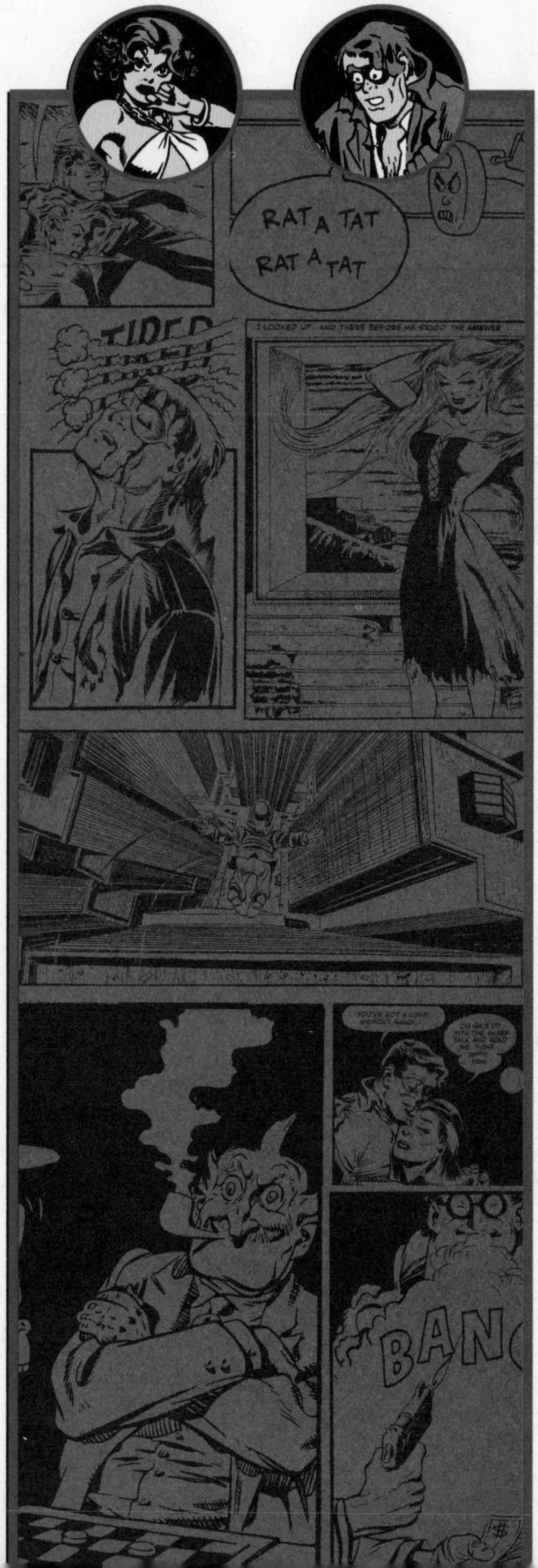
RAT A TAT
RAT A TAT
TIRED
I LOOKED UP ... AND THERE BEFORE ME STOOD THE ANSWER
BAN

It isn't yet easy or comfortable for me to write about Will Eisner. He was too important, and making notes for this introduction reminded me how much I miss Will Eisner my friend, and rereading the stories in here reminded me that I miss Will Eisner the storyteller, the craftsman, the dreamer, the artist. Which is probably the wrong place to start something that is an unabashed celebration of part of Will Eisner's work, but it's nonetheless true.

When Will Eisner died he was as respected and as revered around the world as he would let us respect and revere him. He was a teacher and an innovator. He started out so far ahead of the game that it took the rest of the world literally sixty years to catch up.

Will's life is, in miniature, a history of American comics. He was one of the very first people to run a studio making commercial comic-books, but while his contemporaries dreamed of getting out of the comics ghetto and into more lucrative and respectable places — advertising, perhaps, or illustration, or even fine art — Will had no desire to escape. He was trying to create an artform.

There are arguments today about whether or not Will was actually the first person to coin the term "graphic novel" for his book of short stories *A Contract With God*, the book that kicked off the third act of Will's creative life. There are far fewer arguments about what Will actually did in the 1940s with the Spirit stories, or about the influence Will had on the world of comics all through his creative life — and that his stories had too.

I'll step forward here: I bought my first copy of *The Spirit* in 1975, in a basement comics shop in South London. I saw it hanging on a wall, and I knew that, whatever it was, I wanted it. I would have been about 14. It was the second (and final) issue of Harvey Comics' *Spirit* reprints, and reading it on the train home I had no idea that the stories I was reading were thirty years old at the time. They were fresher and smarter than anything I'd seen in comics — seven-page stories that somehow managed to leave out everything that wasn't the story, while telling wonderful tales of beautiful women and unfortunate men, of human fallibility and of occasional redemption, stories through which the Spirit would wander, bemused and often beaten-up, a McGuffin in a mask and hat.

I loved *The Spirit* then. I loved the choices that Will made, the confidence, the way the art and the story meshed. I read those stories and I wanted to write comics too.

Two or three years later I stopped reading comics, disappointed and disillusioned by the medium as only a sixteen-year-old can be, but even then I kept reading *The*

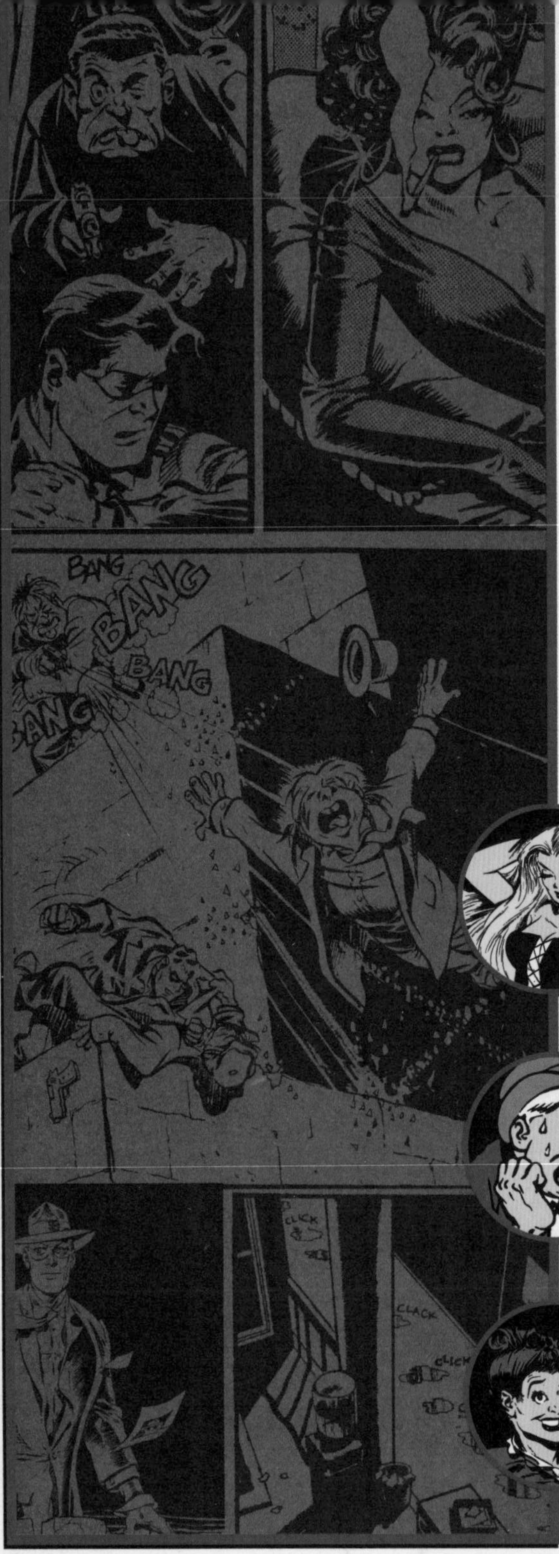
BANG
BANG
BANG
CLICK
CLACK
CLICK

Spirit — I would go to London and bring back copies of the Kitchen Sink reprints, and the Warren reprints, and read them with unalloyed pleasure, such that when, as a twenty-five-year-old, I decided it was time to learn how to write comics, I went out and bought Will Eisner's *Comics and Sequential Art*, and pored over it like a rabbinical student studying his Torah.

Twenty years later, Will Eisner's work on *The Spirit* makes me remember why, as a respectable adult, I wanted to write comics in the first place.

The joy of *The Spirit*, as soon as it had become what it was going to be, which was more or less once Eisner came back from the war in 1945 and reassumed control of the comic (published as a Sunday supplement in newspapers at the time, an avenue that allowed Eisner, who was always a wise businessman, the creative control and ownership he could never have had at that time on the newsstands) was not in the words, nor in the pictures, but in the smoothness and the brilliance and the willingness to experiment of the storytelling. In seven pages — normally less than sixty panels — Eisner could build a short story worthy of O. Henry, funny or tragic, sentimental or hardbitten, or simply odd. The work was uniquely comics, existing neither in the words nor in the pictures but in the place where the words and the pictures come together, commenting on each other, reinforcing each other. Eisner's stories were influenced by film, by theatre, by radio, but were ultimately their own medium, created by a man who thought that comics was an artform, and who was proved right — but who might not have been quite so right if he had not built such a solid body of work, both in *The Spirit* and in the work he did from 1976 until his death, and if he had not taught and inspired along the way.

A lot of the delight in *The Spirit* is in watching Eisner invent and discover new ways of telling stories — the use of white space and panels to represent freedom and captivity in one story, the echoing, reflecting dual panels in another, the use of the murderer's point of view in a third. The stories in this book are, in addition to being astoundingly entertaining, a lesson in how to tell stories in comics form. "ACTION MYSTERY ADVENTURE," the panel on the top right of each *Spirit* splash page tells us — and to those three things one could add humor, craft, pathos, wisdom, and the most beautiful (and dangerous) women in comics.

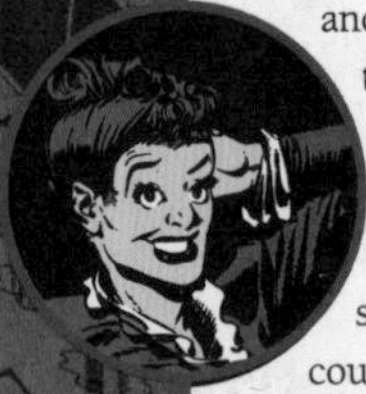

In a world in which the idea of graphic novels — big, thick collections of comics that have heft and value — is becoming widespread and accepted, bookshops, librarians and individuals want to know what the important books are, to know which books are vital to have on their shelves. There are a few books that no self-respecting collection of graphic novels should be without, after all — *Maus*, for example, or *Watchmen*, or *Jimmy Corrigan*, or *Bone*. I'd like to suggest that this book, as an example of what the young Will Eisner could do, should be added to that set and guaranteed a place

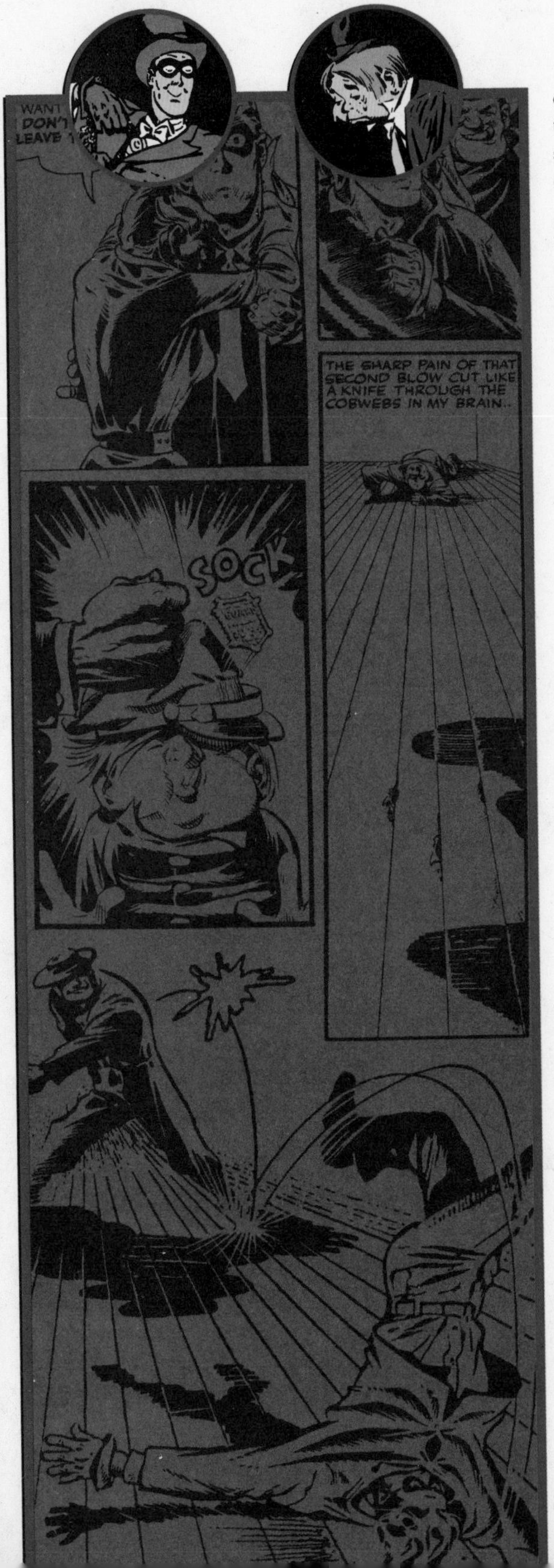
THE SHARP PAIN OF THAT SECOND BLOW CUT LIKE A KNIFE THROUGH THE COBWEBS IN MY BRAIN..
SOCK

on those shelves. The postwar *Spirit* was a masterpiece, in the strict sense of the word — a piece of work that demonstrates that a young journeyman has now become a master of his craft.

If you enjoy these tales there are more where they came from — many more, I'm happy to say. DC Comics has been publishing *The Spirit Archives* for several years now, and the material in the book you are holding is a selection from those volumes: a few early stories to give you context, and some stories, as good as, as interesting as, as exciting as, other Eisner Spirit stories. Which, if you're looking for ACTION MYSTERY ADVENTURE, not to mention the rest, is pretty much as good as it gets

-NEIL GAIMAN

OCTOBER 2005

Creator and writer of the internationally acclaimed comics masterpiece The Sandman, *Neil Gaiman is also the author of the* New York Times *best-selling novels* Anansi Boys *and* American Gods *and the co-writer, with director and longtime collaborator Dave McKean, of the Jim Henson Productions film* MirrorMask. *Among the many awards he has received are the Hugo, the Nebula, the World Fantasy Award, and the Bram Stoker Award. Originally from England, Gaiman now lives in the United States.*

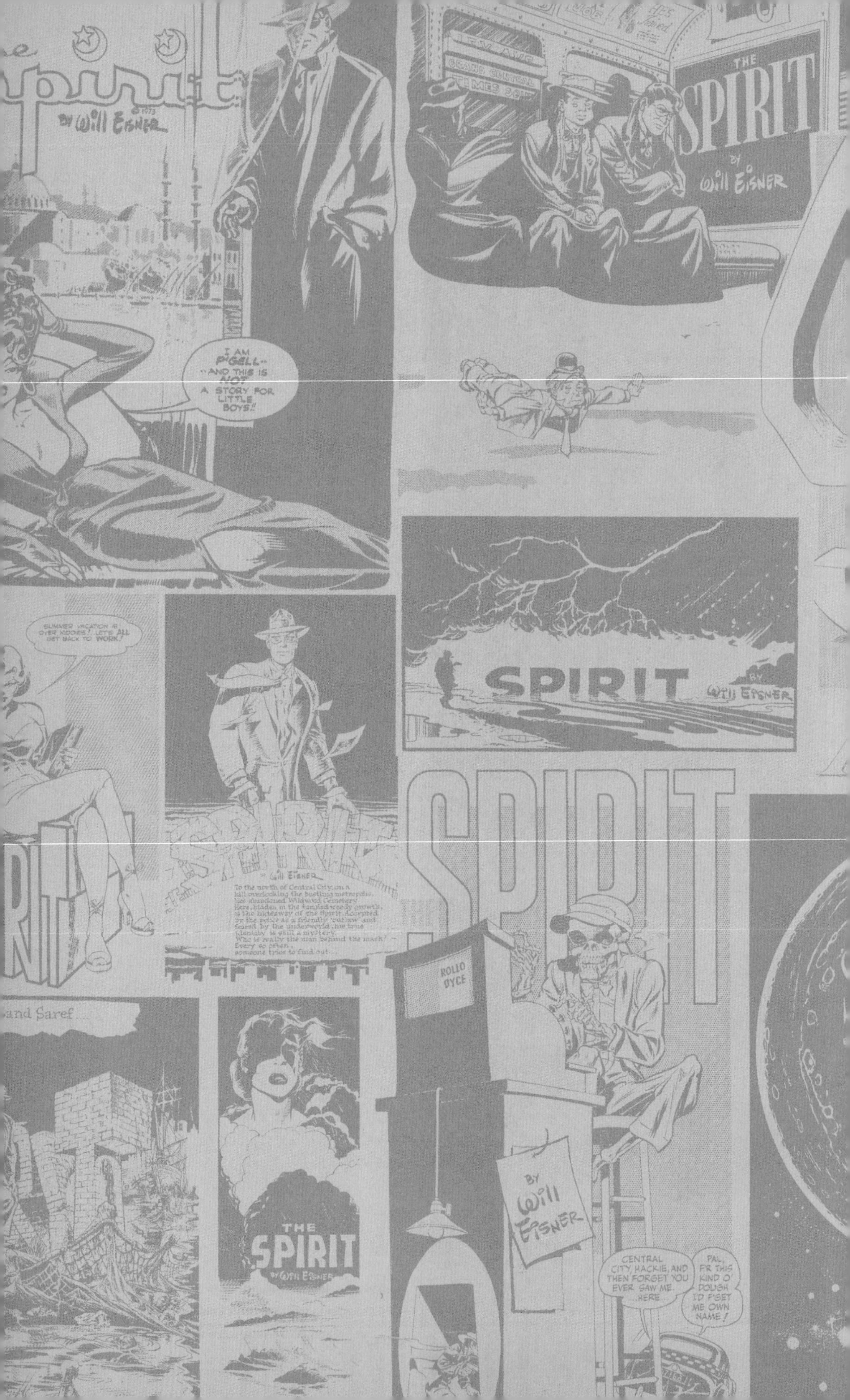
The Spirit
by Will Eisner
I AM P'GELL.. ..AND THIS IS NOT A STORY FOR LITTLE BOYS!!
THE SPIRIT
BY Will Eisner
GRAND CENTRAL
SUMMER VACATION IS OVER KIDDIES! LET'S ALL GET BACK TO WORK!
SPIRIT
BY Will Eisner
SPIRIT
by Will Eisner
To the north of Central City, on a hill overlooking the bustling metropolis, lies abandoned Wildwood Cemetery. Here, hidden in the tangled weedy growth, is the hideaway of the Spirit. Accepted by the police as a friendly 'outlaw' and feared by the underworld, his true identity is still a mystery. Who is really the man behind the mask? — Every so often, someone tries to find out...
THE SPIRIT
ROLLO DYCE
...and Saref...
THE SPIRIT
BY Will Eisner
BY Will Eisner
CENTRAL CITY, HACKIE, AND THEN FORGET YOU EVER SAW ME.. HERE..
PAL, FR THIS KIND O' DOUGH I'D F'GET ME OWN NAME!

COMIC BOOK SECTION

THE ORIGIN OF THE SPIRIT

ACTION Mystery ADVENTURE

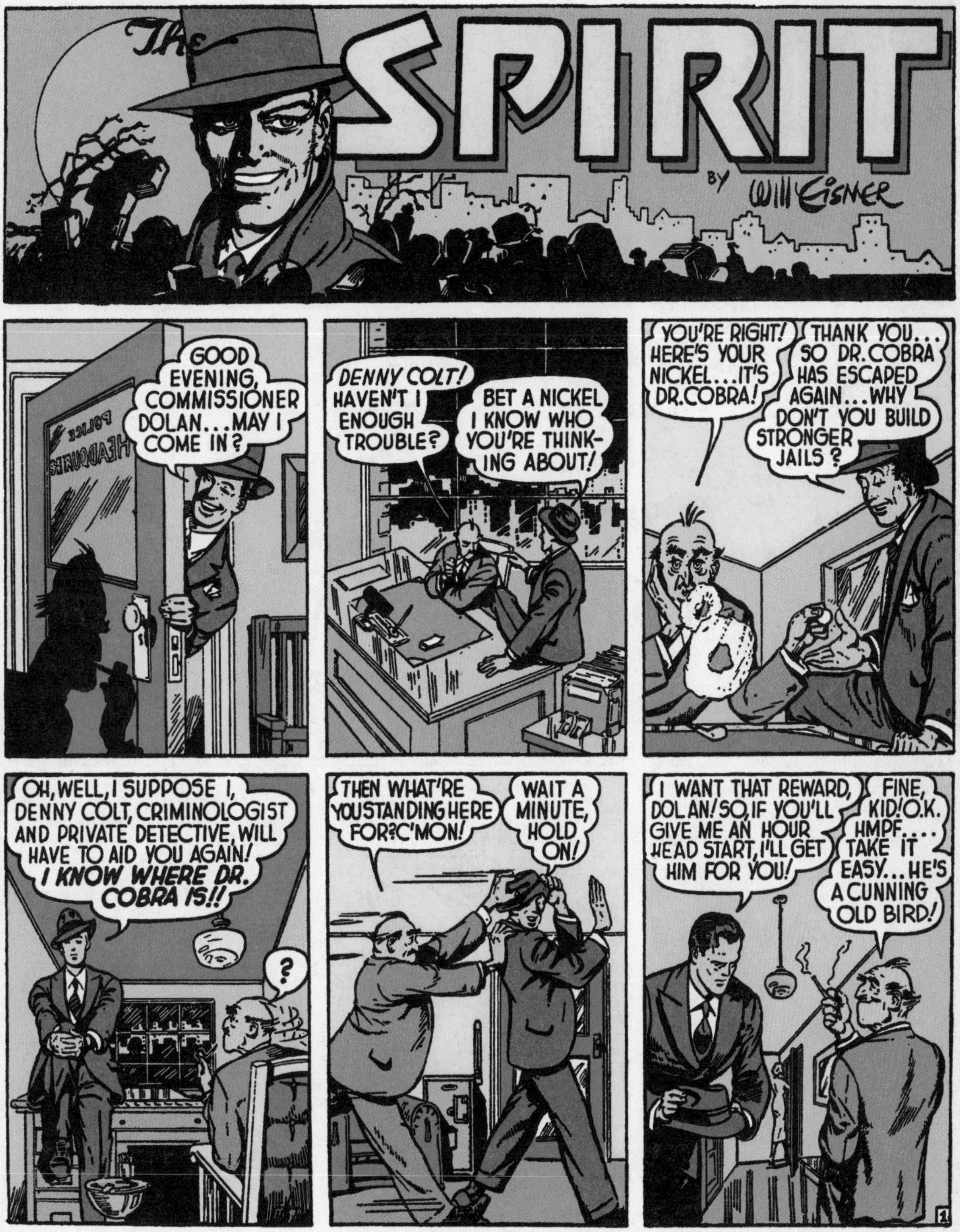
The SPIRIT
BY Will Eisner
GOOD EVENING, COMMISSIONER DOLAN...MAY I COME IN?
DENNY COLT! HAVEN'T I ENOUGH TROUBLE?
BET A NICKEL I KNOW WHO YOU'RE THINKING ABOUT!
YOU'RE RIGHT! HERE'S YOUR NICKEL...IT'S DR.COBRA!
THANK YOU... SO DR. COBRA HAS ESCAPED AGAIN...WHY DON'T YOU BUILD STRONGER JAILS?
OH, WELL, I SUPPOSE I, DENNY COLT, CRIMINOLOGIST AND PRIVATE DETECTIVE, WILL HAVE TO AID YOU AGAIN! I KNOW WHERE DR. COBRA IS!!
?
THEN WHAT'RE YOU STANDING HERE FOR? C'MON!
WAIT A MINUTE, HOLD ON!
I WANT THAT REWARD, DOLAN! SO, IF YOU'LL GIVE ME AN HOUR HEAD START, I'LL GET HIM FOR YOU!
FINE, KID! O.K. HMPF.... TAKE IT EASY...HE'S A CUNNING OLD BIRD!
1

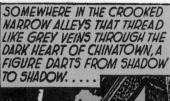
SOMEWHERE IN THE CROOKED NARROW ALLEYS THAT THREAD LIKE GREY VEINS THROUGH THE DARK HEART OF CHINATOWN, A FIGURE DARTS FROM SHADOW TO SHADOW.....

DOWN THROUGH A MANHOLE IN A GUTTER.....

AND AT LAST...

MORE CHLORINE, LEENG, HURRY!... IT'S READY!! HA-HA-HA!

THE GAME'S UP, DR. COBRA I'M TAKING YOU IN!

DENNY COLT!

ALWAYS THE POLICE EENTERFERE WITH MY EXPERIMENTS! SOME DAY THEY WILL BOW DOWN BEFORE ME!

COME DOWN, YOU!!

SUDDENLY..

AGILELY, WITH THE SPEED OF A PANTHER, DR. COBRA LEAPS...

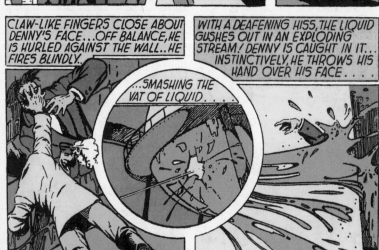

CLAW-LIKE FINGERS CLOSE ABOUT DENNY'S FACE...OFF BALANCE, HE IS HURLED AGAINST THE WALL...HE FIRES BLINDLY..

...SMASHING THE VAT OF LIQUID....

WITH A DEAFENING HISS, THE LIQUID GUSHES OUT IN AN EXPLODING STREAM! DENNY IS CAUGHT IN IT... INSTINCTIVELY, HE THROWS HIS HAND OVER HIS FACE....

2

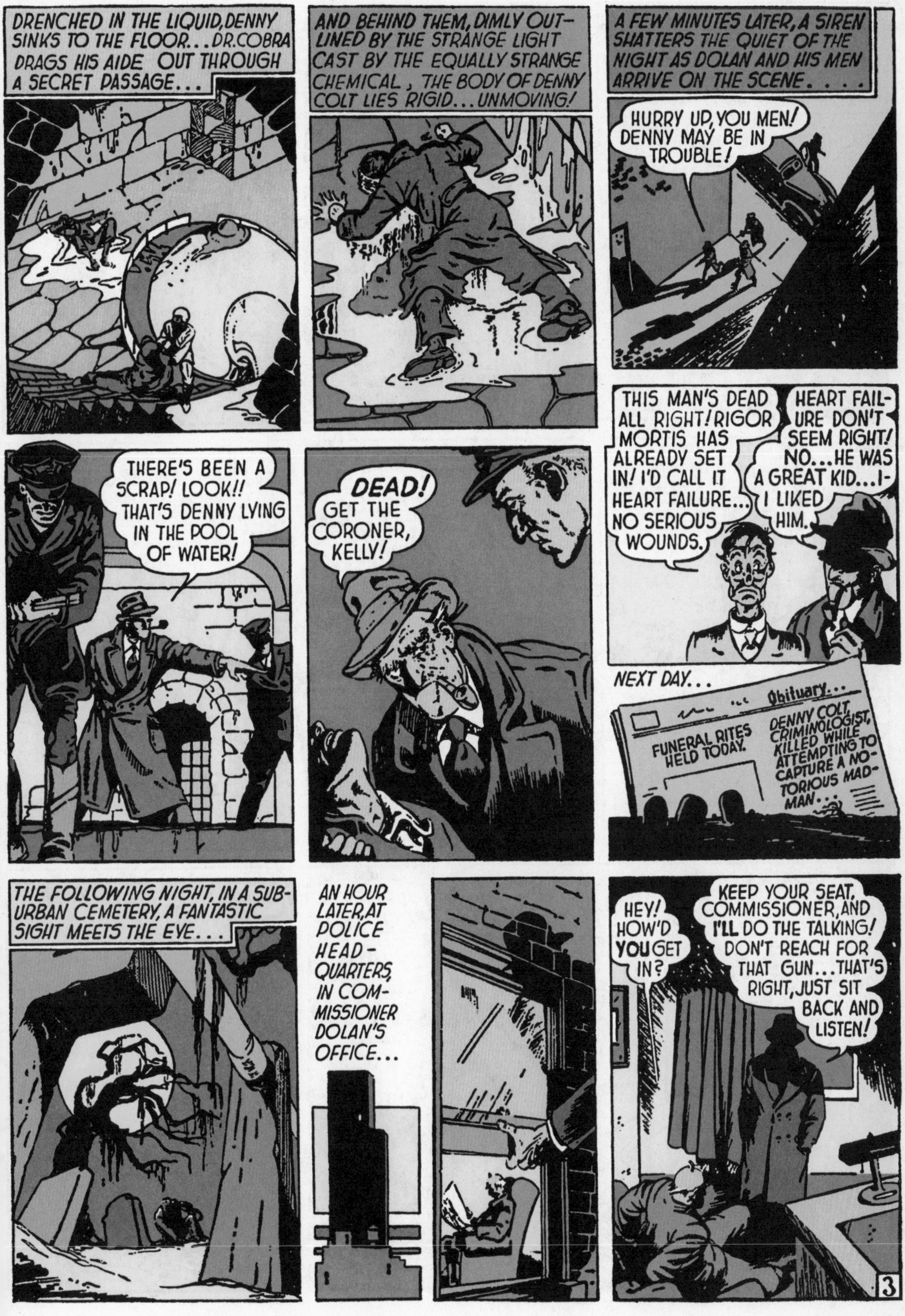

DRENCHED IN THE LIQUID, DENNY SINKS TO THE FLOOR... DR. COBRA DRAGS HIS AIDE OUT THROUGH A SECRET PASSAGE...
AND BEHIND THEM, DIMLY OUTLINED BY THE STRANGE LIGHT CAST BY THE EQUALLY STRANGE CHEMICAL, THE BODY OF DENNY COLT LIES RIGID... UNMOVING!
A FEW MINUTES LATER, A SIREN SHATTERS THE QUIET OF THE NIGHT AS DOLAN AND HIS MEN ARRIVE ON THE SCENE....
HURRY UP, YOU MEN! DENNY MAY BE IN TROUBLE!
THERE'S BEEN A SCRAP! LOOK!! THAT'S DENNY LYING IN THE POOL OF WATER!
DEAD! GET THE CORONER, KELLY!
THIS MAN'S DEAD ALL RIGHT! RIGOR MORTIS HAS ALREADY SET IN! I'D CALL IT HEART FAILURE... NO SERIOUS WOUNDS.
HEART FAILURE DON'T SEEM RIGHT! NO... HE WAS A GREAT KID... I-I LIKED HIM.
NEXT DAY...
Obituary...
FUNERAL RITES HELD TODAY.
DENNY COLT, CRIMINOLOGIST, KILLED WHILE ATTEMPTING TO CAPTURE A NOTORIOUS MADMAN...
THE FOLLOWING NIGHT, IN A SUBURBAN CEMETERY, A FANTASTIC SIGHT MEETS THE EYE...
AN HOUR LATER, AT POLICE HEADQUARTERS, IN COMMISSIONER DOLAN'S OFFICE...
HEY! HOW'D YOU GET IN?
KEEP YOUR SEAT, COMMISSIONER, AND I'LL DO THE TALKING! DON'T REACH FOR THAT GUN... THAT'S RIGHT, JUST SIT BACK AND LISTEN!
3

NOW THEN, THERE'S A BIG REWARD OUT FOR THE CAPTURE OF DR. COBRA... I'VE COME TO CLAIM IT! HAVE THE MONEY HERE AND I'LL DELIVER COBRA IN THREE HOURS!

COME OUT OF THE SHADOWS!

AND LET YOU SEE MY FACE?? HARDLY!! BUT FOR IDENTIFICATION, YOU MIGHT CALL ME... THE "SPIRIT."

THE SPIRIT LEAVES AS QUICKLY AND AS SILENTLY AS HE CAME...

THE SPIRIT, EH?? THAT VOICE...MMM.. SAY, JOE, GET "HAPPY," THE CORONER, IN HERE!

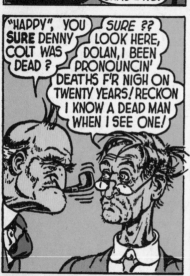

"HAPPY", YOU SURE DENNY COLT WAS DEAD?

SURE?? LOOK HERE, DOLAN, I BEEN PRONOUNCIN' DEATHS F'R NIGH ON TWENTY YEARS! RECKON I KNOW A DEAD MAN WHEN I SEE ONE!

I TELL YOU, O'ROURKE, THE OLD MAN'S BEEN "TECHED" EVER SINCE DENNY COLT DIED!

A FEW MINUTES LATER, DOLAN IS IN THE STREET.

CABBY!!

WILDWOOD CEMETERY, AND HURRY!! OFFICIAL BUSINESS! I'M GOING TO VISIT A DEAD FRIEND.

Y-Y-YAS SUH!

AT THE WILDWOOD GRAVEYARD, TWO MEN TRUDGE FEARFULLY ACROSS A MOONLIT PATH...

WHEN'D YA GIT THE MESSAGE, POKEY?

HOUR AGO, GIMP, I'M SCAIRT!

A GUY SLIPPED DIS INTA ME HAND... A TINY TOMBSTONE!

PUT UP YOUR HANDS! THIS IS THE SPIRIT!

WHAT DO YOU WANT?

GET INTO THAT TOMB! I'LL TELL YOU LATER!

4

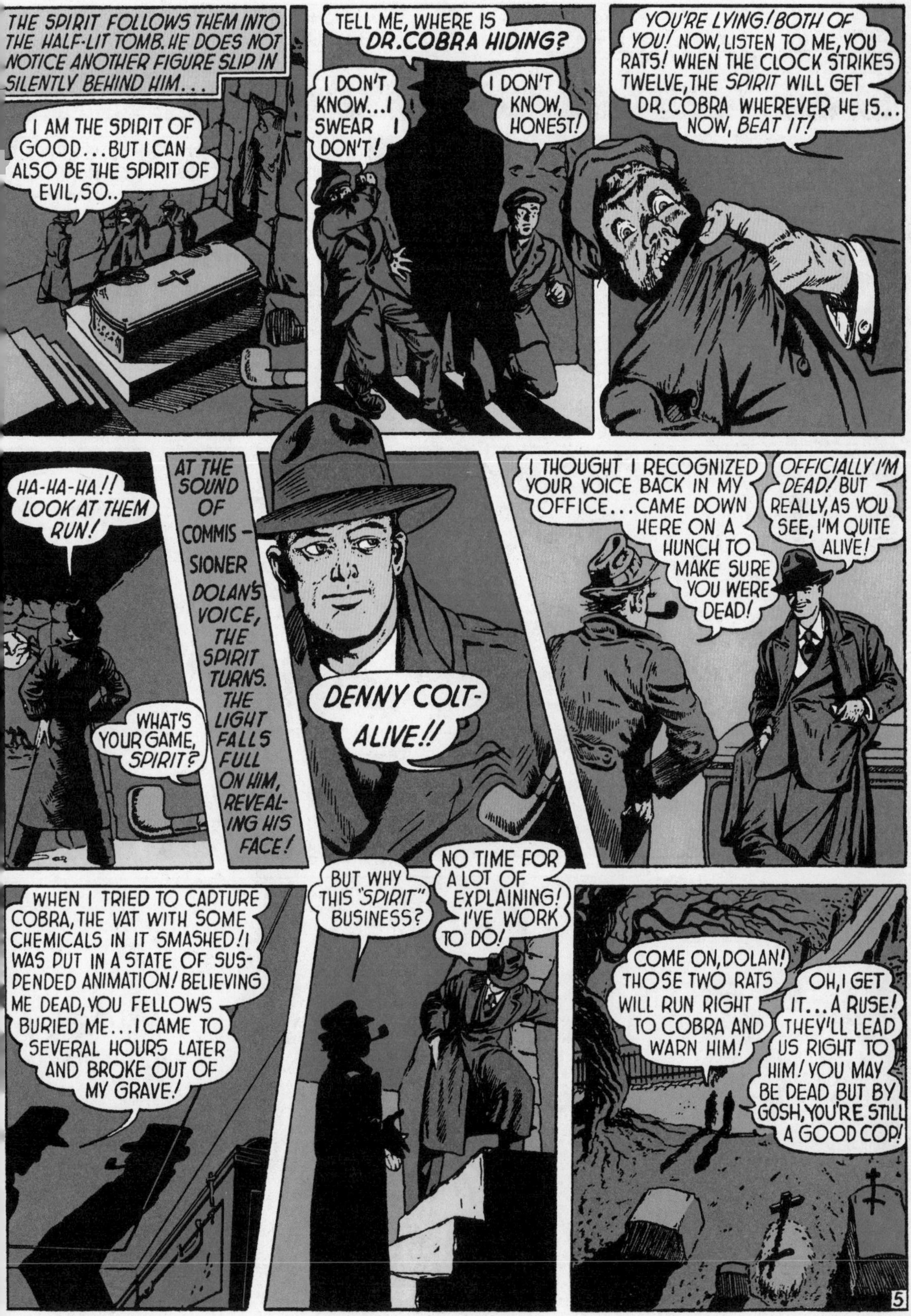
THE SPIRIT FOLLOWS THEM INTO THE HALF-LIT TOMB. HE DOES NOT NOTICE ANOTHER FIGURE SLIP IN SILENTLY BEHIND HIM...
I AM THE SPIRIT OF GOOD... BUT I CAN ALSO BE THE SPIRIT OF EVIL, SO..
TELL ME, WHERE IS DR. COBRA HIDING?
I DON'T KNOW...I SWEAR I DON'T!
I DON'T KNOW, HONEST!
YOU'RE LYING! BOTH OF YOU! NOW, LISTEN TO ME, YOU RATS! WHEN THE CLOCK STRIKES TWELVE, THE SPIRIT WILL GET DR. COBRA WHEREVER HE IS... NOW, BEAT IT!
HA-HA-HA!! LOOK AT THEM RUN!
WHAT'S YOUR GAME, SPIRIT?
AT THE SOUND OF COMMIS-SIONER DOLAN'S VOICE, THE SPIRIT TURNS. THE LIGHT FALLS FULL ON HIM, REVEAL-ING HIS FACE!
DENNY COLT-ALIVE!!
I THOUGHT I RECOGNIZED YOUR VOICE BACK IN MY OFFICE... CAME DOWN HERE ON A HUNCH TO MAKE SURE YOU WERE DEAD!
OFFICIALLY I'M DEAD! BUT REALLY, AS YOU SEE, I'M QUITE ALIVE!
WHEN I TRIED TO CAPTURE COBRA, THE VAT WITH SOME CHEMICALS IN IT SMASHED! I WAS PUT IN A STATE OF SUS-PENDED ANIMATION! BELIEVING ME DEAD, YOU FELLOWS BURIED ME... I CAME TO SEVERAL HOURS LATER AND BROKE OUT OF MY GRAVE!
BUT WHY THIS "SPIRIT" BUSINESS?
NO TIME FOR A LOT OF EXPLAINING! I'VE WORK TO DO!
COME ON, DOLAN! THOSE TWO RATS WILL RUN RIGHT TO COBRA AND WARN HIM!
OH, I GET IT... A RUSE! THEY'LL LEAD US RIGHT TO HIM! YOU MAY BE DEAD BUT BY GOSH, YOU'RE STILL A GOOD COP!
5

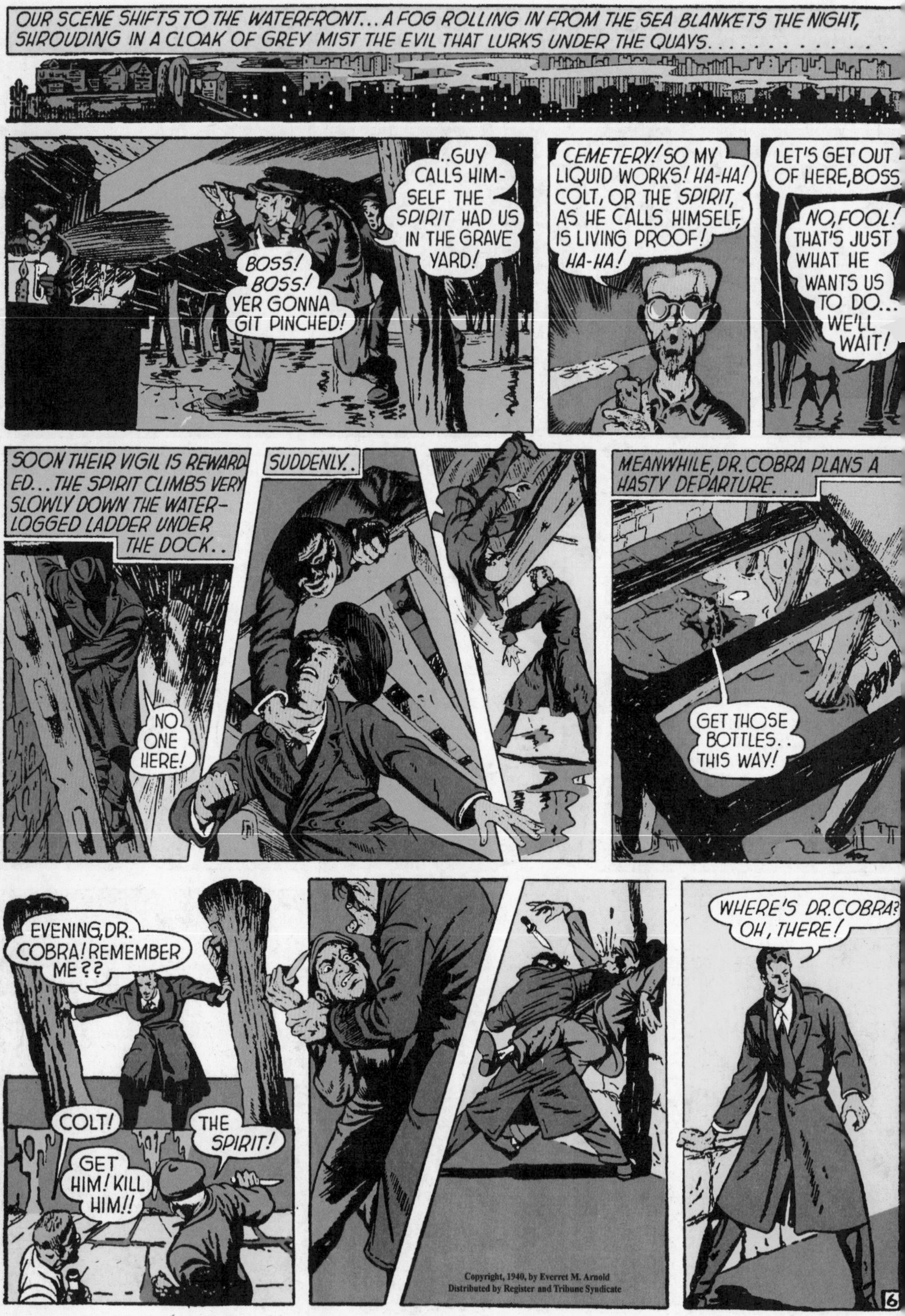
OUR SCENE SHIFTS TO THE WATERFRONT... A FOG ROLLING IN FROM THE SEA BLANKETS THE NIGHT, SHROUDING IN A CLOAK OF GREY MIST THE EVIL THAT LURKS UNDER THE QUAYS..............
BOSS! BOSS! YER GONNA GIT PINCHED!
..GUY CALLS HIMSELF THE SPIRIT HAD US IN THE GRAVE YARD!
CEMETERY! SO MY LIQUID WORKS! HA-HA! COLT, OR THE SPIRIT, AS HE CALLS HIMSELF, IS LIVING PROOF! HA-HA!
LET'S GET OUT OF HERE, BOSS.
NO, FOOL! THAT'S JUST WHAT HE WANTS US TO DO... WE'LL WAIT!
SOON THEIR VIGIL IS REWARDED... THE SPIRIT CLIMBS VERY SLOWLY DOWN THE WATER-LOGGED LADDER UNDER THE DOCK..
NO ONE HERE!
SUDDENLY..
MEANWHILE, DR. COBRA PLANS A HASTY DEPARTURE...
GET THOSE BOTTLES.. THIS WAY!
EVENING, DR. COBRA! REMEMBER ME??
COLT!
THE SPIRIT!
GET HIM! KILL HIM!!
WHERE'S DR. COBRA? OH, THERE!
Copyright, 1940, by Everret M. Arnold
Distributed by Register and Tribune Syndicate
6

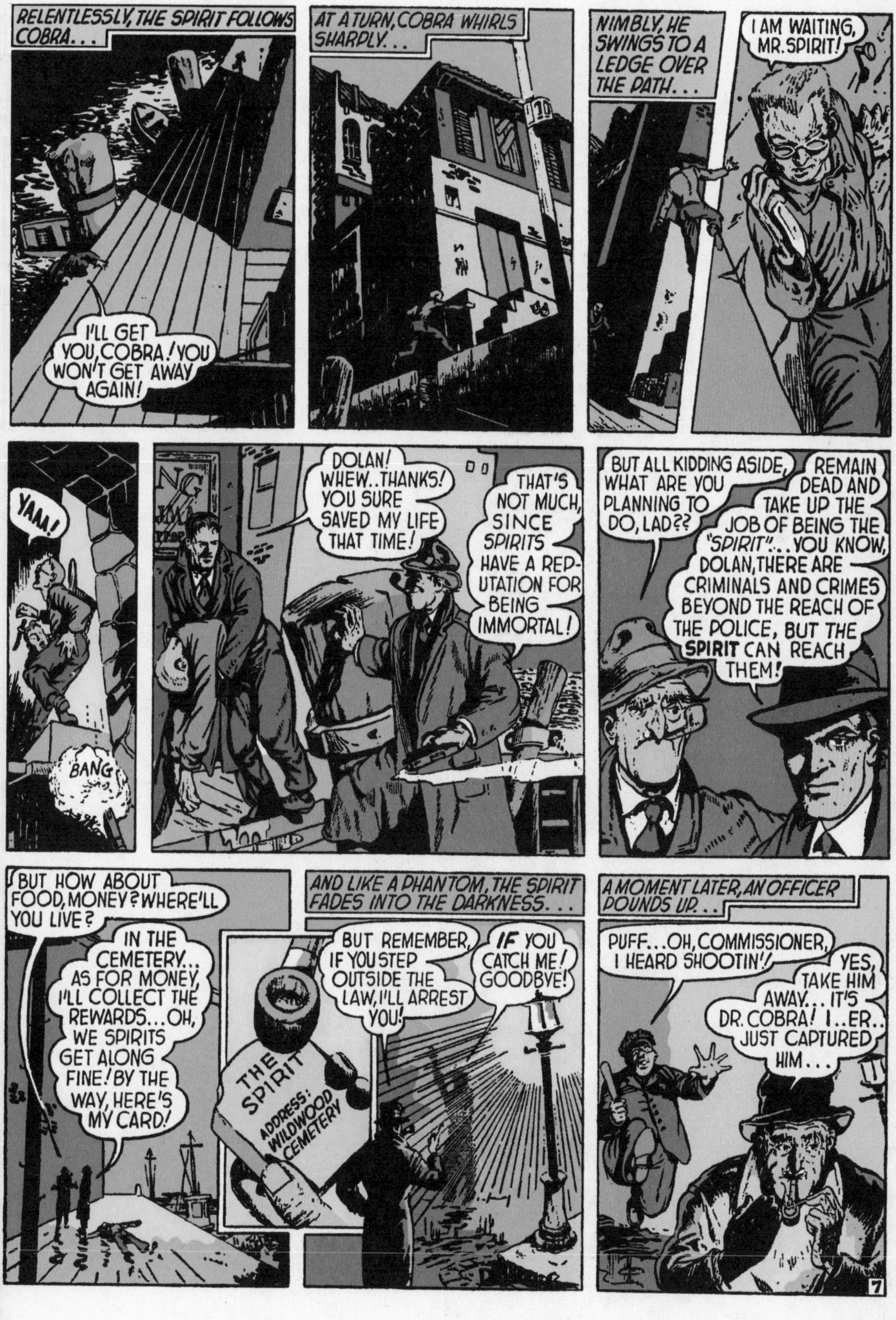
RELENTLESSLY, THE SPIRIT FOLLOWS COBRA...
I'LL GET YOU, COBRA! YOU WON'T GET AWAY AGAIN!
AT A TURN, COBRA WHIRLS SHARPLY...
NIMBLY, HE SWINGS TO A LEDGE OVER THE PATH...
I AM WAITING, MR. SPIRIT!
YAAA!
BANG
DOLAN! WHEW..THANKS! YOU SURE SAVED MY LIFE THAT TIME!
THAT'S NOT MUCH, SINCE SPIRITS HAVE A REPUTATION FOR BEING IMMORTAL!
BUT ALL KIDDING ASIDE, WHAT ARE YOU PLANNING TO DO, LAD??
REMAIN DEAD AND TAKE UP THE JOB OF BEING THE "SPIRIT"... YOU KNOW, DOLAN, THERE ARE CRIMINALS AND CRIMES BEYOND THE REACH OF THE POLICE, BUT THE SPIRIT CAN REACH THEM!
BUT HOW ABOUT FOOD, MONEY? WHERE'LL YOU LIVE?
IN THE CEMETERY... AS FOR MONEY, I'LL COLLECT THE REWARDS... OH, WE SPIRITS GET ALONG FINE! BY THE WAY, HERE'S MY CARD!
AND LIKE A PHANTOM, THE SPIRIT FADES INTO THE DARKNESS...
THE SPIRIT
ADDRESS: WILDWOOD CEMETERY
BUT REMEMBER, IF YOU STEP OUTSIDE THE LAW, I'LL ARREST YOU!
IF YOU CATCH ME! GOODBYE!
A MOMENT LATER, AN OFFICER POUNDS UP...
PUFF...OH, COMMISSIONER, I HEARD SHOOTIN'!
YES, TAKE HIM AWAY... IT'S DR. COBRA! I..ER.. JUST CAPTURED HIM...
7

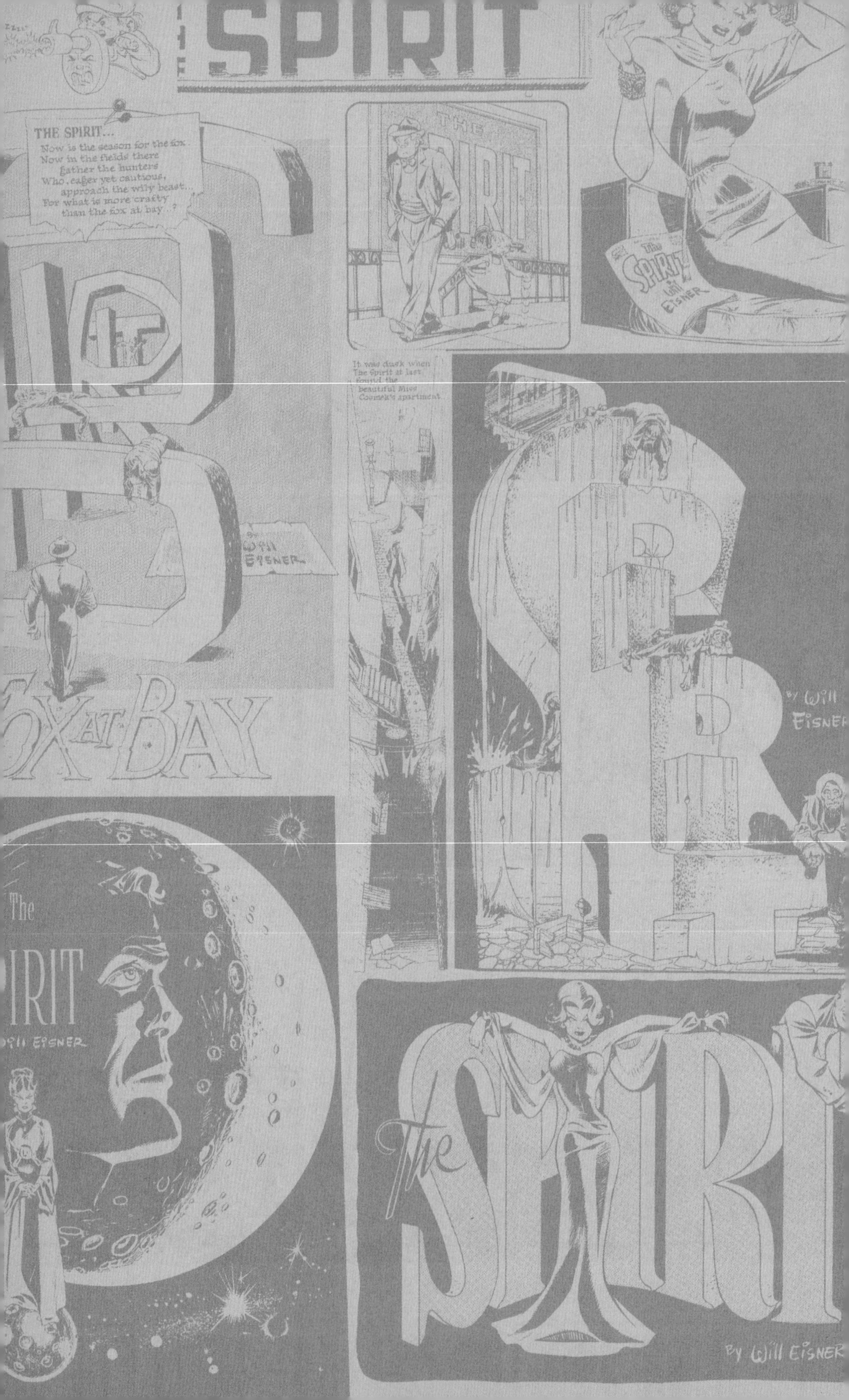
SPIRIT
THE SPIRIT...
Now is the season for the fox.
Now in the fields there
gather the hunters
Who, eager yet cautious,
approach the wily beast...
For what is more crafty
than the fox at bay?
By Will Eisner
OX AT BAY
The
SPIRIT
Will
Eisner
It was dusk when
The Spirit at last
found the
beautiful Miss
Cosmek's apartment
By Will
Eisner
The
IRIT
Will Eisner
The
SPIRIT
By Will Eisner

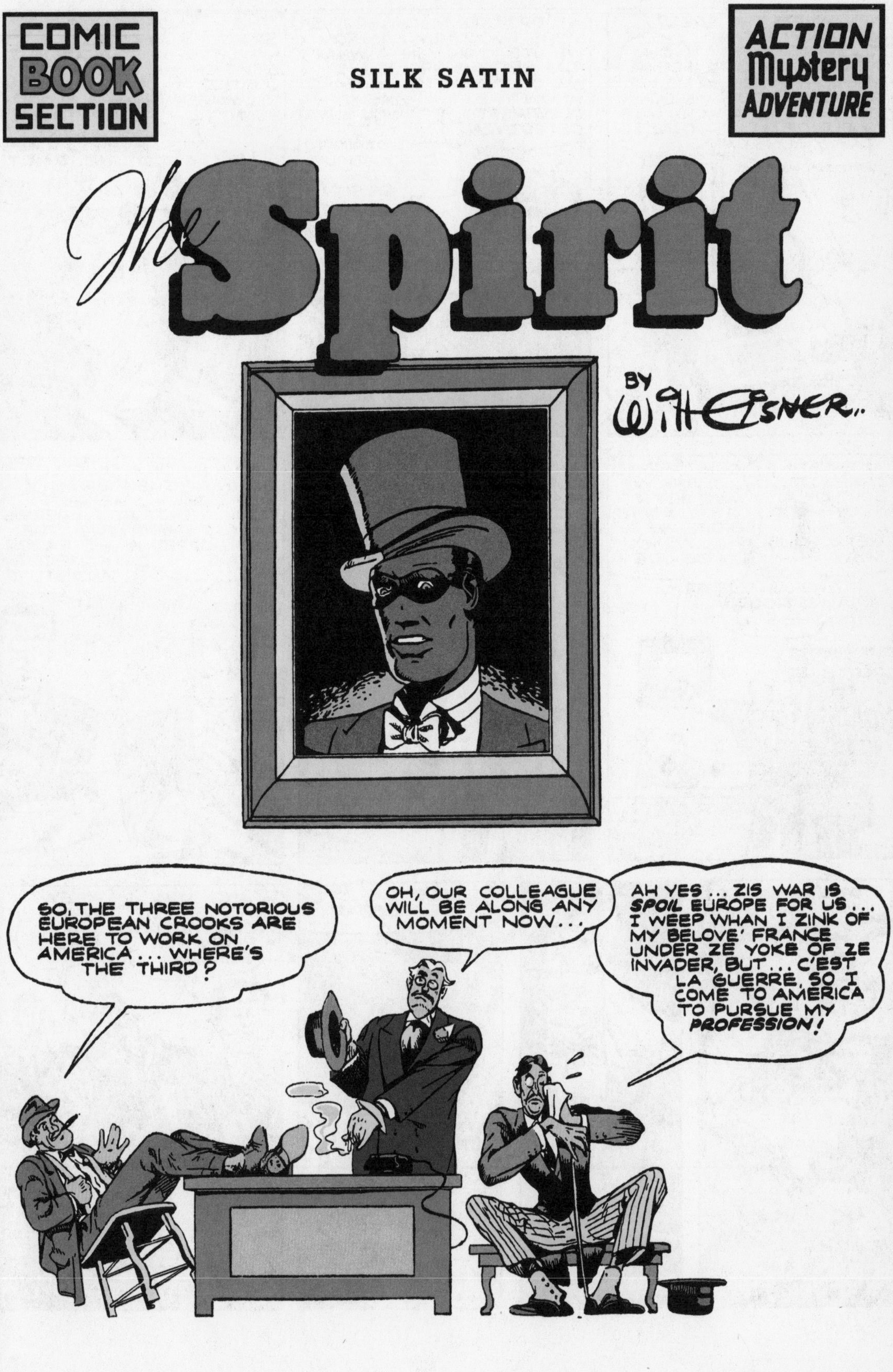
COMIC BOOK SECTION
SILK SATIN
ACTION Mystery ADVENTURE
The Spirit
BY Will Eisner
SO, THE THREE NOTORIOUS EUROPEAN CROOKS ARE HERE TO WORK ON AMERICA... WHERE'S THE THIRD?
OH, OUR COLLEAGUE WILL BE ALONG ANY MOMENT NOW...
AH YES... ZIS WAR IS SPOIL EUROPE FOR US... I WEEP WHAN I ZINK OF MY BELOVE' FRANCE UNDER ZE YOKE OF ZE INVADER, BUT... C'EST LA GUERRE, SO I COME TO AMERICA TO PURSUE MY PROFESSION!

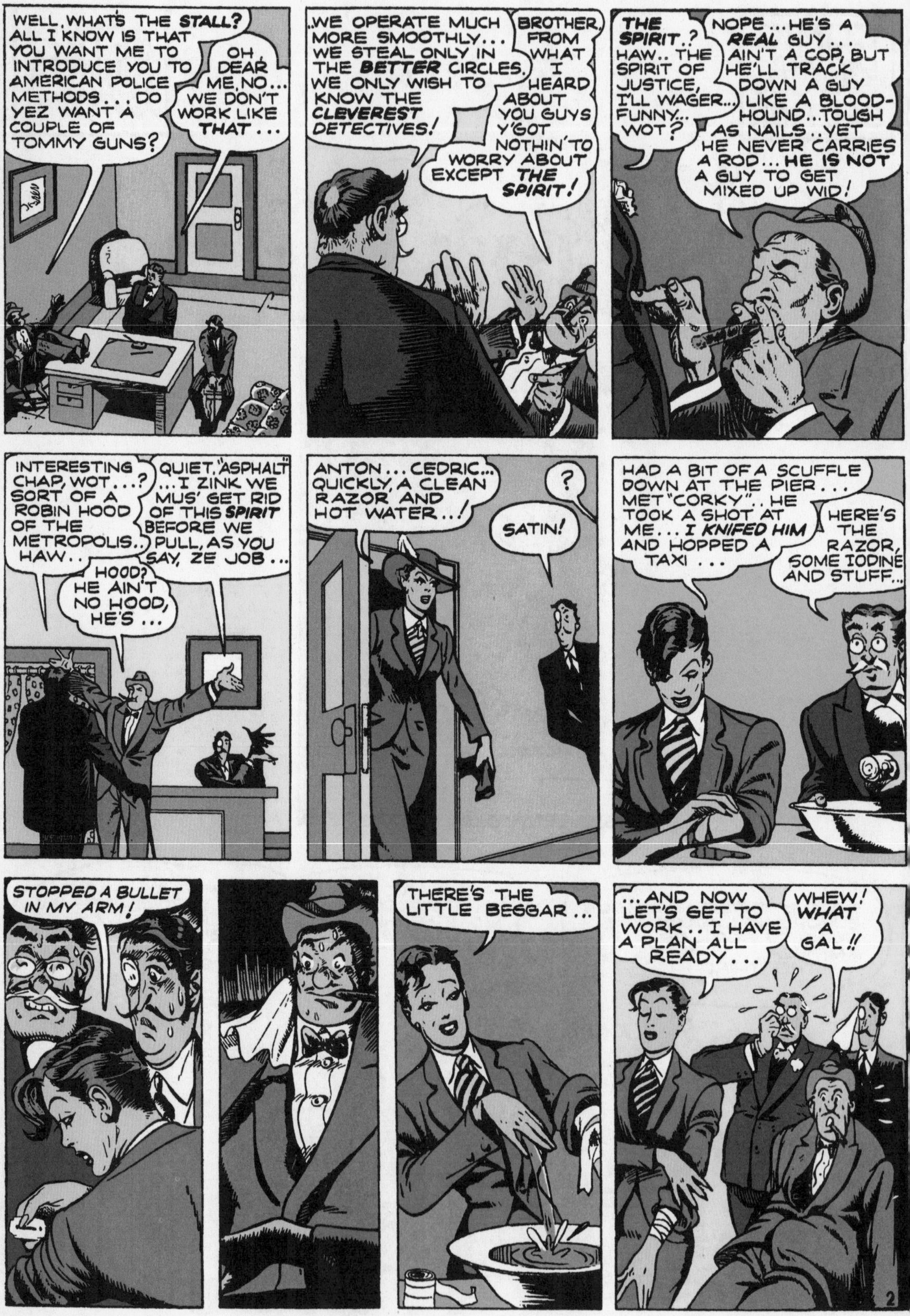
WELL, WHAT'S THE **STALL?** ALL I KNOW IS THAT YOU WANT ME TO INTRODUCE YOU TO AMERICAN POLICE METHODS... DO YEZ WANT A COUPLE OF TOMMY GUNS?
OH, DEAR ME, NO... WE DON'T WORK LIKE **THAT**...
..WE OPERATE MUCH MORE SMOOTHLY... WE STEAL ONLY IN THE **BETTER** CIRCLES. WE ONLY WISH TO KNOW THE **CLEVEREST DETECTIVES!**
BROTHER, FROM WHAT I HEARD ABOUT YOU GUYS Y'GOT NOTHIN' TO WORRY ABOUT EXCEPT **THE SPIRIT!**
THE SPIRIT..? HAW.. THE SPIRIT OF JUSTICE, I'LL WAGER... FUNNY... WOT?
NOPE... HE'S A **REAL** GUY... AIN'T A COP, BUT HE'LL TRACK DOWN A GUY LIKE A BLOOD-HOUND... TOUGH AS NAILS.. YET HE NEVER CARRIES A ROD... **HE IS NOT** A GUY TO GET MIXED UP WID!
INTERESTING CHAP, WOT...? SORT OF A ROBIN HOOD OF THE METROPOLIS.. HAW..
HOOD? HE AIN'T NO HOOD, HE'S...
QUIET, "ASPHALT" ... I ZINK WE MUS' GET RID OF THIS **SPIRIT** BEFORE WE PULL, AS YOU SAY, ZE JOB...
ANTON... CEDRIC... QUICKLY, A CLEAN RAZOR AND HOT WATER..!
?
SATIN!
HAD A BIT OF A SCUFFLE DOWN AT THE PIER... MET "CORKY".. HE TOOK A SHOT AT ME... **I KNIFED HIM** AND HOPPED A TAXI...
HERE'S THE RAZOR, SOME IODINE AND STUFF...
STOPPED A BULLET IN MY ARM!
THERE'S THE LITTLE BEGGAR...
...AND NOW LET'S GET TO WORK.. I HAVE A PLAN ALL READY...
WHEW! **WHAT** A GAL!!
2

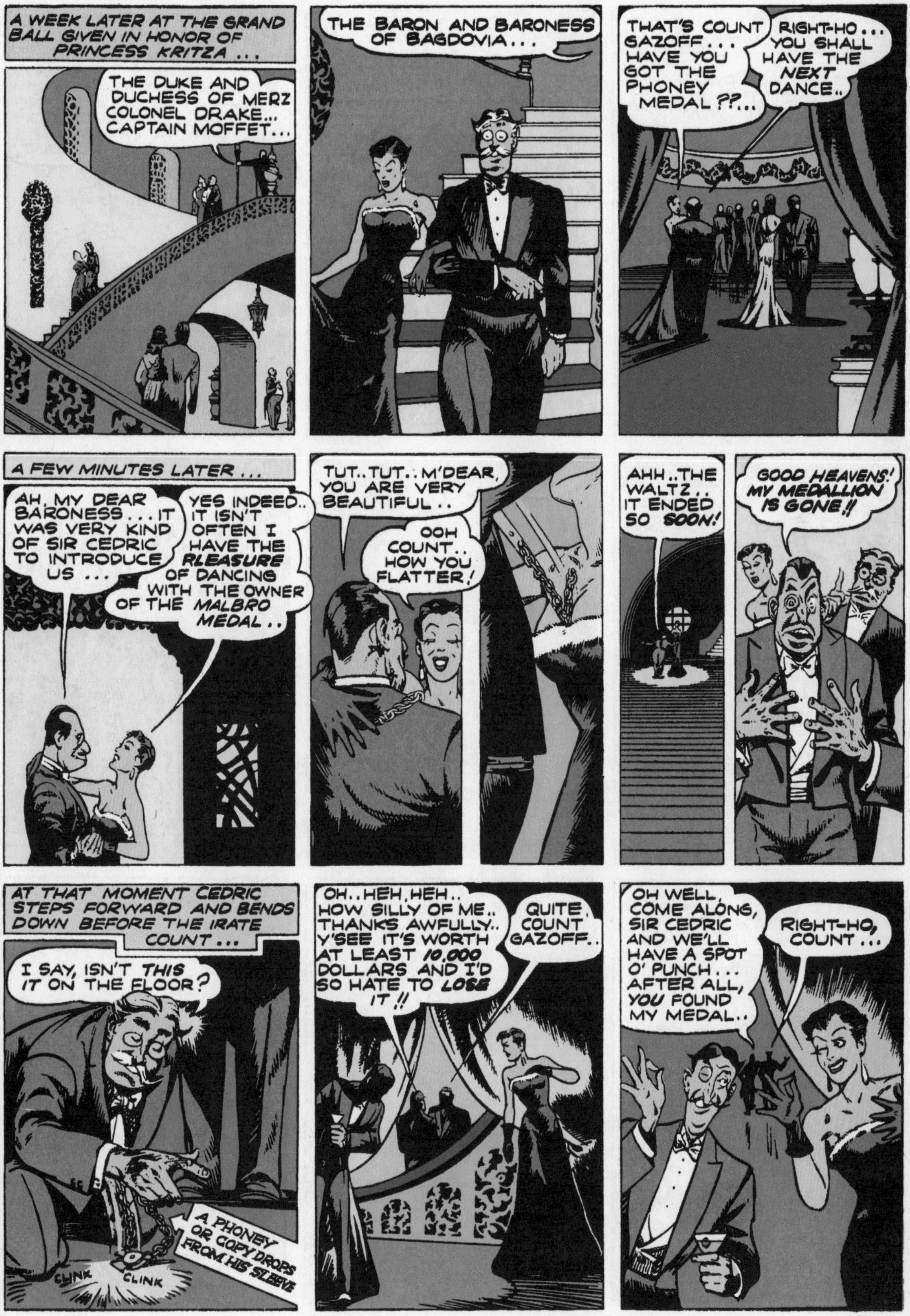

A WEEK LATER AT THE GRAND BALL GIVEN IN HONOR OF PRINCESS KRITZA ...
THE DUKE AND DUCHESS OF MERZ COLONEL DRAKE... CAPTAIN MOFFET...
THE BARON AND BARONESS OF BAGDOVIA ...
THAT'S COUNT GAZOFF ... HAVE YOU GOT THE PHONEY MEDAL ??...
RIGHT-HO ... YOU SHALL HAVE THE NEXT DANCE..
A FEW MINUTES LATER ...
AH, MY DEAR BARONESS ... IT WAS VERY KIND OF SIR CEDRIC TO INTRODUCE US ...
YES INDEED.. IT ISN'T OFTEN I HAVE THE RLEASURE OF DANCING WITH THE OWNER OF THE MALBRO MEDAL ..
TUT..TUT..M'DEAR, YOU ARE VERY BEAUTIFUL ..
OOH COUNT.. HOW YOU FLATTER!
AHH..THE WALTZ.. IT ENDED SO SOON!
GOOD HEAVENS! MY MEDALLION IS GONE!!
AT THAT MOMENT CEDRIC STEPS FORWARD AND BENDS DOWN BEFORE THE IRATE COUNT ...
I SAY, ISN'T THIS IT ON THE FLOOR?
A PHONEY OR COPY DROPS FROM HIS SLEEVE
CLINK CLINK
OH..HEH,HEH.. HOW SILLY OF ME.. THANKS AWFULLY.. Y'SEE IT'S WORTH AT LEAST 10,000 DOLLARS AND I'D SO HATE TO LOSE IT !!
QUITE, COUNT GAZOFF..
OH WELL, COME ALONG, SIR CEDRIC AND WE'LL HAVE A SPOT O' PUNCH ... AFTER ALL, YOU FOUND MY MEDAL..
RIGHT-HO, COUNT ...

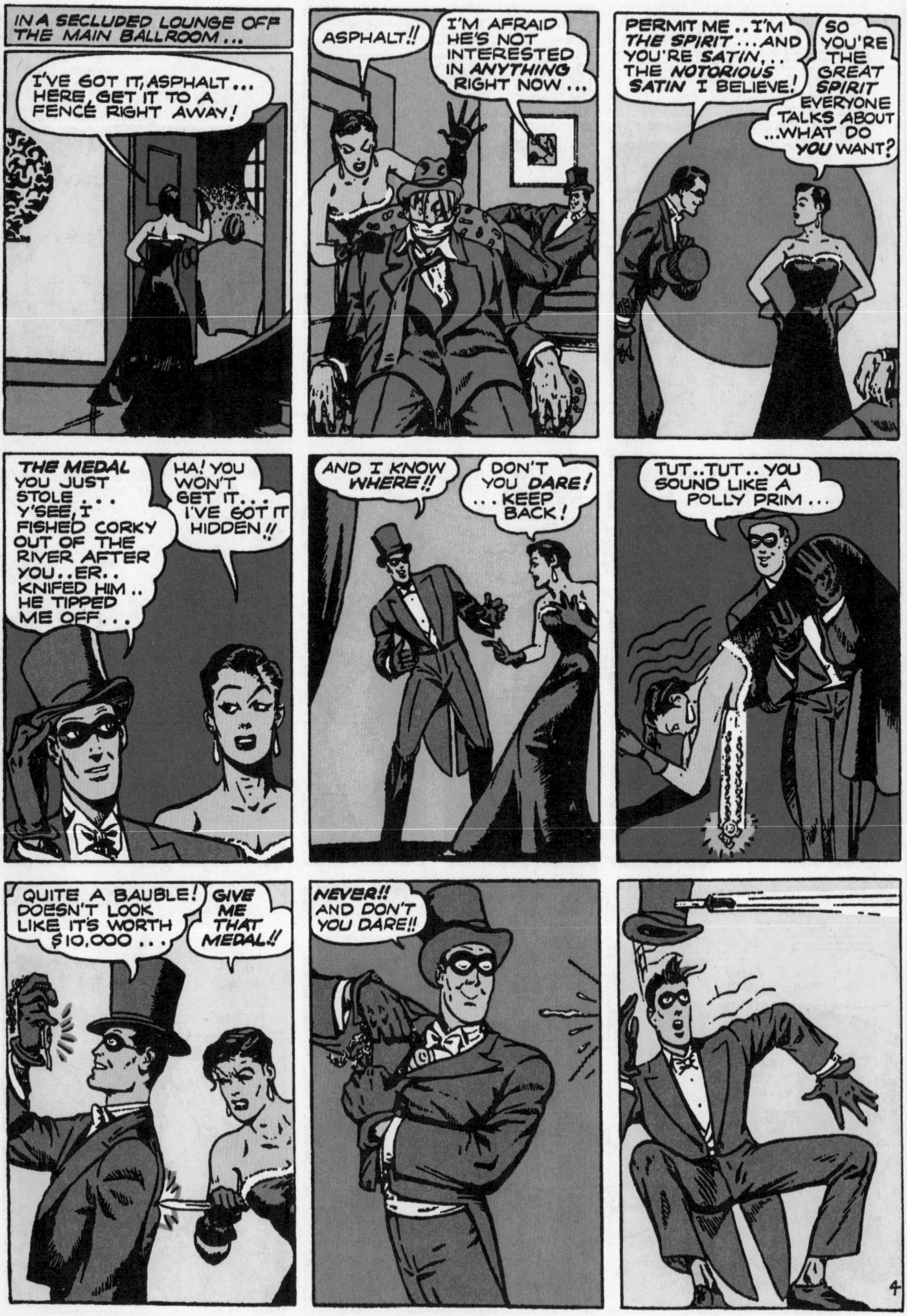
IN A SECLUDED LOUNGE OFF THE MAIN BALLROOM...
I'VE GOT IT, ASPHALT... HERE, GET IT TO A FENCE RIGHT AWAY!
ASPHALT!!
I'M AFRAID HE'S NOT INTERESTED IN ANYTHING RIGHT NOW...
PERMIT ME.. I'M THE SPIRIT ...AND YOU'RE SATIN,.. THE NOTORIOUS SATIN I BELIEVE!
SO YOU'RE THE GREAT SPIRIT EVERYONE TALKS ABOUT ...WHAT DO YOU WANT?
THE MEDAL YOU JUST STOLE... Y'SEE, I FISHED CORKY OUT OF THE RIVER AFTER YOU..ER.. KNIFED HIM.. HE TIPPED ME OFF...
HA! YOU WON'T GET IT... I'VE GOT IT HIDDEN!!
AND I KNOW WHERE!!
DON'T YOU DARE! ...KEEP BACK!
TUT..TUT.. YOU SOUND LIKE A POLLY PRIM...
QUITE A BAUBLE! DOESN'T LOOK LIKE IT'S WORTH $10,000...
GIVE ME THAT MEDAL!!
NEVER!! AND DON'T YOU DARE!!
4

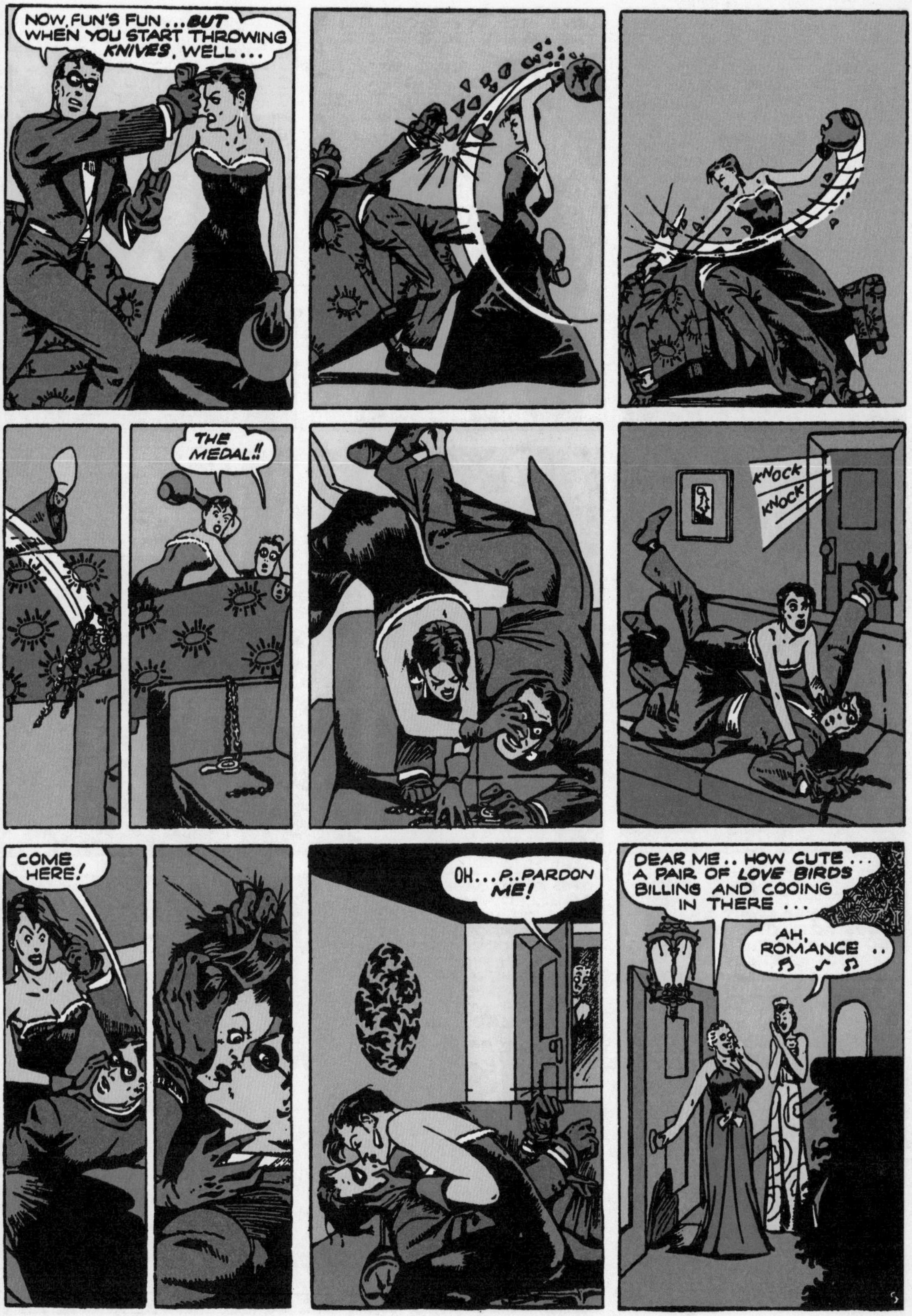
NOW, FUN'S FUN ... BUT WHEN YOU START THROWING KNIVES, WELL ...
THE MEDAL!!
KNOCK
KNOCK
COME HERE!
OH... P..PARDON ME!
DEAR ME.. HOW CUTE... A PAIR OF LOVE BIRDS BILLING AND COOING IN THERE ...
AH, ROMANCE ..

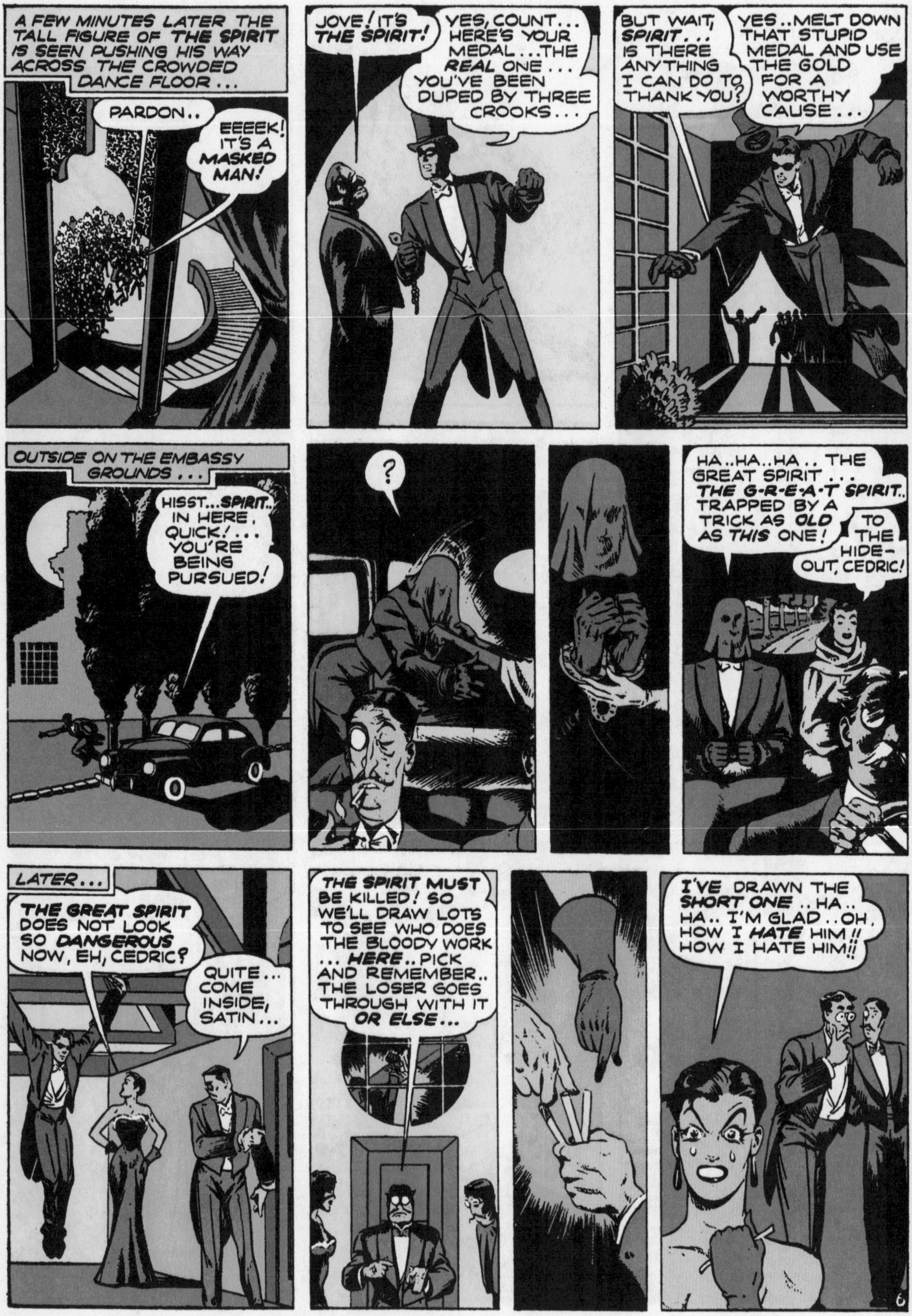
A FEW MINUTES LATER THE TALL FIGURE OF THE SPIRIT IS SEEN PUSHING HIS WAY ACROSS THE CROWDED DANCE FLOOR ...
PARDON..
EEEEK! IT'S A MASKED MAN!
JOVE! IT'S THE SPIRIT!
YES, COUNT... HERE'S YOUR MEDAL ...THE REAL ONE ... YOU'VE BEEN DUPED BY THREE CROOKS ...
BUT WAIT, SPIRIT... IS THERE ANYTHING I CAN DO TO THANK YOU?
YES..MELT DOWN THAT STUPID MEDAL AND USE THE GOLD FOR A WORTHY CAUSE ...
OUTSIDE ON THE EMBASSY GROUNDS ...
HISST...SPIRIT.. IN HERE, QUICK!... YOU'RE BEING PURSUED!
?
HA..HA..HA.. THE GREAT SPIRIT ... THE G-R-E-A-T SPIRIT.. TRAPPED BY A TRICK AS OLD AS THIS ONE!
TO THE HIDE-OUT, CEDRIC!
LATER...
THE GREAT SPIRIT DOES NOT LOOK SO DANGEROUS NOW, EH, CEDRIC?
QUITE... COME INSIDE, SATIN...
THE SPIRIT MUST BE KILLED! SO WE'LL DRAW LOTS TO SEE WHO DOES THE BLOODY WORK ... HERE.. PICK AND REMEMBER.. THE LOSER GOES THROUGH WITH IT OR ELSE...
I'VE DRAWN THE SHORT ONE .. HA.. HA.. I'M GLAD ..OH, HOW I HATE HIM!! HOW I HATE HIM!!
6

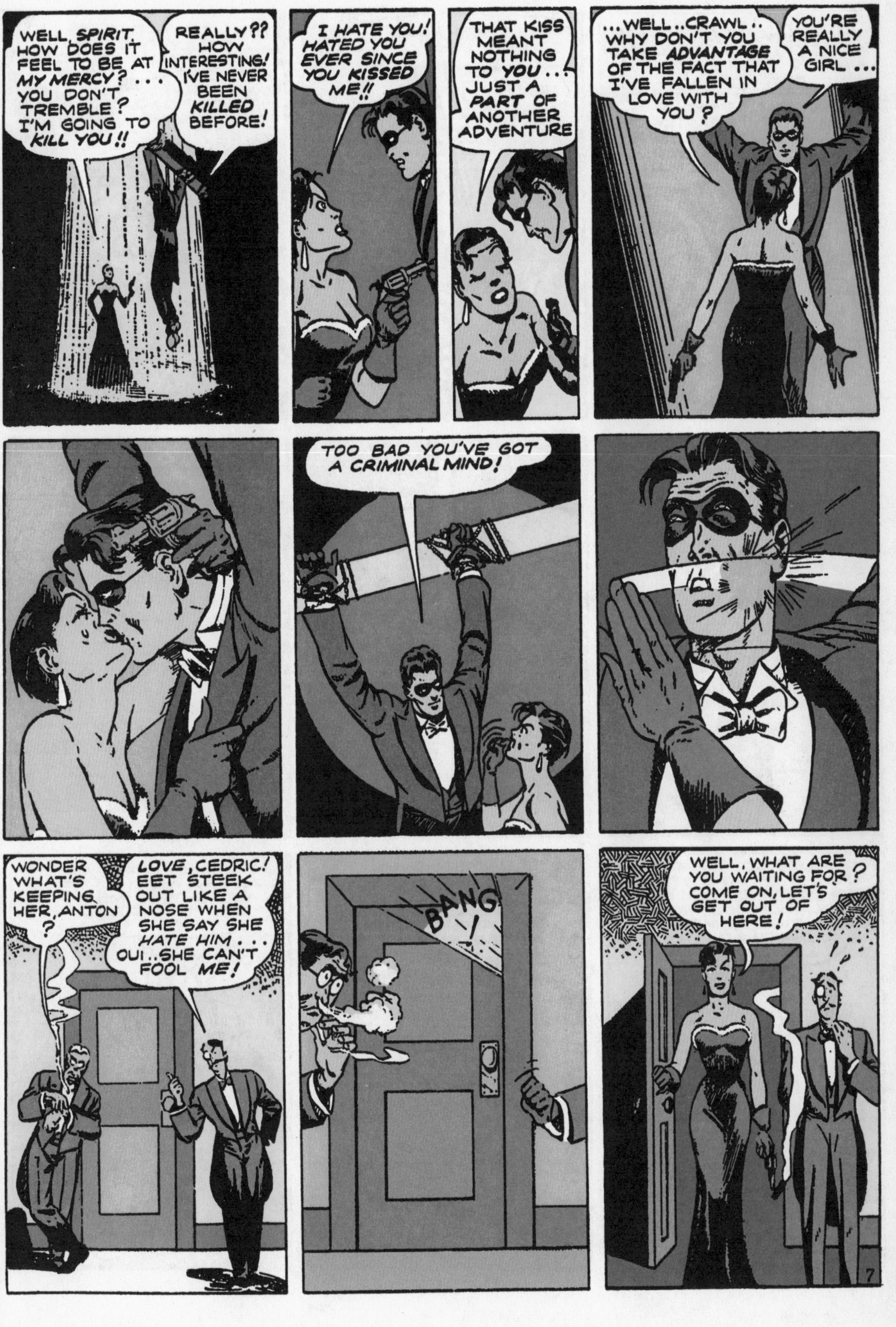
WELL, SPIRIT, HOW DOES IT FEEL TO BE AT MY MERCY? ... YOU DON'T TREMBLE? I'M GOING TO KILL YOU!!
REALLY?? HOW INTERESTING! I'VE NEVER BEEN KILLED BEFORE!
I HATE YOU! HATED YOU EVER SINCE YOU KISSED ME!!
THAT KISS MEANT NOTHING TO YOU... JUST A PART OF ANOTHER ADVENTURE
...WELL..CRAWL.. WHY DON'T YOU TAKE ADVANTAGE OF THE FACT THAT I'VE FALLEN IN LOVE WITH YOU?
YOU'RE REALLY A NICE GIRL ...
TOO BAD YOU'VE GOT A CRIMINAL MIND!
WONDER WHAT'S KEEPING HER, ANTON?
LOVE, CEDRIC! EET STEEK OUT LIKE A NOSE WHEN SHE SAY SHE HATE HIM... OUI..SHE CAN'T FOOL ME!
BANG!
WELL, WHAT ARE YOU WAITING FOR? COME ON, LET'S GET OUT OF HERE!
7

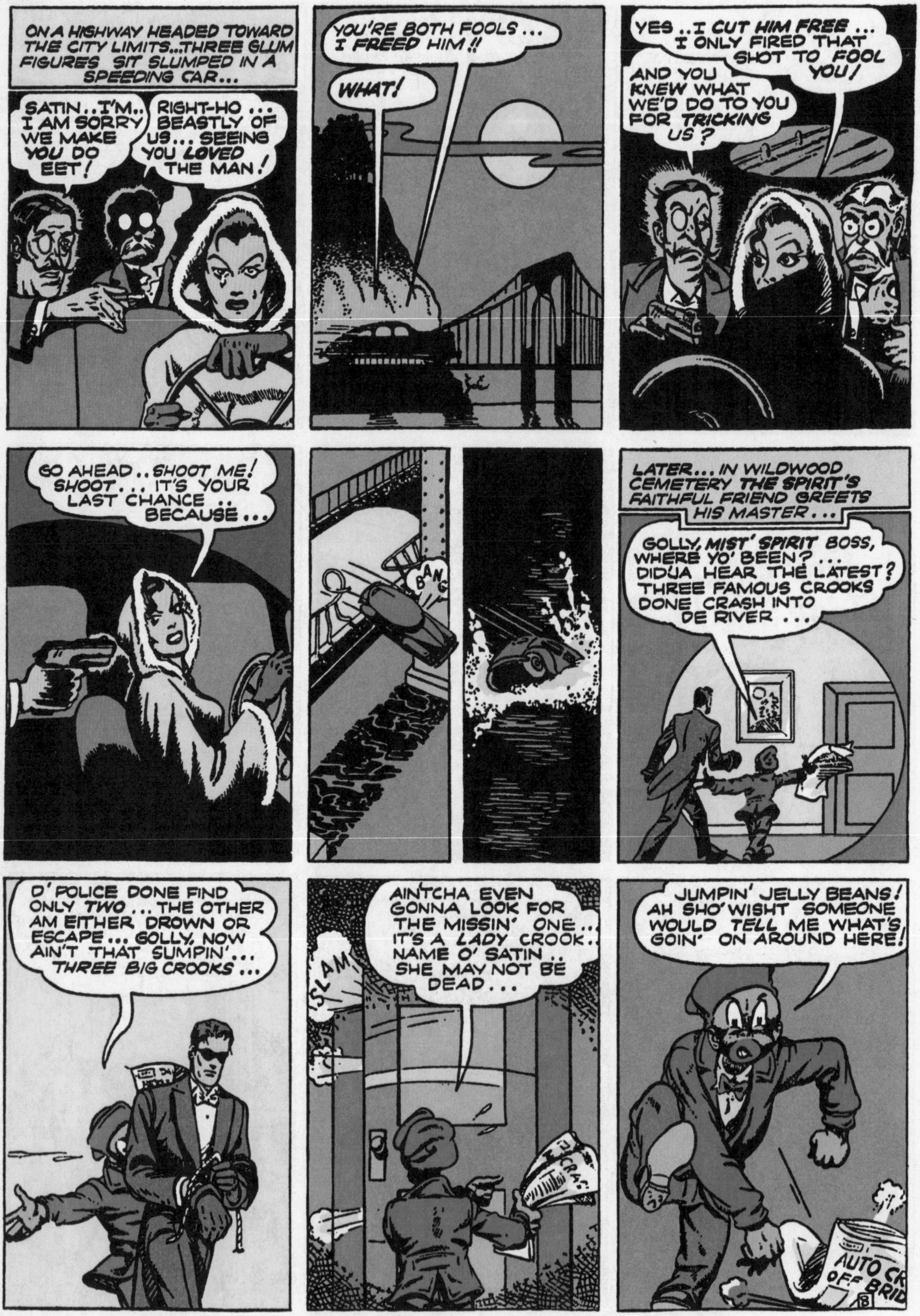
ON A HIGHWAY HEADED TOWARD THE CITY LIMITS...THREE GLUM FIGURES SIT SLUMPED IN A SPEEDING CAR...
SATIN..I'M.. I AM SORRY WE MAKE YOU DO EET!
RIGHT-HO ... BEASTLY OF US... SEEING YOU LOVED THE MAN!
YOU'RE BOTH FOOLS ... I FREED HIM!!
WHAT!
YES ..I CUT HIM FREE ... I ONLY FIRED THAT SHOT TO FOOL YOU!
AND YOU KNEW WHAT WE'D DO TO YOU FOR TRICKING US?
GO AHEAD..SHOOT ME! SHOOT... IT'S YOUR LAST CHANCE .. BECAUSE...
BANG
LATER... IN WILDWOOD CEMETERY THE SPIRIT'S FAITHFUL FRIEND GREETS HIS MASTER...
GOLLY, MIST' SPIRIT BOSS, WHERE YO' BEEN?... DIDJA HEAR THE LATEST? THREE FAMOUS CROOKS DONE CRASH INTO DE RIVER...
D' POLICE DONE FIND ONLY TWO... THE OTHER AM EITHER DROWN OR ESCAPE... GOLLY, NOW AIN'T THAT SUMPIN'... THREE BIG CROOKS...
SLAM
AINTCHA EVEN GONNA LOOK FOR THE MISSIN' ONE... IT'S A LADY CROOK.. NAME O' SATIN.. SHE MAY NOT BE DEAD...
JUMPIN' JELLY BEANS! AH SHO' WISHT SOMEONE WOULD TELL ME WHAT'S GOIN' ON AROUND HERE!
AUTO CR OFF BRID

THE LAST TROLLEY

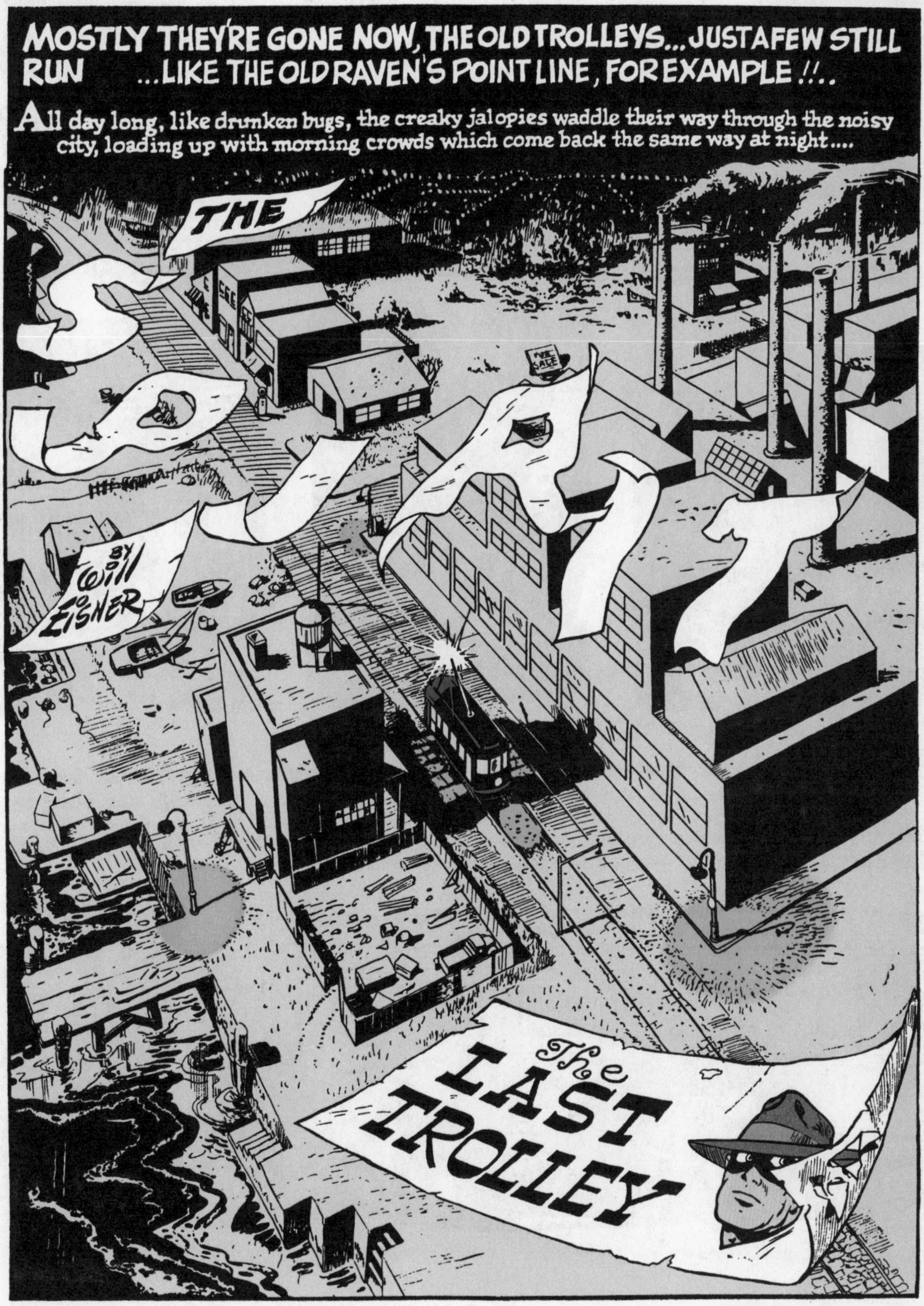
MOSTLY THEY'RE GONE NOW, THE OLD TROLLEYS... JUST A FEW STILL RUN ...LIKE THE OLD RAVEN'S POINT LINE, FOR EXAMPLE !!..
All day long, like drunken bugs, the creaky jalopies waddle their way through the noisy city, loading up with morning crowds which come back the same way at night....
THE SPIRIT
BY Will EISNER
The LAST TROLLEY

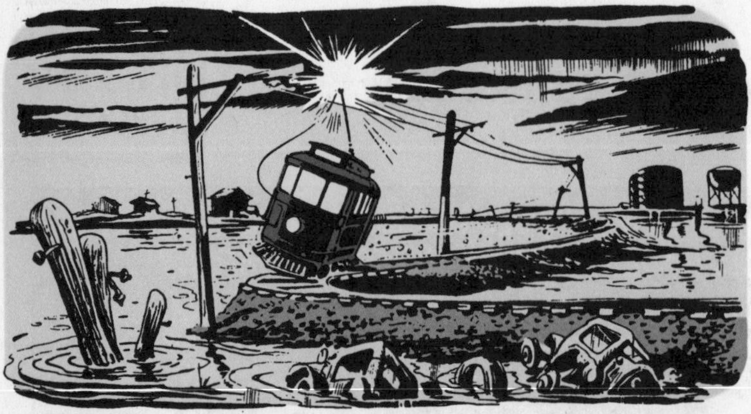

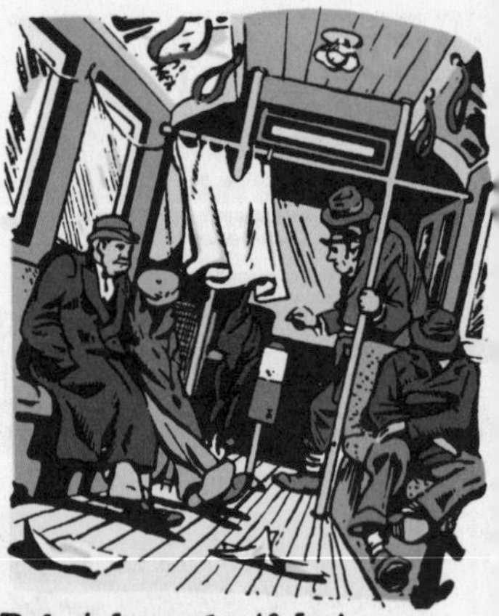

The trolley-run from the heart of Central City to Raven's Point is only thirty twisted miles and can hardly be called A Great Adventure....

CLACKITY CLACK... CLACKITY CLACK... CLACKITY CLACK... CLACKITY CLACK... CLACKITY CLACK...

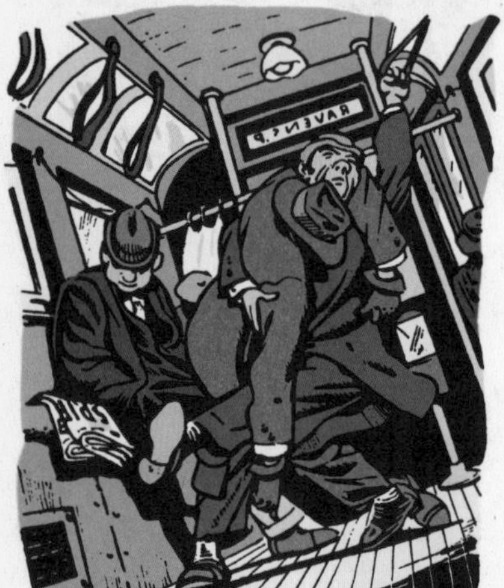

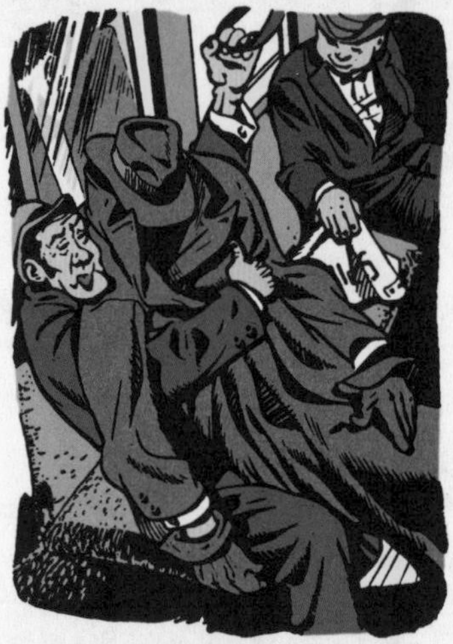

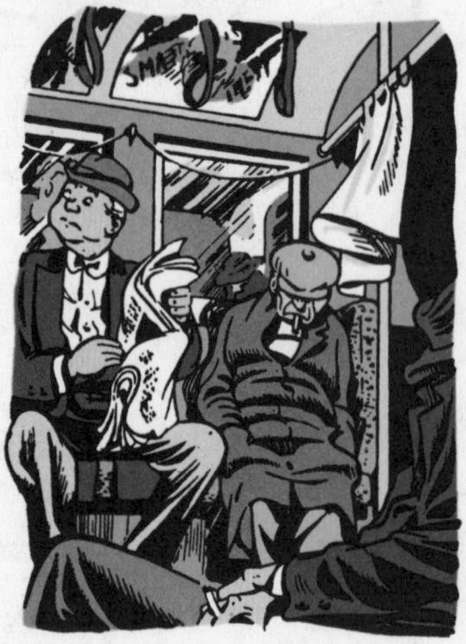

CLACKITY CLACKK CLACKITY CLACK CLACKITY CLACK

Until 3 a.m.... the trolleys come and go, getting emptier and emptier as the night grows deeper.... then, the last trolley--"The 29 Car"--clatters through the sleeping metropolis, rattles noisily across Central River Bridge, and with its cargo of human flotsam clickety-clacks for the Raven's Point barns.... From here until the end of the line there are no stops -- it is the dullest part of the trip!

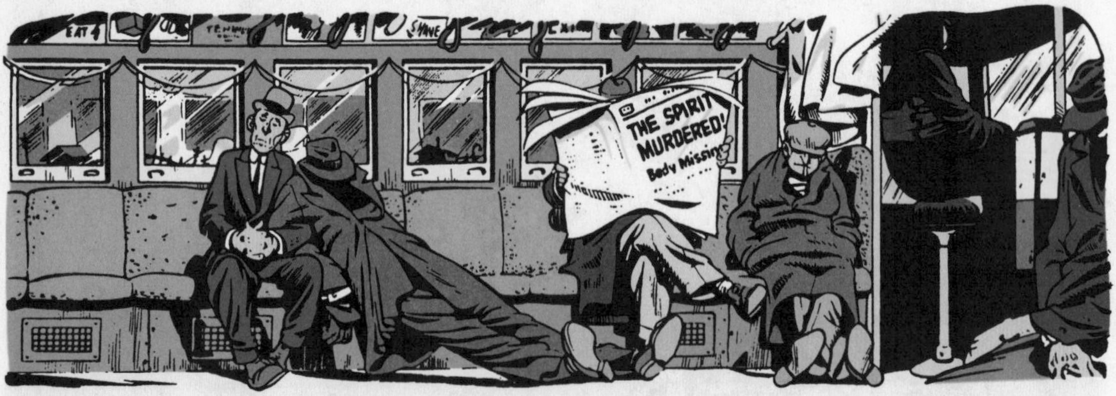
THE SPIRIT MURDERED!

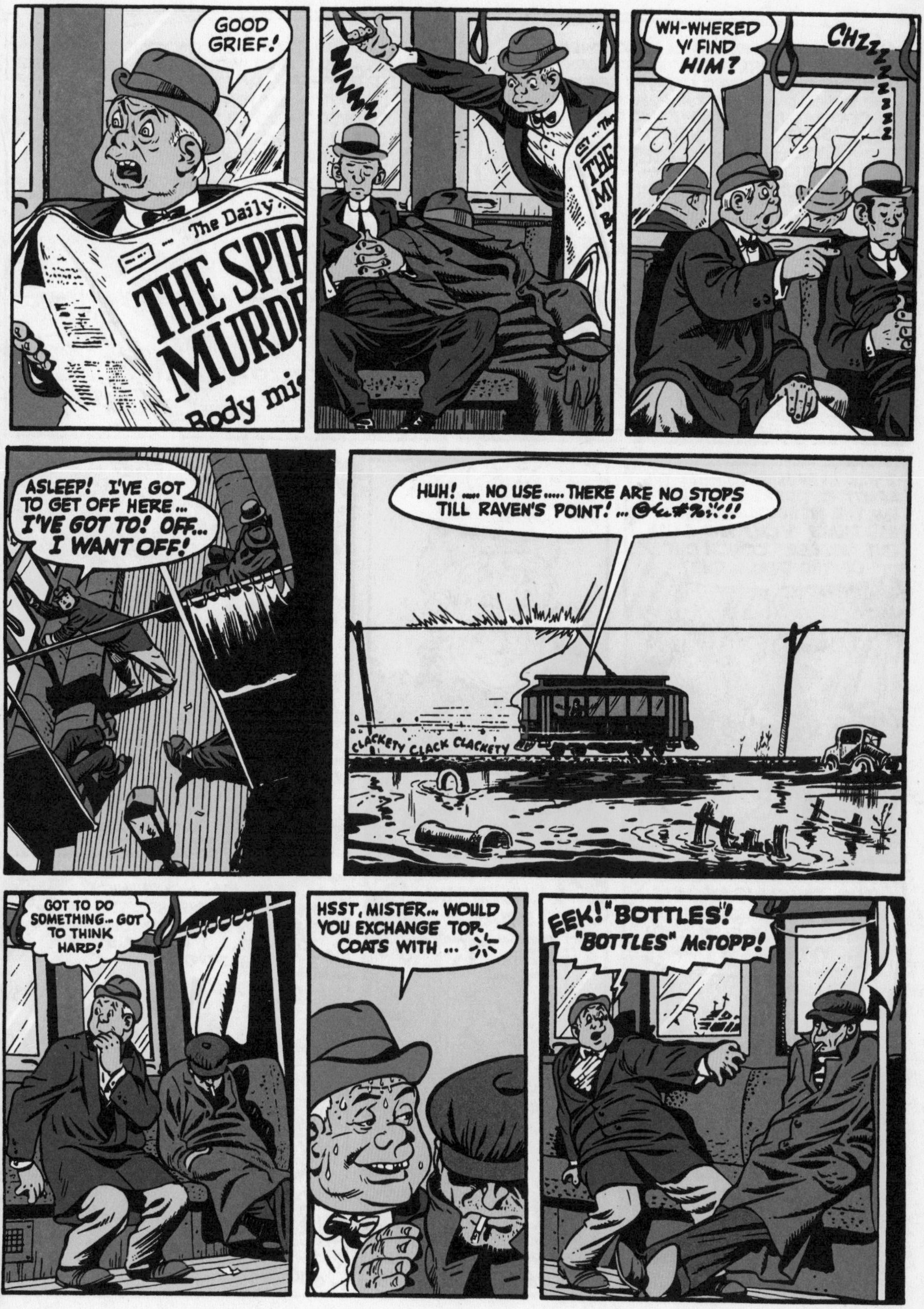
GOOD GRIEF!
ZZZZZ
WH-WHERED Y' FIND HIM?
CHZZZZZZZZZZ
ASLEEP! I'VE GOT TO GET OFF HERE... I'VE GOT TO! OFF... I WANT OFF!
HUH! ..... NO USE..... THERE ARE NO STOPS TILL RAVEN'S POINT! ...@¢#%!!
CLACKETY CLACK CLACKETY
GOT TO DO SOMETHING.. GOT TO THINK HARD!
HSST, MISTER.. WOULD YOU EXCHANGE TOP-COATS WITH ...
EEK! "BOTTLES"! "BOTTLES" McTOPP!

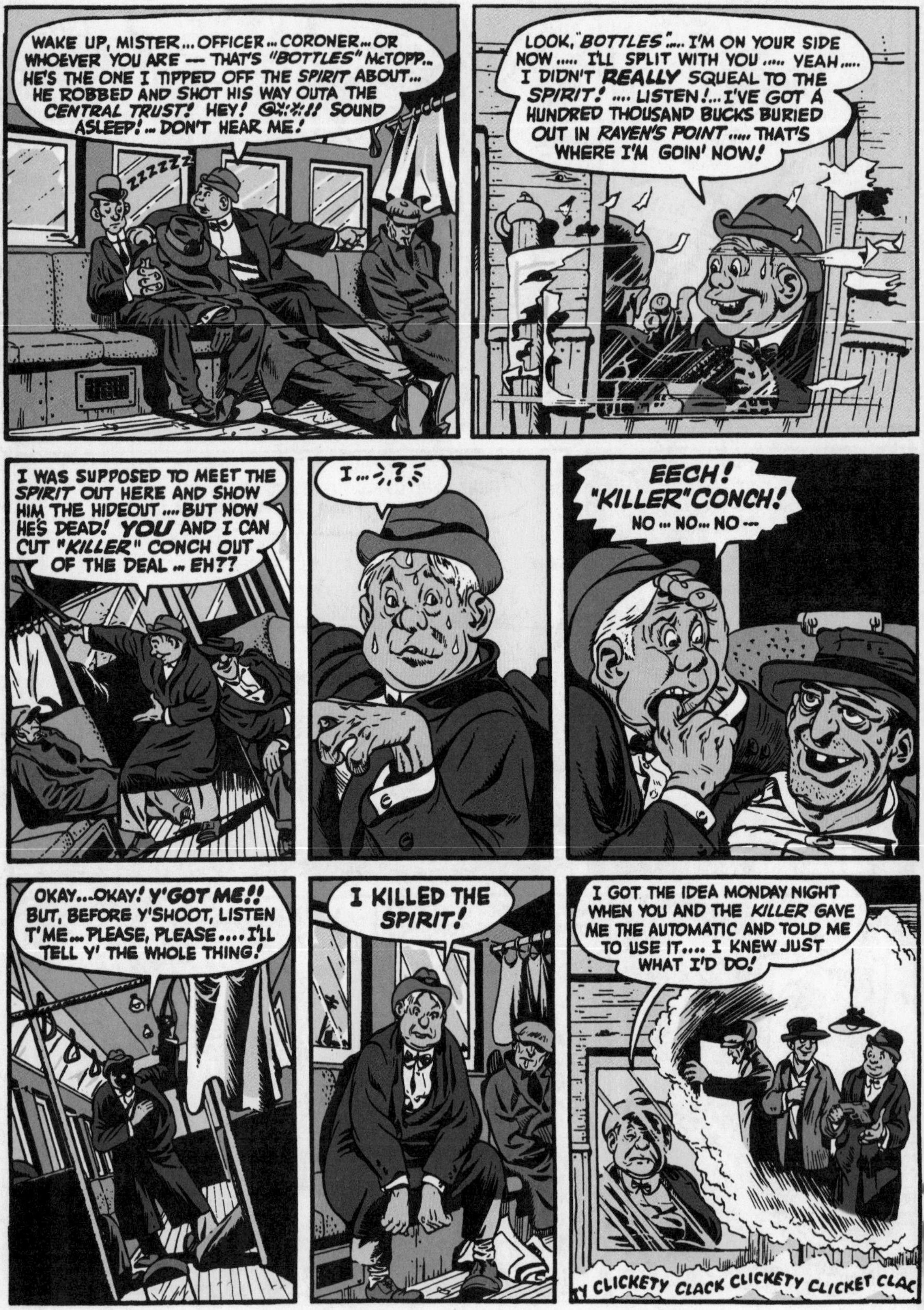
WAKE UP, MISTER... OFFICER... CORONER... OR WHOEVER YOU ARE — THAT'S "BOTTLES" McTOPP.. HE'S THE ONE I TIPPED OFF THE SPIRIT ABOUT... HE ROBBED AND SHOT HIS WAY OUTA THE CENTRAL TRUST! HEY! @%:%:!! SOUND ASLEEP!.. DON'T HEAR ME!
ZZZZZZ
LOOK, "BOTTLES"..... I'M ON YOUR SIDE NOW..... I'LL SPLIT WITH YOU..... YEAH..... I DIDN'T REALLY SQUEAL TO THE SPIRIT!.... LISTEN!... I'VE GOT A HUNDRED THOUSAND BUCKS BURIED OUT IN RAVEN'S POINT..... THAT'S WHERE I'M GOIN' NOW!
I WAS SUPPOSED TO MEET THE SPIRIT OUT HERE AND SHOW HIM THE HIDEOUT.... BUT NOW HE'S DEAD! YOU AND I CAN CUT "KILLER" CONCH OUT OF THE DEAL.. EH??
I... ?
EECH! "KILLER" CONCH! NO... NO... NO—
OKAY...OKAY! Y'GOT ME!! BUT, BEFORE Y'SHOOT, LISTEN T'ME... PLEASE, PLEASE.... I'LL TELL Y' THE WHOLE THING!
I KILLED THE SPIRIT!
I GOT THE IDEA MONDAY NIGHT WHEN YOU AND THE KILLER GAVE ME THE AUTOMATIC AND TOLD ME TO USE IT.... I KNEW JUST WHAT I'D DO!
Y CLICKETY CLACK CLICKETY CLICKET CLAC

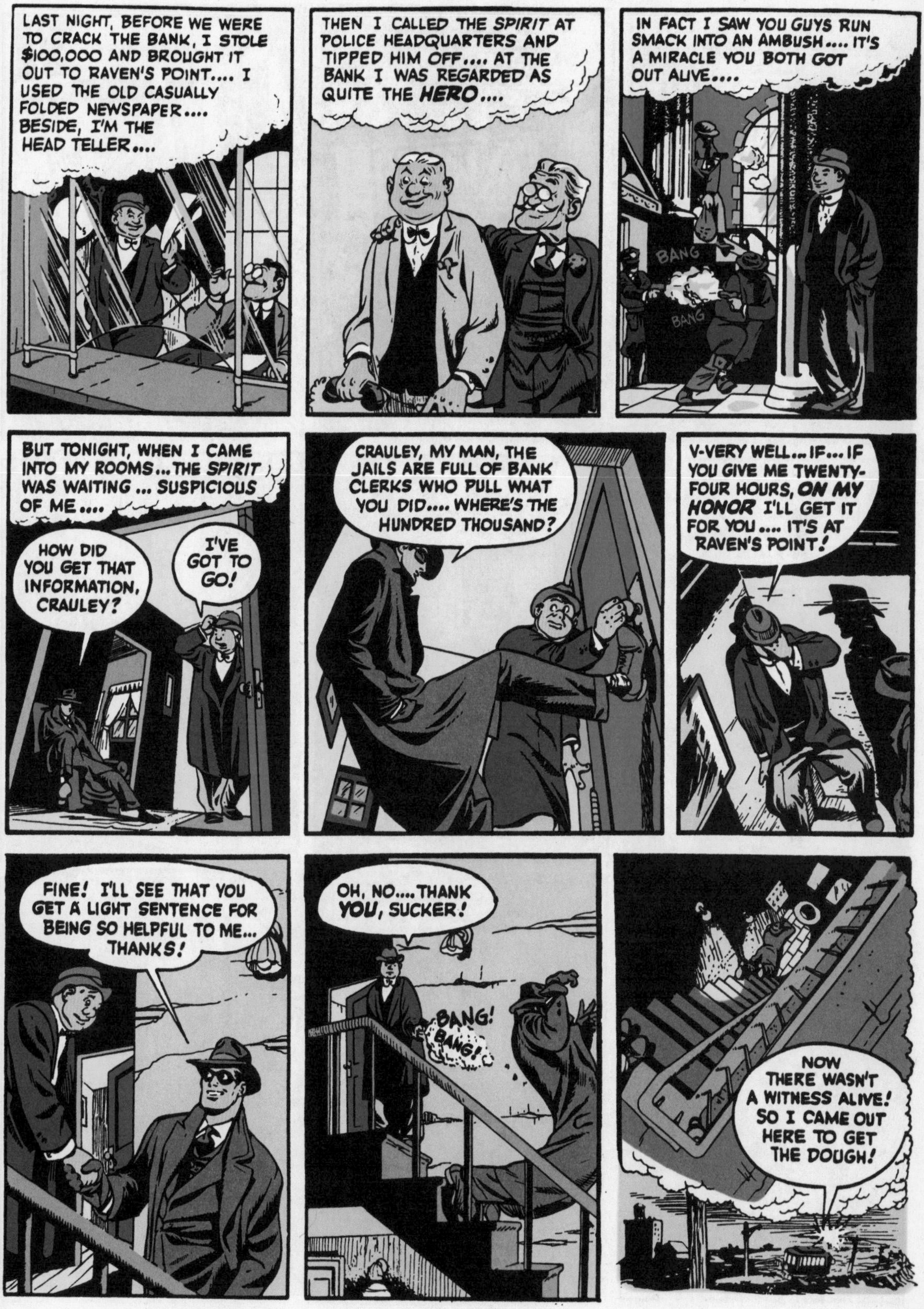
LAST NIGHT, BEFORE WE WERE TO CRACK THE BANK, I STOLE $100,000 AND BROUGHT IT OUT TO RAVEN'S POINT.... I USED THE OLD CASUALLY FOLDED NEWSPAPER.... BESIDE, I'M THE HEAD TELLER....
THEN I CALLED THE SPIRIT AT POLICE HEADQUARTERS AND TIPPED HIM OFF.... AT THE BANK I WAS REGARDED AS QUITE THE HERO....
IN FACT I SAW YOU GUYS RUN SMACK INTO AN AMBUSH.... IT'S A MIRACLE YOU BOTH GOT OUT ALIVE....
BANG
BANG
BUT TONIGHT, WHEN I CAME INTO MY ROOMS...THE SPIRIT WAS WAITING ... SUSPICIOUS OF ME....
HOW DID YOU GET THAT INFORMATION, CRAULEY?
I'VE GOT TO GO!
CRAULEY, MY MAN, THE JAILS ARE FULL OF BANK CLERKS WHO PULL WHAT YOU DID.... WHERE'S THE HUNDRED THOUSAND?
V-VERY WELL...IF...IF YOU GIVE ME TWENTY-FOUR HOURS, ON MY HONOR I'LL GET IT FOR YOU .... IT'S AT RAVEN'S POINT!
FINE! I'LL SEE THAT YOU GET A LIGHT SENTENCE FOR BEING SO HELPFUL TO ME... THANKS!
OH, NO....THANK YOU, SUCKER!
BANG!
BANG!
NOW THERE WASN'T A WITNESS ALIVE! SO I CAME OUT HERE TO GET THE DOUGH!

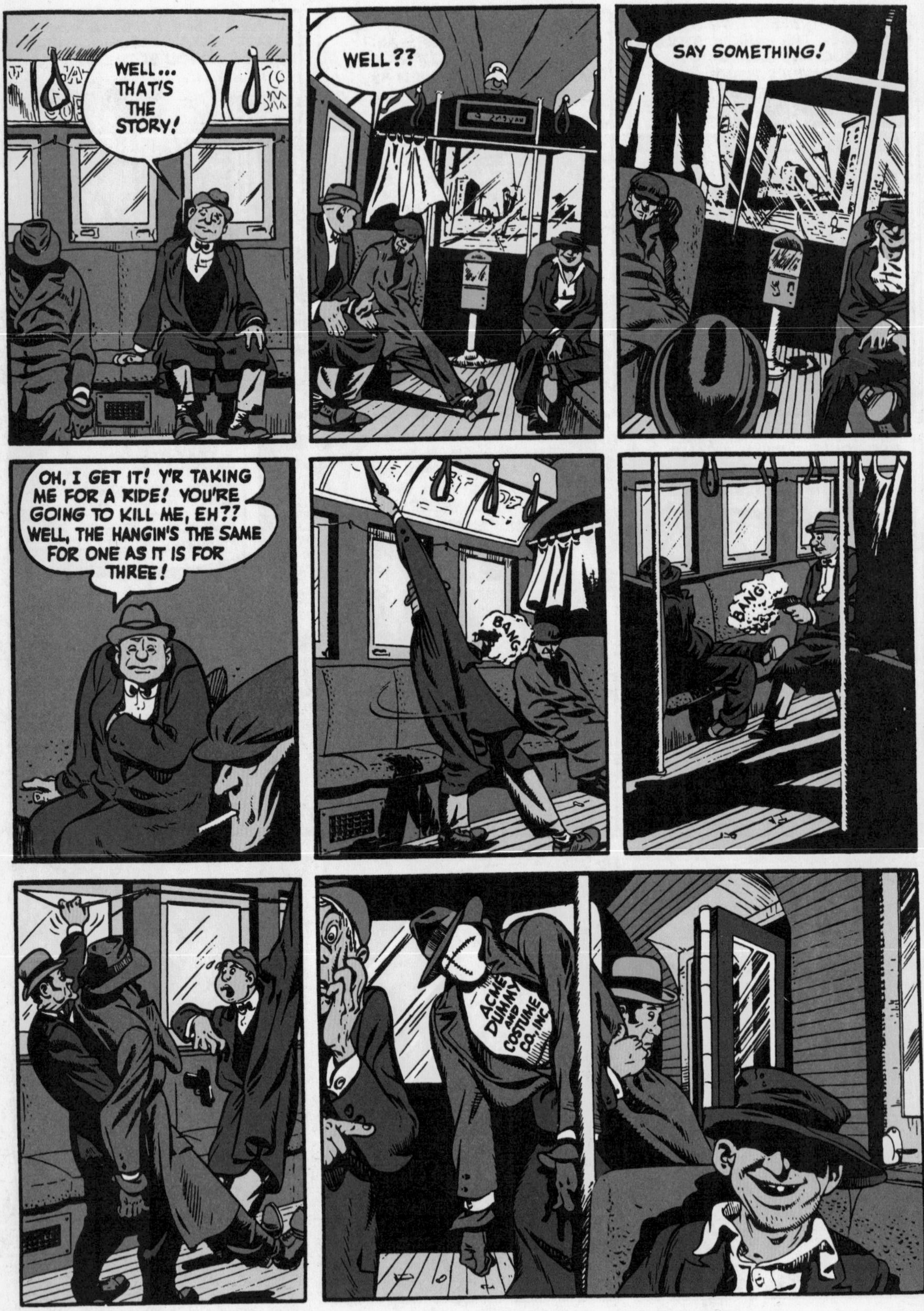
WELL... THAT'S THE STORY!
WELL??
SAY SOMETHING!
OH, I GET IT! Y'R TAKING ME FOR A RIDE! YOU'RE GOING TO KILL ME, EH?? WELL, THE HANGIN'S THE SAME FOR ONE AS IT IS FOR THREE!
BANG
BANG
ACME DUMMY AND COSTUME CO. INC

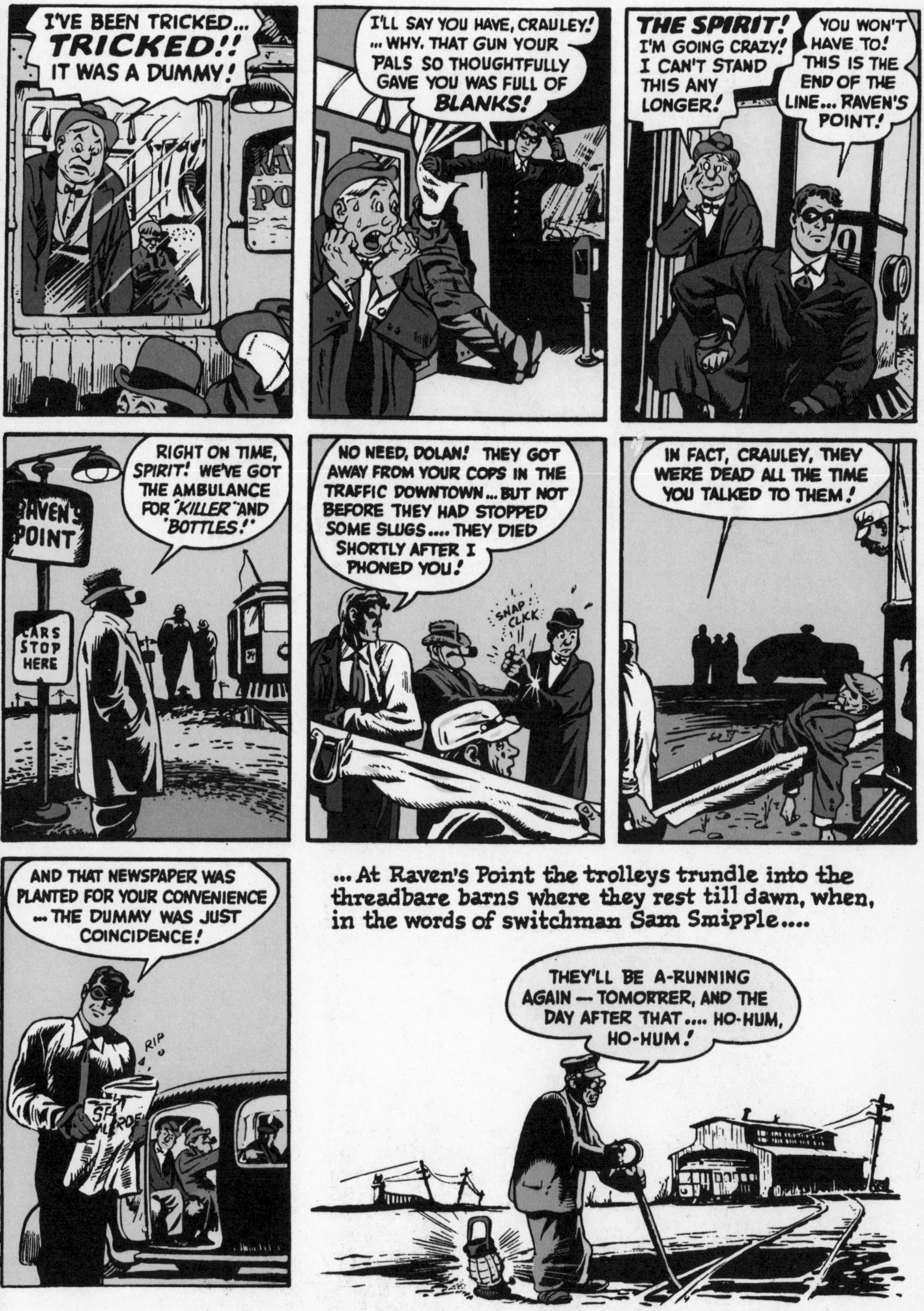
I'VE BEEN TRICKED... TRICKED!! IT WAS A DUMMY!
I'LL SAY YOU HAVE, CRAULEY! ... WHY, THAT GUN YOUR PALS SO THOUGHTFULLY GAVE YOU WAS FULL OF BLANKS!
THE SPIRIT! I'M GOING CRAZY! I CAN'T STAND THIS ANY LONGER!
YOU WON'T HAVE TO! THIS IS THE END OF THE LINE... RAVEN'S POINT!
RIGHT ON TIME, SPIRIT! WE'VE GOT THE AMBULANCE FOR "KILLER" AND "BOTTLES!"
RAVEN'S POINT
CARS STOP HERE
NO NEED, DOLAN! THEY GOT AWAY FROM YOUR COPS IN THE TRAFFIC DOWNTOWN... BUT NOT BEFORE THEY HAD STOPPED SOME SLUGS.... THEY DIED SHORTLY AFTER I PHONED YOU!
SNAP CLKK
IN FACT, CRAULEY, THEY WERE DEAD ALL THE TIME YOU TALKED TO THEM!
AND THAT NEWSPAPER WAS PLANTED FOR YOUR CONVENIENCE ... THE DUMMY WAS JUST COINCIDENCE!
RIP
... At Raven's Point the trolleys trundle into the threadbare barns where they rest till dawn, when, in the words of switchman Sam Smipple....
THEY'LL BE A-RUNNING AGAIN — TOMORRER, AND THE DAY AFTER THAT.... HO-HUM, HO-HUM!

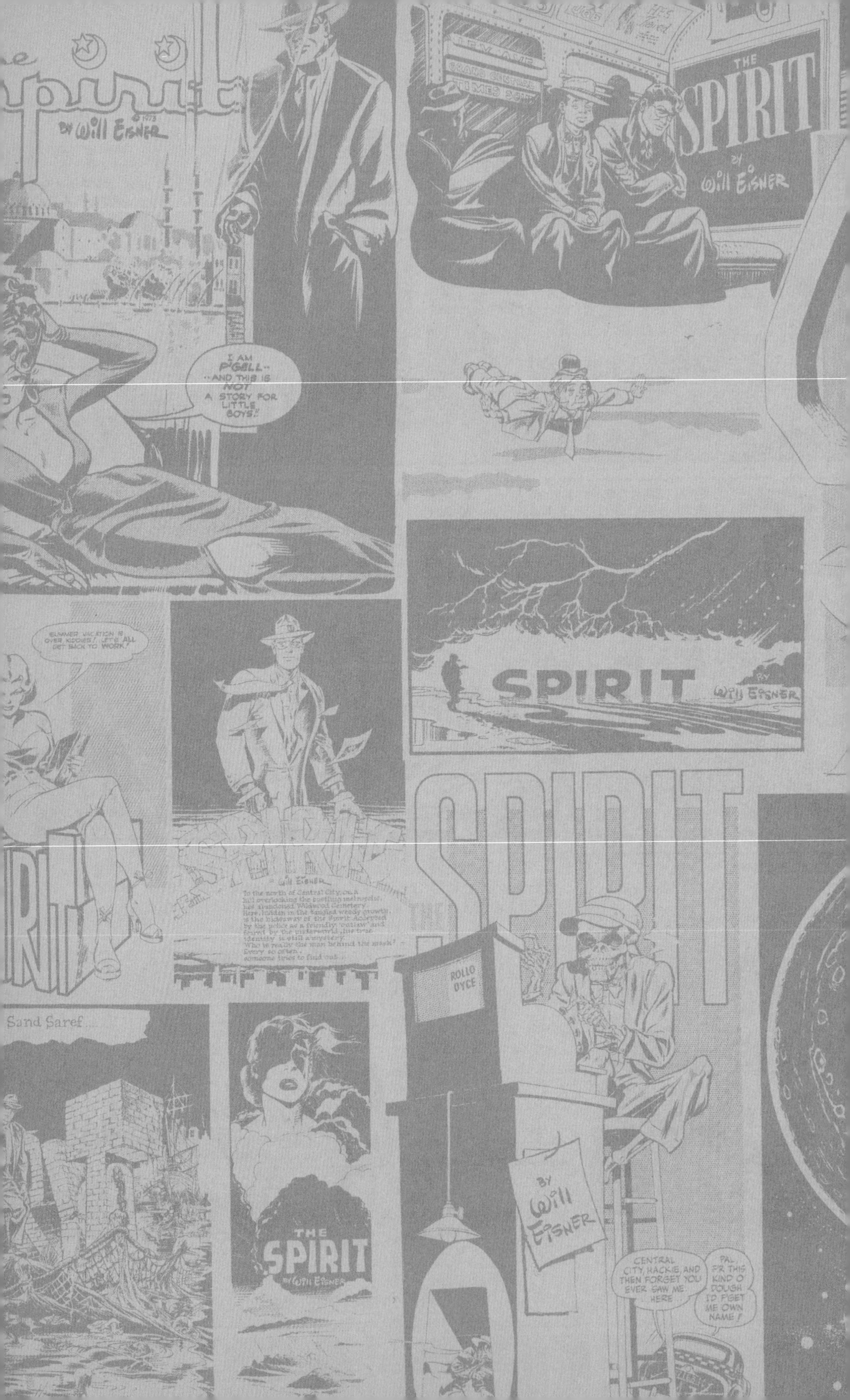
The Spirit
BY Will Eisner
I AM P'GELL-- ..AND THIS IS NOT A STORY FOR LITTLE BOYS!!
THE SPIRIT
BY Will Eisner
SUMMER VACATION IS OVER KIDDIES! LET'S ALL GET BACK TO WORK!
SPIRIT
BY Will Eisner
THE SPIRIT
Sand Saref....
ROLLO DYCE
THE SPIRIT
BY Will Eisner
BY Will Eisner
CENTRAL CITY, HACKIE, AND THEN FORGET YOU EVER SAW ME HERE.
PAL, FR THIS KIND O DOUGH I'D F'GET ME OWN NAME!

COMIC BOOK SECTION

THE POSTAGE STAMP

ACTION Mystery ADVENTURE

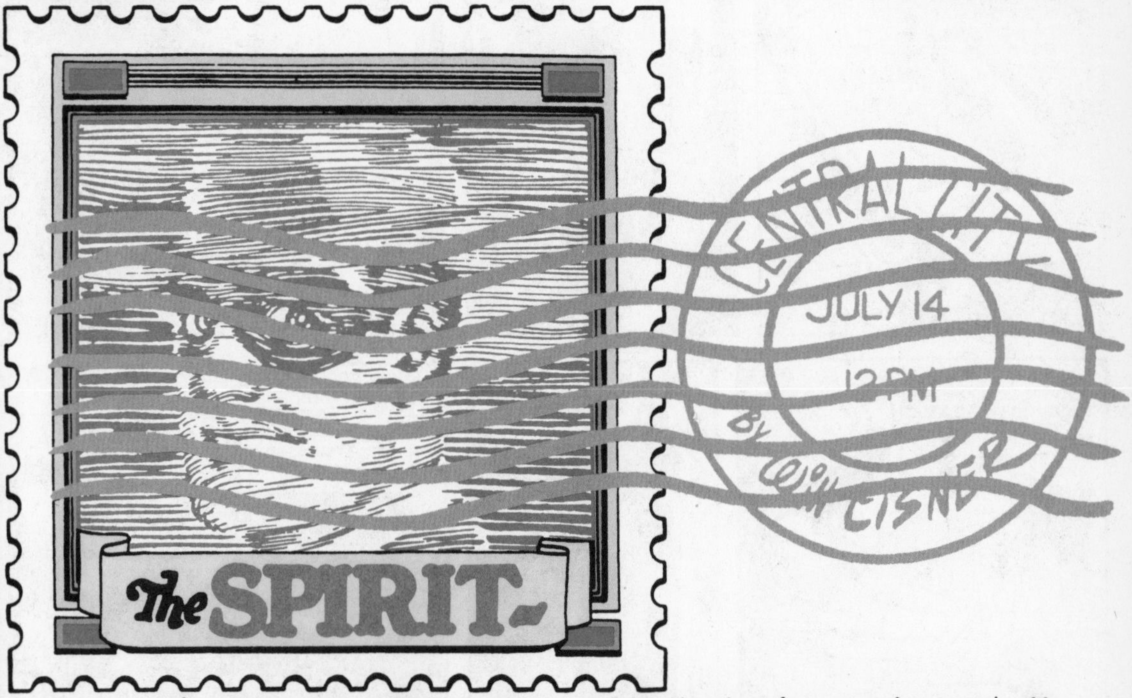
The SPIRIT
CENTRAL CITY
JULY 14
12 PM
BY WILL EISNER

The waterfront, unlike any other part of the city, lives a life unto itself! Mystery and unfathomable intrigue seems to cling to it with the tenacity of sea moss. Here, while you and I slumber, those who wish can do a brisk traffic in sudden death. For sometimes, the ships that come and go in the night bring cargos that none but the mad could conceive.

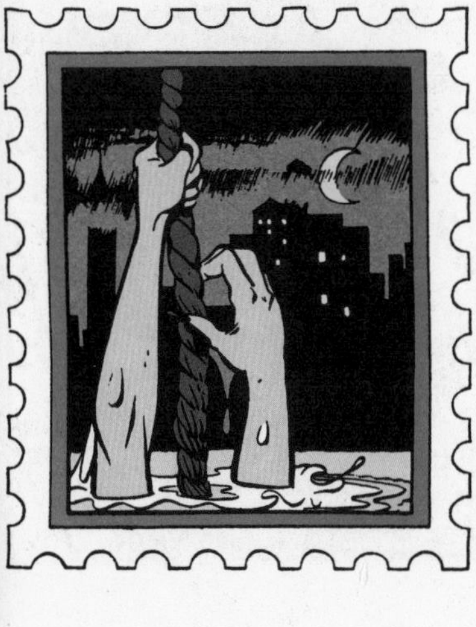

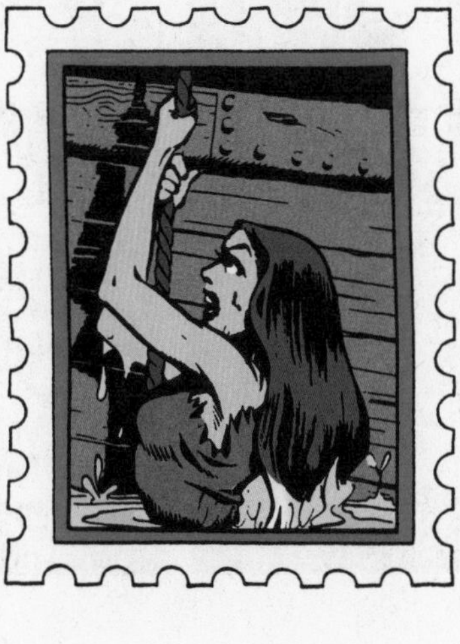

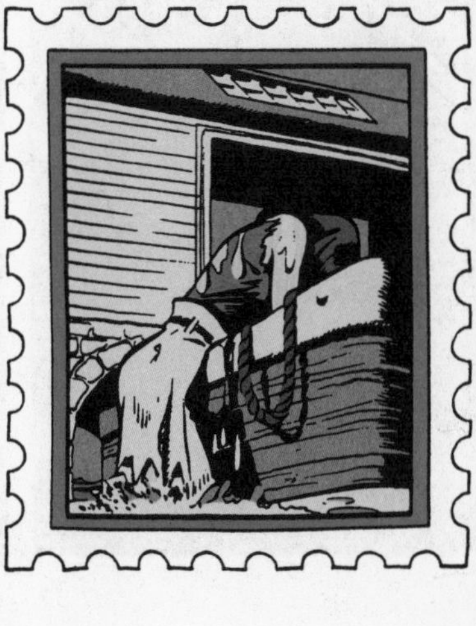

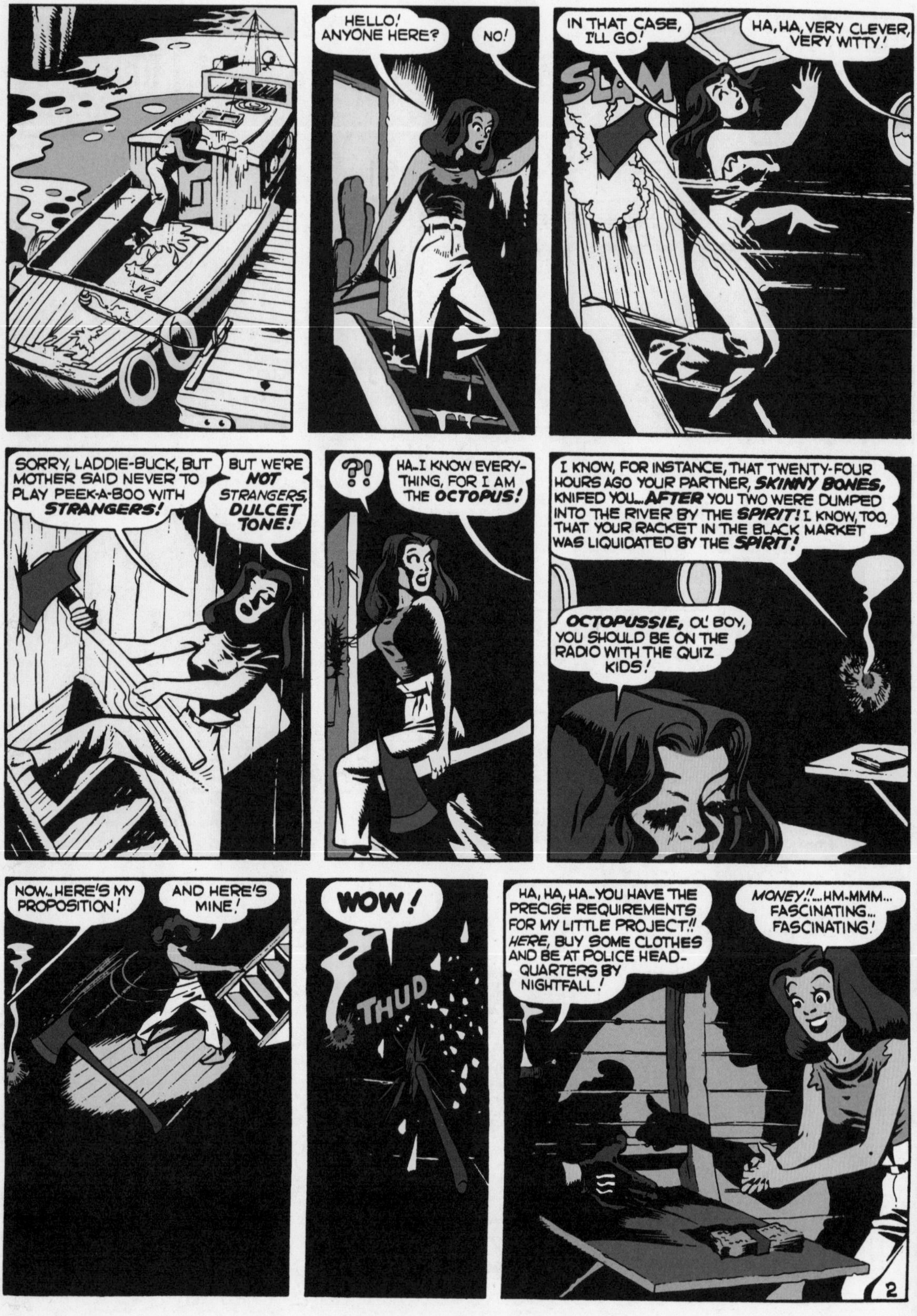

HELLO! ANYONE HERE?
NO!
IN THAT CASE, I'LL GO!
SLAM
HA, HA, VERY CLEVER, VERY WITTY!
SORRY, LADDIE-BUCK, BUT MOTHER SAID NEVER TO PLAY PEEK-A-BOO WITH STRANGERS!
BUT WE'RE NOT STRANGERS, DULCET TONE!
?!
HA-I KNOW EVERY-THING, FOR I AM THE OCTOPUS!
I KNOW, FOR INSTANCE, THAT TWENTY-FOUR HOURS AGO YOUR PARTNER, SKINNY BONES, KNIFED YOU...AFTER YOU TWO WERE DUMPED INTO THE RIVER BY THE SPIRIT! I KNOW, TOO, THAT YOUR RACKET IN THE BLACK MARKET WAS LIQUIDATED BY THE SPIRIT!
OCTOPUSSIE, OL' BOY, YOU SHOULD BE ON THE RADIO WITH THE QUIZ KIDS!
NOW...HERE'S MY PROPOSITION!
AND HERE'S MINE!
WOW!
THUD
HA, HA, HA-YOU HAVE THE PRECISE REQUIREMENTS FOR MY LITTLE PROJECT!! HERE, BUY SOME CLOTHES AND BE AT POLICE HEAD-QUARTERS BY NIGHTFALL!
MONEY!!...HM-MMM... FASCINATING... FASCINATING!
2

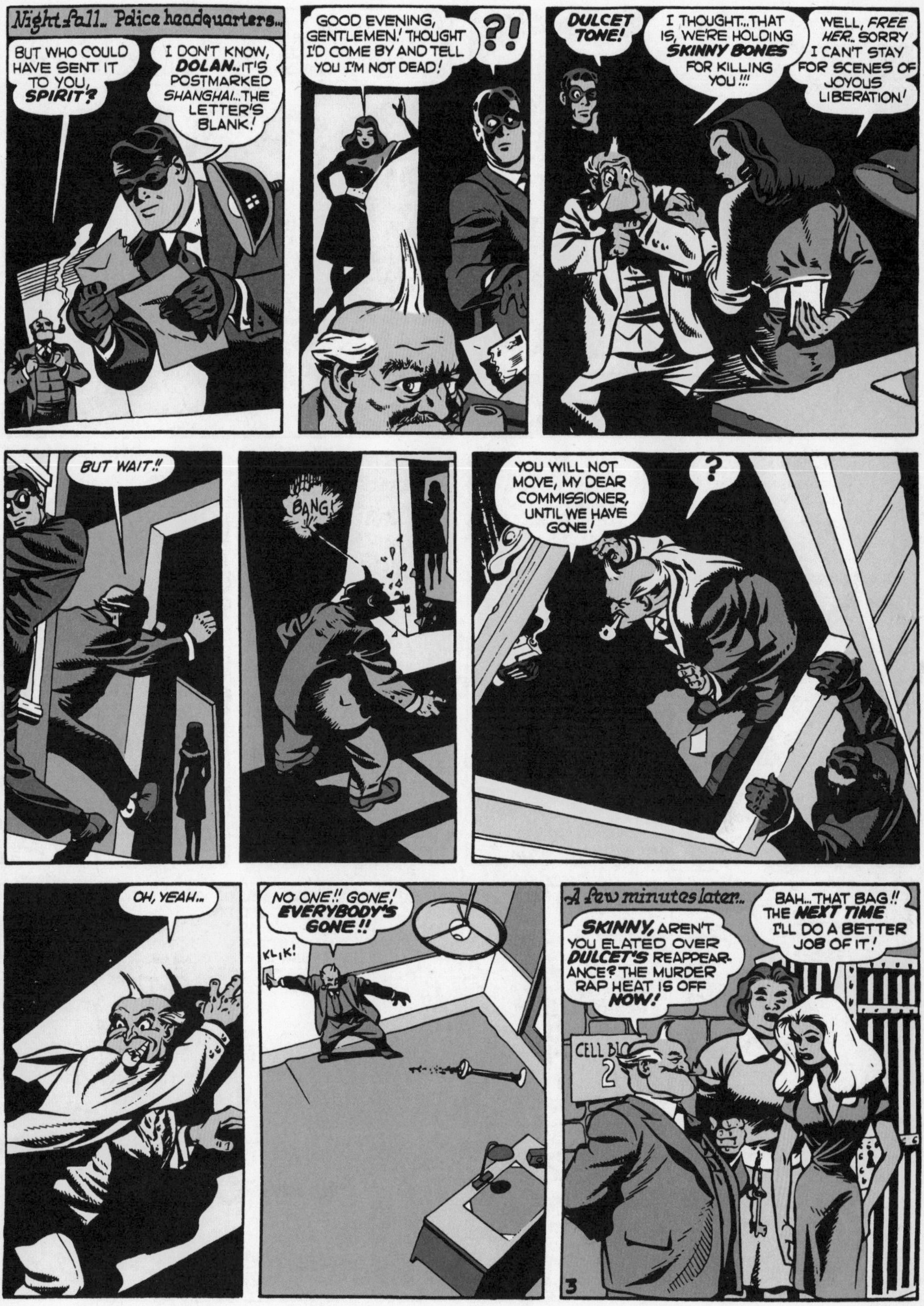
Nightfall.. Police headquarters...
BUT WHO COULD HAVE SENT IT TO YOU, SPIRIT?
I DON'T KNOW, DOLAN.. IT'S POSTMARKED SHANGHAI... THE LETTER'S BLANK!
GOOD EVENING, GENTLEMEN! THOUGHT I'D COME BY AND TELL YOU I'M NOT DEAD!
?!
DULCET TONE!
I THOUGHT... THAT IS, WE'RE HOLDING SKINNY BONES FOR KILLING YOU!!!
WELL, FREE HER.. SORRY I CAN'T STAY FOR SCENES OF JOYOUS LIBERATION!
BUT WAIT!!
BANG!
YOU WILL NOT MOVE, MY DEAR COMMISSIONER, UNTIL WE HAVE GONE!
?
OH, YEAH..
NO ONE!! GONE! EVERYBODY'S GONE!!
KLIK!
A few minutes later..
SKINNY, AREN'T YOU ELATED OVER DULCET'S REAPPEARANCE? THE MURDER RAP HEAT IS OFF NOW!
BAH... THAT BAG!! THE NEXT TIME I'LL DO A BETTER JOB OF IT!
CELL BL
2
3

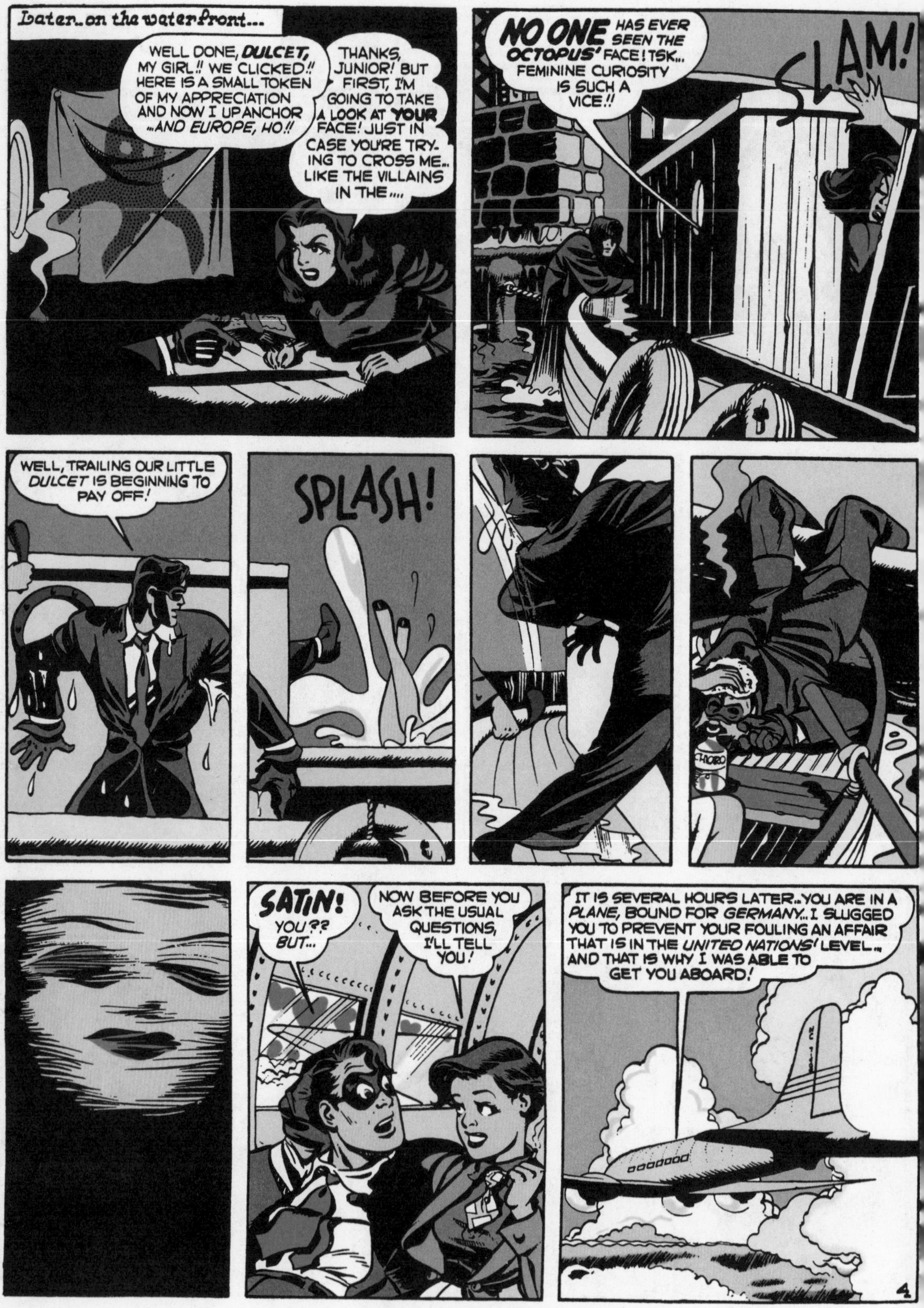
Later.. on the waterfront...
WELL DONE, DULCET, MY GIRL!! WE CLICKED!! HERE IS A SMALL TOKEN OF MY APPRECIATION AND NOW I UP ANCHOR ...AND EUROPE, HO!!
THANKS, JUNIOR! BUT FIRST, I'M GOING TO TAKE A LOOK AT YOUR FACE! JUST IN CASE YOU'RE TRYING TO CROSS ME.. LIKE THE VILLAINS IN THE....
NO ONE HAS EVER SEEN THE OCTOPUS' FACE! TSK... FEMININE CURIOSITY IS SUCH A VICE!!
SLAM!
WELL, TRAILING OUR LITTLE DULCET IS BEGINNING TO PAY OFF!
SPLASH!
CHLORO
SATIN! YOU?? BUT...
NOW BEFORE YOU ASK THE USUAL QUESTIONS, I'LL TELL YOU!
IT IS SEVERAL HOURS LATER.. YOU ARE IN A PLANE, BOUND FOR GERMANY... I SLUGGED YOU TO PREVENT YOUR FOULING AN AFFAIR THAT IS IN THE UNITED NATIONS' LEVEL... AND THAT IS WHY I WAS ABLE TO GET YOU ABOARD!
4

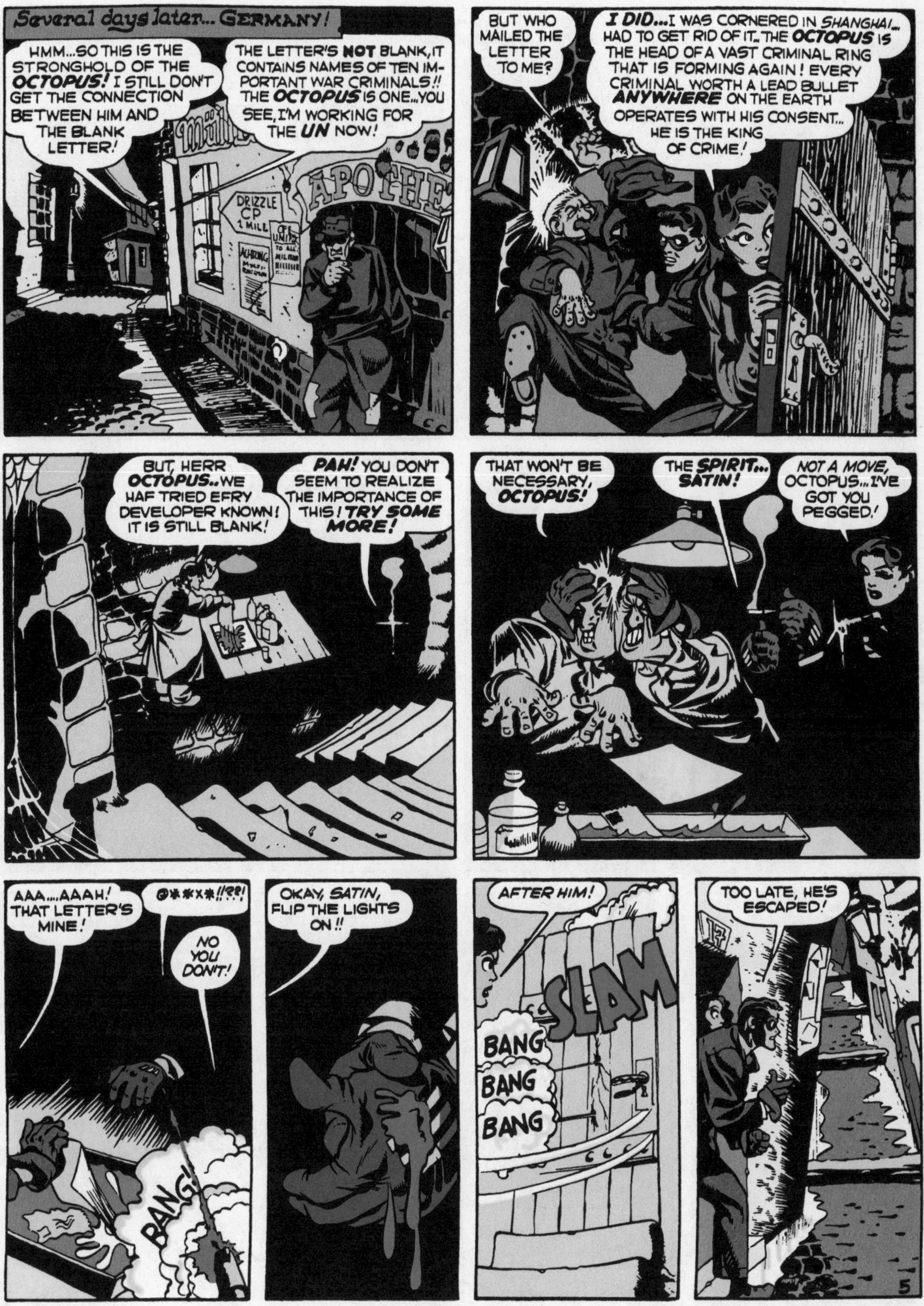
Several days later... GERMANY!
HMM...SO THIS IS THE STRONGHOLD OF THE OCTOPUS! I STILL DON'T GET THE CONNECTION BETWEEN HIM AND THE BLANK LETTER!
THE LETTER'S NOT BLANK, IT CONTAINS NAMES OF TEN IMPORTANT WAR CRIMINALS!! THE OCTOPUS IS ONE...YOU SEE, I'M WORKING FOR THE UN NOW!
DRIZZLE CP 1 MILE
APOTHE
BUT WHO MAILED THE LETTER TO ME?
I DID...I WAS CORNERED IN SHANGHAI... HAD TO GET RID OF IT.. THE OCTOPUS IS THE HEAD OF A VAST CRIMINAL RING THAT IS FORMING AGAIN! EVERY CRIMINAL WORTH A LEAD BULLET ANYWHERE ON THE EARTH OPERATES WITH HIS CONSENT... HE IS THE KING OF CRIME!
BUT, HERR OCTOPUS..WE HAF TRIED EFRY DEVELOPER KNOWN! IT IS STILL BLANK!
PAH! YOU DON'T SEEM TO REALIZE THE IMPORTANCE OF THIS! TRY SOME MORE!
THAT WON'T BE NECESSARY, OCTOPUS!
THE SPIRIT... SATIN!
NOT A MOVE, OCTOPUS...I'VE GOT YOU PEGGED!
AAA....AAAH! THAT LETTER'S MINE!
@**X*!!??!
NO YOU DON'T!
BANG!
OKAY, SATIN, FLIP THE LIGHTS ON!!
AFTER HIM!
SLAM
BANG
BANG
BANG
TOO LATE, HE'S ESCAPED!

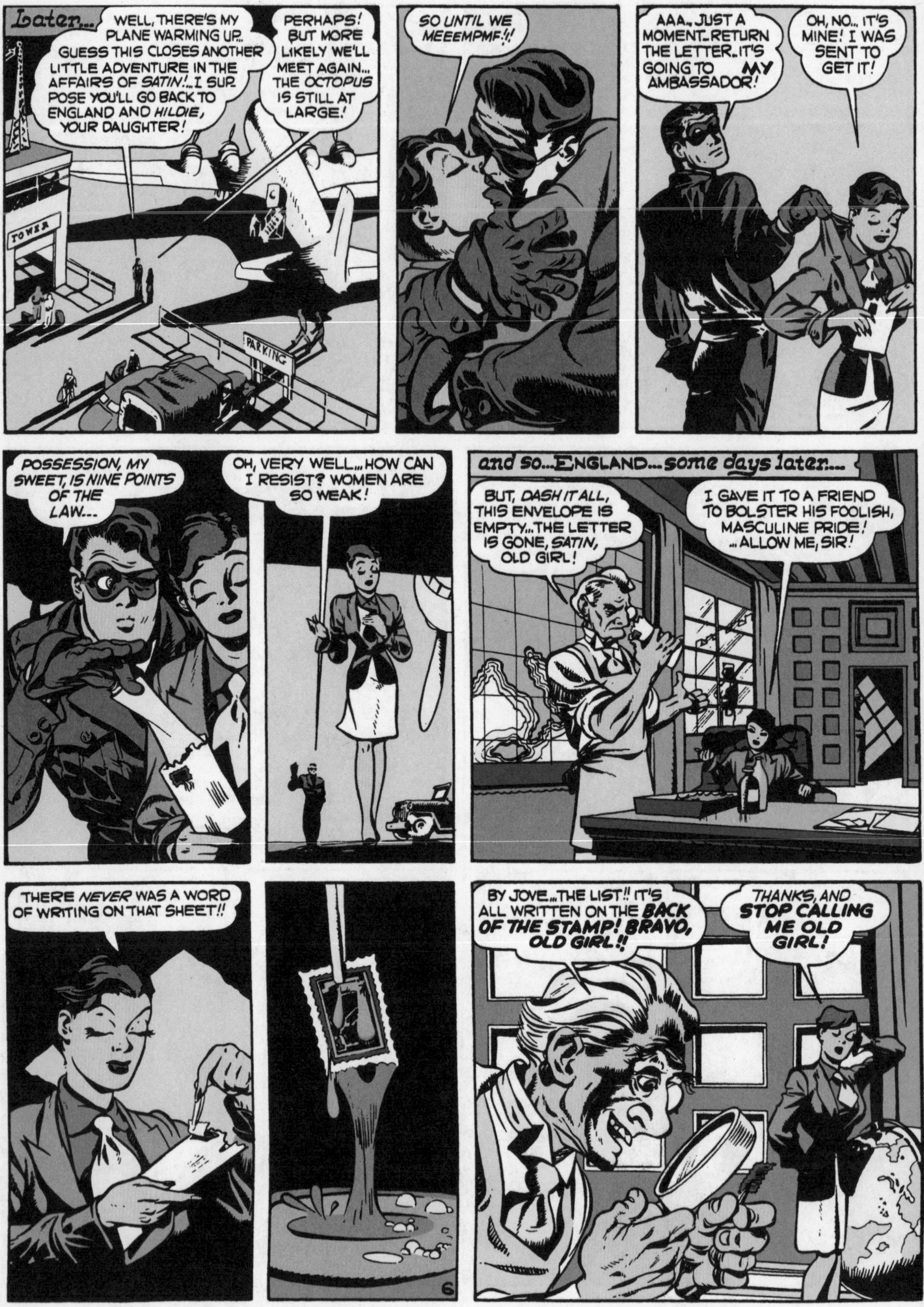
Later...
WELL, THERE'S MY PLANE WARMING UP... GUESS THIS CLOSES ANOTHER LITTLE ADVENTURE IN THE AFFAIRS OF SATIN!... I SUPPOSE YOU'LL GO BACK TO ENGLAND AND HILDIE, YOUR DAUGHTER!
PERHAPS! BUT MORE LIKELY WE'LL MEET AGAIN... THE OCTOPUS IS STILL AT LARGE!
TOWER
PARKING
SO UNTIL WE MEEEMPMF!!
AAA.. JUST A MOMENT... RETURN THE LETTER... IT'S GOING TO MY AMBASSADOR!
OH, NO... IT'S MINE! I WAS SENT TO GET IT!
POSSESSION, MY SWEET, IS NINE POINTS OF THE LAW...
OH, VERY WELL... HOW CAN I RESIST? WOMEN ARE SO WEAK!
and so...ENGLAND... some days later....
BUT, DASH IT ALL, THIS ENVELOPE IS EMPTY... THE LETTER IS GONE, SATIN, OLD GIRL!
I GAVE IT TO A FRIEND TO BOLSTER HIS FOOLISH, MASCULINE PRIDE! ...ALLOW ME, SIR!
THERE NEVER WAS A WORD OF WRITING ON THAT SHEET!!
6
BY JOVE... THE LIST!! IT'S ALL WRITTEN ON THE BACK OF THE STAMP! BRAVO, OLD GIRL!!
THANKS, AND STOP CALLING ME OLD GIRL!

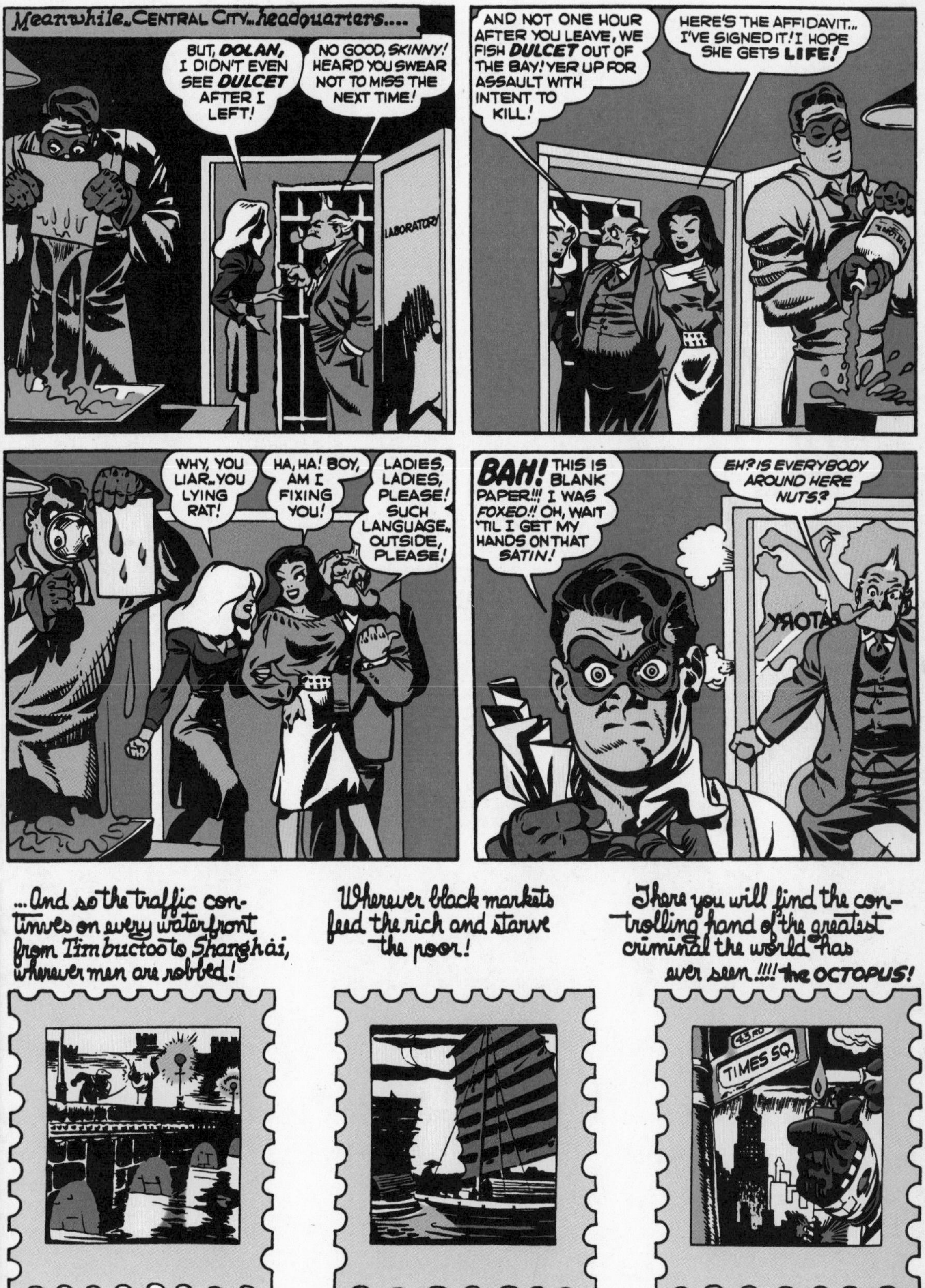
Meanwhile.. CENTRAL CITY.. headquarters....
BUT, DOLAN, I DIDN'T EVEN SEE DULCET AFTER I LEFT!
NO GOOD, SKINNY! HEARD YOU SWEAR NOT TO MISS THE NEXT TIME!
LABORATORY
AND NOT ONE HOUR AFTER YOU LEAVE, WE FISH DULCET OUT OF THE BAY! YER UP FOR ASSAULT WITH INTENT TO KILL!
HERE'S THE AFFIDAVIT... I'VE SIGNED IT! I HOPE SHE GETS LIFE!
WHY, YOU LIAR.. YOU LYING RAT!
HA, HA! BOY, AM I FIXING YOU!
LADIES, LADIES, PLEASE! SUCH LANGUAGE.. OUTSIDE, PLEASE!
BAH! THIS IS BLANK PAPER!!! I WAS FOXED!! OH, WAIT 'TIL I GET MY HANDS ON THAT SATIN!
EH? IS EVERYBODY AROUND HERE NUTS?
...And so the traffic continues on every waterfront from Timbuctoo to Shanghai, wherever men are robbed!
Wherever black markets feed the rich and starve the poor!
There you will find the controlling hand of the greatest criminal the world has ever seen!!!! the OCTOPUS!
43 RD
TIMES SQ.

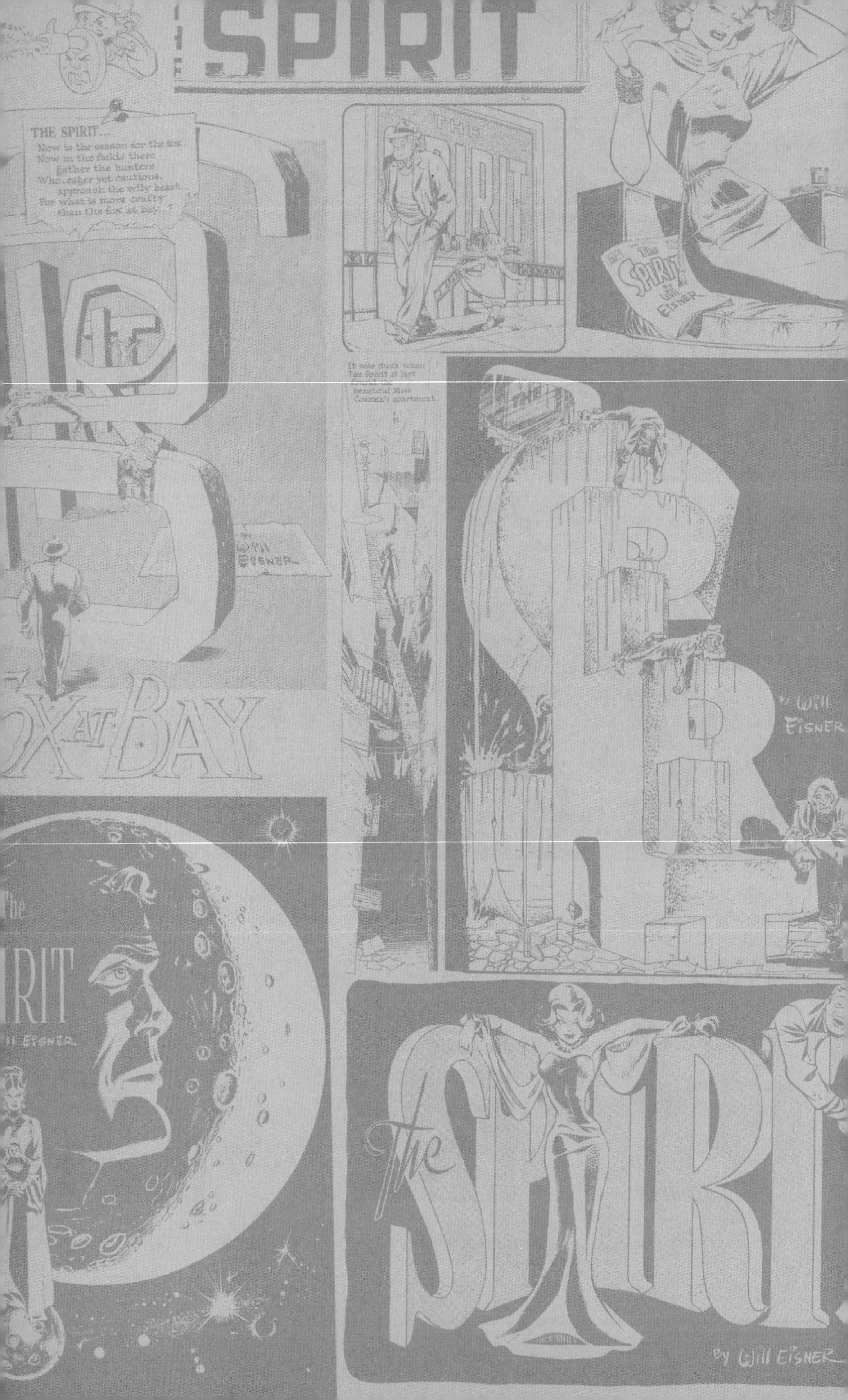
SPIRIT
THE SPIRIT...
Now is the season for the fox.
Now in the fields there gather the hunters
Who, eager yet cautious, approach the wily beast...
For what is more crafty than the fox at bay...?
THE SPIRIT
By Will Eisner
AT BAY
It was dusk when The Spirit at last found the beautiful Miss Cosmek's apartment.
THE
By Will Eisner
The SPIRIT
Will Eisner
The SPIRIT
By Will Eisner

MEET P'GELL

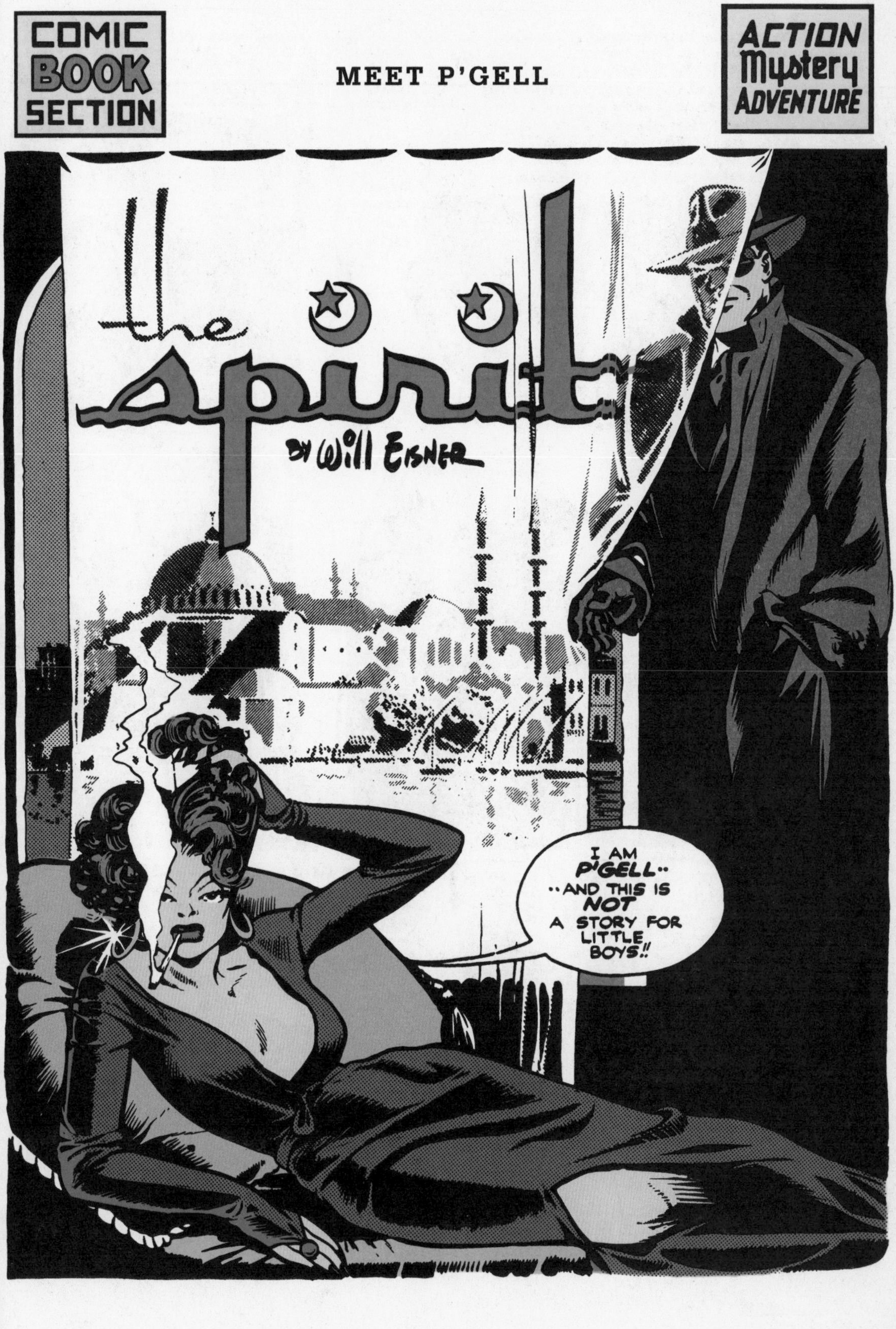

COMIC BOOK SECTION
ACTION Mystery ADVENTURE
the spirit
BY Will Eisner
I AM P'GELL.. ..AND THIS IS NOT A STORY FOR LITTLE BOYS!!

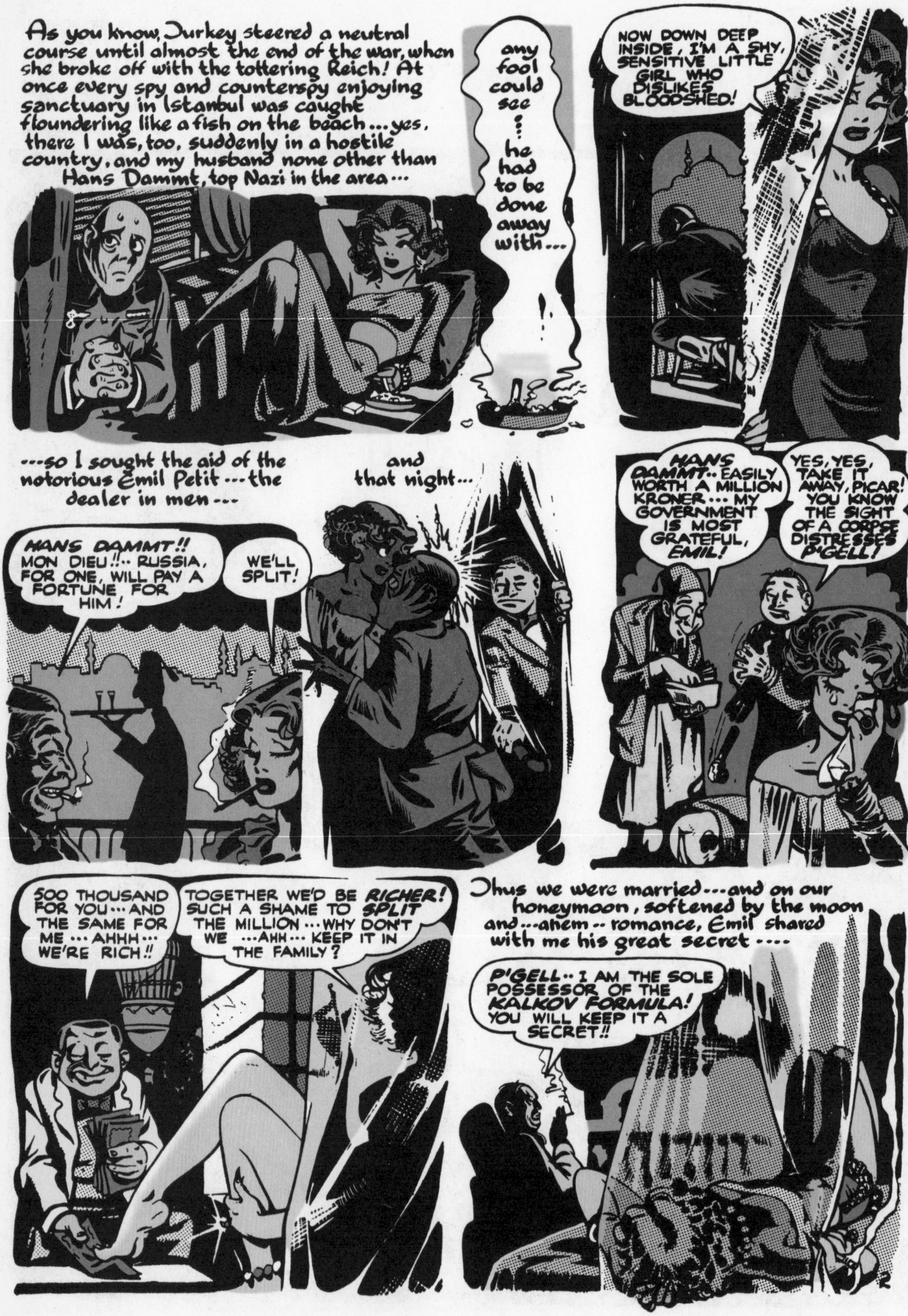

As you know, Turkey steered a neutral course until almost the end of the war, when she broke off with the tottering Reich! At once every spy and counterspy enjoying sanctuary in Istanbul was caught floundering like a fish on the beach ... yes, there I was, too, suddenly in a hostile country, and my husband none other than Hans Dammt, top Nazi in the area ...
any fool could see ... he had to be done away with ...
NOW DOWN DEEP INSIDE, I'M A SHY, SENSITIVE LITTLE GIRL WHO DISLIKES BLOODSHED!
--- so I sought the aid of the notorious Emil Petit --- the dealer in men ---
HANS DAMMT!! MON DIEU!! .. RUSSIA, FOR ONE, WILL PAY A FORTUNE FOR HIM!
WE'LL SPLIT!
and that night ...
HANS DAMMT .. EASILY WORTH A MILLION KRONER ... MY GOVERNMENT IS MOST GRATEFUL, EMIL!
YES, YES, TAKE IT AWAY, PICAR! YOU KNOW THE SIGHT OF A CORPSE DISTRESSES P'GELL!
500 THOUSAND FOR YOU ... AND THE SAME FOR ME ... AHHH ... WE'RE RICH!!
TOGETHER WE'D BE RICHER! SUCH A SHAME TO SPLIT THE MILLION ... WHY DON'T WE ... AHH ... KEEP IT IN THE FAMILY?
Thus we were married ... and on our honeymoon, softened by the moon and ... ahem .. romance, Emil shared with me his great secret ....
P'GELL .. I AM THE SOLE POSSESSOR OF THE KALKOV FORMULA! YOU WILL KEEP IT A SECRET!!
2

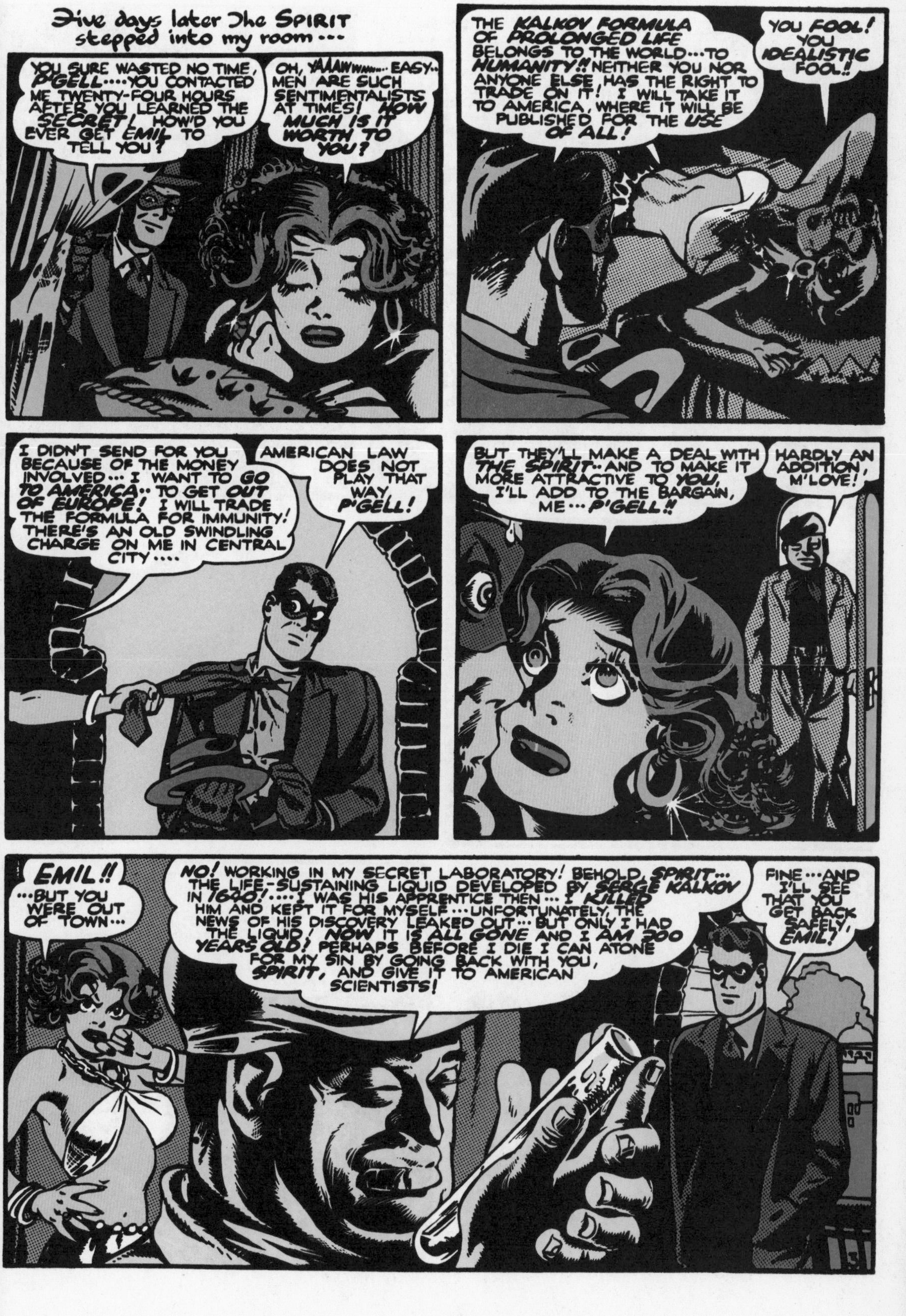
Five days later The Spirit stepped into my room...
YOU SURE WASTED NO TIME, P'GELL....YOU CONTACTED ME TWENTY-FOUR HOURS AFTER YOU LEARNED THE SECRET! HOW'D YOU EVER GET EMIL TO TELL YOU?
OH, YAAAWWW.... EASY.. MEN ARE SUCH SENTIMENTALISTS AT TIMES! HOW MUCH IS IT WORTH TO YOU?
THE KALKOV FORMULA OF PROLONGED LIFE BELONGS TO THE WORLD...TO HUMANITY!! NEITHER YOU NOR ANYONE ELSE HAS THE RIGHT TO TRADE ON IT! I WILL TAKE IT TO AMERICA, WHERE IT WILL BE PUBLISHED FOR THE USE OF ALL!
YOU FOOL! YOU IDEALISTIC FOOL!!
I DIDN'T SEND FOR YOU BECAUSE OF THE MONEY INVOLVED... I WANT TO GO TO AMERICA.. TO GET OUT OF EUROPE! I WILL TRADE THE FORMULA FOR IMMUNITY! THERE'S AN OLD SWINDLING CHARGE ON ME IN CENTRAL CITY....
AMERICAN LAW DOES NOT PLAY THAT WAY P'GELL!
BUT THEY'LL MAKE A DEAL WITH THE SPIRIT.. AND TO MAKE IT MORE ATTRACTIVE TO YOU, I'LL ADD TO THE BARGAIN, ME... P'GELL!!
HARDLY AN ADDITION, M'LOVE!
EMIL!! ...BUT YOU WERE OUT OF TOWN...
NO! WORKING IN MY SECRET LABORATORY! BEHOLD, SPIRIT... THE LIFE-SUSTAINING LIQUID DEVELOPED BY SERGE KALKOV IN 1600!.... I WAS HIS APPRENTICE THEN... I KILLED HIM AND KEPT IT FOR MYSELF... UNFORTUNATELY, THE NEWS OF HIS DISCOVERY LEAKED OUT... BUT ONLY I HAD THE LIQUID! NOW IT IS ALL GONE AND I AM 300 YEARS OLD! PERHAPS BEFORE I DIE I CAN ATONE FOR MY SIN BY GOING BACK WITH YOU, SPIRIT, AND GIVE IT TO AMERICAN SCIENTISTS!
FINE... AND I'LL SEE THAT YOU GET BACK SAFELY, EMIL!

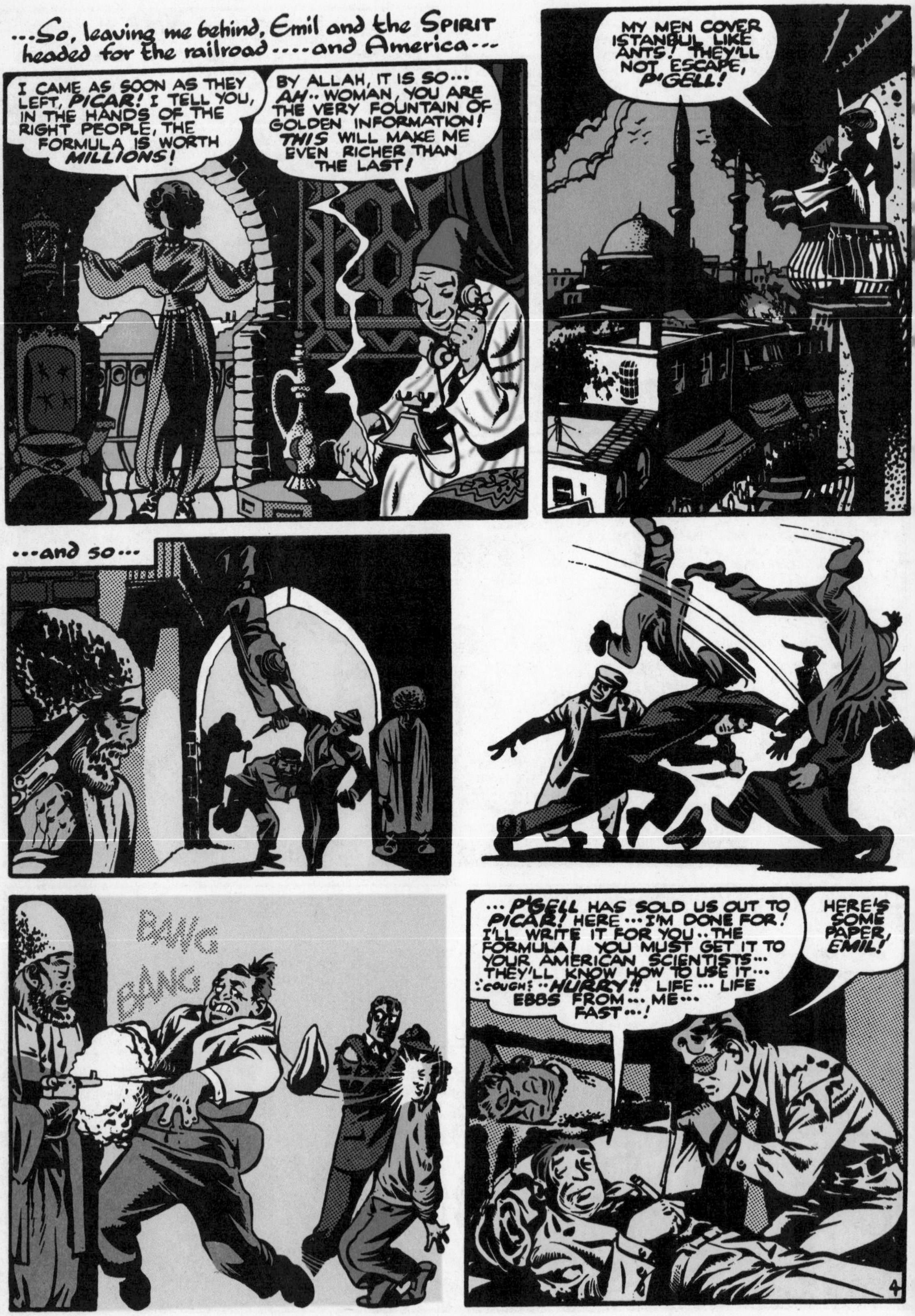
...So, leaving me behind, Emil and the SPIRIT headed for the railroad....and America...
I CAME AS SOON AS THEY LEFT, PICAR! I TELL YOU, IN THE HANDS OF THE RIGHT PEOPLE, THE FORMULA IS WORTH MILLIONS!
BY ALLAH, IT IS SO... AH.. WOMAN, YOU ARE THE VERY FOUNTAIN OF GOLDEN INFORMATION! THIS WILL MAKE ME EVEN RICHER THAN THE LAST!
MY MEN COVER ISTANBUL LIKE ANTS! THEY'LL NOT ESCAPE, P'GELL!
...and so...
BANG
BANG
...P'GELL HAS SOLD US OUT TO PICAR! HERE...I'M DONE FOR! I'LL WRITE IT FOR YOU..THE FORMULA! YOU MUST GET IT TO YOUR AMERICAN SCIENTISTS... THEY'LL KNOW HOW TO USE IT... COUGH!..HURRY!! LIFE... LIFE EBBS FROM... ME... FAST...!
HERE'S SOME PAPER, EMIL!
4

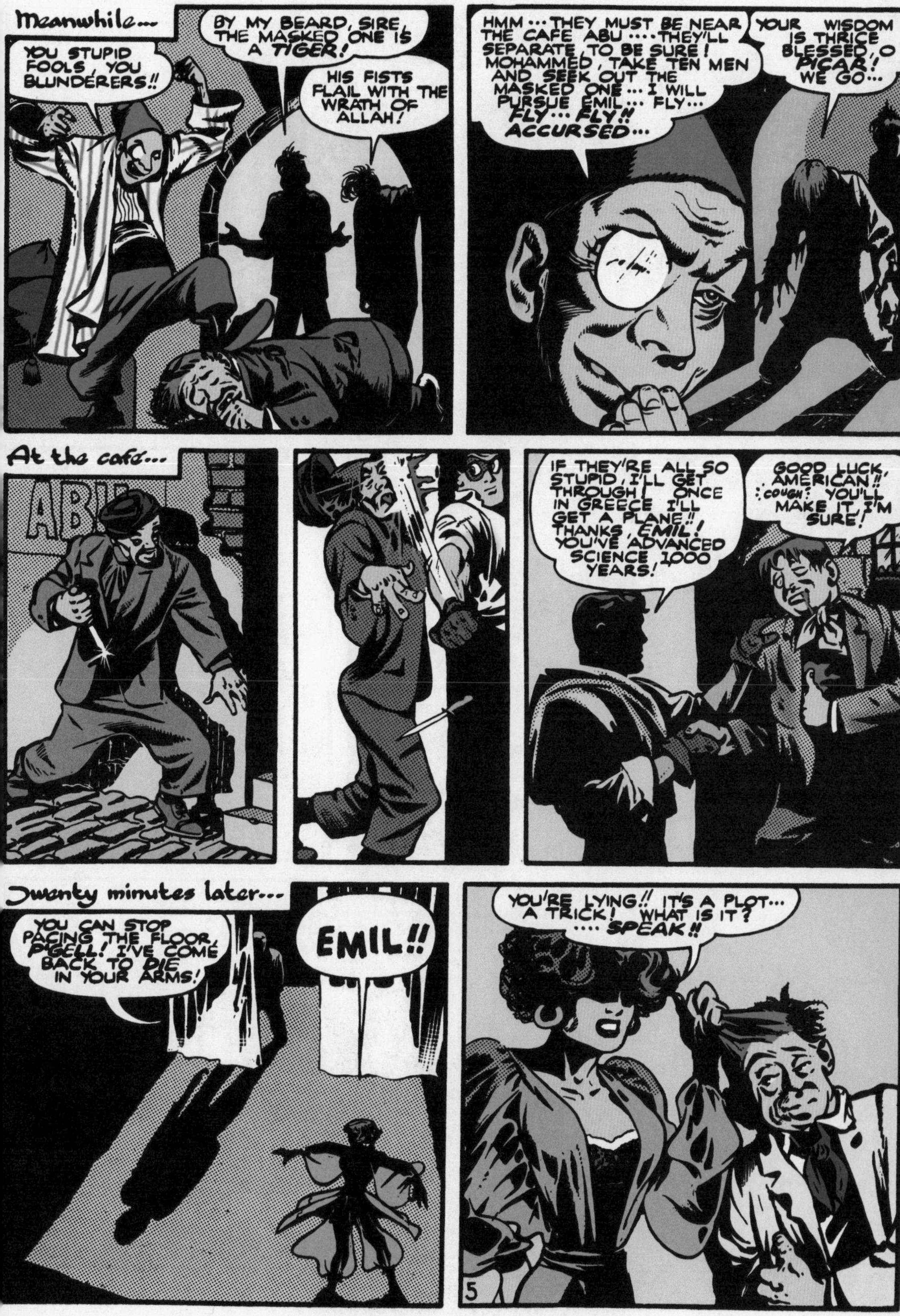
Meanwhile...
YOU STUPID FOOLS, YOU BLUNDERERS!!
BY MY BEARD, SIRE, THE MASKED ONE IS A TIGER!
HIS FISTS FLAIL WITH THE WRATH OF ALLAH!
HMM ... THEY MUST BE NEAR THE CAFE ABU .... THEY'LL SEPARATE, TO BE SURE! MOHAMMED, TAKE TEN MEN AND SEEK OUT THE MASKED ONE ... I WILL PURSUE EMIL ... FLY ... FLY ... FLY!! ACCURSED ...
YOUR WISDOM IS THRICE BLESSED, O PICAR! WE GO...
At the café...
IF THEY'RE ALL SO STUPID, I'LL GET THROUGH! ONCE IN GREECE I'LL GET A PLANE!! THANKS, EMIL! YOU'VE ADVANCED SCIENCE 1000 YEARS!
GOOD LUCK, AMERICAN!! :COUGH: YOU'LL MAKE IT, I'M SURE!
Twenty minutes later...
YOU CAN STOP PACING THE FLOOR, PIGELL! I'VE COME BACK TO DIE IN YOUR ARMS!
EMIL!!
YOU'RE LYING!! IT'S A PLOT... A TRICK! WHAT IS IT? .... SPEAK!!
5

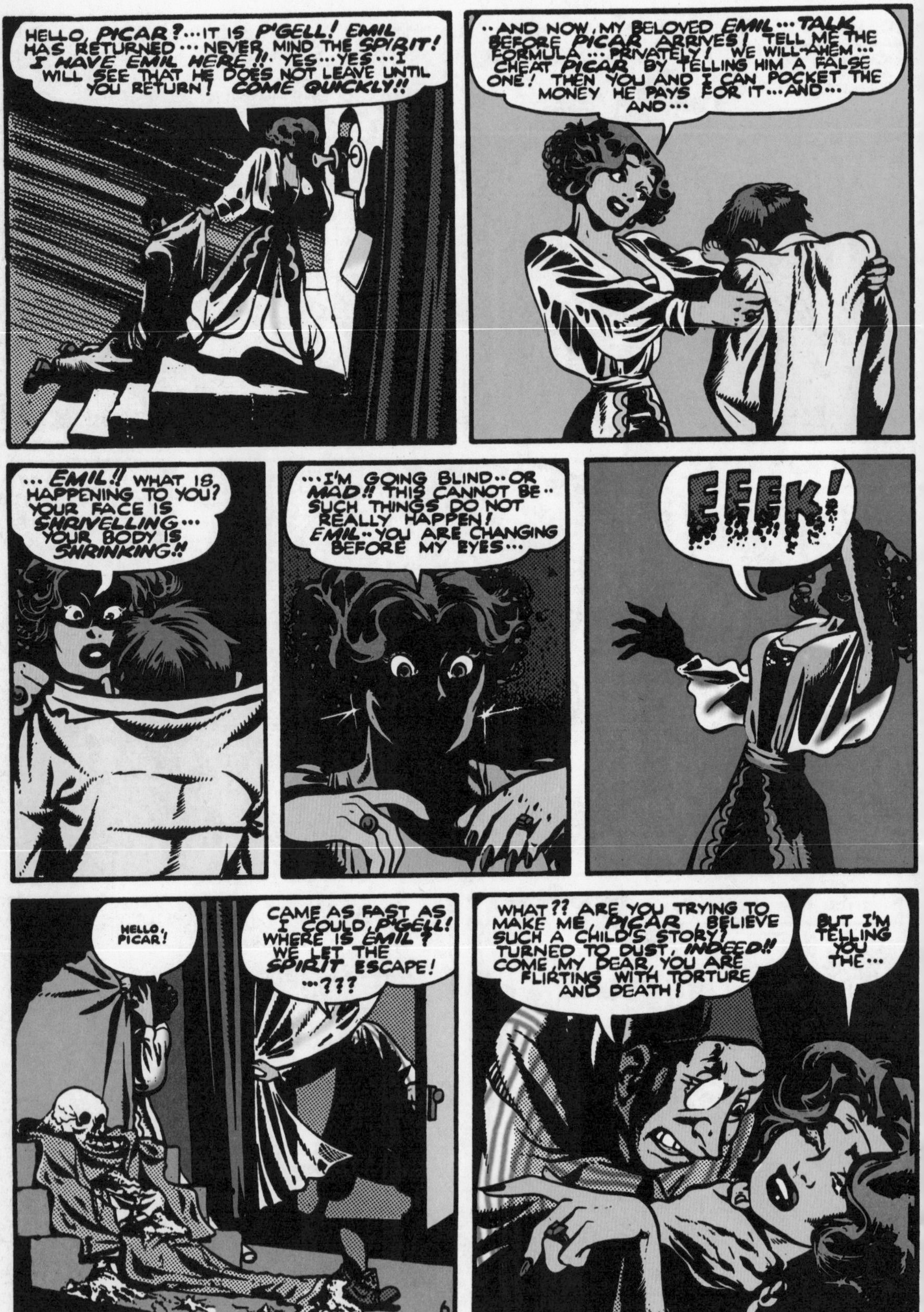
HELLO, PICAR?...IT IS P'GELL! EMIL HAS RETURNED... NEVER MIND THE SPIRIT! I HAVE EMIL HERE!!. YES...YES...I WILL SEE THAT HE DOES NOT LEAVE UNTIL YOU RETURN! COME QUICKLY!!
..AND NOW, MY BELOVED EMIL...TALK BEFORE PICAR ARRIVES! TELL ME THE FORMULA...PRIVATELY! WE WILL-AHEM... CHEAT PICAR BY TELLING HIM A FALSE ONE! THEN YOU AND I CAN POCKET THE MONEY HE PAYS FOR IT...AND... AND...
...EMIL!! WHAT IS HAPPENING TO YOU? YOUR FACE IS SHRIVELLING... YOUR BODY IS SHRINKING!!
...I'M GOING BLIND..OR MAD!! THIS CANNOT BE.. SUCH THINGS DO NOT REALLY HAPPEN! EMIL..YOU ARE CHANGING BEFORE MY EYES...
EEEK!
HELLO, PICAR!
CAME AS FAST AS I COULD, P'GELL! WHERE IS EMIL? WE LET THE SPIRIT ESCAPE! ...???
6
WHAT?? ARE YOU TRYING TO MAKE ME, PICAR, BELIEVE SUCH A CHILD'S STORY? TURNED TO DUST, INDEED!! COME MY DEAR, YOU ARE FLIRTING WITH TORTURE AND DEATH!
BUT I'M TELLING YOU THE...

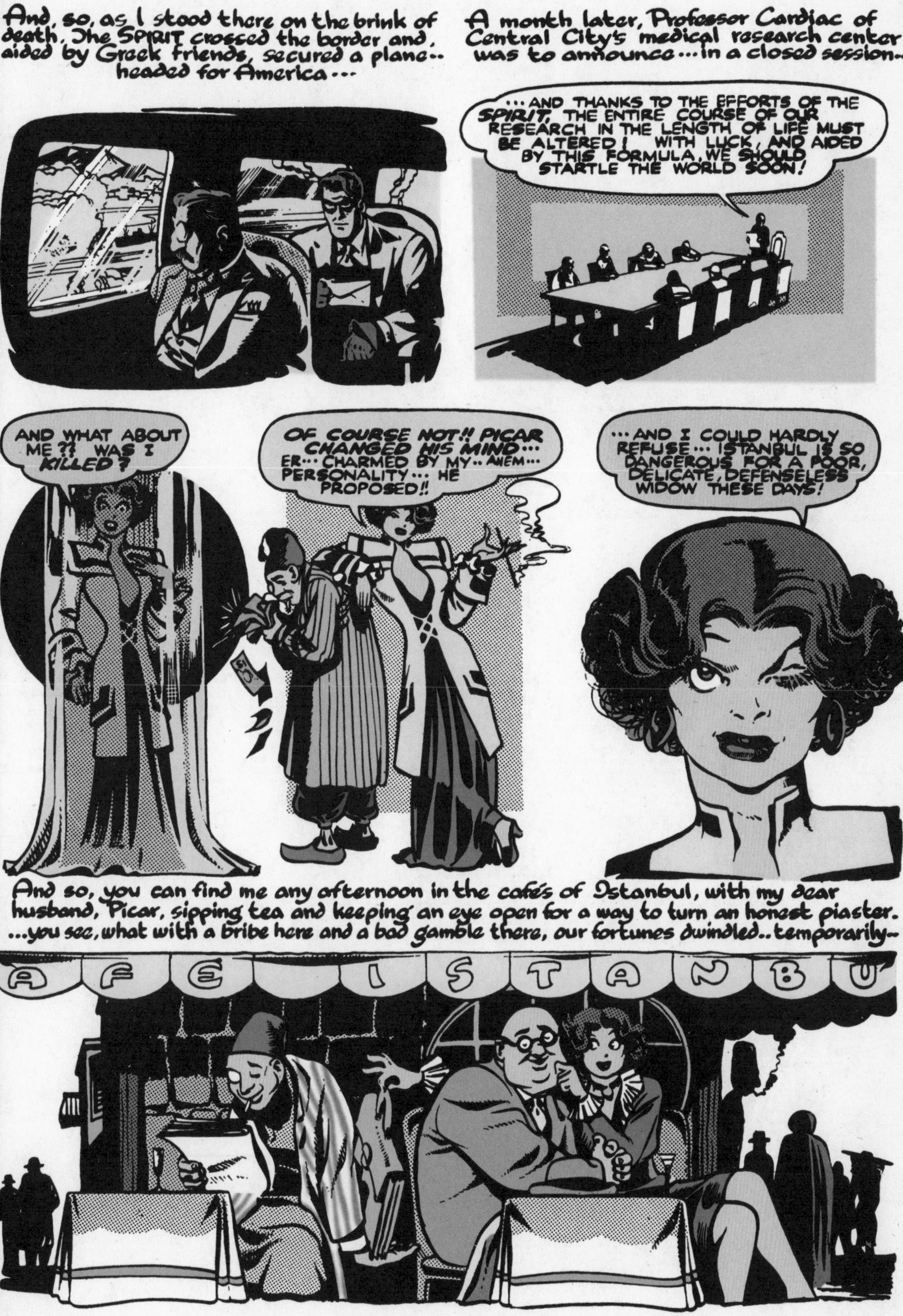
And, so, as I stood there on the brink of death, The SPIRIT crossed the border and, aided by Greek friends, secured a plane.. headed for America...
A month later, Professor Cardiac of Central City's medical research center was to announce... in a closed session..
...AND THANKS TO THE EFFORTS OF THE SPIRIT, THE ENTIRE COURSE OF OUR RESEARCH IN THE LENGTH OF LIFE MUST BE ALTERED! WITH LUCK, AND AIDED BY THIS FORMULA, WE SHOULD STARTLE THE WORLD SOON!
AND WHAT ABOUT ME?? WAS I KILLED?
OF COURSE NOT!! PICAR CHANGED HIS MIND... ER... CHARMED BY MY.. AHEM... PERSONALITY... HE PROPOSED!!
...AND I COULD HARDLY REFUSE... ISTANBUL IS SO DANGEROUS FOR A POOR, DELICATE, DEFENSELESS WIDOW THESE DAYS!
And so, you can find me any afternoon in the cafés of Istanbul, with my dear husband, Picar, sipping tea and keeping an eye open for a way to turn an honest piaster. ...you see, what with a bribe here and a bad gamble there, our fortunes dwindled.. temporarily..
A F E I S T A N B U

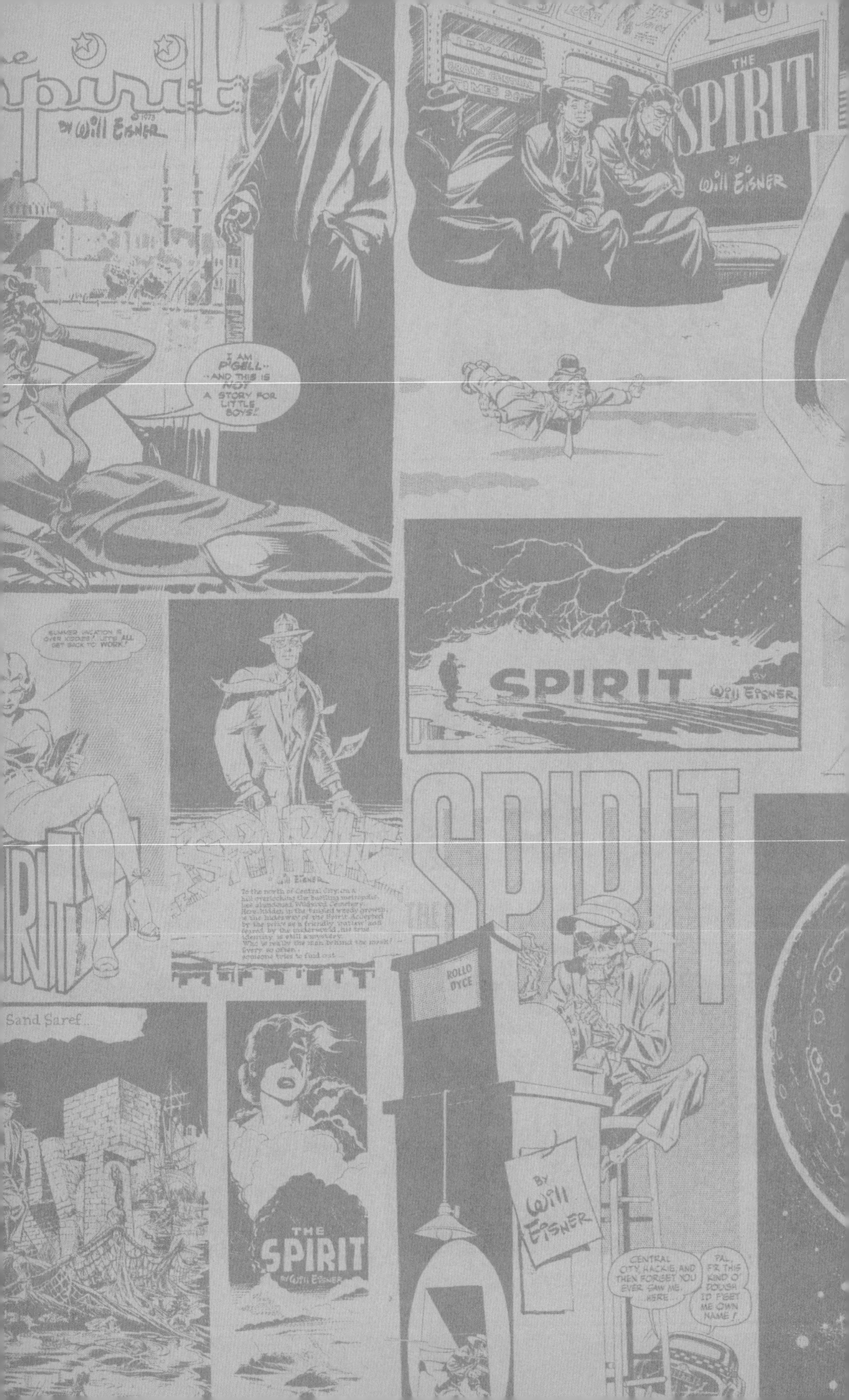
Spirit
© 1973
By Will Eisner
I AM P'GELL -- AND THIS IS NOT A STORY FOR LITTLE BOYS!
THE SPIRIT
BY Will Eisner
SUMMER VACATION IS OVER KIDDIES! LET'S ALL GET BACK TO WORK!
SPIRIT
BY Will Eisner
Sand Saref...
THE SPIRIT
BY Will Eisner
THE SPIRIT
ROLLO DYCE
BY Will Eisner
CENTRAL CITY HACKIE, AND THEN FORGET YOU EVER SAW ME HERE...
PAL, FR THIS KIND O' DOUGH I'D FIGET ME OWN NAME!

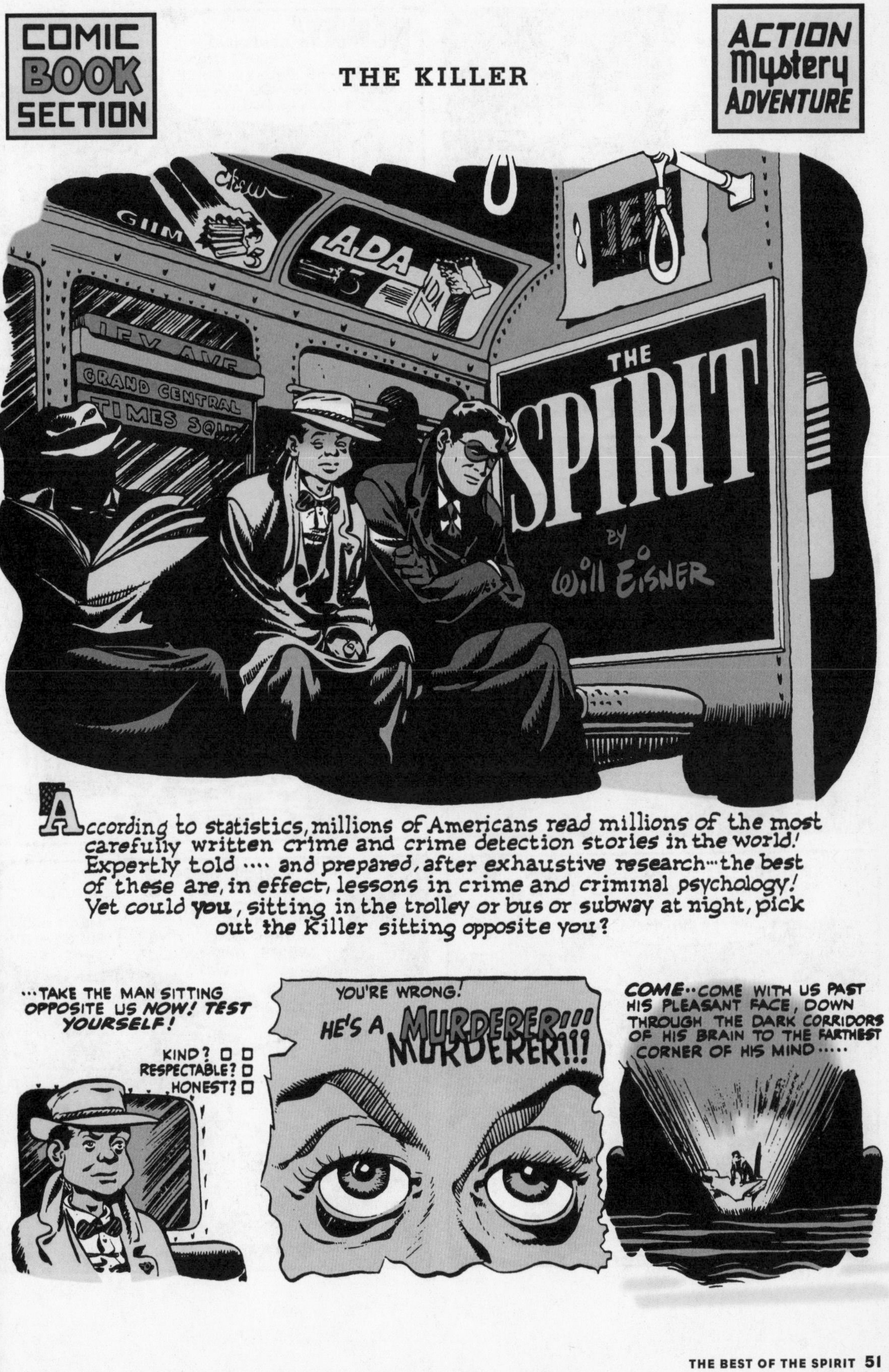
COMIC BOOK SECTION
THE KILLER
ACTION Mystery ADVENTURE
GUM
ADA
LEX AVE
GRAND CENTRAL
TIMES SQU
THE SPIRIT
BY Will Eisner
According to statistics, millions of Americans read millions of the most carefully written crime and crime detection stories in the world! Expertly told .... and prepared, after exhaustive research...the best of these are, in effect, lessons in crime and criminal psychology! Yet could you, sitting in the trolley or bus or subway at night, pick out the Killer sitting opposite you?
...TAKE THE MAN SITTING OPPOSITE US NOW! TEST YOURSELF!
KIND?
RESPECTABLE?
HONEST?
YOU'RE WRONG!
HE'S A MURDERER!!! MURDERER!!!
COME.. COME WITH US PAST HIS PLEASANT FACE, DOWN THROUGH THE DARK CORRIDORS OF HIS BRAIN TO THE FARTHEST CORNER OF HIS MIND.....

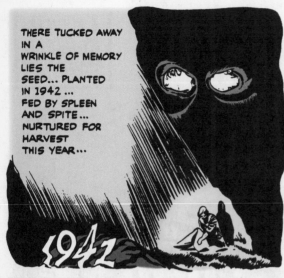

THERE TUCKED AWAY IN A WRINKLE OF MEMORY LIES THE SEED... PLANTED IN 1942... FED BY SPLEEN AND SPITE... NURTURED FOR HARVEST THIS YEAR...

1942

HENRY! CONFOUND YOUR LAZY HIDE! ONLY SIX BOXES PACKED SINCE NOON ... ARE YOU NEVER GONNA FINISH?

YES, MISTER JAMES! ER...I...I MEAN, NO, MISTER JAMES!

1942

WHY MY SISTER EVER MARRIED SUCH A SAP BEATS ME! HO HUM! LEND ME ANOTHER FIN, AND IF Y'OPEN YA TRAP TO MARY ABOUT THIS I'LL BEAT YOUR HEAD IN!

O.K., JOE, O.K.!

STILL MAKIN' THE SAME OLD SALARY, EH, HENRY? OH, WELL...

I'M WORKIN' AS HARD AS I CAN, MARY! I BEEN WORKIN' MY HEART OUT AT THAT DRUDGE JOB SINCE I WAS TEN... PUSHED AROUND DAY AND NIGHT! I'M FED UP!! I'M QUITTING... I'M LEAVING TOWN ...I...

BET YER LIFE YOU ARE ... HAW, HAW! HERE'S YOUR GREETINGS NOTICE! YOU'RE GOING ... INTO THE ARMY! HA, HA, HA, HA, HA!

?

AND SO...

HENRY! CONFOUND YOUR G.I. HIDE ... AIN'T YOU FINISHED PACKIN' YET? WE'RE SHIPPIN' OUT T'NIGHT!

YES, SERGEANT! ...ER...I MEAN, NO, SERGEANT! THAT IS ...

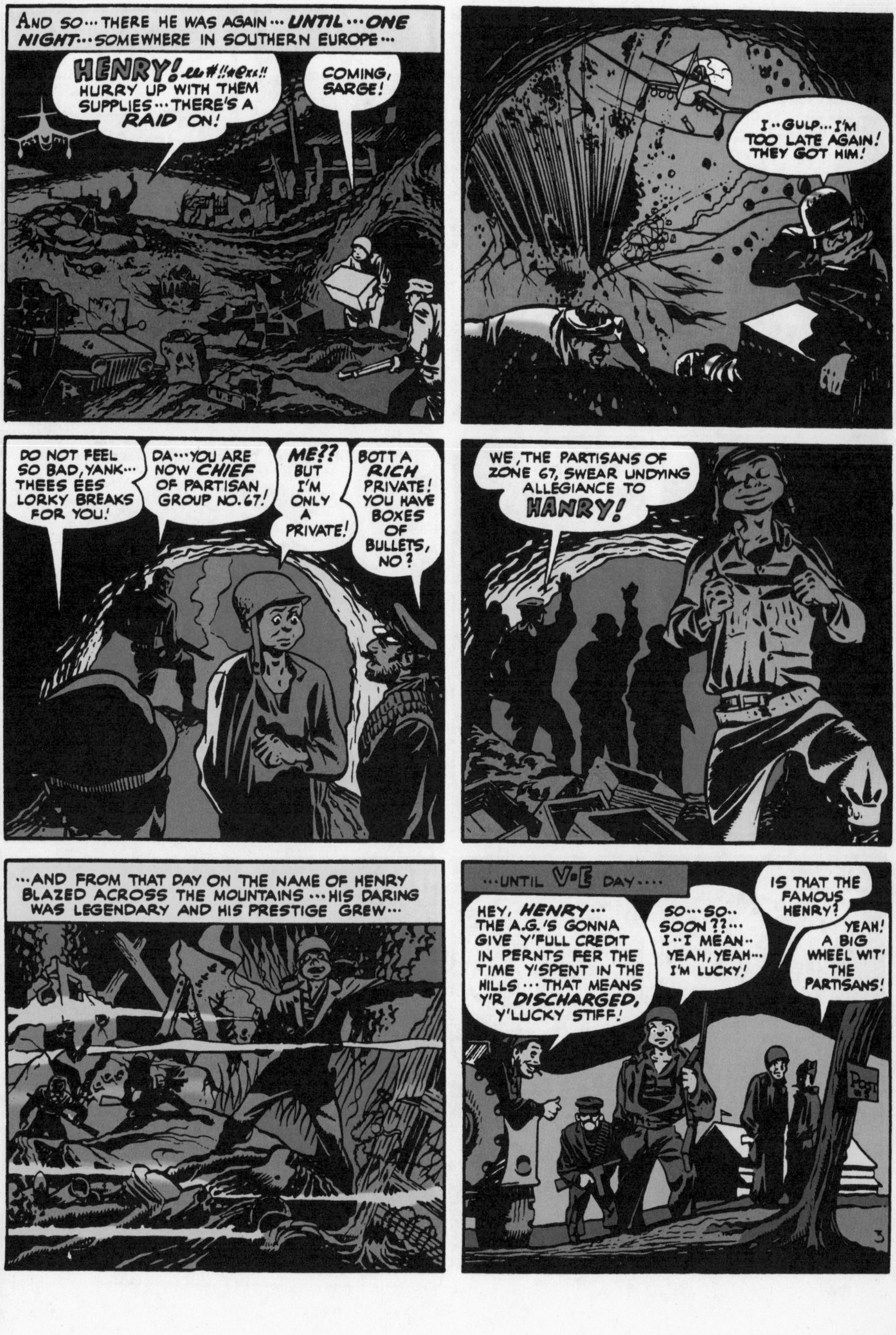

AND SO... THERE HE WAS AGAIN... UNTIL... ONE NIGHT... SOMEWHERE IN SOUTHERN EUROPE...
HENRY! HURRY UP WITH THEM SUPPLIES... THERE'S A RAID ON!
COMING, SARGE!
I.. GULP... I'M TOO LATE AGAIN! THEY GOT HIM!
DO NOT FEEL SO BAD, YANK... THEES EES LORKY BREAKS FOR YOU!
DA... YOU ARE NOW CHIEF OF PARTISAN GROUP NO. 67!
ME?? BUT I'M ONLY A PRIVATE!
BOTT A RICH PRIVATE! YOU HAVE BOXES OF BULLETS, NO?
WE, THE PARTISANS OF ZONE 67, SWEAR UNDYING ALLEGIANCE TO HANRY!
...AND FROM THAT DAY ON THE NAME OF HENRY BLAZED ACROSS THE MOUNTAINS... HIS DARING WAS LEGENDARY AND HIS PRESTIGE GREW...
...UNTIL V-E DAY....
HEY, HENRY... THE A.G.'S GONNA GIVE Y'FULL CREDIT IN PERNTS FER THE TIME Y'SPENT IN THE HILLS... THAT MEANS Y'R DISCHARGED, Y'LUCKY STIFF!
SO... SO.. SOON??... I.. I MEAN.. YEAH, YEAH... I'M LUCKY!
IS THAT THE FAMOUS HENRY?
YEAH! A BIG WHEEL WIT' THE PARTISANS!
POST

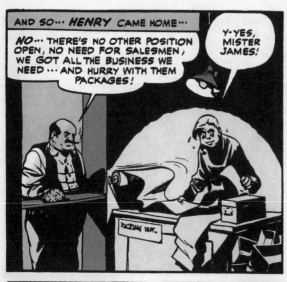

AND SO... *HENRY* CAME HOME...

NO... THERE'S NO OTHER POSITION OPEN, NO NEED FOR SALESMEN, WE GOT ALL THE BUSINESS WE NEED... AND HURRY WITH THEM PACKAGES!

Y-YES, MISTER JAMES!

...Y'MAY HAVE BEEN A HOT-SHOT SOLDIER...

...BUT YOU'RE JUST A PUNK SHIPPING CLERK TO ME... *HEY!!* YOU CAN'T QUIT! I'LL BLACKBALL YOU IN THE INDUSTRY!

ALL ABOARD...

...LOTSA ROOM, FOLKS... UGH!

HSST! SLIP IT IN TH' JOIK'S POCKET, ATAWAY, TRIGG!

DAILY NE

HENRY'S A CRACK SHOT...

HENRY'S PARTISANS LEFT NO NAZIS

"ALIVE"... "PUNK!"... "FOOL"... BACK IN THE SAME OLD RUT... FOR THE REST OF YOUR LIFE... DAY AFTER DAY... PUSHED AROUND... *HEY!!* WHAT'S THIS IN MY POCKET?

4

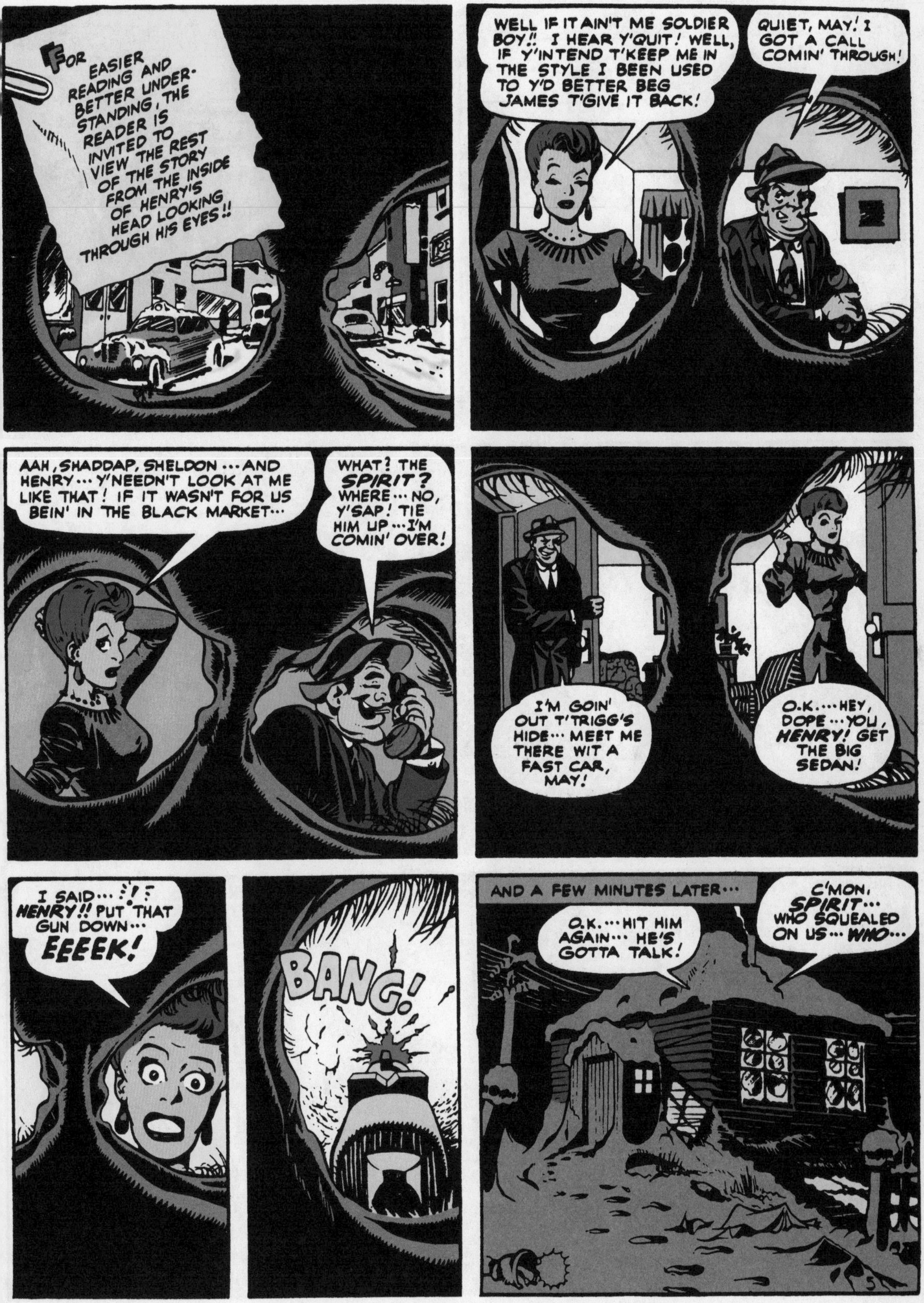
FOR EASIER READING AND BETTER UNDER-STANDING, THE READER IS INVITED TO VIEW THE REST OF THE STORY FROM THE INSIDE OF HENRY'S HEAD LOOKING THROUGH HIS EYES!!
WELL IF IT AIN'T ME SOLDIER BOY!! I HEAR Y'QUIT! WELL, IF Y'INTEND T'KEEP ME IN THE STYLE I BEEN USED TO Y'D BETTER BEG JAMES T'GIVE IT BACK!
QUIET, MAY! I GOT A CALL COMIN' THROUGH!
AAH, SHADDAP, SHELDON ... AND HENRY ... Y'NEEDN'T LOOK AT ME LIKE THAT! IF IT WASN'T FOR US BEIN' IN THE BLACK MARKET...
WHAT? THE SPIRIT? WHERE ... NO, Y'SAP! TIE HIM UP ... I'M COMIN' OVER!
I'M GOIN' OUT T'TRIGG'S HIDE... MEET ME THERE WIT A FAST CAR, MAY!
O.K. ... HEY, DOPE ... YOU, HENRY! GET THE BIG SEDAN!
I SAID... !! HENRY!! PUT THAT GUN DOWN... EEEEK!
BANG!
AND A FEW MINUTES LATER...
O.K. ... HIT HIM AGAIN... HE'S GOTTA TALK!
C'MON, SPIRIT... WHO SQUEALED ON US... WHO...

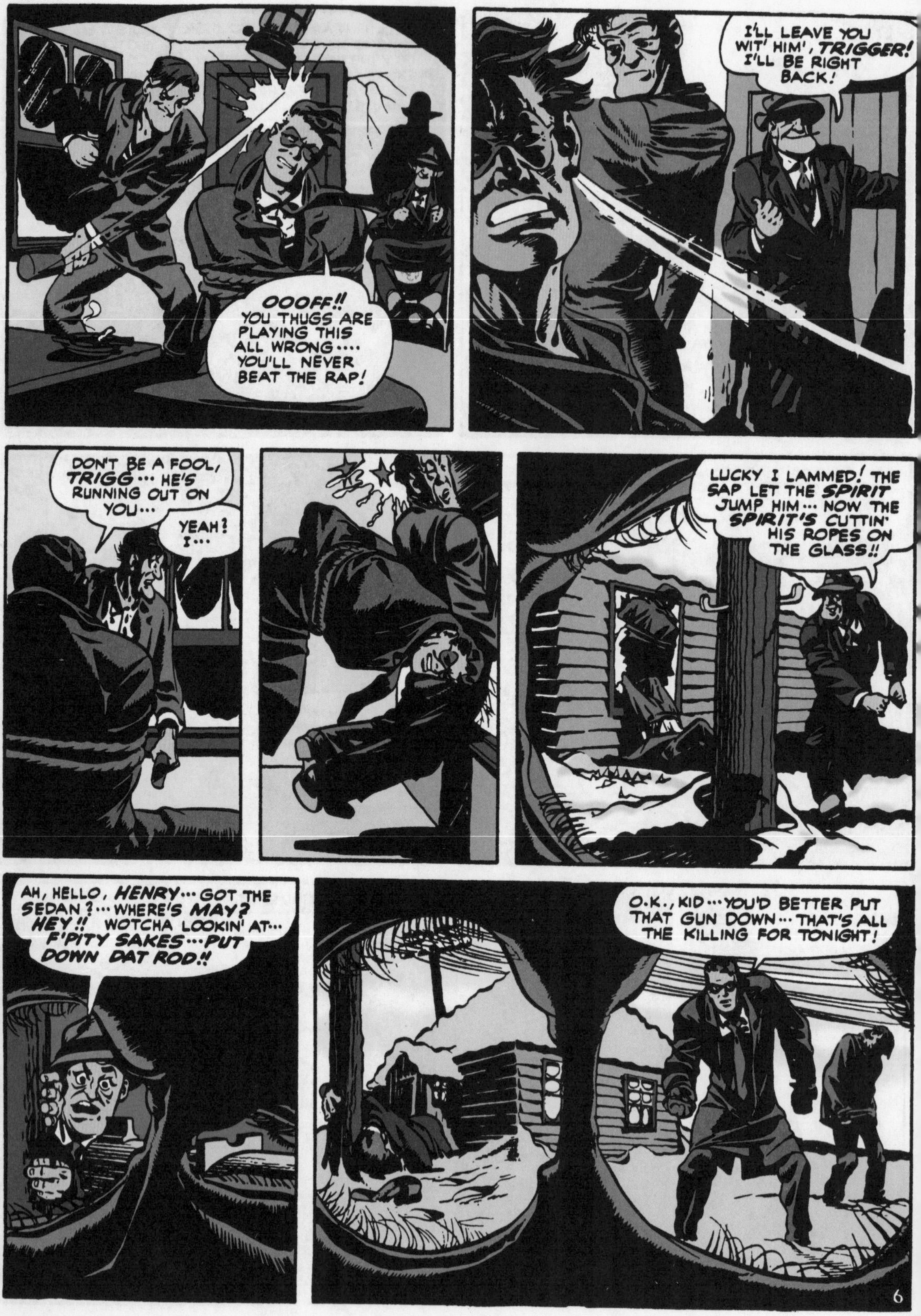
OOOFF!! YOU THUGS ARE PLAYING THIS ALL WRONG.... YOU'LL NEVER BEAT THE RAP!
I'LL LEAVE YOU WIT' HIM', TRIGGER! I'LL BE RIGHT BACK!
DON'T BE A FOOL, TRIGG... HE'S RUNNING OUT ON YOU...
YEAH? I...
LUCKY I LAMMED! THE SAP LET THE SPIRIT JUMP HIM... NOW THE SPIRIT'S CUTTIN' HIS ROPES ON THE GLASS!!
AH, HELLO, HENRY... GOT THE SEDAN?... WHERE'S MAY? HEY!! WOTCHA LOOKIN' AT... F'PITY SAKES... PUT DOWN DAT ROD!!
O.K., KID... YOU'D BETTER PUT THAT GUN DOWN... THAT'S ALL THE KILLING FOR TONIGHT!
6

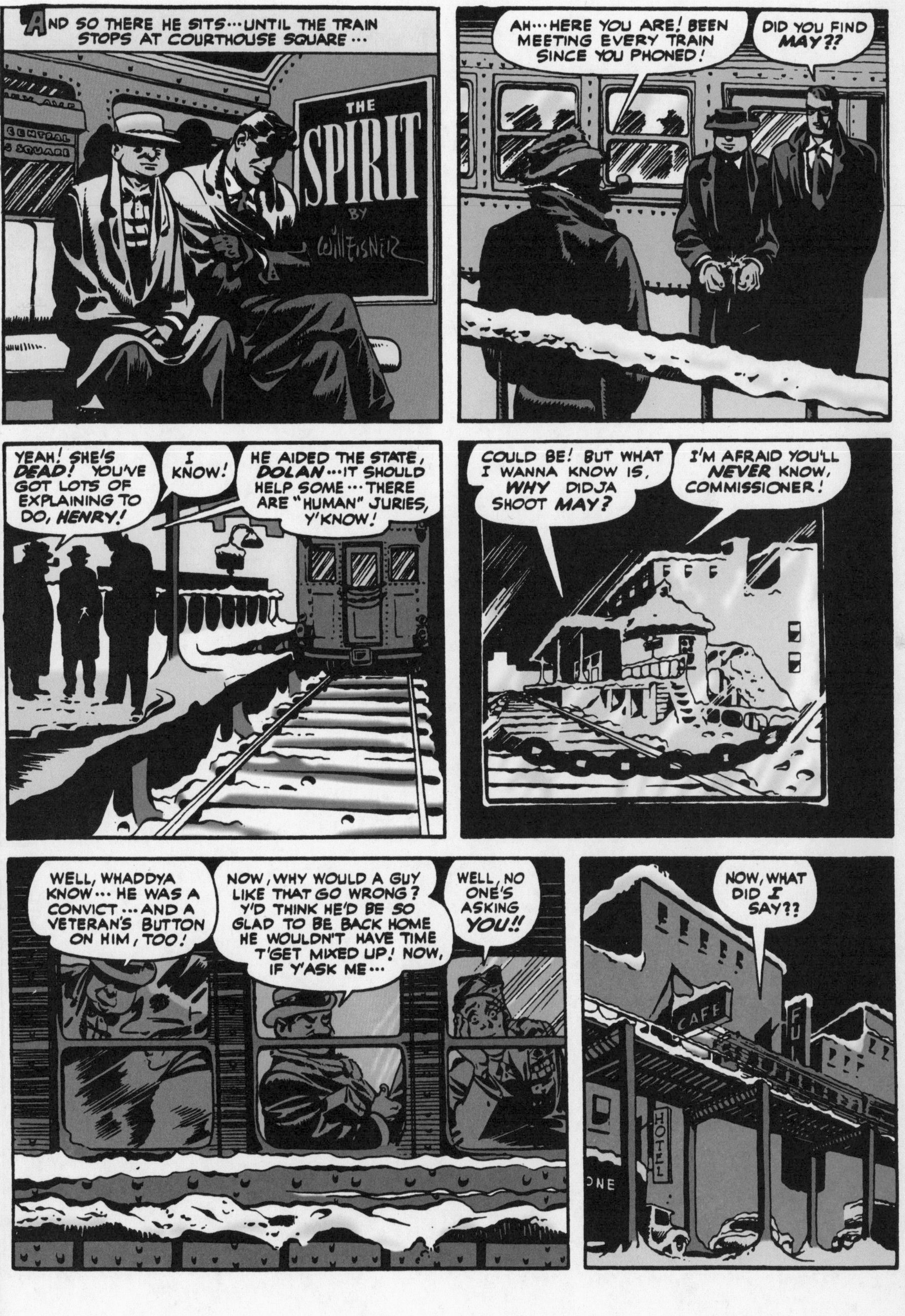
AND SO THERE HE SITS··· UNTIL THE TRAIN STOPS AT COURTHOUSE SQUARE ···
THE SPIRIT BY WILL EISNER
AH··· HERE YOU ARE! BEEN MEETING EVERY TRAIN SINCE YOU PHONED!
DID YOU FIND MAY??
YEAH! SHE'S DEAD! YOU'VE GOT LOTS OF EXPLAINING TO DO, HENRY!
I KNOW!
HE AIDED THE STATE, DOLAN··· IT SHOULD HELP SOME··· THERE ARE "HUMAN" JURIES, Y'KNOW!
COULD BE! BUT WHAT I WANNA KNOW IS, WHY DIDJA SHOOT MAY?
I'M AFRAID YOU'LL NEVER KNOW, COMMISSIONER!
WELL, WHADDYA KNOW··· HE WAS A CONVICT··· AND A VETERAN'S BUTTON ON HIM, TOO!
NOW, WHY WOULD A GUY LIKE THAT GO WRONG? Y'D THINK HE'D BE SO GLAD TO BE BACK HOME HE WOULDN'T HAVE TIME T'GET MIXED UP! NOW, IF Y'ASK ME···
WELL, NO ONE'S ASKING YOU!!
NOW, WHAT DID I SAY??
CAFE
HOTEL

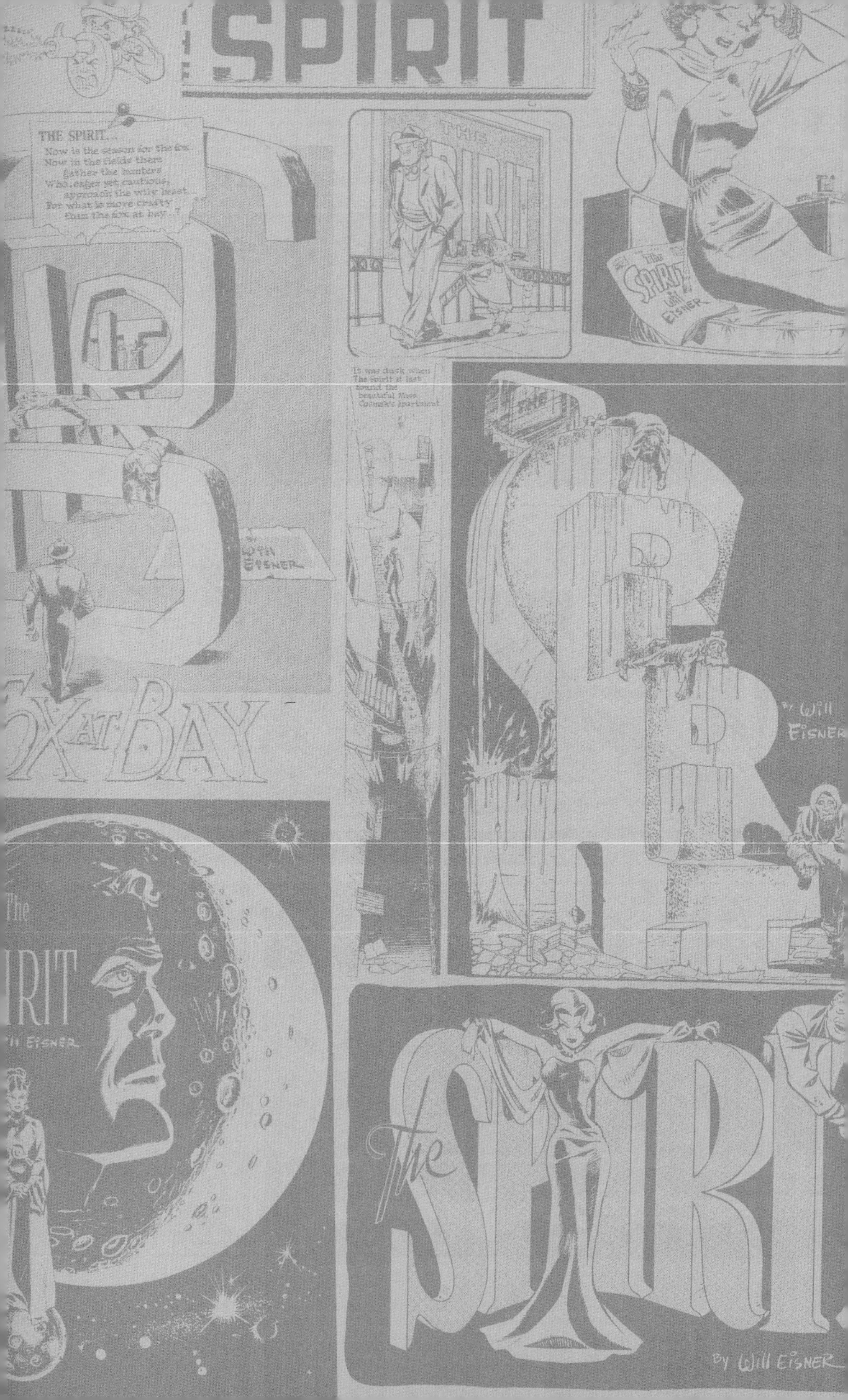

THE SPIRIT
THE SPIRIT...
Now is the season for the fox.
Now in the fields there
gather the hunters
Who, eager yet cautious,
approach the wily beast.
For what is more crafty
than the fox at bay...?
By Will Eisner
AT BAY
THE SPIRIT
The Spirit by Will Eisner
It was dusk when
The Spirit at last
found the
beautiful Miss
THE
By Will Eisner
The
SPIRIT
Will Eisner
The
By Will Eisner

COMIC BOOK SECTION

LIFE BELOW

ACTION Mystery ADVENTURE

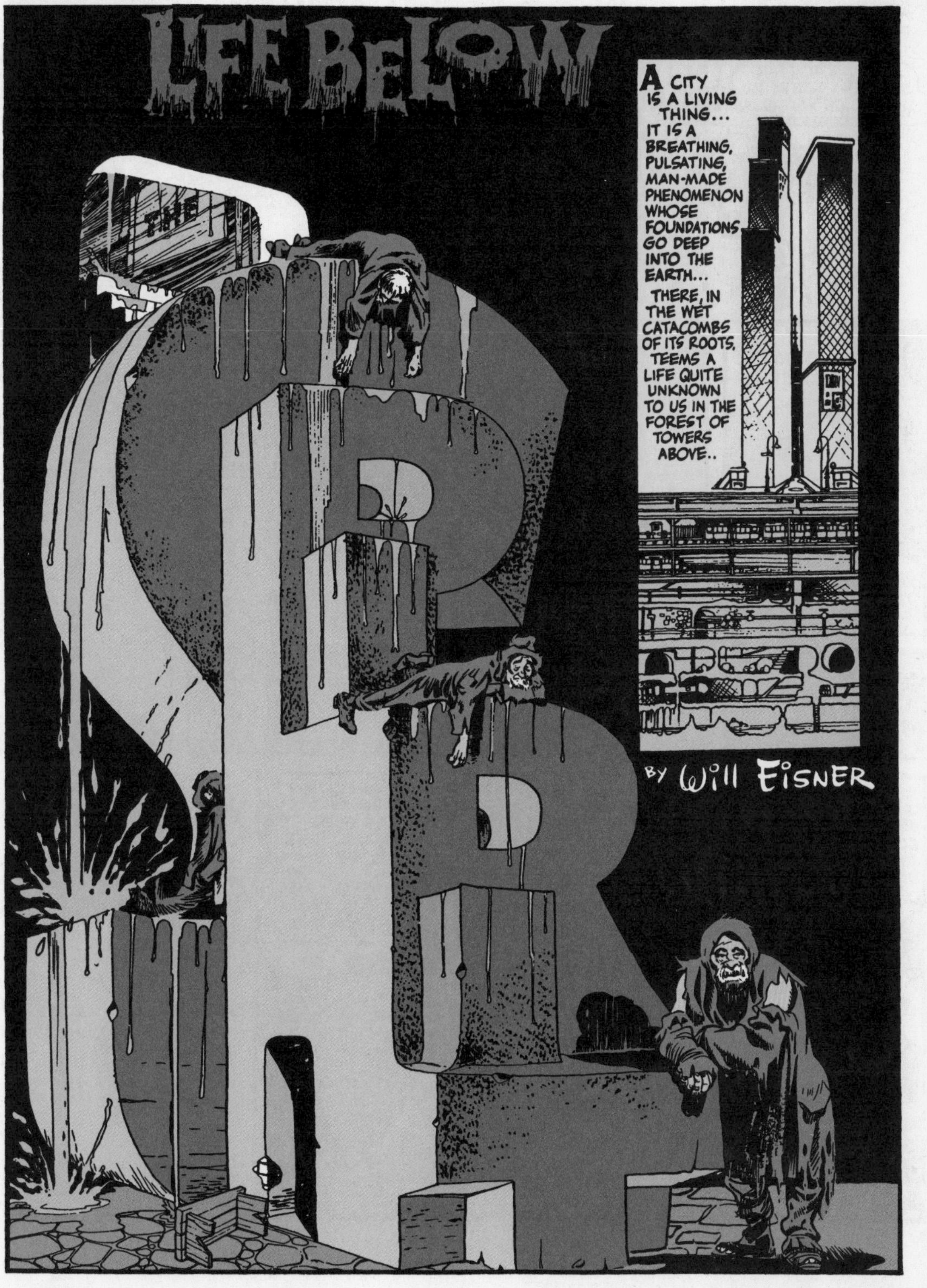
LIFE BELOW
A CITY IS A LIVING THING... IT IS A BREATHING, PULSATING, MAN-MADE PHENOMENON WHOSE FOUNDATIONS GO DEEP INTO THE EARTH...
THERE, IN THE WET CATACOMBS OF ITS ROOTS, TEEMS A LIFE QUITE UNKNOWN TO US IN THE FOREST OF TOWERS ABOVE..
THE
BY Will EISNER

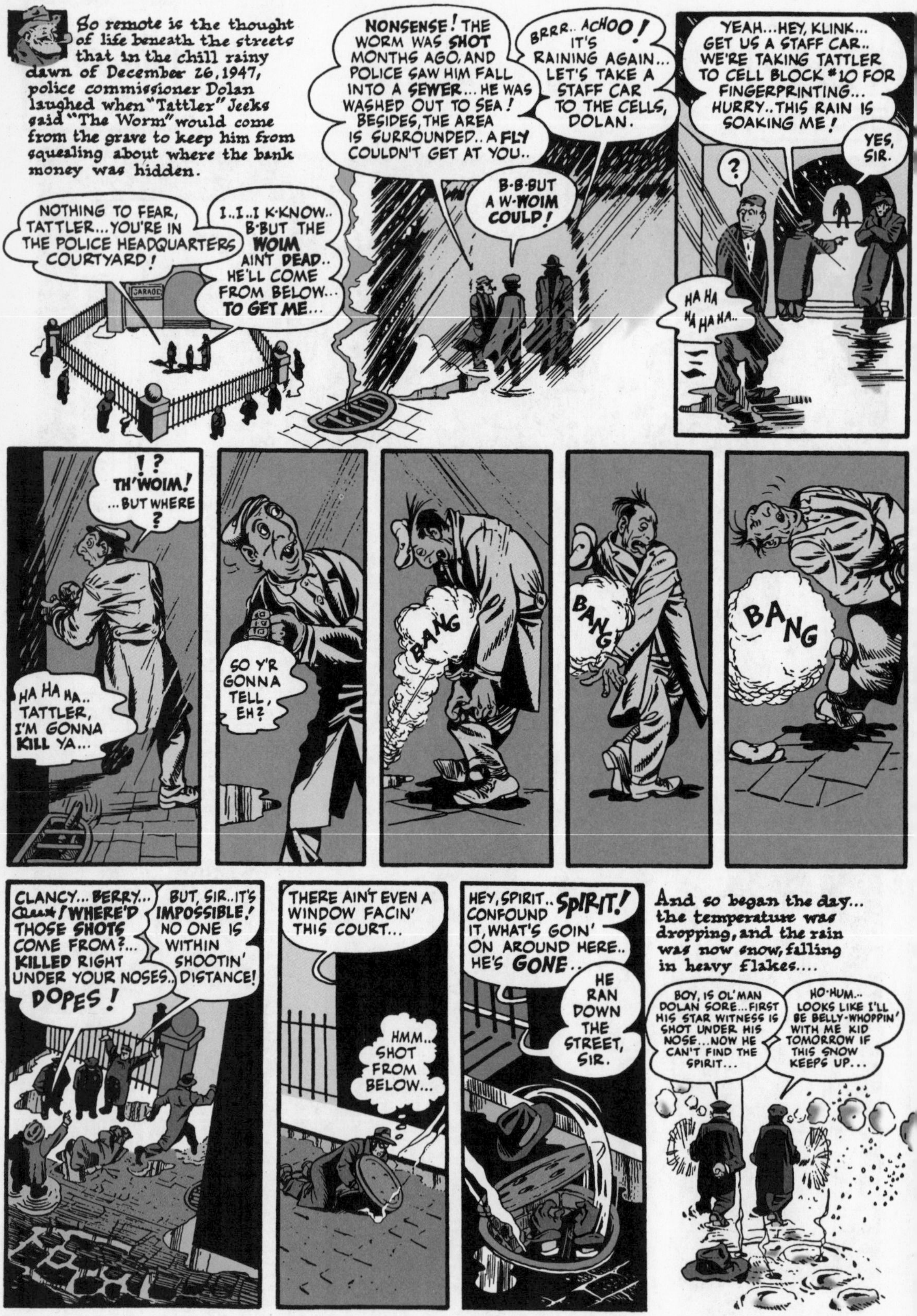
So remote is the thought of life beneath the streets that in the chill rainy dawn of December 26, 1947, police commissioner Dolan laughed when "Tattler" Jeeks said "The Worm" would come from the grave to keep him from squealing about where the bank money was hidden.
NOTHING TO FEAR, TATTLER... YOU'RE IN THE POLICE HEADQUARTERS COURTYARD!
I..I..I K-KNOW.. B-BUT THE WOIM AIN'T DEAD.. HE'LL COME FROM BELOW... TO GET ME...
GARAGE
NONSENSE! THE WORM WAS SHOT MONTHS AGO, AND POLICE SAW HIM FALL INTO A SEWER... HE WAS WASHED OUT TO SEA! BESIDES, THE AREA IS SURROUNDED.. A FLY COULDN'T GET AT YOU..
BRRR.. ACHOO! IT'S RAINING AGAIN... LET'S TAKE A STAFF CAR TO THE CELLS, DOLAN.
B-B-BUT A W-WOIM COULD!
YEAH... HEY, KLINK... GET US A STAFF CAR.. WE'RE TAKING TATTLER TO CELL BLOCK #10 FOR FINGERPRINTING... HURRY.. THIS RAIN IS SOAKING ME!
?
YES, SIR.
HA HA HA HA HA..
!? TH'WOIM! ...BUT WHERE ?
HA HA HA.. TATTLER, I'M GONNA KILL YA...
SO Y'R GONNA TELL, EH?
BANG
BANG
BANG
CLANCY... BERRY... ! WHERE'D THOSE SHOTS COME FROM?... KILLED RIGHT UNDER YOUR NOSES.. DOPES!
BUT, SIR.. IT'S IMPOSSIBLE! NO ONE IS WITHIN SHOOTIN' DISTANCE!
THERE AIN'T EVEN A WINDOW FACIN' THIS COURT...
HMM.. SHOT FROM BELOW...
HEY, SPIRIT.. SPIRIT! CONFOUND IT, WHAT'S GOIN' ON AROUND HERE.. HE'S GONE..
HE RAN DOWN THE STREET, SIR.
And so began the day... the temperature was dropping, and the rain was now snow, falling in heavy flakes....
BOY, IS OL' MAN DOLAN SORE... FIRST HIS STAR WITNESS IS SHOT UNDER HIS NOSE... NOW HE CAN'T FIND THE SPIRIT...
HO-HUM.. LOOKS LIKE I'LL BE BELLY-WHOPPIN' WITH ME KID TOMORROW IF THIS SNOW KEEPS UP...

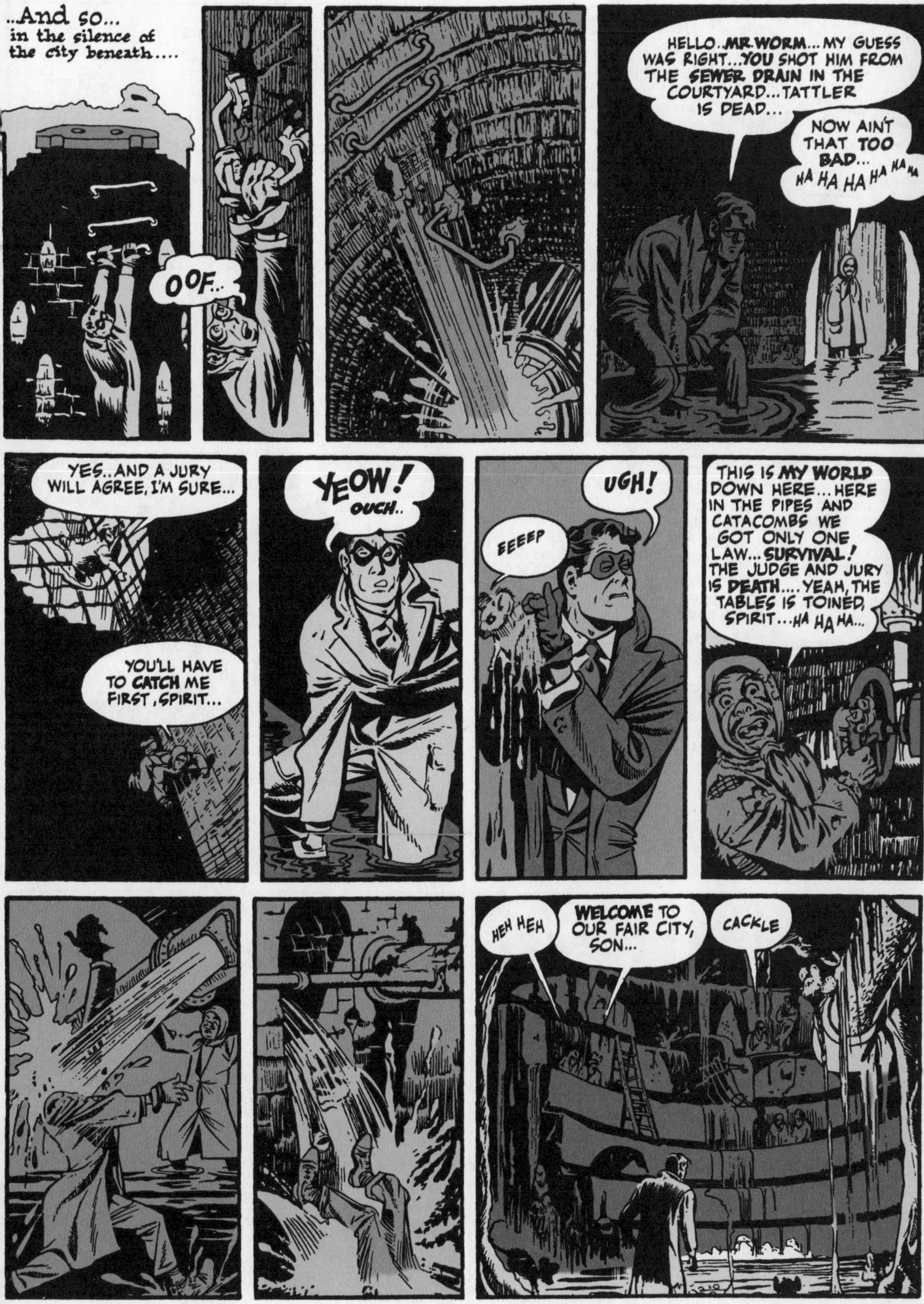

..And so...
in the silence of
the city beneath....
OOF..
HELLO..MR.WORM...MY GUESS WAS RIGHT...YOU SHOT HIM FROM THE SEWER DRAIN IN THE COURTYARD...TATTLER IS DEAD...
NOW AIN'T THAT TOO BAD... HA HA HA HA HA HA HA
YES..AND A JURY WILL AGREE, I'M SURE...
YOU'LL HAVE TO CATCH ME FIRST, SPIRIT...
YEOW! OUCH..
UGH!
EEEEP
THIS IS MY WORLD DOWN HERE...HERE IN THE PIPES AND CATACOMBS WE GOT ONLY ONE LAW...SURVIVAL! THE JUDGE AND JURY IS DEATH....YEAH, THE TABLES IS TOINED, SPIRIT...HA HA HA...
HEH HEH
WELCOME TO OUR FAIR CITY, SON...
CACKLE

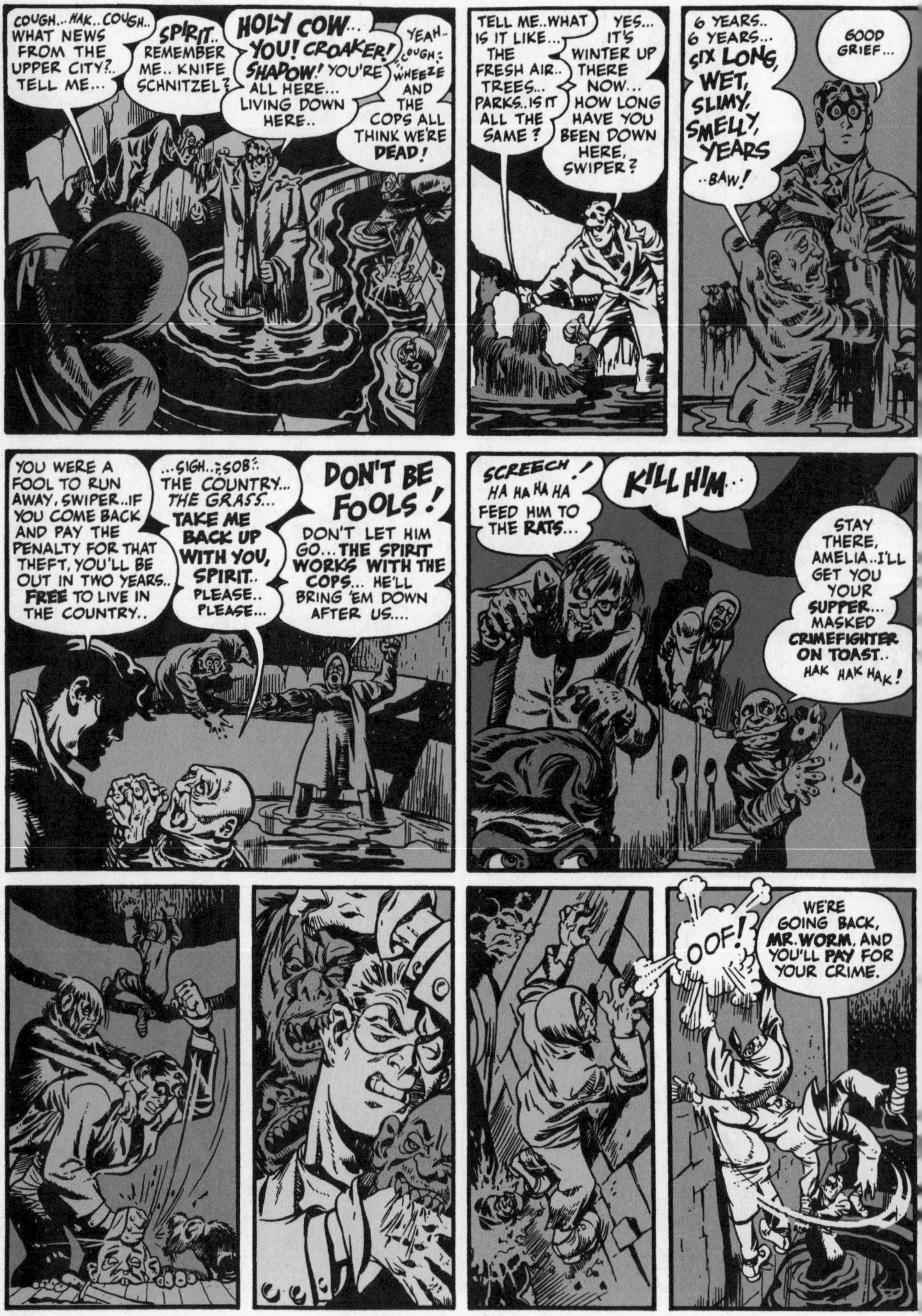
COUGH.. HAK.. COUGH.. WHAT NEWS FROM THE UPPER CITY?.. TELL ME...
SPIRIT.. REMEMBER ME.. KNIFE SCHNITZEL?
HOLY COW... YOU! CROAKER! SHADOW! YOU'RE ALL HERE... LIVING DOWN HERE..
YEAH.. COUGH.. WHEEZE AND THE COPS ALL THINK WE'RE DEAD!
TELL ME..WHAT IS IT LIKE... THE FRESH AIR.. TREES... PARKS..IS IT ALL THE SAME?
YES... IT'S WINTER UP THERE NOW... HOW LONG HAVE YOU BEEN DOWN HERE, SWIPER?
6 YEARS.. 6 YEARS... SIX LONG, WET, SLIMY, SMELLY, YEARS ..BAW!
GOOD GRIEF...
YOU WERE A FOOL TO RUN AWAY, SWIPER..IF YOU COME BACK AND PAY THE PENALTY FOR THAT THEFT, YOU'LL BE OUT IN TWO YEARS.. FREE TO LIVE IN THE COUNTRY..
...SIGH.. SOB.. THE COUNTRY... THE GRASS... TAKE ME BACK UP WITH YOU, SPIRIT.. PLEASE.. PLEASE...
DON'T BE FOOLS! DON'T LET HIM GO... THE SPIRIT WORKS WITH THE COPS... HE'LL BRING 'EM DOWN AFTER US....
SCREECH! HA HA HA HA FEED HIM TO THE RATS...
KILL HIM...
STAY THERE, AMELIA..I'LL GET YOU YOUR SUPPER... MASKED CRIMEFIGHTER ON TOAST.. HAK HAK HAK!
OOF!
WE'RE GOING BACK, MR. WORM, AND YOU'LL PAY FOR YOUR CRIME.

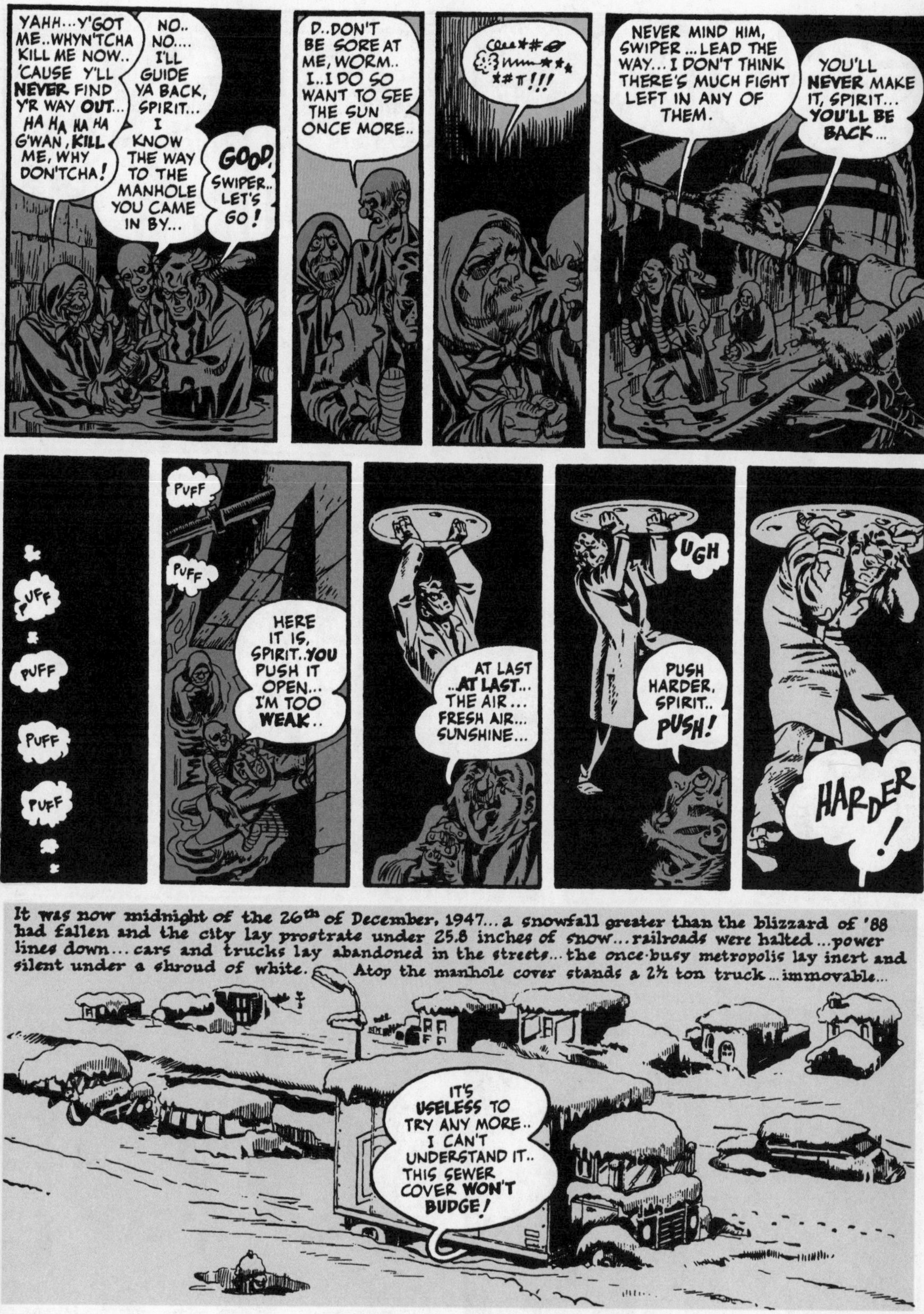
YAHH... Y'GOT ME..WHYN'TCHA KILL ME NOW.. 'CAUSE Y'LL NEVER FIND Y'R WAY OUT... HA HA HA HA G'WAN, KILL ME, WHY DON'TCHA!
NO.. NO.... I'LL GUIDE YA BACK, SPIRIT... I KNOW THE WAY TO THE MANHOLE YOU CAME IN BY...
GOOD, SWIPER.. LET'S GO!
D..DON'T BE SORE AT ME, WORM.. I..I DO SO WANT TO SEE THE SUN ONCE MORE..
NEVER MIND HIM, SWIPER... LEAD THE WAY... I DON'T THINK THERE'S MUCH FIGHT LEFT IN ANY OF THEM.
YOU'LL NEVER MAKE IT, SPIRIT... YOU'LL BE BACK...
PUFF
PUFF
PUFF
PUFF
PUFF
PUFF
PUFF
HERE IT IS, SPIRIT..YOU PUSH IT OPEN... I'M TOO WEAK..
AT LAST ..AT LAST... THE AIR... FRESH AIR... SUNSHINE...
UGH
PUSH HARDER, SPIRIT.. PUSH!
HARDER!
It was now midnight of the 26th of December, 1947... a snowfall greater than the blizzard of '88 had fallen and the city lay prostrate under 25.8 inches of snow... railroads were halted... power lines down... cars and trucks lay abandoned in the streets... the once-busy metropolis lay inert and silent under a shroud of white. Atop the manhole cover stands a 2½ ton truck... immovable...
IT'S USELESS TO TRY ANY MORE.. I CAN'T UNDERSTAND IT.. THIS SEWER COVER WON'T BUDGE!

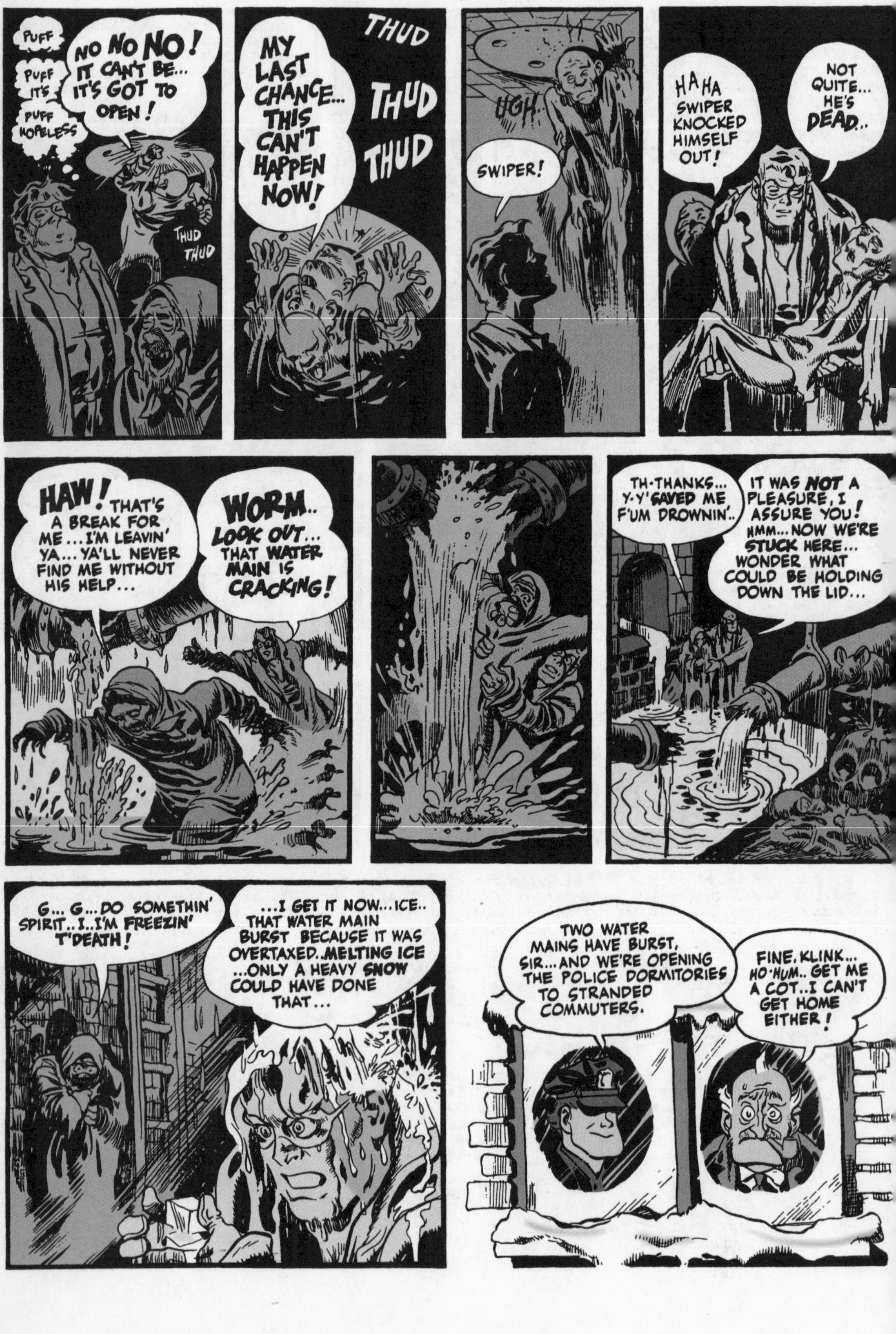
PUFF
PUFF IT'S
PUFF HOPELESS
NO NO NO! IT CAN'T BE... IT'S GOT TO OPEN!
THUD THUD
MY LAST CHANCE... THIS CAN'T HAPPEN NOW!
THUD
THUD
THUD
UGH
SWIPER!
HA HA SWIPER KNOCKED HIMSELF OUT!
NOT QUITE... HE'S DEAD...
HAW! THAT'S A BREAK FOR ME... I'M LEAVIN' YA... YA'LL NEVER FIND ME WITHOUT HIS HELP...
WORM.. LOOK OUT... THAT WATER MAIN IS CRACKING!
TH-THANKS... Y-Y'SAVED ME F'UM DROWNIN'..
IT WAS NOT A PLEASURE, I ASSURE YOU! HMM... NOW WE'RE STUCK HERE... WONDER WHAT COULD BE HOLDING DOWN THE LID...
G... G... DO SOMETHIN' SPIRIT.. I..I'M FREEZIN' T'DEATH!
...I GET IT NOW... ICE.. THAT WATER MAIN BURST BECAUSE IT WAS OVERTAXED..MELTING ICE ...ONLY A HEAVY SNOW COULD HAVE DONE THAT...
TWO WATER MAINS HAVE BURST, SIR... AND WE'RE OPENING THE POLICE DORMITORIES TO STRANDED COMMUTERS.
FINE, KLINK... HO-HUM.. GET ME A COT.. I CAN'T GET HOME EITHER!

On the morning of the 27th, the city with military precision moved huge equipment into the streets and began the million-dollar job of snow removal ... life began to regain its tempo, and things long buried under the drifts began to move....

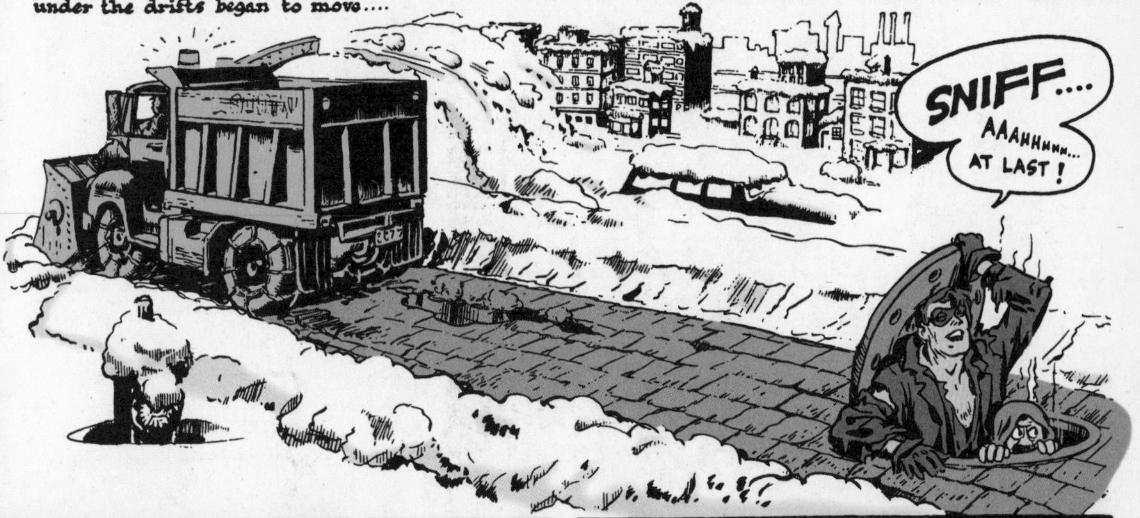
SNIFF....
AAAHHHHH...
AT LAST!

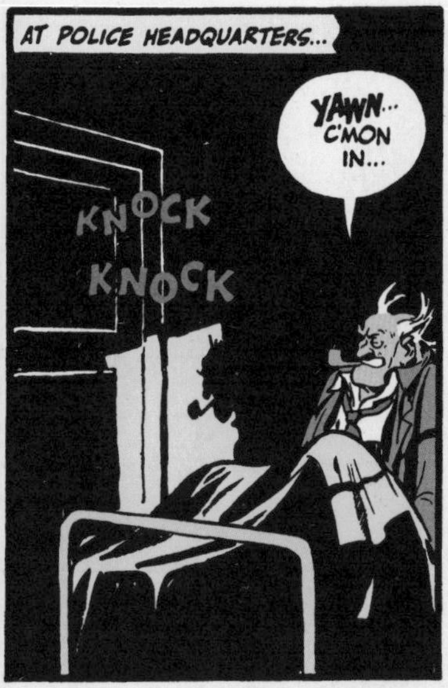
AT POLICE HEADQUARTERS...
KNOCK
KNOCK
YAWN... C'MON IN...

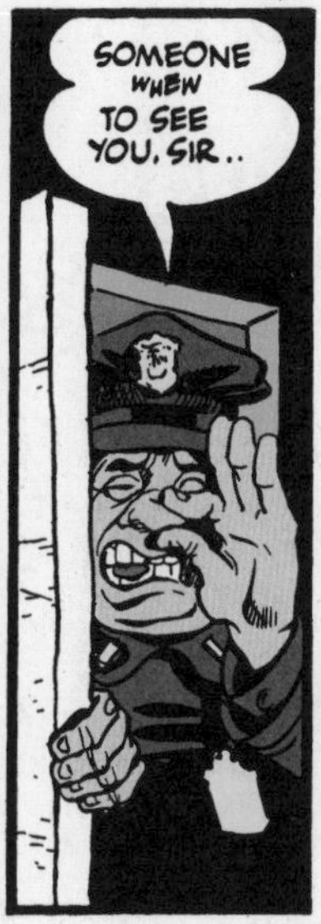
SOMEONE WHEW TO SEE YOU, SIR..

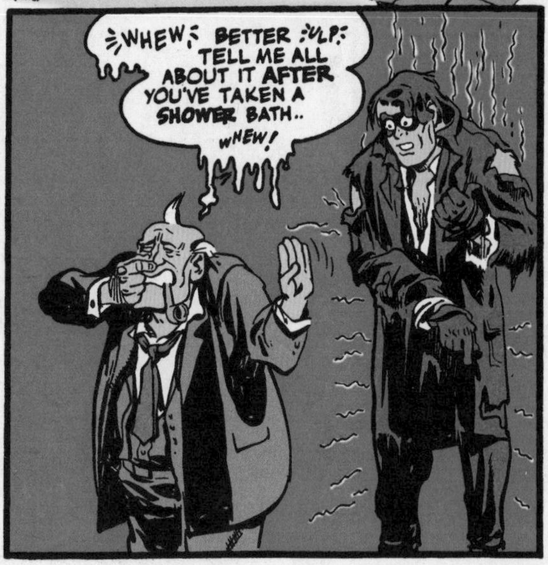
WHEW BETTER GULP TELL ME ALL ABOUT IT AFTER YOU'VE TAKEN A SHOWER BATH.. WHEW!

Within 48 hours the temperature dropped ... a soft rain melted the snow, saving the city millions of dollars...

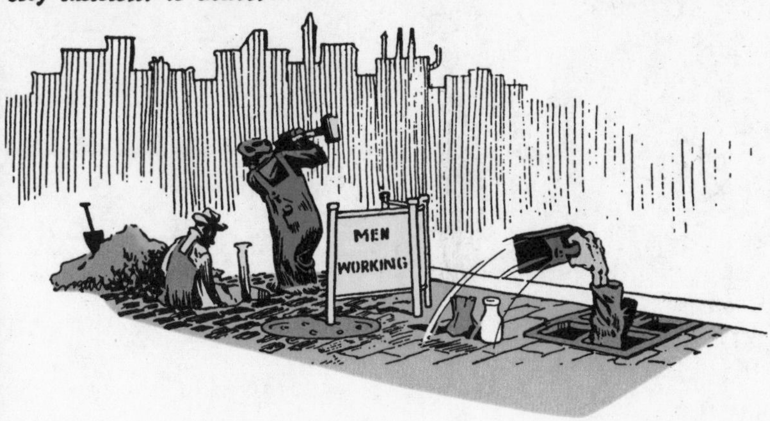
MEN
WORKING

....and all was normal above...

... and below the city..

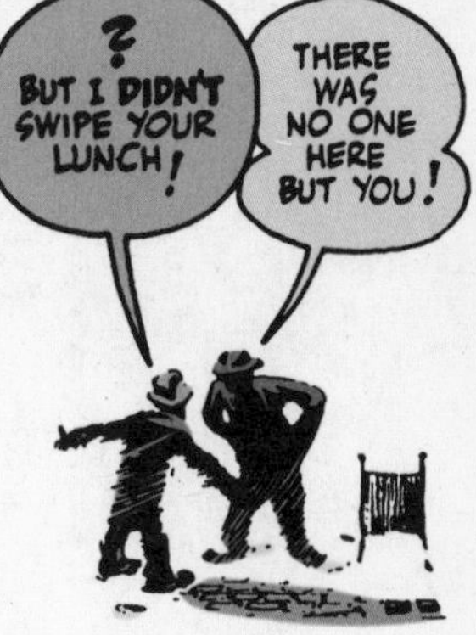
? BUT I DIDN'T SWIPE YOUR LUNCH!
THERE WAS NO ONE HERE BUT YOU!

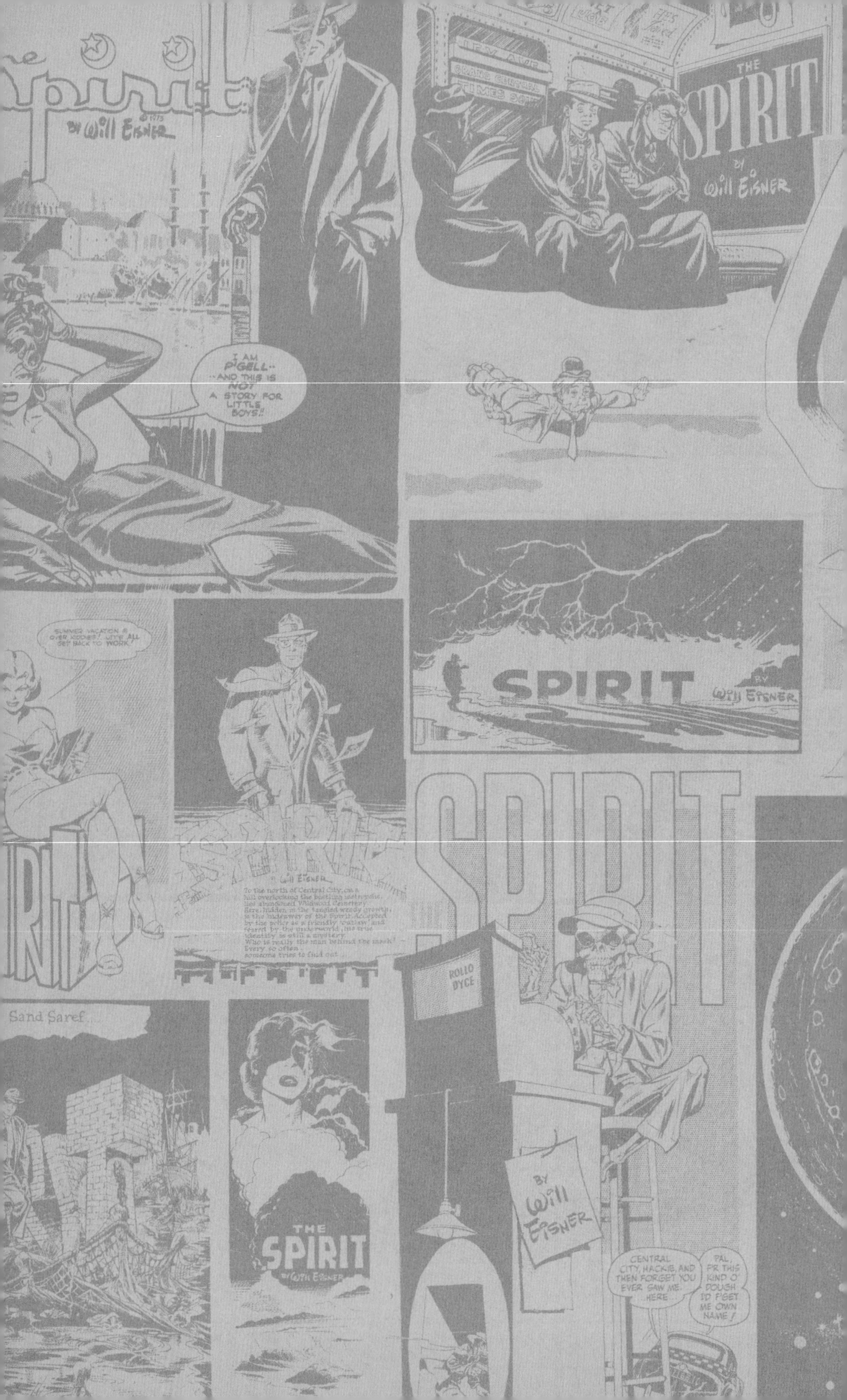
Spirit
©1973
BY Will Eisner
I AM P'GELL.. ..AND THIS IS NOT A STORY FOR LITTLE BOYS!!
THE SPIRIT BY Will Eisner
SUMMER VACATION IS OVER KIDDIES! LET'S ALL GET BACK TO WORK!
SPIRIT BY Will Eisner
SPIRIT
Will Eisner
To the north of Central City, on a hill overlooking the bustling metropolis, lies abandoned Wildwood Cemetery. Here, hidden in the tangled weedy growth, is the hideaway of the Spirit. Accepted by the police as a friendly 'outlaw' and feared by the underworld, his true identity is still a mystery. Who is really the man behind the mask? - Every so often someone tries to find out...
SPIRIT
ROLLO DYCE
Sand Saref...
THE SPIRIT BY Will Eisner
BY Will Eisner
CENTRAL CITY, HACKIE, AND THEN FORGET YOU EVER SAW ME. ..HERE
PAL, FR THIS KIND O' DOUGH I'D F'GET ME OWN NAME!

WILD RICE

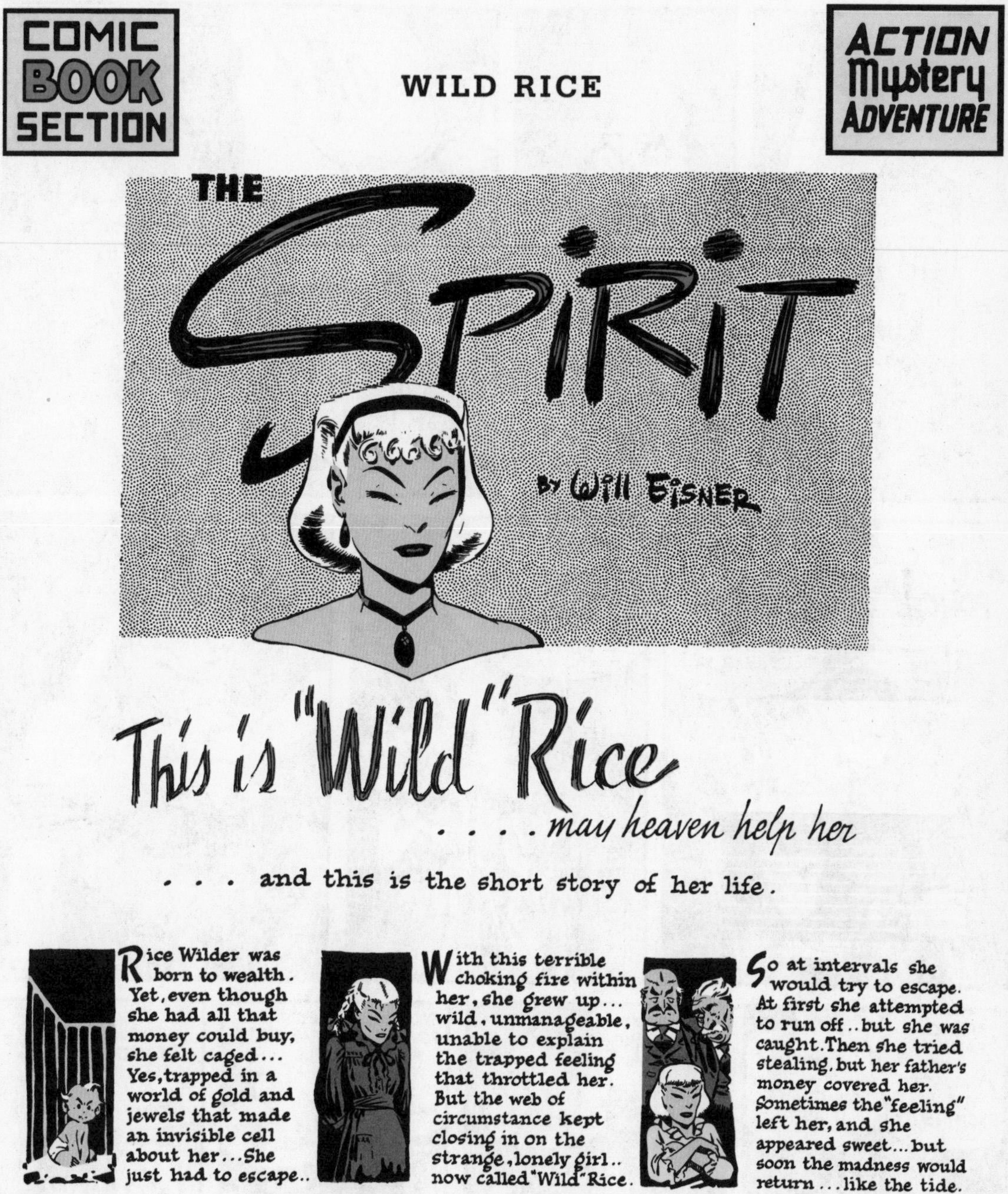

COMIC BOOK SECTION
ACTION Mystery ADVENTURE
THE SPIRIT
by Will Eisner
This is "Wild" Rice
. . . . may heaven help her
. . . and this is the short story of her life.
Rice Wilder was born to wealth. Yet, even though she had all that money could buy, she felt caged... Yes, trapped in a world of gold and jewels that made an invisible cell about her... She just had to escape..
With this terrible choking fire within her, she grew up... wild, unmanageable, unable to explain the trapped feeling that throttled her. But the web of circumstance kept closing in on the strange, lonely girl.. now called "Wild" Rice.
So at intervals she would try to escape. At first she attempted to run off.. but she was caught. Then she tried stealing, but her father's money covered her. Sometimes the "feeling" left her, and she appeared sweet... but soon the madness would return... like the tide.
At last...by the time she was 24 years old, the inner fires seemed to subside... and though they lay like glowing coals within her, she surrendered. Her father arranged a profitable marriage and a wedding day was set.
On the evening of the reception, however, the slumbering volcano burst within her, and the force of it sent her flying from the dance.. propelled her from her husband's arms and upstairs to her room...
I CAN'T... I CAN'T GO THROUGH WITH IT... JUST ANOTHER LINK IN THE CHAIN..!

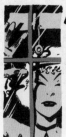

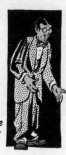

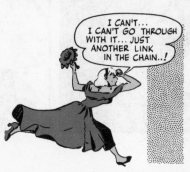

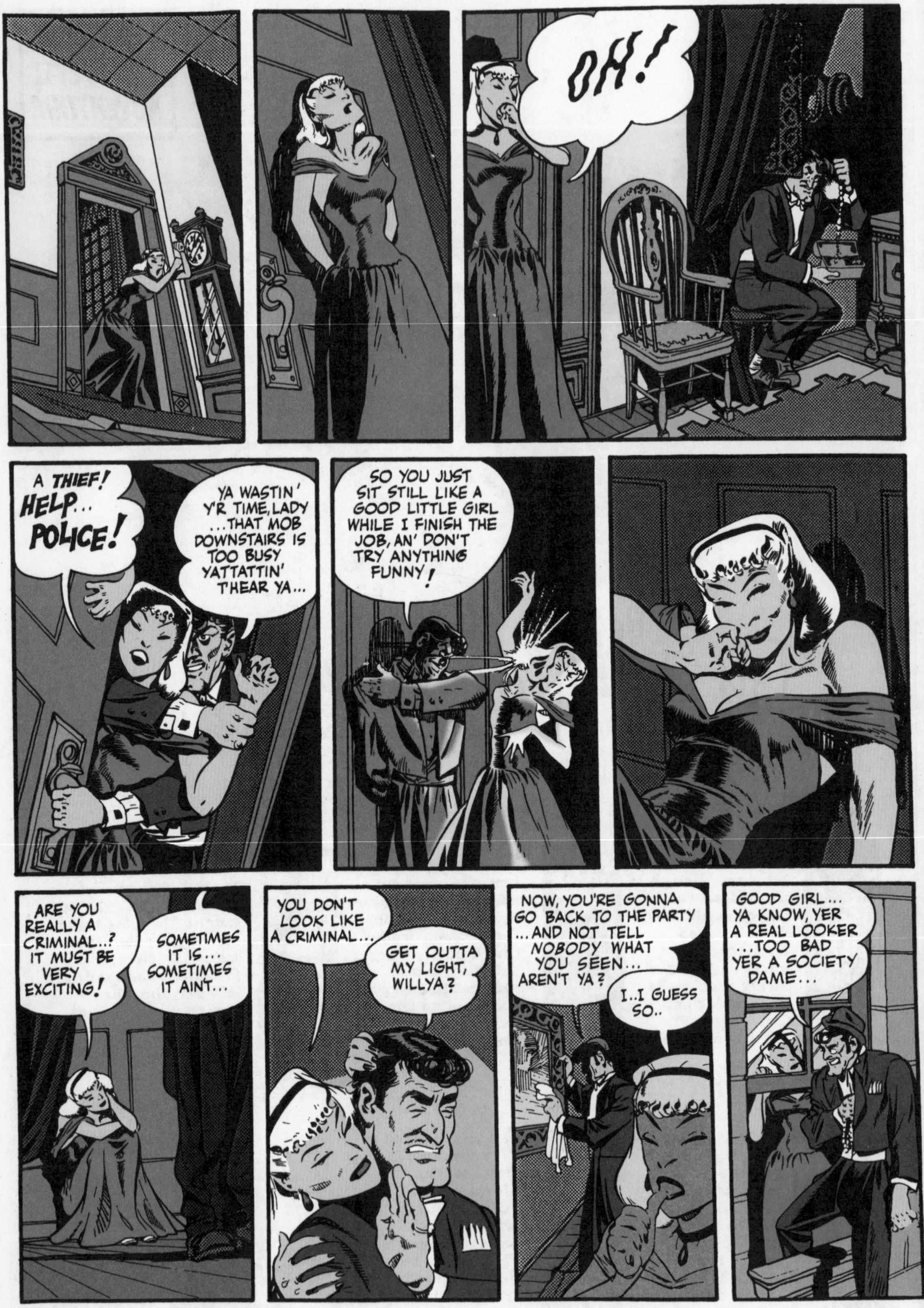
OH!
A THIEF! HELP... POLICE!
YA WASTIN' Y'R TIME, LADY ...THAT MOB DOWNSTAIRS IS TOO BUSY YATTATTIN' T'HEAR YA...
SO YOU JUST SIT STILL LIKE A GOOD LITTLE GIRL WHILE I FINISH THE JOB, AN' DON'T TRY ANYTHING FUNNY!
ARE YOU REALLY A CRIMINAL..? IT MUST BE VERY EXCITING!
SOMETIMES IT IS... SOMETIMES IT AIN'T...
YOU DON'T LOOK LIKE A CRIMINAL...
GET OUTTA MY LIGHT, WILLYA?
NOW, YOU'RE GONNA GO BACK TO THE PARTY ...AND NOT TELL NOBODY WHAT YOU SEEN... AREN'T YA?
I..I GUESS SO..
GOOD GIRL... YA KNOW, YER A REAL LOOKER ...TOO BAD YER A SOCIETY DAME...

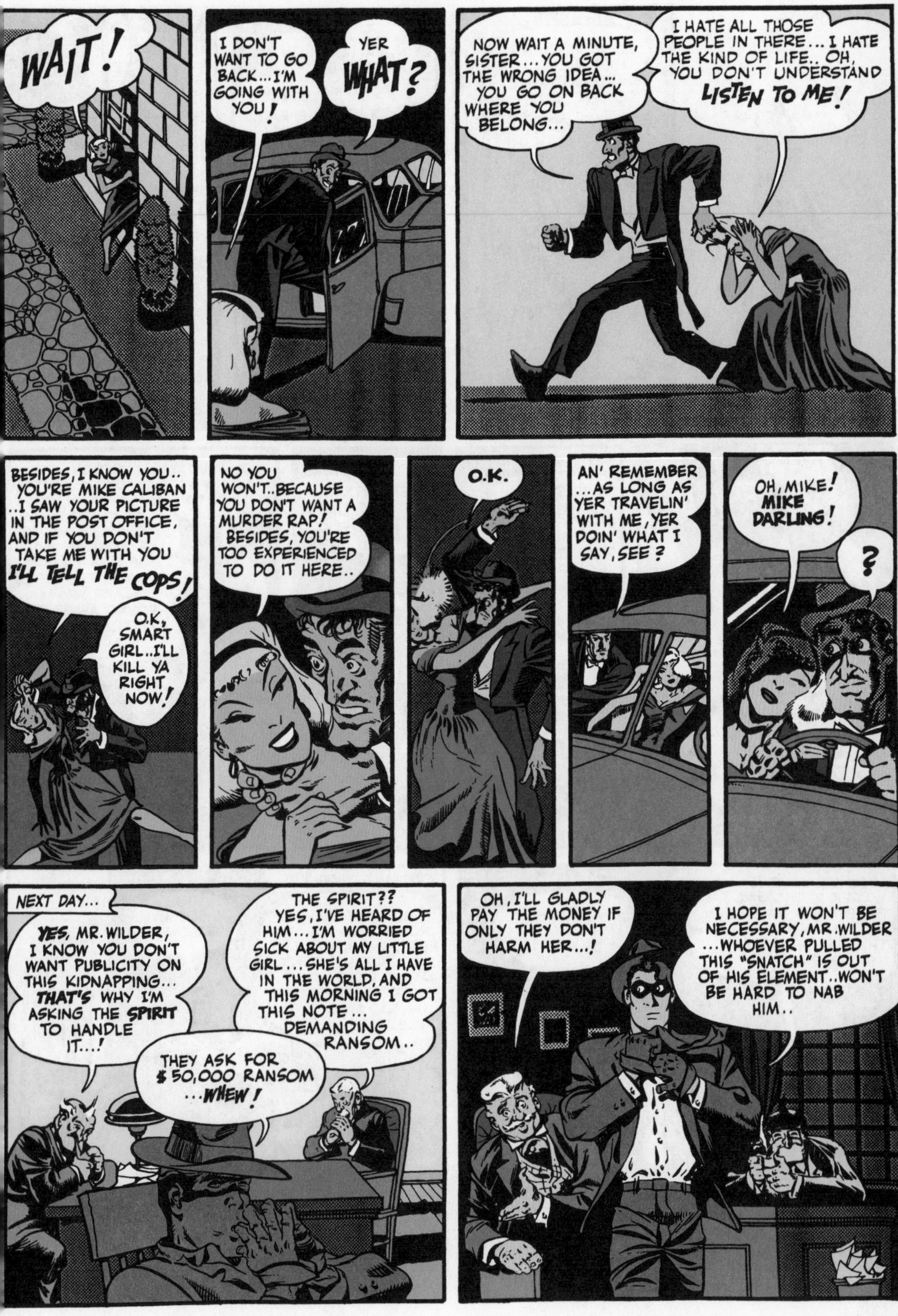
WAIT!
I DON'T WANT TO GO BACK...I'M GOING WITH YOU!
YER WHAT?
NOW WAIT A MINUTE, SISTER...YOU GOT THE WRONG IDEA... YOU GO ON BACK WHERE YOU BELONG...
I HATE ALL THOSE PEOPLE IN THERE... I HATE THE KIND OF LIFE.. OH, YOU DON'T UNDERSTAND LISTEN TO ME!
BESIDES, I KNOW YOU.. YOU'RE MIKE CALIBAN ..I SAW YOUR PICTURE IN THE POST OFFICE, AND IF YOU DON'T TAKE ME WITH YOU I'LL TELL THE COPS!
O.K., SMART GIRL..I'LL KILL YA RIGHT NOW!
NO YOU WON'T..BECAUSE YOU DON'T WANT A MURDER RAP! BESIDES, YOU'RE TOO EXPERIENCED TO DO IT HERE..
O.K.
AN' REMEMBER ...AS LONG AS YER TRAVELIN' WITH ME, YER DOIN' WHAT I SAY, SEE?
OH, MIKE! MIKE DARLING!
?
NEXT DAY...
YES, MR. WILDER, I KNOW YOU DON'T WANT PUBLICITY ON THIS KIDNAPPING... THAT'S WHY I'M ASKING THE SPIRIT TO HANDLE IT...!
THE SPIRIT?? YES, I'VE HEARD OF HIM... I'M WORRIED SICK ABOUT MY LITTLE GIRL... SHE'S ALL I HAVE IN THE WORLD, AND THIS MORNING I GOT THIS NOTE... DEMANDING RANSOM..
THEY ASK FOR $50,000 RANSOM ...WHEW!
OH, I'LL GLADLY PAY THE MONEY IF ONLY THEY DON'T HARM HER...!
I HOPE IT WON'T BE NECESSARY, MR. WILDER ...WHOEVER PULLED THIS "SNATCH" IS OUT OF HIS ELEMENT..WON'T BE HARD TO NAB HIM..

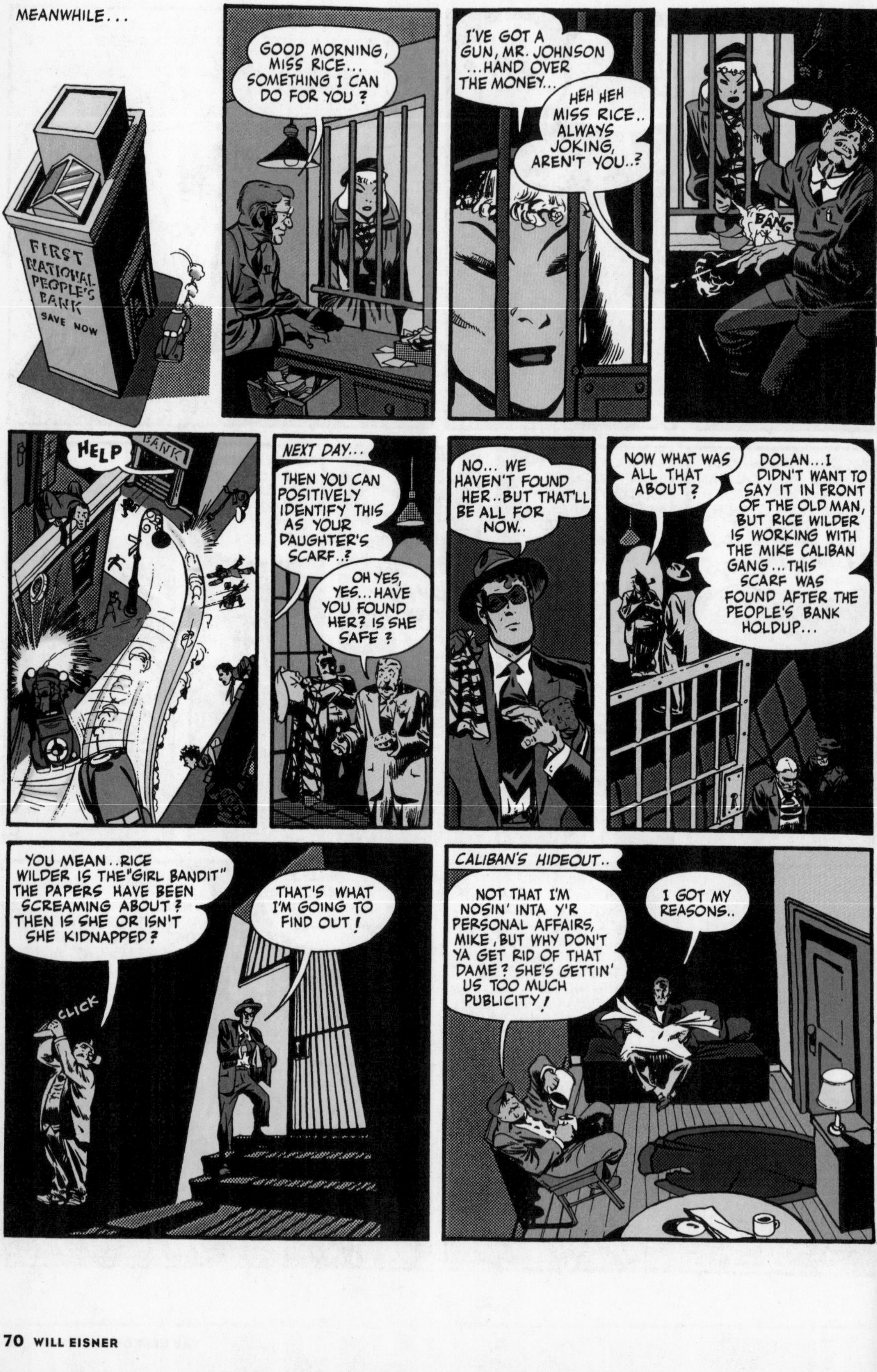
MEANWHILE...
FIRST NATIONAL PEOPLE'S BANK
SAVE NOW
GOOD MORNING, MISS RICE... SOMETHING I CAN DO FOR YOU ?
I'VE GOT A GUN, MR. JOHNSON ...HAND OVER THE MONEY...
HEH HEH MISS RICE.. ALWAYS JOKING, AREN'T YOU..?
BANG
HELP
BANK
NEXT DAY...
THEN YOU CAN POSITIVELY IDENTIFY THIS AS YOUR DAUGHTER'S SCARF..?
OH YES, YES... HAVE YOU FOUND HER? IS SHE SAFE ?
NO... WE HAVEN'T FOUND HER.. BUT THAT'LL BE ALL FOR NOW..
NOW WHAT WAS ALL THAT ABOUT ?
DOLAN...I DIDN'T WANT TO SAY IT IN FRONT OF THE OLD MAN, BUT RICE WILDER IS WORKING WITH THE MIKE CALIBAN GANG... THIS SCARF WAS FOUND AFTER THE PEOPLE'S BANK HOLDUP...
YOU MEAN..RICE WILDER IS THE "GIRL BANDIT" THE PAPERS HAVE BEEN SCREAMING ABOUT ? THEN IS SHE OR ISN'T SHE KIDNAPPED ?
CLICK
THAT'S WHAT I'M GOING TO FIND OUT !
CALIBAN'S HIDEOUT..
NOT THAT I'M NOSIN' INTA Y'R PERSONAL AFFAIRS, MIKE, BUT WHY DON'T YA GET RID OF THAT DAME ? SHE'S GETTIN' US TOO MUCH PUBLICITY !
I GOT MY REASONS..

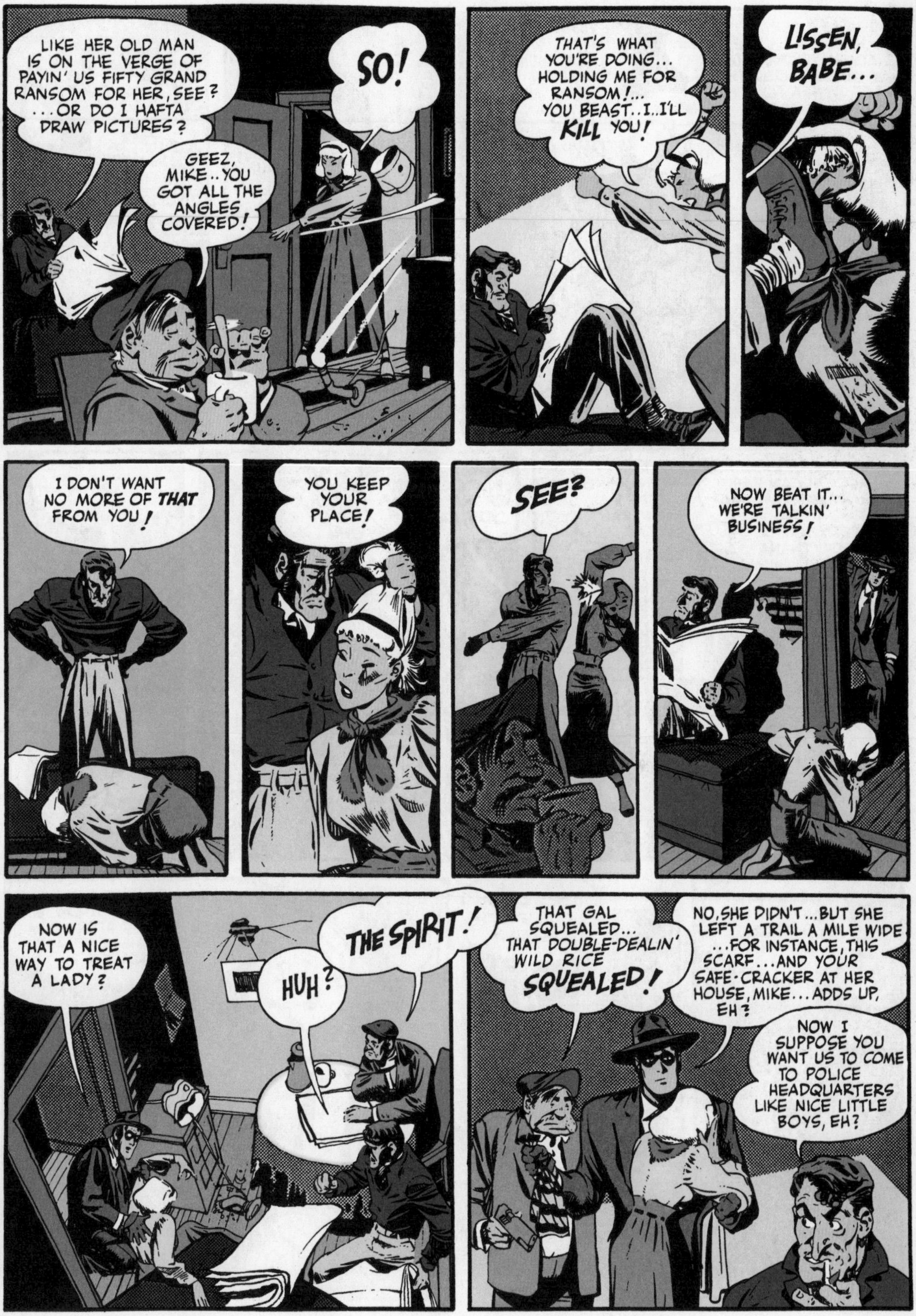
LIKE HER OLD MAN IS ON THE VERGE OF PAYIN' US FIFTY GRAND RANSOM FOR HER, SEE? ...OR DO I HAFTA DRAW PICTURES?
GEEZ, MIKE..YOU GOT ALL THE ANGLES COVERED!
SO!
THAT'S WHAT YOU'RE DOING... HOLDING ME FOR RANSOM!... YOU BEAST..I..I'LL KILL YOU!
LISSEN, BABE...
I DON'T WANT NO MORE OF THAT FROM YOU!
YOU KEEP YOUR PLACE!
SEE?
NOW BEAT IT... WE'RE TALKIN' BUSINESS!
NOW IS THAT A NICE WAY TO TREAT A LADY?
THE SPIRIT!
HUH?
THAT GAL SQUEALED... THAT DOUBLE-DEALIN' WILD RICE SQUEALED!
NO, SHE DIDN'T...BUT SHE LEFT A TRAIL A MILE WIDE ...FOR INSTANCE, THIS SCARF...AND YOUR SAFE-CRACKER AT HER HOUSE, MIKE...ADDS UP, EH?
NOW I SUPPOSE YOU WANT US TO COME TO POLICE HEADQUARTERS LIKE NICE LITTLE BOYS, EH?

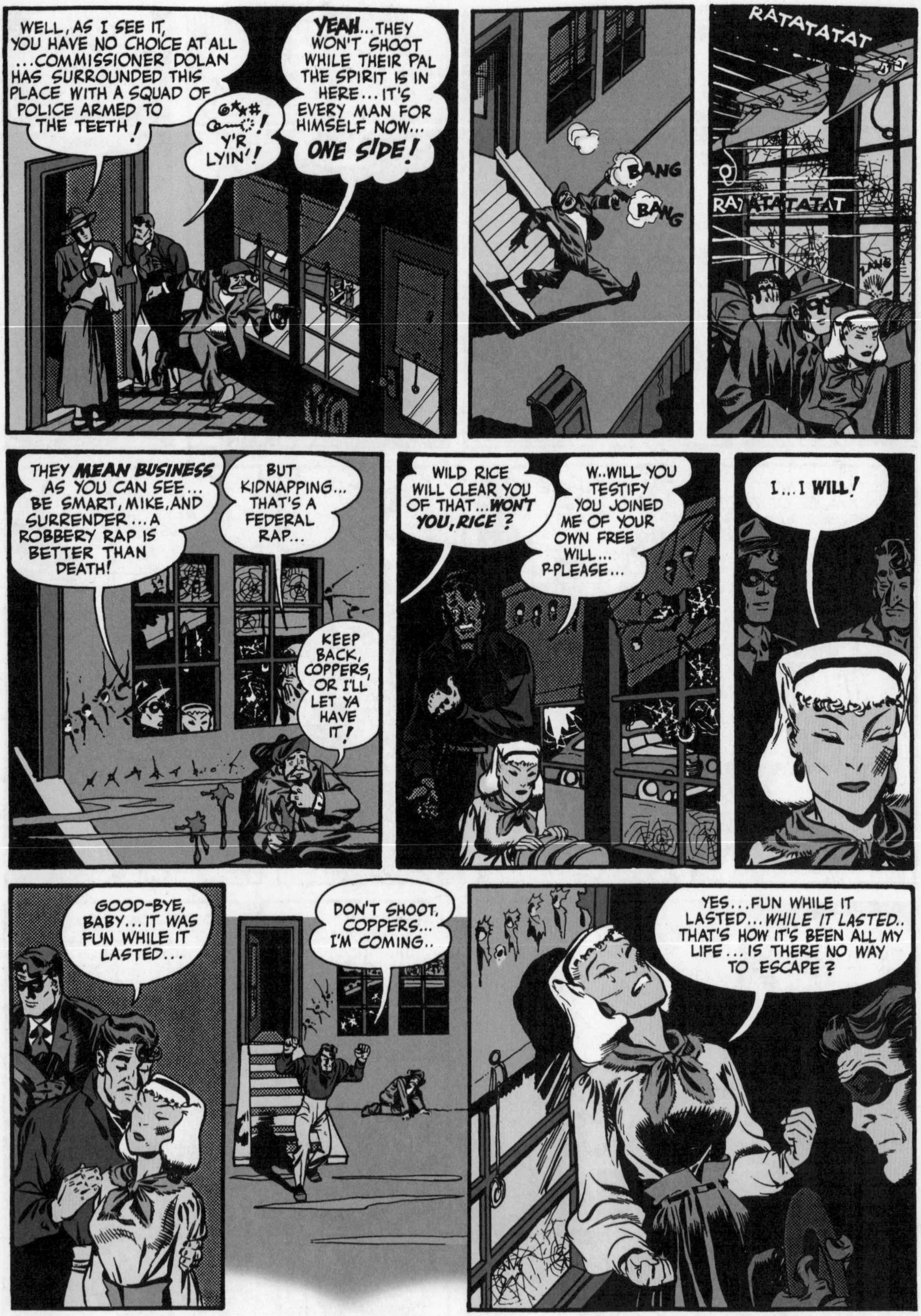
WELL, AS I SEE IT, YOU HAVE NO CHOICE AT ALL ...COMMISSIONER DOLAN HAS SURROUNDED THIS PLACE WITH A SQUAD OF POLICE ARMED TO THE TEETH!
Y'R LYIN'!
YEAH... THEY WON'T SHOOT WHILE THEIR PAL THE SPIRIT IS IN HERE... IT'S EVERY MAN FOR HIMSELF NOW... ONE SIDE!
BANG
BANG
RATATATAT
RATATATATAT
THEY MEAN BUSINESS AS YOU CAN SEE... BE SMART, MIKE, AND SURRENDER... A ROBBERY RAP IS BETTER THAN DEATH!
BUT KIDNAPPING... THAT'S A FEDERAL RAP...
KEEP BACK, COPPERS, OR I'LL LET YA HAVE IT!
WILD RICE WILL CLEAR YOU OF THAT...WON'T YOU, RICE?
W..WILL YOU TESTIFY YOU JOINED ME OF YOUR OWN FREE WILL... P-PLEASE...
I... I WILL!
GOOD-BYE, BABY... IT WAS FUN WHILE IT LASTED...
DON'T SHOOT, COPPERS... I'M COMING..
YES... FUN WHILE IT LASTED... WHILE IT LASTED.. THAT'S HOW IT'S BEEN ALL MY LIFE... IS THERE NO WAY TO ESCAPE?

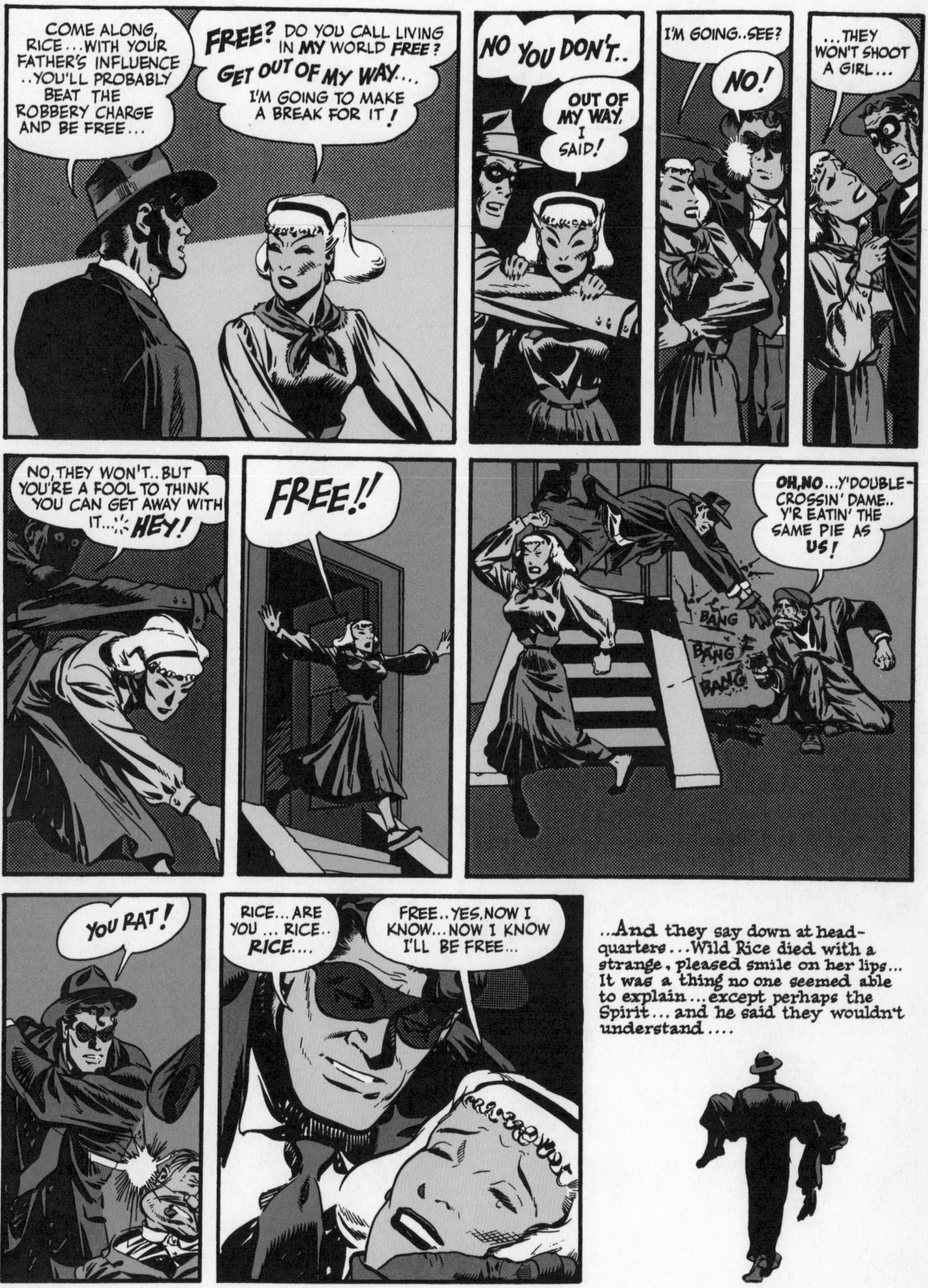
COME ALONG, RICE... WITH YOUR FATHER'S INFLUENCE ..YOU'LL PROBABLY BEAT THE ROBBERY CHARGE AND BE FREE...
FREE? DO YOU CALL LIVING IN MY WORLD FREE? GET OUT OF MY WAY.... I'M GOING TO MAKE A BREAK FOR IT!
NO YOU DON'T..
OUT OF MY WAY, I SAID!
I'M GOING..SEE?
NO!
...THEY WON'T SHOOT A GIRL...
NO, THEY WON'T.. BUT YOU'RE A FOOL TO THINK YOU CAN GET AWAY WITH IT... HEY!
FREE!!
OH, NO...Y'DOUBLE-CROSSIN' DAME.. Y'R EATIN' THE SAME PIE AS US!
BANG
BANG
BANG
YOU RAT!
RICE... ARE YOU ... RICE.. RICE....
FREE.. YES, NOW I KNOW... NOW I KNOW I'LL BE FREE...
...And they say down at head-quarters...Wild Rice died with a strange, pleased smile on her lips... It was a thing no one seemed able to explain... except perhaps the Spirit... and he said they wouldn't understand....

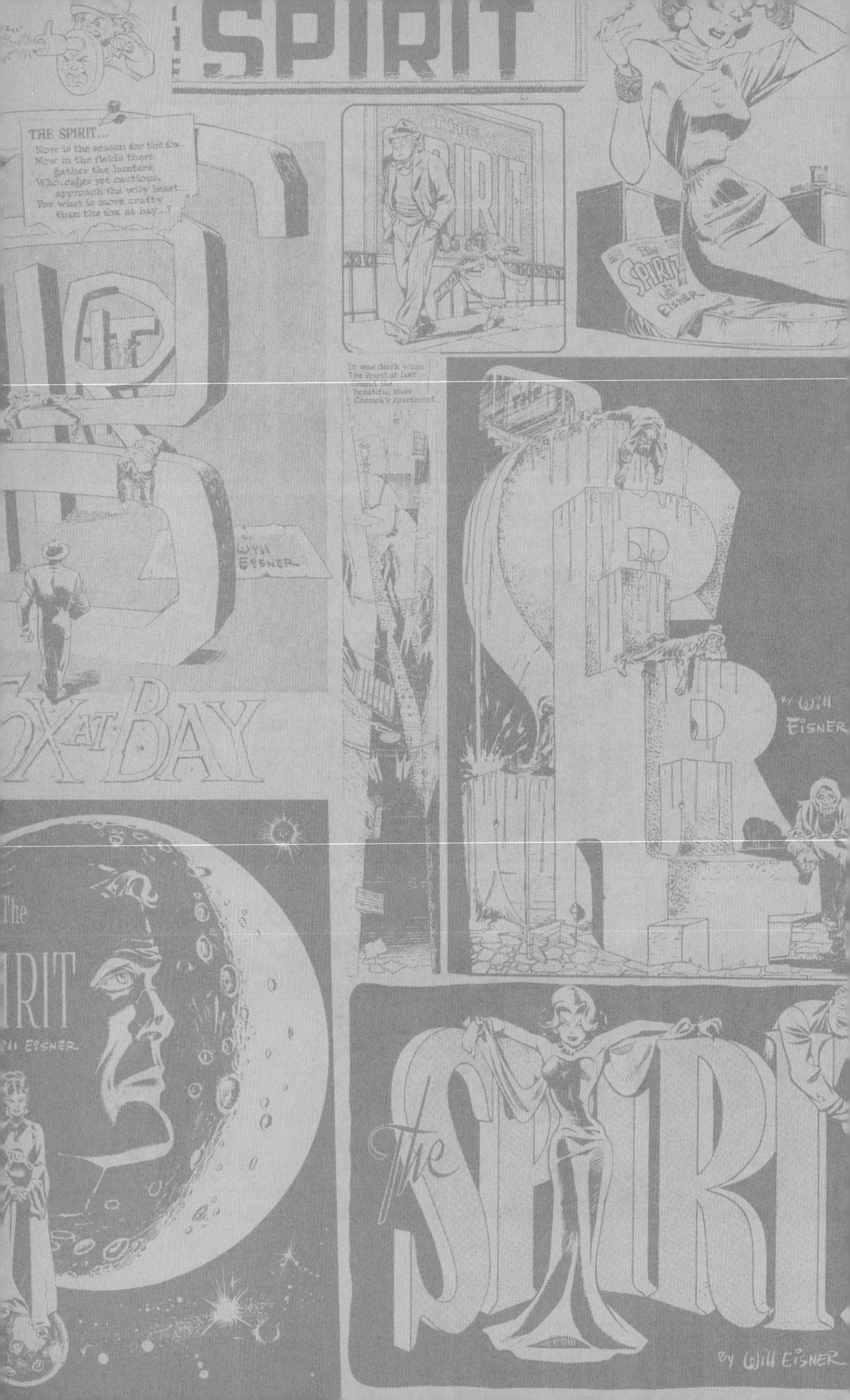
SPIRIT
THE SPIRIT...
Now is the season for the fox.
Now in the fields there gather the hunters
Who, eager yet cautious, approach the wily beast...
For what is more crafty than the fox at bay..?
by Will Eisner
X AT BAY
THE SPIRIT
The Spirit by Will Eisner
It was dusk when
The Spirit at last
beautiful Miss
Cosmek's apartment...
THE
by Will Eisner
The
IRIT
Will Eisner
The SPIRIT
by Will Eisner

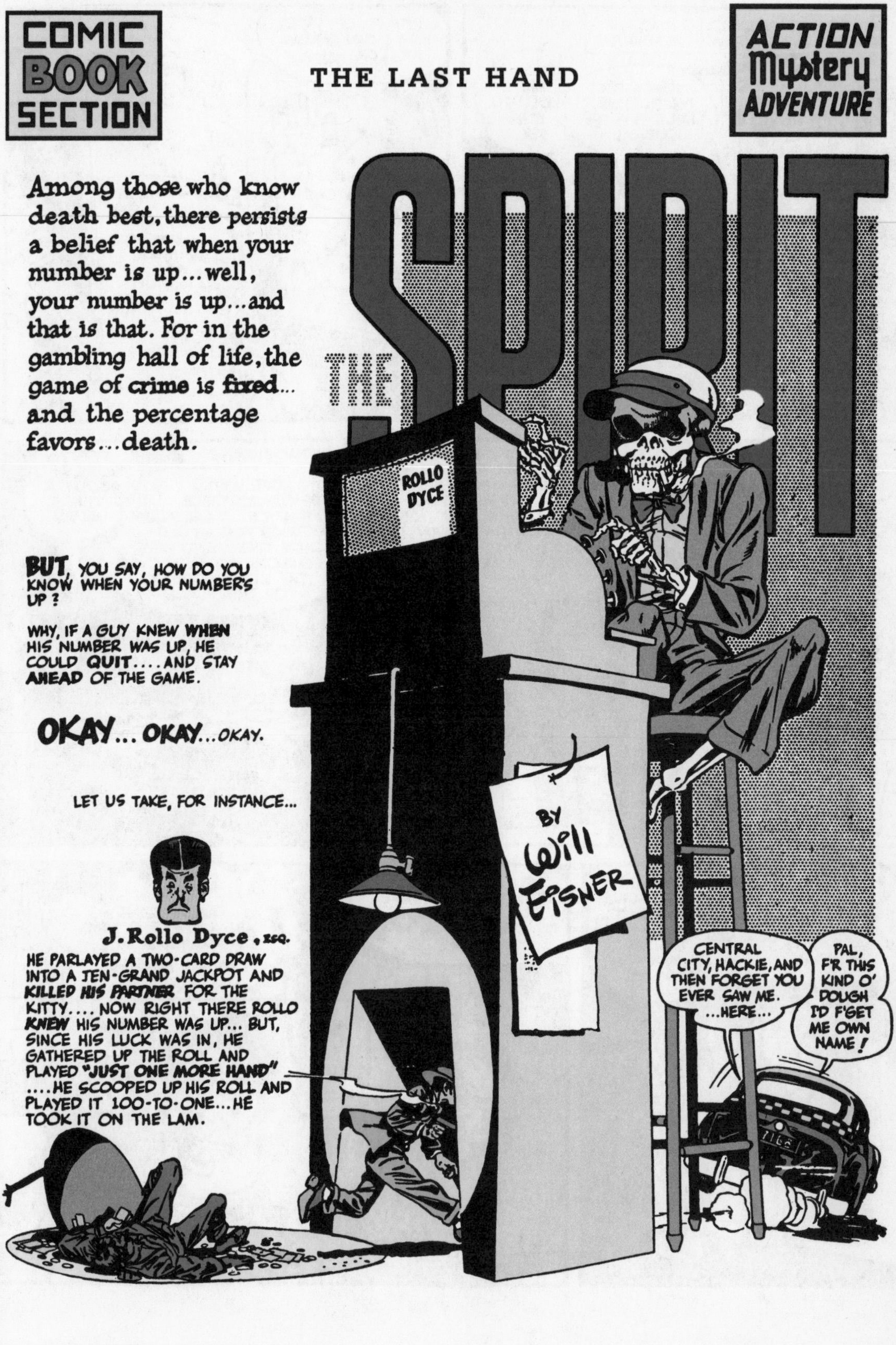
COMIC BOOK SECTION
THE LAST HAND
ACTION Mystery ADVENTURE
THE SPIRIT
Among those who know death best, there persists a belief that when your number is up... well, your number is up... and that is that. For in the gambling hall of life, the game of crime is fixed... and the percentage favors... death.
ROLLO DYCE
BUT, YOU SAY, HOW DO YOU KNOW WHEN YOUR NUMBER'S UP ?
WHY, IF A GUY KNEW WHEN HIS NUMBER WAS UP, HE COULD QUIT.... AND STAY AHEAD OF THE GAME.
OKAY... OKAY... OKAY.
LET US TAKE, FOR INSTANCE...
BY Will Eisner
J. Rollo Dyce, ESQ.
HE PARLAYED A TWO-CARD DRAW INTO A TEN-GRAND JACKPOT AND KILLED HIS PARTNER FOR THE KITTY.... NOW RIGHT THERE ROLLO KNEW HIS NUMBER WAS UP... BUT, SINCE HIS LUCK WAS IN, HE GATHERED UP THE ROLL AND PLAYED "JUST ONE MORE HAND" ....HE SCOOPED UP HIS ROLL AND PLAYED IT 100-TO-ONE... HE TOOK IT ON THE LAM.
CENTRAL CITY, HACKIE, AND THEN FORGET YOU EVER SAW ME. ...HERE...
PAL, F'R THIS KIND O' DOUGH I'D F'GET ME OWN NAME!

AND SO... WE FIND ROLLO DYCE IN CENTRAL CITY THE NEXT MORNING..

OUT OF TOWN PAPERS •

GARTER CITY GANG SEEKS KILLER OF GAMBLER SHARP

HEADS IT'S THE TRIBUNE, TAILS IT'S THE JOURNAL.

TAILS. THE JOURNAL IT IS, SIR.

HMMM... LET'S SEE HOW I CAN PARLAY MY LUCK ..AH !

HOUSEHOLD HELP WANTED

couple elderly ??X Rogers Rd after 5 p.m

Elderly woman needs capable man to man age country estate. Mrs Morrison..RPD 3 Bald Mountain Box 34

uple wanted eep in light ework time reference all HE 290-93B

YESSIR THERE'S A SURE BET... IT CAN'T LOSE.

...THAT JOB WILL KEEP ME UNDER COVER FOR A FEW DAYS, AND WHEN THE HEAT'S OFF, I'LL CROAK THE OLD GAL AND TAKE HER WAD WHICH SHE SURELY HAS... HAW LOOKS LIKE IT'S HER NUMBER THAT'S UP!

THAT EVENING

I HOPE YOU'LL BE COMFORTABLE, MR. DYCE IT CERTAINLY IS NICE FOR AN OLD LADY LIKE ME TO HAVE SOMEONE TO TAKE OVER THE RESPONSIBILITY OF THIS PLACE

DON'T WORRY ABOUT A THING, MA'AM

BY THE WAY.. YOU'LL HAVE TO SHIFT FOR YOURSELF ... THE SERVANTS DON'T ARRIVE TILL MONDAY.

REALLY...? ER...HOW CONVENIENT... AHEM...I MEAN TCH TCH! I'LL MANAGE SOMEHOW.

I'LL LOCK THE DOORS...CAN'T TAKE A CHANCE ON ROBBERS OR MURDERERS WAY OUT HERE

HA HA HA . Y'R PRECAUTIONS ARE A WASTE O'TIME. Y'R NUMBER'S UP ! CHUCKLE CHUCKLE AND Y'DON'T KNOW IT.

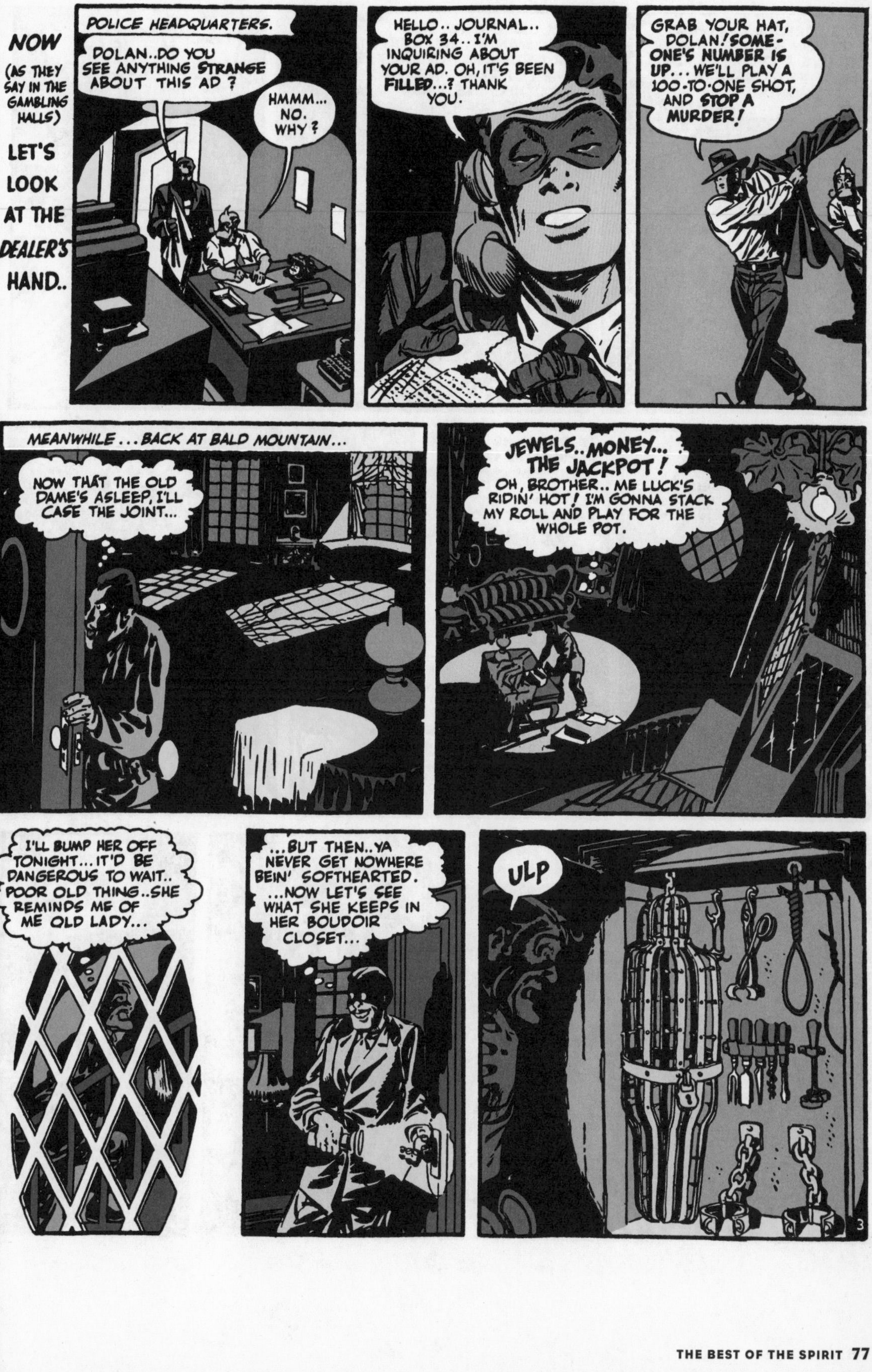
NOW (AS THEY SAY IN THE GAMBLING HALLS) LET'S LOOK AT THE DEALER'S HAND..
POLICE HEADQUARTERS.
DOLAN..DO YOU SEE ANYTHING STRANGE ABOUT THIS AD ?
HMMM... NO. WHY ?
HELLO.. JOURNAL.. BOX 34.. I'M INQUIRING ABOUT YOUR AD. OH, IT'S BEEN FILLED...? THANK YOU.
GRAB YOUR HAT, DOLAN! SOME-ONE'S NUMBER IS UP... WE'LL PLAY A 100-TO-ONE SHOT, AND STOP A MURDER!
MEANWHILE ... BACK AT BALD MOUNTAIN...
NOW THAT THE OLD DAME'S ASLEEP, I'LL CASE THE JOINT...
JEWELS..MONEY... THE JACKPOT!
OH, BROTHER.. ME LUCK'S RIDIN' HOT! I'M GONNA STACK MY ROLL AND PLAY FOR THE WHOLE POT.
I'LL BUMP HER OFF TONIGHT....IT'D BE DANGEROUS TO WAIT.. POOR OLD THING..SHE REMINDS ME OF ME OLD LADY...
...BUT THEN..YA NEVER GET NOWHERE BEIN' SOFTHEARTED. ...NOW LET'S SEE WHAT SHE KEEPS IN HER BOUDOIR CLOSET...
ULP
3

A TORTURE CHAMBER! NO WONDER SHE'S SCARED TO LIVE ALONE..THIS PLACE MUST BE CRAWLIN' WITH GHOSTS.

I'LL USE ONE OF THE INSTRUMENTS...THIS GARROTE, FOR INSTANCE... IT'LL BAFFLE THE COPS. HA..THERE'S NOTHIN' LIKE A RUN OF LUCK!

AAH...OLD GAL'S FAST ASLEEP...

AT THAT SAME MOMENT.. DOWN IN THE VALLEY...

CAN'T YOU GO ANY FASTER..? FASTER! EVERY SECOND COUNTS!

THIS DOGGONE TRAFFIC, SPIRIT...I CAN'T...

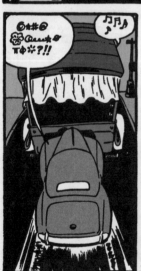

Θ⏀#ϴ ⁂Ⓠⓐⓐⓐⓐ⏀ �⏀⁂?!! ♫♪♬

AND BACK AT BALD MOUNTAIN...

WELL I'LL BE ★ϴ☀ⓉΘ Θ🜨 Cm! SHE AIN'T IN BED AT ALL!!

♫ OH, MRS. MORRISON... ♫

4

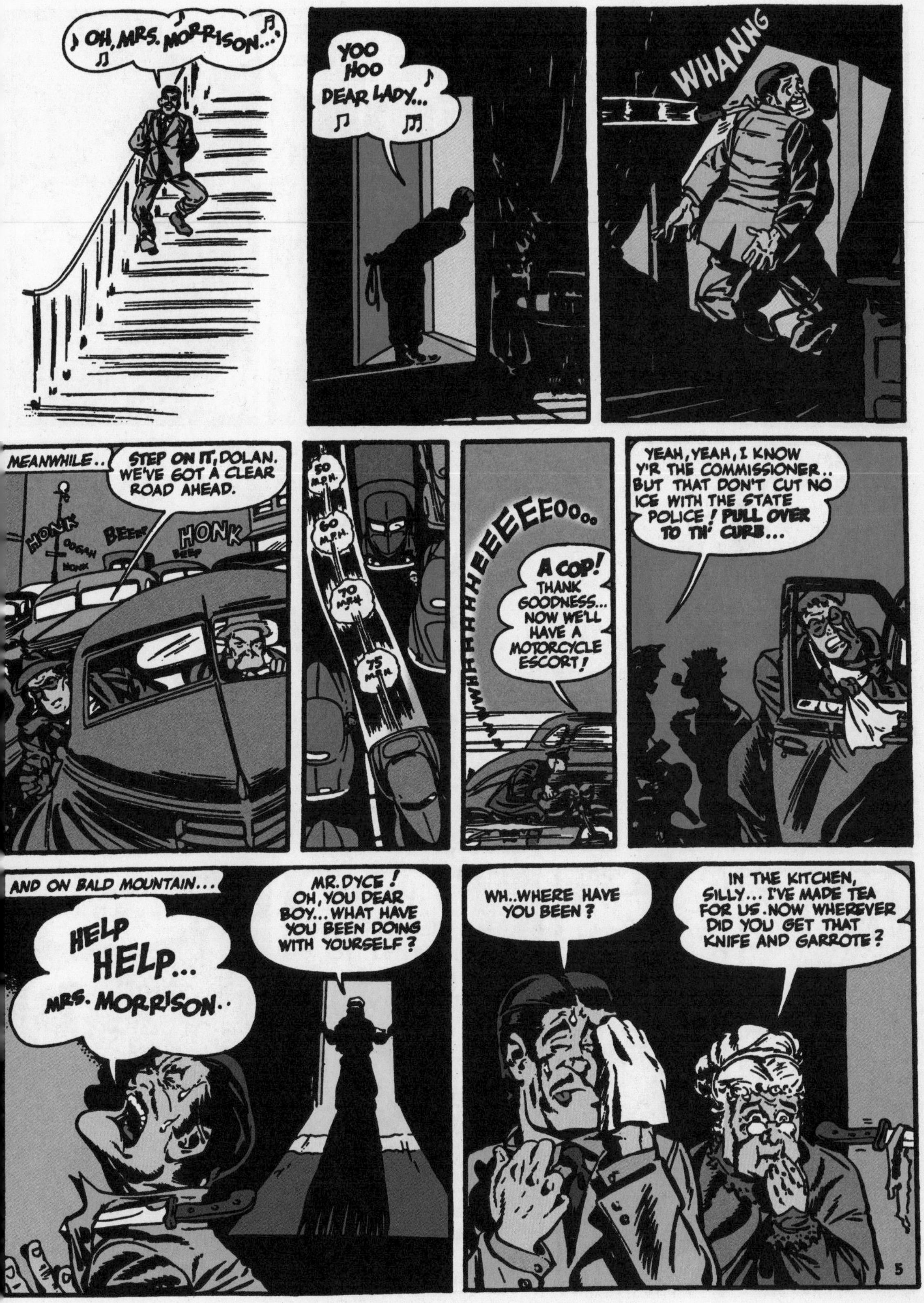
OH, MRS. MORRISON...
YOO HOO DEAR LADY...
WHANNG
MEANWHILE..
STEP ON IT, DOLAN. WE'VE GOT A CLEAR ROAD AHEAD.
HONK
OOGAH
HONK
BEEP
HONK
BEEP
50 M.P.H.
60 M.P.H.
70 M.P.H.
75 M.P.H.
WHHHHHHHEEEEEEOOoo
A COP! THANK GOODNESS... NOW WE'LL HAVE A MOTORCYCLE ESCORT!
YEAH, YEAH, I KNOW Y'R THE COMMISSIONER.. BUT THAT DON'T CUT NO ICE WITH THE STATE POLICE! PULL OVER TO TH' CURB...
AND ON BALD MOUNTAIN...
HELP HELP... MRS. MORRISON..
MR. DYCE! OH, YOU DEAR BOY... WHAT HAVE YOU BEEN DOING WITH YOURSELF?
WH..WHERE HAVE YOU BEEN?
IN THE KITCHEN, SILLY... I'VE MADE TEA FOR US. NOW WHEREVER DID YOU GET THAT KNIFE AND GARROTE?
5

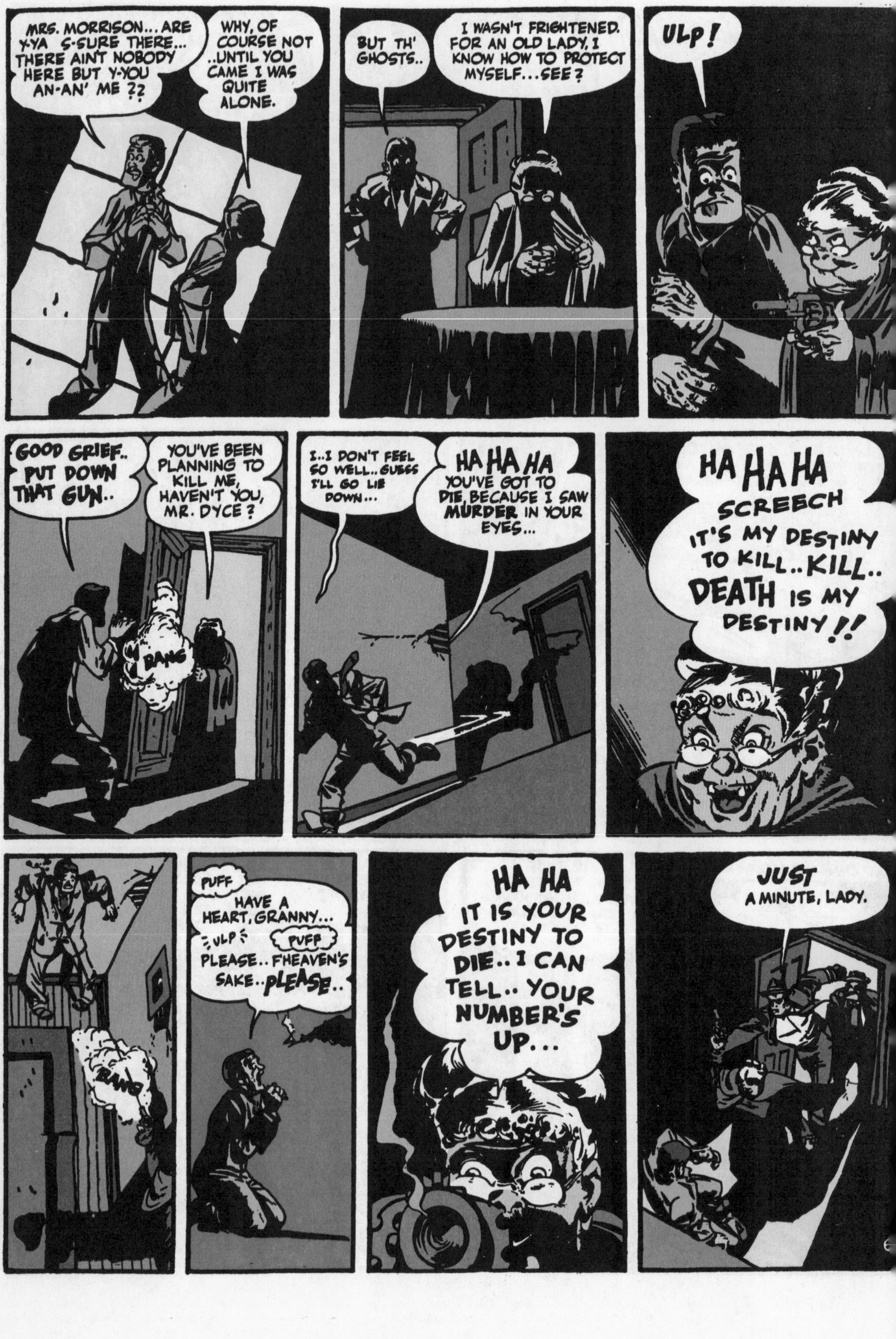
MRS. MORRISON... ARE Y-YA S-SURE THERE... THERE AIN'T NOBODY HERE BUT Y-YOU AN-AN' ME ??
WHY, OF COURSE NOT ..UNTIL YOU CAME I WAS QUITE ALONE.
BUT TH' GHOSTS..
I WASN'T FRIGHTENED. FOR AN OLD LADY, I KNOW HOW TO PROTECT MYSELF...SEE?
ULP!
GOOD GRIEF.. PUT DOWN THAT GUN..
YOU'VE BEEN PLANNING TO KILL ME, HAVEN'T YOU, MR. DYCE?
BANG
I..I DON'T FEEL SO WELL..GUESS I'LL GO LIE DOWN...
HA HA HA YOU'VE GOT TO DIE, BECAUSE I SAW MURDER IN YOUR EYES...
HA HA HA SCREECH IT'S MY DESTINY TO KILL..KILL.. DEATH IS MY DESTINY!!
BANG
PUFF
HAVE A HEART, GRANNY...
ULP
PUFF
PLEASE.. FHEAVEN'S SAKE..PLEASE..
HA HA IT IS YOUR DESTINY TO DIE.. I CAN TELL.. YOUR NUMBER'S UP...
JUST A MINUTE, LADY.

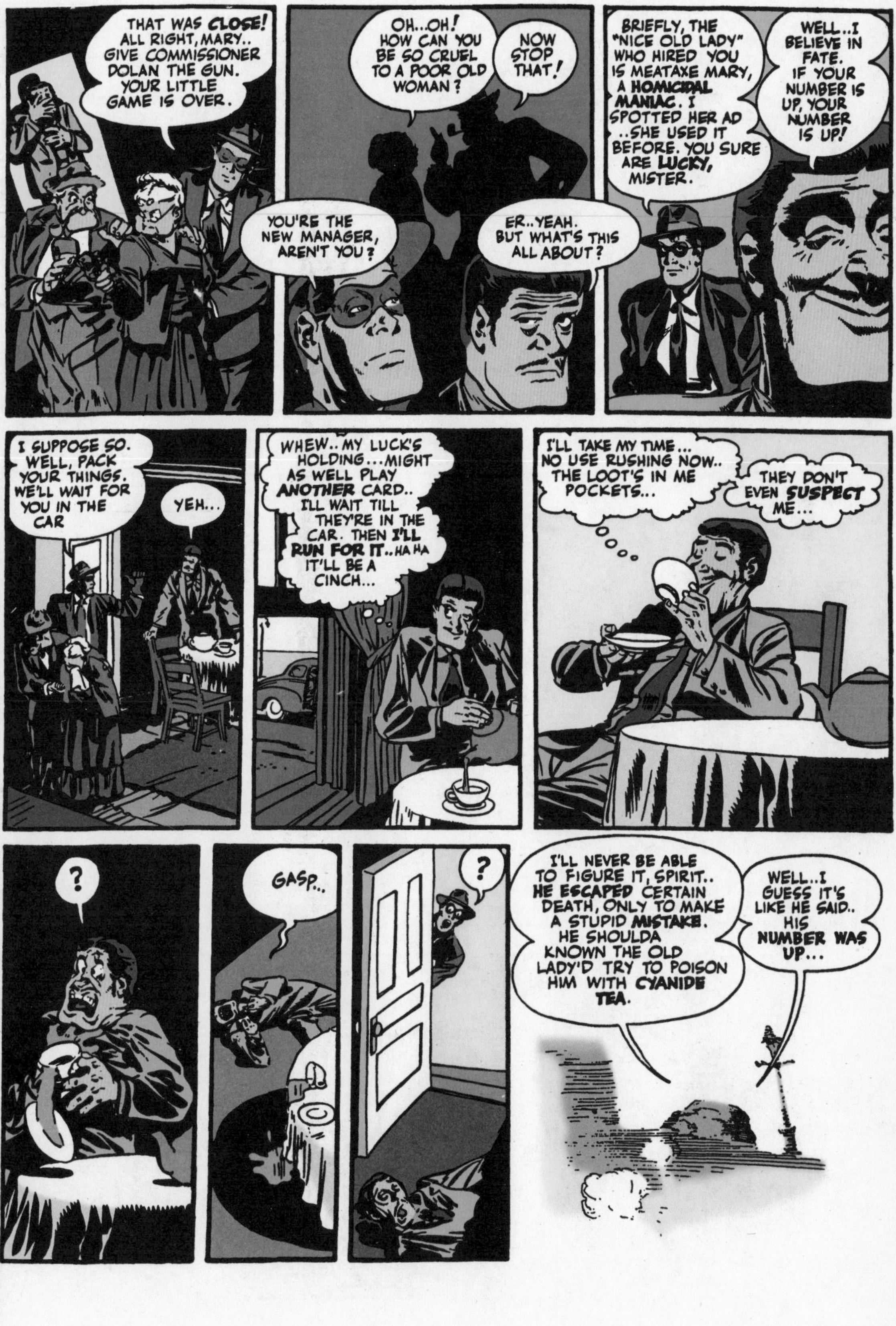
THAT WAS CLOSE! ALL RIGHT, MARY.. GIVE COMMISSIONER DOLAN THE GUN. YOUR LITTLE GAME IS OVER.
OH...OH! HOW CAN YOU BE SO CRUEL TO A POOR OLD WOMAN?
NOW STOP THAT!
YOU'RE THE NEW MANAGER, AREN'T YOU?
ER..YEAH. BUT WHAT'S THIS ALL ABOUT?
BRIEFLY, THE "NICE OLD LADY" WHO HIRED YOU IS MEATAXE MARY, A HOMICIDAL MANIAC. I SPOTTED HER AD ..SHE USED IT BEFORE. YOU SURE ARE LUCKY, MISTER.
WELL..I BELIEVE IN FATE. IF YOUR NUMBER IS UP, YOUR NUMBER IS UP!
I SUPPOSE SO. WELL, PACK YOUR THINGS. WE'LL WAIT FOR YOU IN THE CAR
YEH...
WHEW.. MY LUCK'S HOLDING...MIGHT AS WELL PLAY ANOTHER CARD.. I'LL WAIT TILL THEY'RE IN THE CAR. THEN I'LL RUN FOR IT..HA HA IT'LL BE A CINCH...
I'LL TAKE MY TIME... NO USE RUSHING NOW.. THE LOOT'S IN ME POCKETS...
THEY DON'T EVEN SUSPECT ME...
?
GASP...
?
I'LL NEVER BE ABLE TO FIGURE IT, SPIRIT.. HE ESCAPED CERTAIN DEATH, ONLY TO MAKE A STUPID MISTAKE. HE SHOULDA KNOWN THE OLD LADY'D TRY TO POISON HIM WITH CYANIDE TEA.
WELL..I GUESS IT'S LIKE HE SAID.. HIS NUMBER WAS UP...

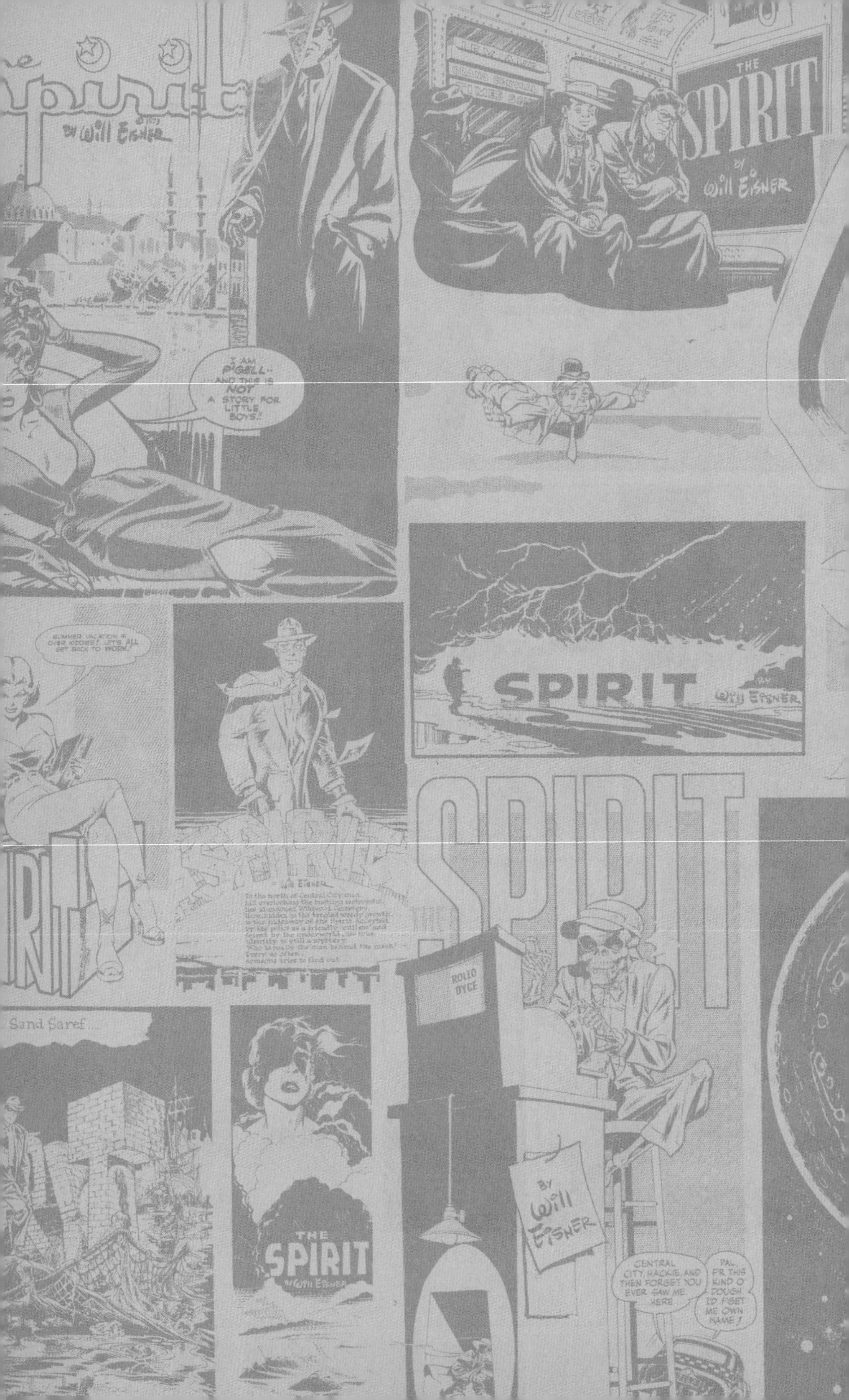
The Spirit
by Will Eisner
©1973
I AM P'GELL... AND THIS IS NOT A STORY FOR LITTLE BOYS!
THE SPIRIT BY Will EISNER
SUMMER VACATION IS OVER KIDDIES! LET'S ALL GET BACK TO WORK!
SPIRIT
BY Will EISNER
SPIRIT
THE SPIRIT
Sand Saref...
THE SPIRIT BY Will EISNER
ROLLO DYCE
BY Will EISNER
CENTRAL CITY, HACKIE, AND THEN FORGET YOU EVER SAW ME. HERE.
PAL, FR THIS KIND O' DOUGH I'D FIGET ME OWN NAME!

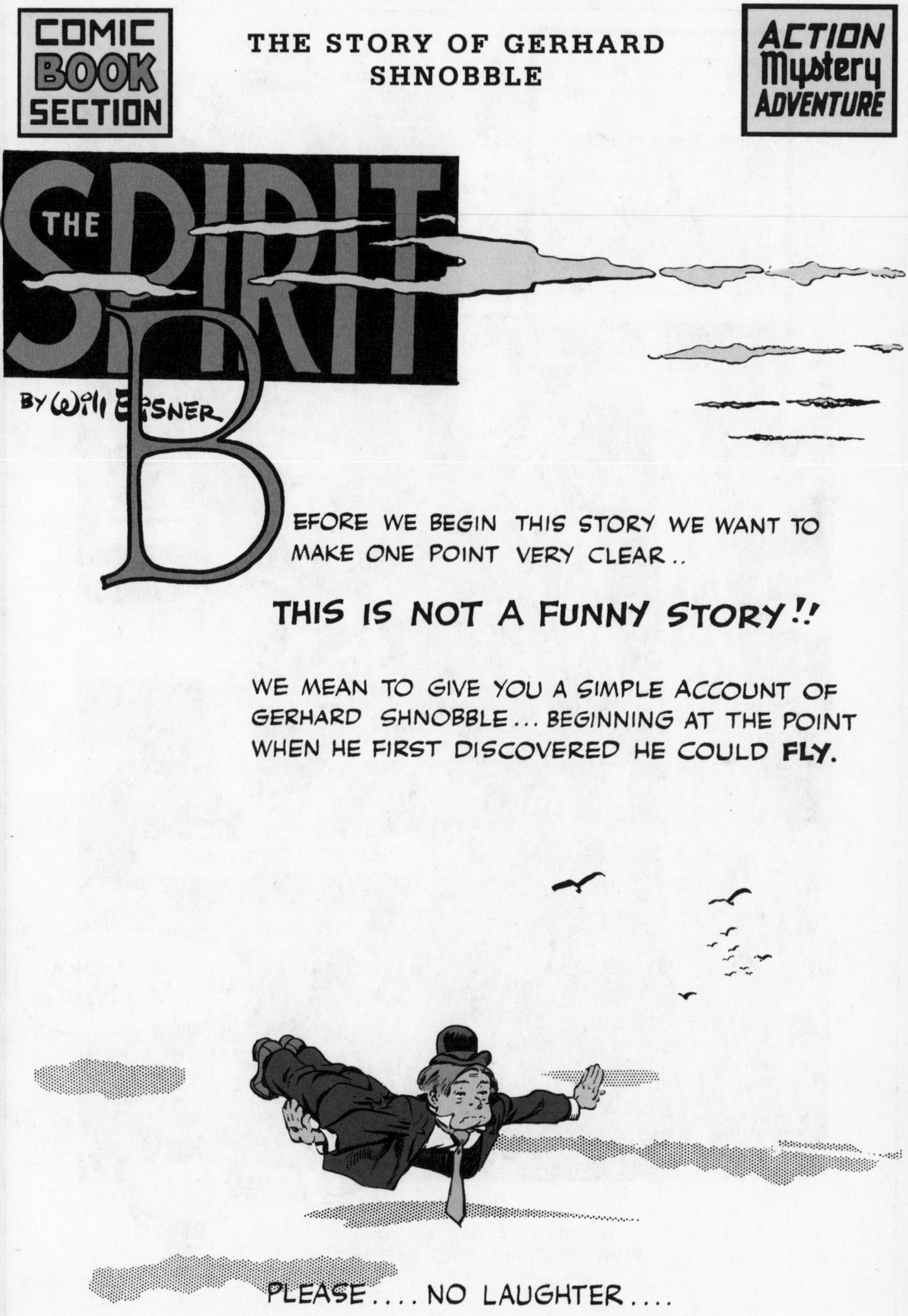
COMIC BOOK SECTION
THE STORY OF GERHARD SHNOBBLE
ACTION Mystery ADVENTURE
THE SPIRIT
BY Will Eisner
BEFORE WE BEGIN THIS STORY WE WANT TO MAKE ONE POINT VERY CLEAR..
THIS IS NOT A FUNNY STORY!!
WE MEAN TO GIVE YOU A SIMPLE ACCOUNT OF GERHARD SHNOBBLE... BEGINNING AT THE POINT WHEN HE FIRST DISCOVERED HE COULD FLY.
PLEASE.... NO LAUGHTER....

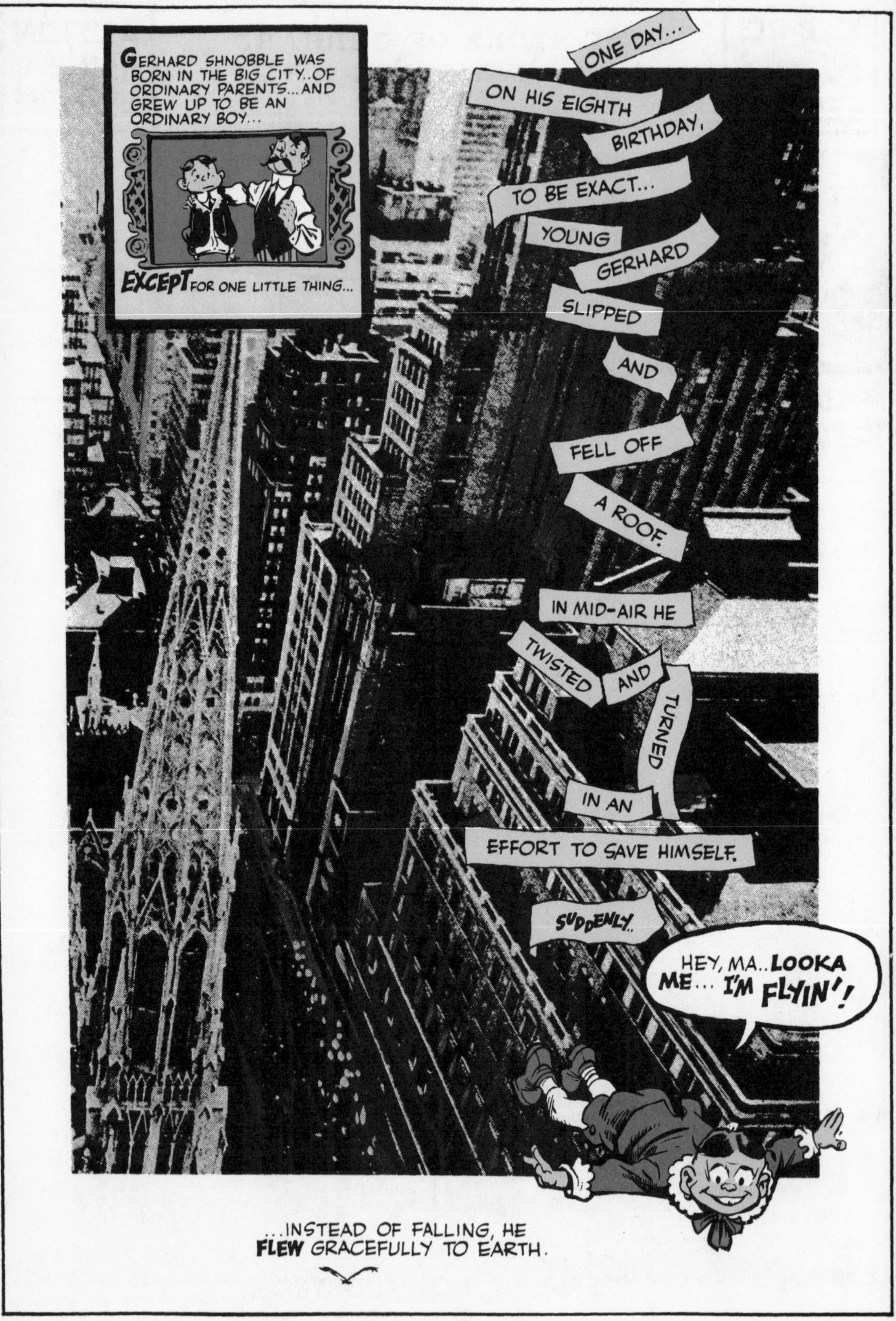
GERHARD SHNOBBLE WAS BORN IN THE BIG CITY..OF ORDINARY PARENTS...AND GREW UP TO BE AN ORDINARY BOY...
EXCEPT FOR ONE LITTLE THING...
ONE DAY...
ON HIS EIGHTH
BIRTHDAY,
TO BE EXACT...
YOUNG
GERHARD
SLIPPED
AND
FELL OFF
A ROOF.
IN MID-AIR HE
TWISTED
AND
TURNED
IN AN
EFFORT TO SAVE HIMSELF.
SUDDENLY..
HEY, MA..LOOKA ME... I'M FLYIN'!
...INSTEAD OF FALLING, HE FLEW GRACEFULLY TO EARTH.

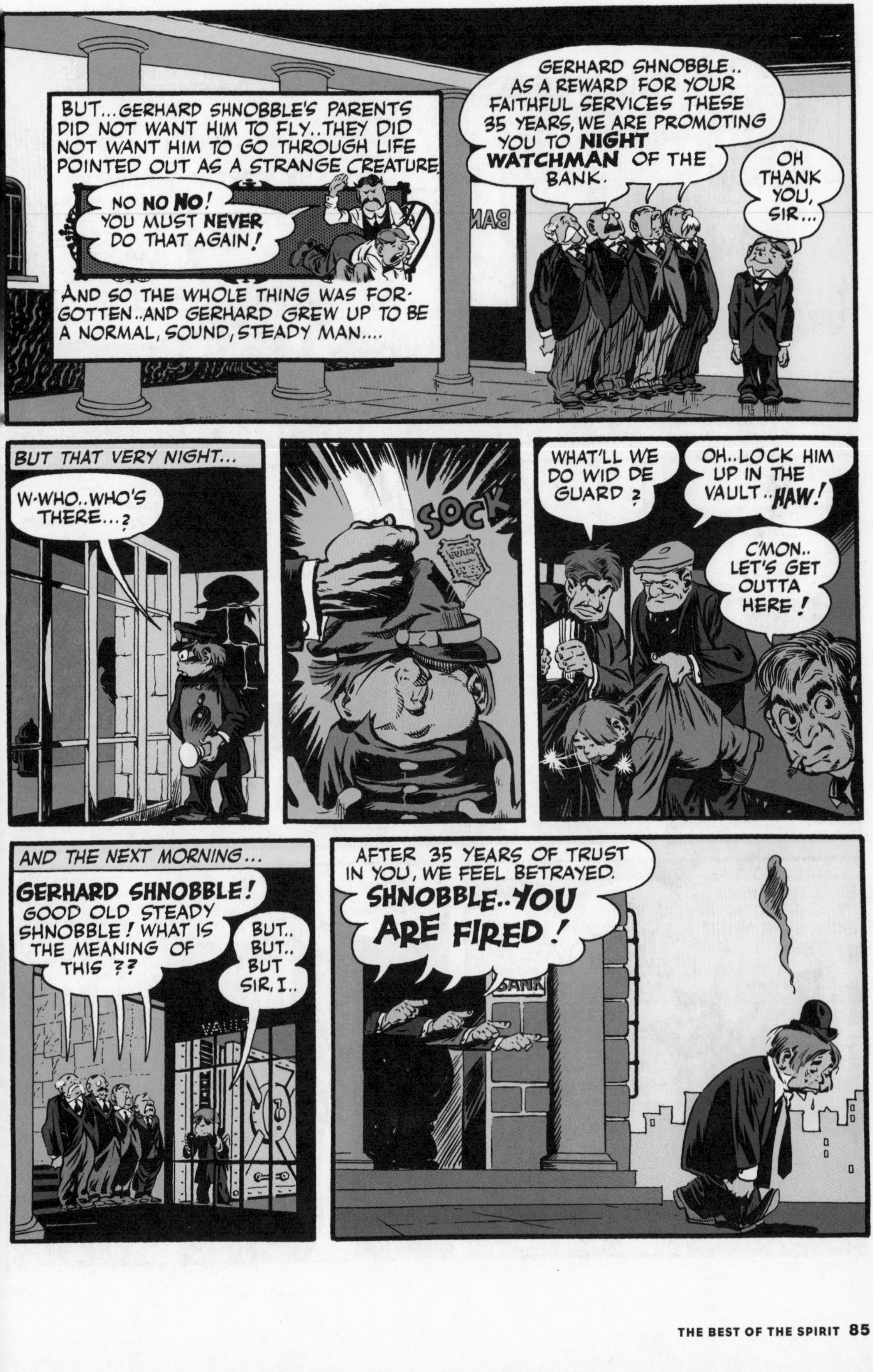
BUT...GERHARD SHNOBBLE'S PARENTS DID NOT WANT HIM TO FLY..THEY DID NOT WANT HIM TO GO THROUGH LIFE POINTED OUT AS A STRANGE CREATURE.
NO **NO NO**! YOU MUST **NEVER** DO THAT AGAIN!
AND SO THE WHOLE THING WAS FORGOTTEN..AND GERHARD GREW UP TO BE A NORMAL, SOUND, STEADY MAN....
GERHARD SHNOBBLE.. AS A REWARD FOR YOUR FAITHFUL SERVICES THESE 35 YEARS, WE ARE PROMOTING YOU TO **NIGHT WATCHMAN** OF THE BANK.
OH THANK YOU, SIR...
BUT THAT VERY NIGHT...
W-WHO..WHO'S THERE...?
SOCK
WHAT'LL WE DO WID DE GUARD?
OH..LOCK HIM UP IN THE VAULT..**HAW!**
C'MON.. LET'S GET OUTTA HERE!
AND THE NEXT MORNING...
GERHARD SHNOBBLE! GOOD OLD STEADY SHNOBBLE! WHAT IS THE MEANING OF THIS ??
BUT.. BUT.. BUT SIR, I..
AFTER 35 YEARS OF TRUST IN YOU, WE FEEL BETRAYED.
SHNOBBLE..YOU ARE FIRED!
BANK
VAULT

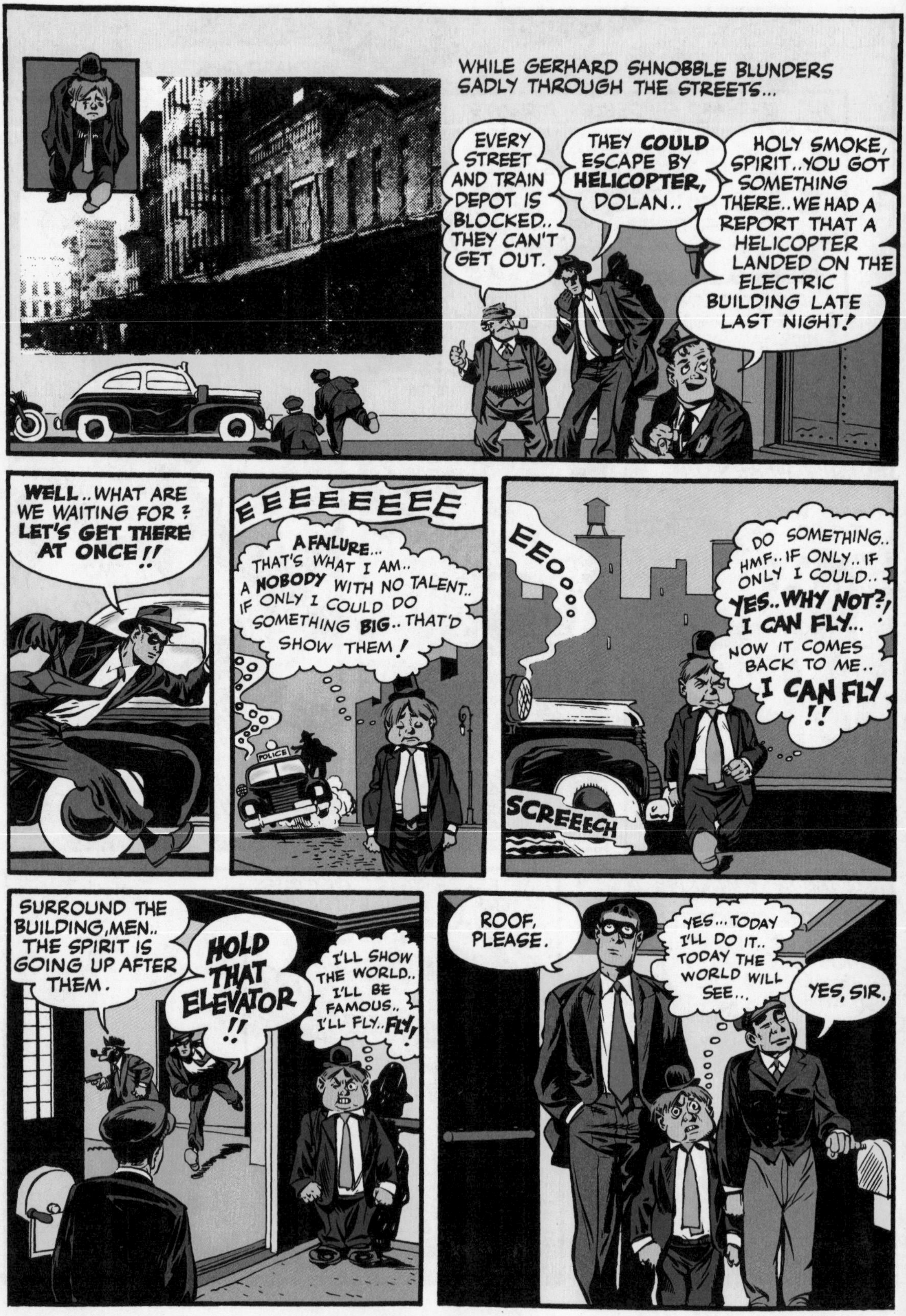

WHILE GERHARD SHNOBBLE BLUNDERS SADLY THROUGH THE STREETS...
EVERY STREET AND TRAIN DEPOT IS BLOCKED.. THEY CAN'T GET OUT.
THEY COULD ESCAPE BY HELICOPTER, DOLAN..
HOLY SMOKE, SPIRIT..YOU GOT SOMETHING THERE..WE HAD A REPORT THAT A HELICOPTER LANDED ON THE ELECTRIC BUILDING LATE LAST NIGHT!
WELL..WHAT ARE WE WAITING FOR? LET'S GET THERE AT ONCE!!
EEEEEEEEE
A FAILURE... THAT'S WHAT I AM.. A NOBODY WITH NO TALENT.. IF ONLY I COULD DO SOMETHING BIG.. THAT'D SHOW THEM!
POLICE
EEOoooo
DO SOMETHING.. HMF.. IF ONLY.. IF ONLY I COULD.. YES..WHY NOT?! I CAN FLY... NOW IT COMES BACK TO ME.. I CAN FLY!!
SCREEECH
SURROUND THE BUILDING,MEN.. THE SPIRIT IS GOING UP AFTER THEM.
HOLD THAT ELEVATOR!!
I'LL SHOW THE WORLD.. I'LL BE FAMOUS.. I'LL FLY..FLY!
ROOF, PLEASE.
YES...TODAY I'LL DO IT.. TODAY THE WORLD WILL SEE...
YES, SIR.

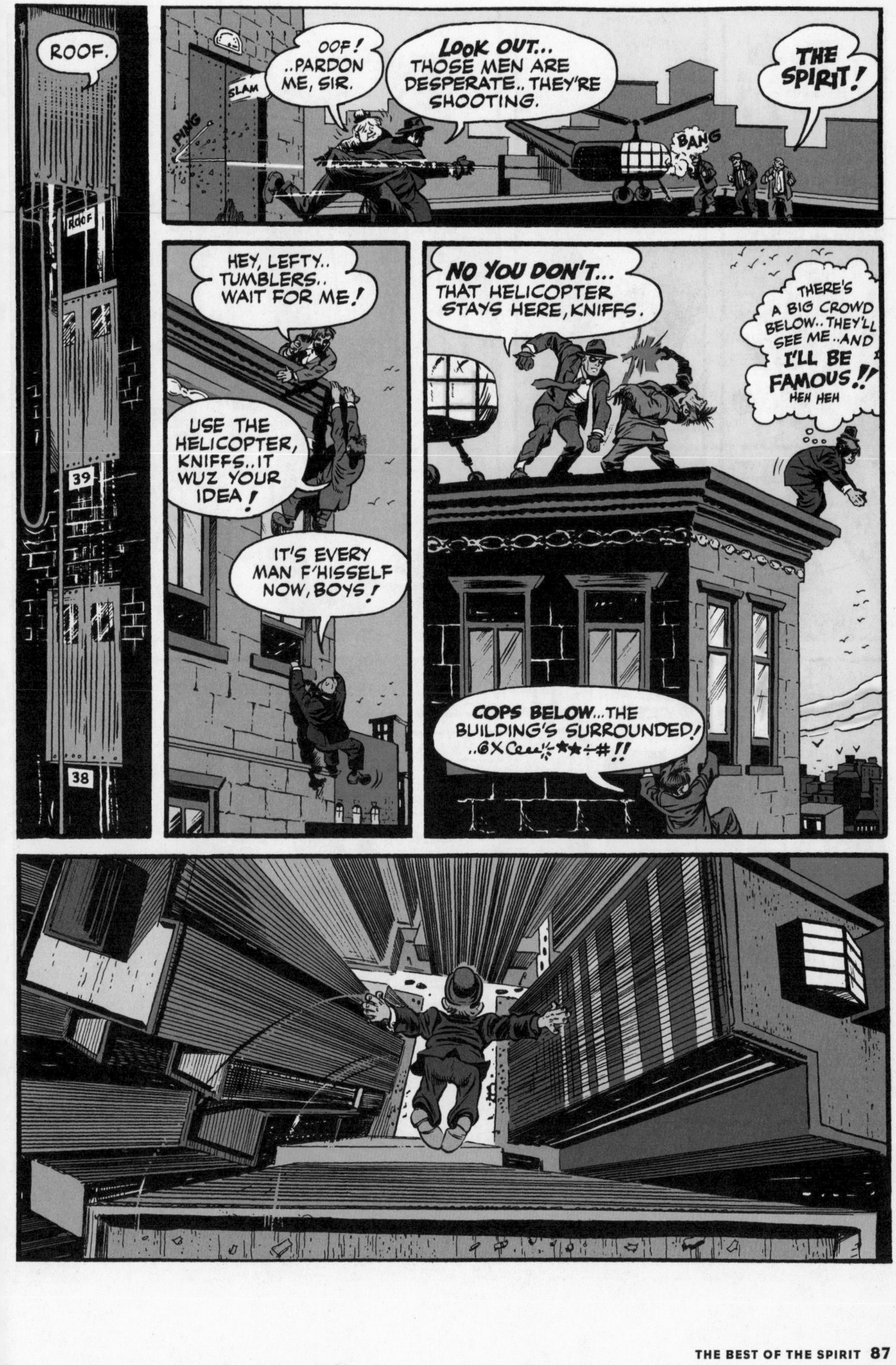
ROOF.
ROOF
39
38
SLAM
PING
OOF! ..PARDON ME, SIR.
LOOK OUT... THOSE MEN ARE DESPERATE.. THEY'RE SHOOTING.
BANG
THE SPIRIT!
HEY, LEFTY.. TUMBLERS.. WAIT FOR ME!
USE THE HELICOPTER, KNIFFS..IT WUZ YOUR IDEA!
IT'S EVERY MAN F'HISSELF NOW, BOYS!
NO YOU DON'T... THAT HELICOPTER STAYS HERE, KNIFFS.
THERE'S A BIG CROWD BELOW.. THEY'LL SEE ME ..AND I'LL BE FAMOUS!! HEH HEH
COPS BELOW...THE BUILDING'S SURROUNDED!

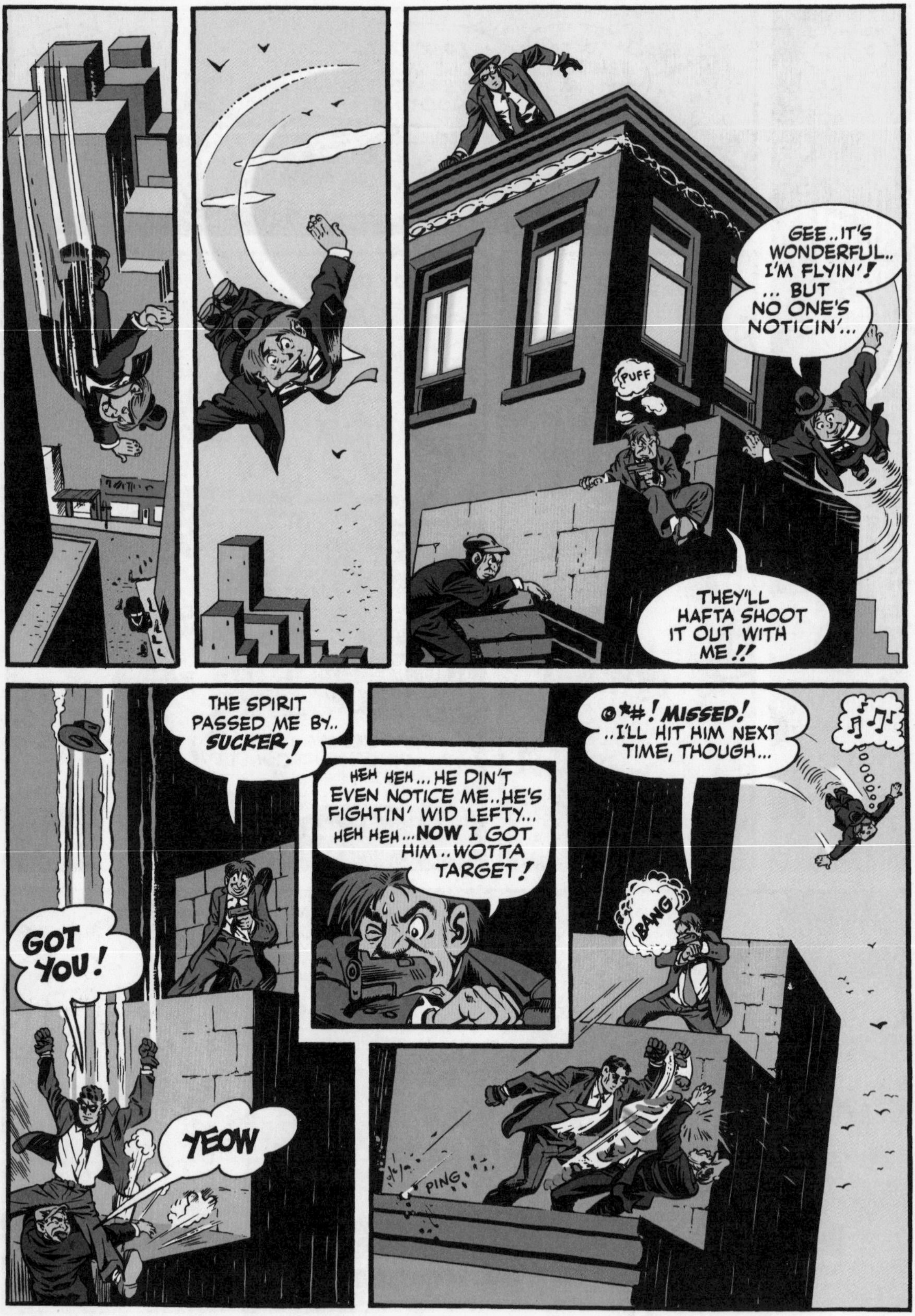
GEE.. IT'S WONDERFUL.. I'M FLYIN'! ... BUT NO ONE'S NOTICIN'...
PUFF
THEY'LL HAFTA SHOOT IT OUT WITH ME!!
THE SPIRIT PASSED ME BY.. SUCKER!
GOT YOU!
YEOW
HEH HEH... HE DIN'T EVEN NOTICE ME.. HE'S FIGHTIN' WID LEFTY... HEH HEH... NOW I GOT HIM.. WOTTA TARGET!
@*#! MISSED! ..I'LL HIT HIM NEXT TIME, THOUGH...
BANG
PING

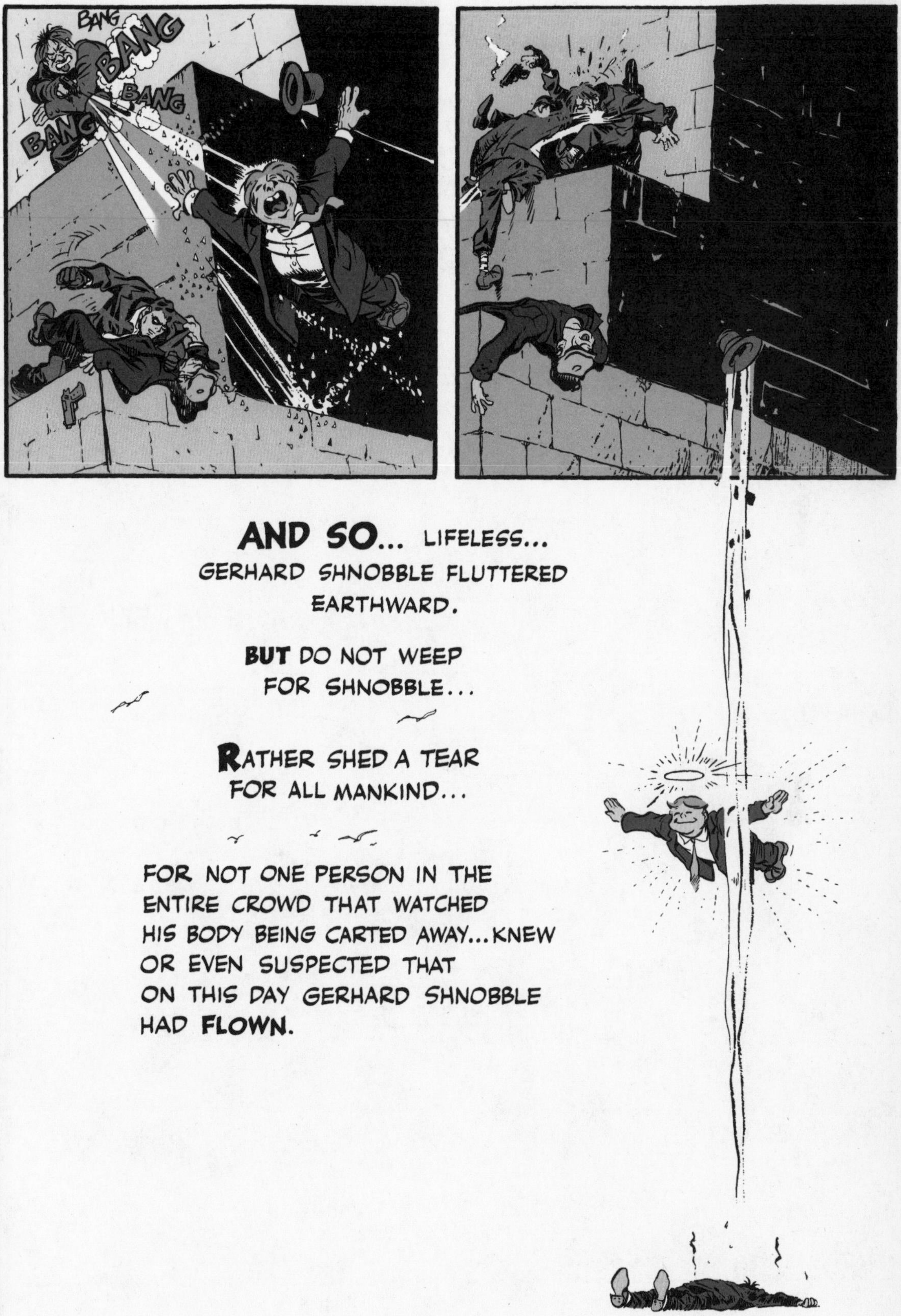
BANG
BANG
BANG
BANG
AND SO... LIFELESS...
GERHARD SHNOBBLE FLUTTERED
EARTHWARD.
BUT DO NOT WEEP
FOR SHNOBBLE...
RATHER SHED A TEAR
FOR ALL MANKIND...
FOR NOT ONE PERSON IN THE
ENTIRE CROWD THAT WATCHED
HIS BODY BEING CARTED AWAY...KNEW
OR EVEN SUSPECTED THAT
ON THIS DAY GERHARD SHNOBBLE
HAD FLOWN.

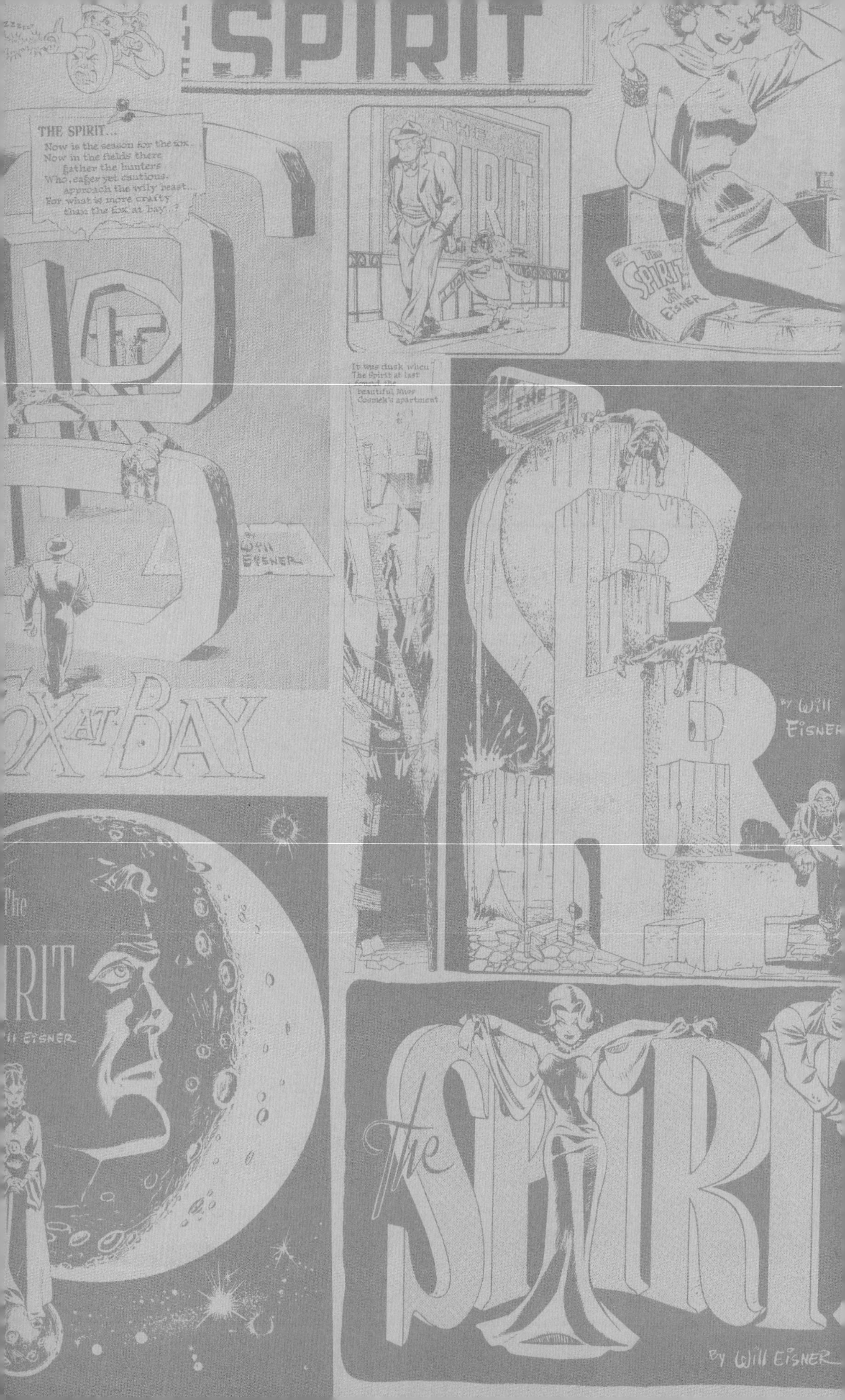
SPIRIT
THE SPIRIT...
Now is the season for the fox. Now in the fields there gather the hunters. Who, eager yet cautious, approach the wily beast... For what is more crafty than the fox at bay...?
By Will Eisner
AT BAY
The Spirit By Will Eisner
It was dusk when The Spirit at last found the beautiful Miss Cosmek's apartment...
By Will Eisner
The
Will Eisner
The Spirit
By Will Eisner

COMIC BOOK SECTION

LORELEI ROX

ACTION Mystery ADVENTURE

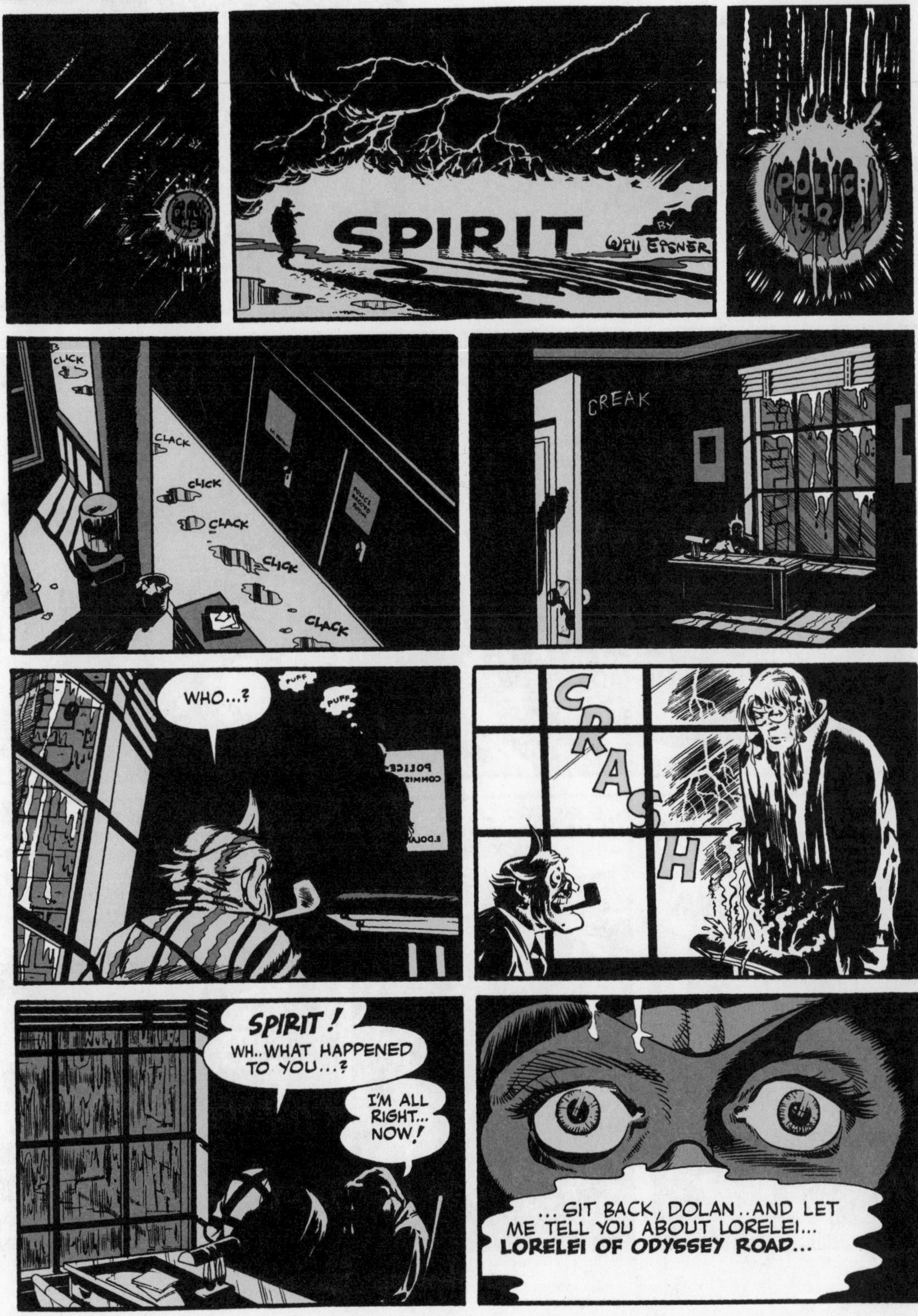
SPIRIT
BY Will Eisner
CLICK
CLACK
CLICK
CLACK
CLICK
CLACK
CREAK
WHO...?
PUFF
PUFF
CRASH
SPIRIT! WH.. WHAT HAPPENED TO YOU...?
I'M ALL RIGHT... NOW!
... SIT BACK, DOLAN.. AND LET ME TELL YOU ABOUT LORELEI... LORELEI OF ODYSSEY ROAD...

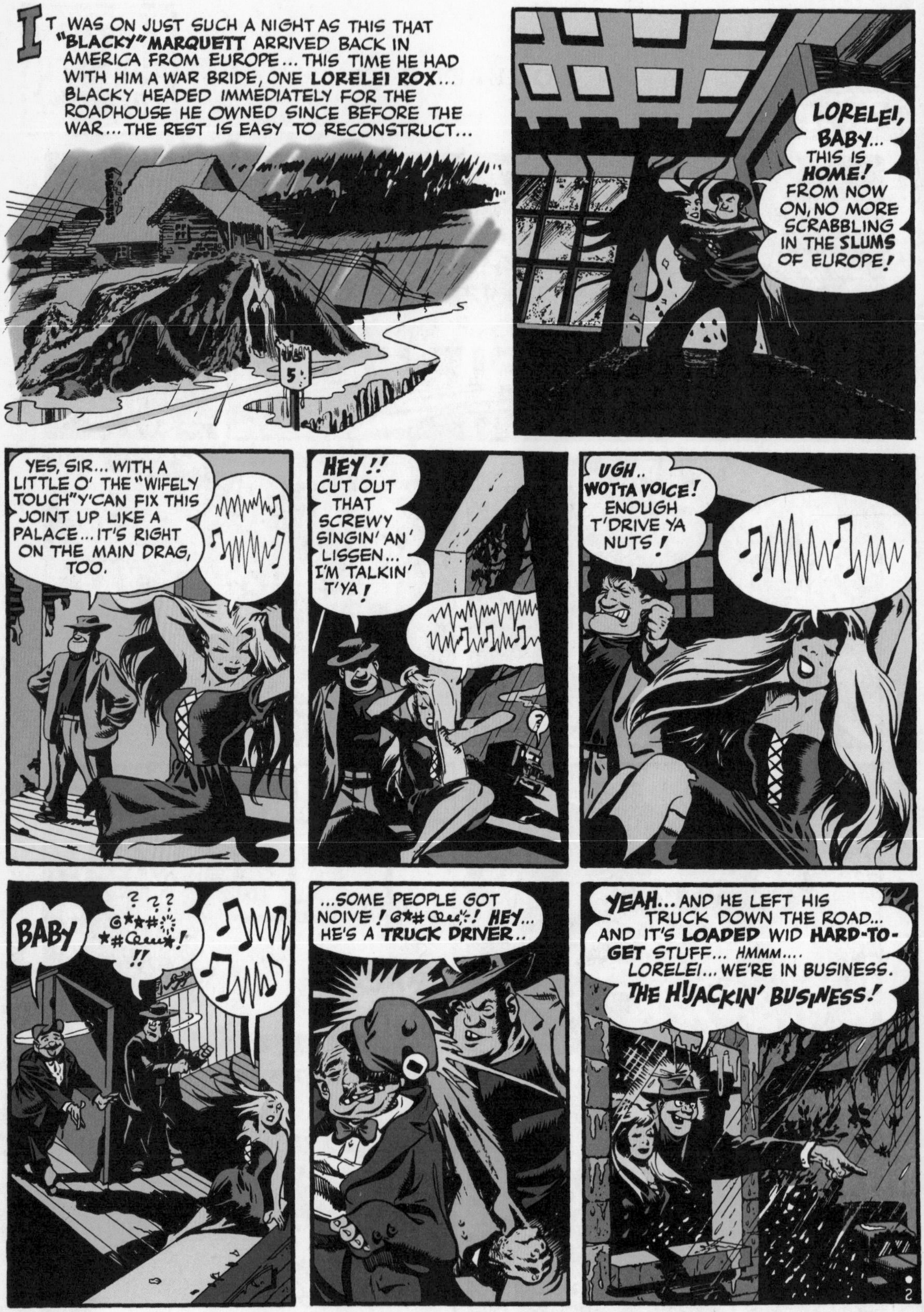
IT WAS ON JUST SUCH A NIGHT AS THIS THAT "BLACKY" MARQUETT ARRIVED BACK IN AMERICA FROM EUROPE... THIS TIME HE HAD WITH HIM A WAR BRIDE, ONE LORELEI ROX... BLACKY HEADED IMMEDIATELY FOR THE ROADHOUSE HE OWNED SINCE BEFORE THE WAR... THE REST IS EASY TO RECONSTRUCT...
5
LORELEI, BABY... THIS IS HOME! FROM NOW ON, NO MORE SCRABBLING IN THE SLUMS OF EUROPE!
YES, SIR... WITH A LITTLE O' THE "WIFELY TOUCH" Y'CAN FIX THIS JOINT UP LIKE A PALACE... IT'S RIGHT ON THE MAIN DRAG, TOO.
HEY!! CUT OUT THAT SCREWY SINGIN' AN' LISSEN... I'M TALKIN' T'YA!
UGH.. WOTTA VOICE! ENOUGH T'DRIVE YA NUTS!
BABY
? ? ? @*#*#☼ *#*! !!
...SOME PEOPLE GOT NOIVE! @*#*! HEY... HE'S A TRUCK DRIVER..
YEAH... AND HE LEFT HIS TRUCK DOWN THE ROAD... AND IT'S LOADED WID HARD-TO-GET STUFF... HMMM.... LORELEI... WE'RE IN BUSINESS. THE HIJACKIN' BUSINESS!
2

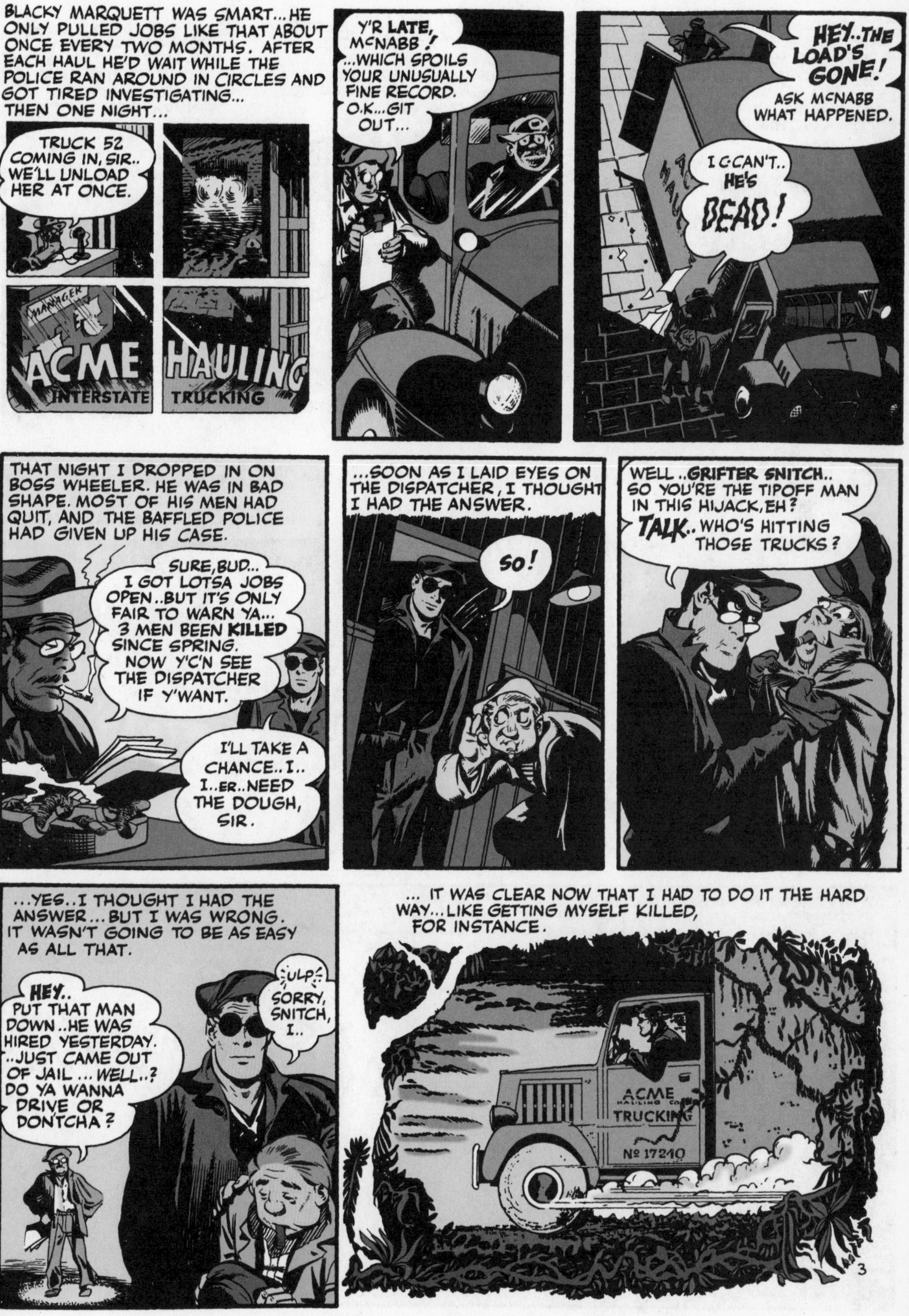
BLACKY MARQUETT WAS SMART...HE ONLY PULLED JOBS LIKE THAT ABOUT ONCE EVERY TWO MONTHS. AFTER EACH HAUL HE'D WAIT WHILE THE POLICE RAN AROUND IN CIRCLES AND GOT TIRED INVESTIGATING... THEN ONE NIGHT...
TRUCK 52 COMING IN, SIR.. WE'LL UNLOAD HER AT ONCE.
MANAGER
ACME
INTERSTATE
HAULING
TRUCKING
Y'R LATE, McNABB! ...WHICH SPOILS YOUR UNUSUALLY FINE RECORD. O.K...GIT OUT...
HEY..THE LOAD'S GONE!
ASK McNABB WHAT HAPPENED.
I C-CAN'T.. HE'S DEAD!
THAT NIGHT I DROPPED IN ON BOSS WHEELER. HE WAS IN BAD SHAPE. MOST OF HIS MEN HAD QUIT, AND THE BAFFLED POLICE HAD GIVEN UP HIS CASE.
SURE, BUD... I GOT LOTSA JOBS OPEN..BUT IT'S ONLY FAIR TO WARN YA... 3 MEN BEEN KILLED SINCE SPRING. NOW Y'C'N SEE THE DISPATCHER IF Y'WANT.
I'LL TAKE A CHANCE..I.. I..ER..NEED THE DOUGH, SIR.
...SOON AS I LAID EYES ON THE DISPATCHER, I THOUGHT I HAD THE ANSWER.
SO!
WELL ..GRIFTER SNITCH.. SO YOU'RE THE TIPOFF MAN IN THIS HIJACK, EH? TALK.. WHO'S HITTING THOSE TRUCKS?
...YES..I THOUGHT I HAD THE ANSWER... BUT I WAS WRONG. IT WASN'T GOING TO BE AS EASY AS ALL THAT.
HEY.. PUT THAT MAN DOWN..HE WAS HIRED YESTERDAY. ..JUST CAME OUT OF JAIL ... WELL..? DO YA WANNA DRIVE OR DONTCHA?
ULP SORRY, SNITCH, I..
... IT WAS CLEAR NOW THAT I HAD TO DO IT THE HARD WAY...LIKE GETTING MYSELF KILLED, FOR INSTANCE.
ACME
TRUCKING
No 17240
3

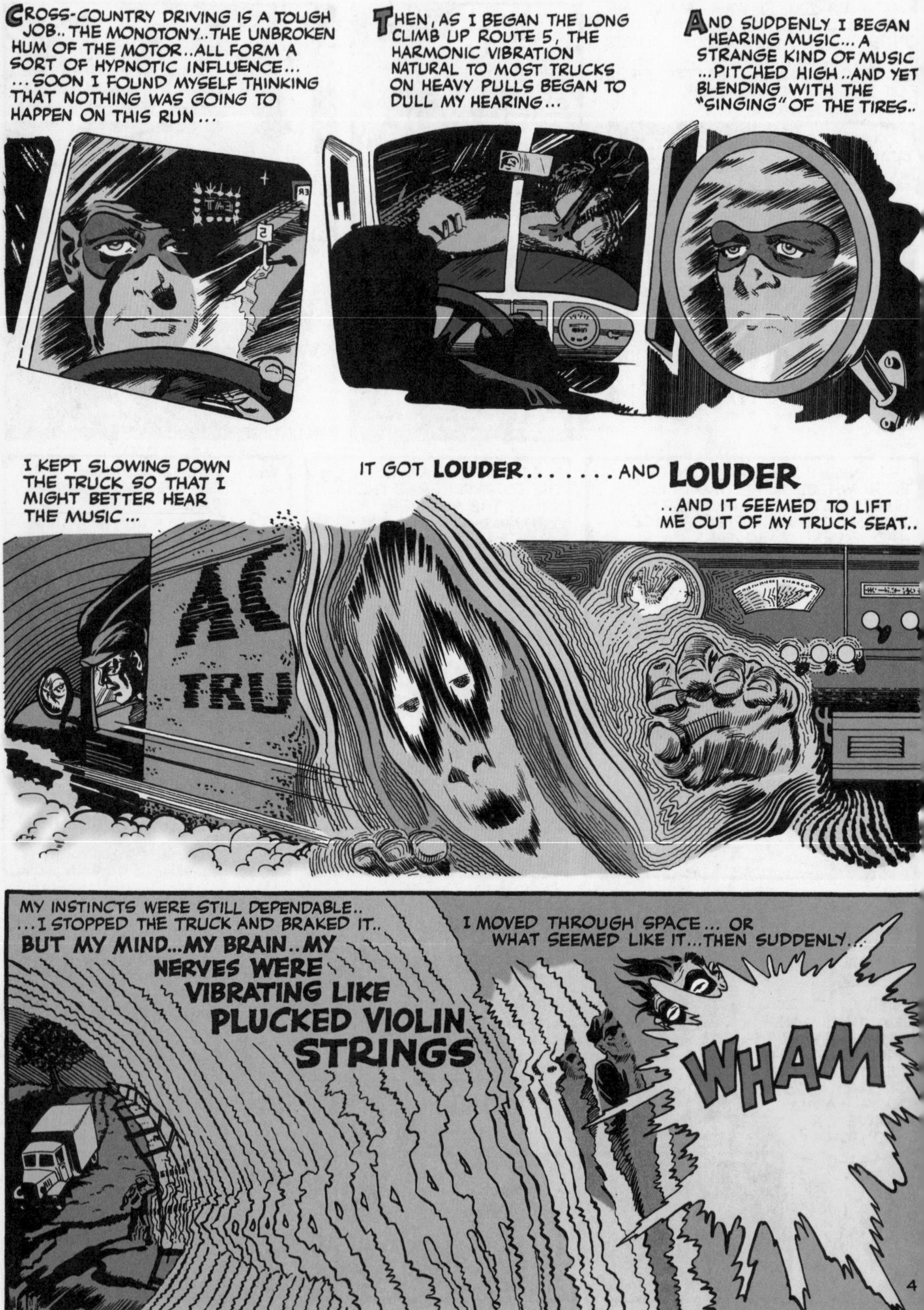
CROSS-COUNTRY DRIVING IS A TOUGH JOB.. THE MONOTONY..THE UNBROKEN HUM OF THE MOTOR..ALL FORM A SORT OF HYPNOTIC INFLUENCE... ...SOON I FOUND MYSELF THINKING THAT NOTHING WAS GOING TO HAPPEN ON THIS RUN...
THEN, AS I BEGAN THE LONG CLIMB UP ROUTE 5, THE HARMONIC VIBRATION NATURAL TO MOST TRUCKS ON HEAVY PULLS BEGAN TO DULL MY HEARING...
AND SUDDENLY I BEGAN HEARING MUSIC... A STRANGE KIND OF MUSIC ...PITCHED HIGH..AND YET BLENDING WITH THE "SINGING" OF THE TIRES..
I KEPT SLOWING DOWN THE TRUCK SO THAT I MIGHT BETTER HEAR THE MUSIC...
IT GOT LOUDER.......AND LOUDER
..AND IT SEEMED TO LIFT ME OUT OF MY TRUCK SEAT..
AC
TRU
MY INSTINCTS WERE STILL DEPENDABLE.. ...I STOPPED THE TRUCK AND BRAKED IT.. BUT MY MIND...MY BRAIN..MY NERVES WERE VIBRATING LIKE PLUCKED VIOLIN STRINGS
I MOVED THROUGH SPACE... OR WHAT SEEMED LIKE IT...THEN SUDDENLY...
WHAM
4

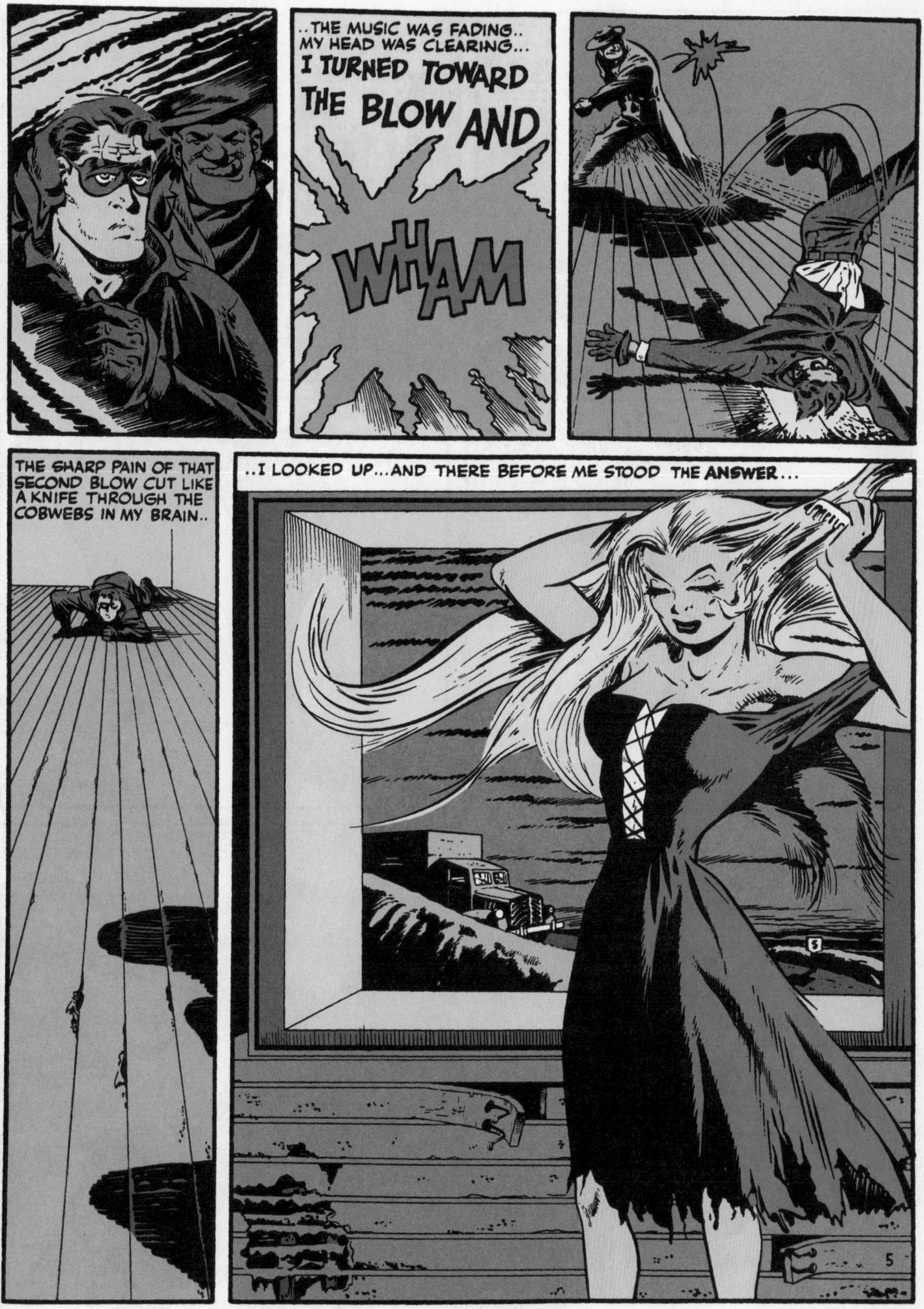
..THE MUSIC WAS FADING..
MY HEAD WAS CLEARING...
I TURNED TOWARD THE BLOW AND
WHAM
THE SHARP PAIN OF THAT SECOND BLOW CUT LIKE A KNIFE THROUGH THE COBWEBS IN MY BRAIN..
..I LOOKED UP...AND THERE BEFORE ME STOOD THE ANSWER...
5

I GET IT NOW... YOU LURE THE DAZED DRIVERS UP HERE...AND KILL THEM...A..COZY.. HIJACK GIMMICK...

YEAH..YEAH..YEAH. GIMME DAT CHAIR, LORELEI..DIS ONE'S GOT A HEAD LIKE CONCRETE...

..AIDED BY..A REAL-LIFE LORELEI... UGH!

G#**@#! WHATSAMATTA WID YOU? AIN'T YOU GOT NO FEELINGS??

YOU MUST LIKE GITTIN' HIT, SUCKER!!

I FELT, MORE THAN HEARD, BLACKY DROP TO THE FLOOR...I TRIED HARD TO KEEP GOING..BUT I WAS

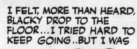

TIRED

...SO TIRED...THAT IT SEEMED MINUTES BEFORE I SLOWLY REALIZED THE PRESENCE

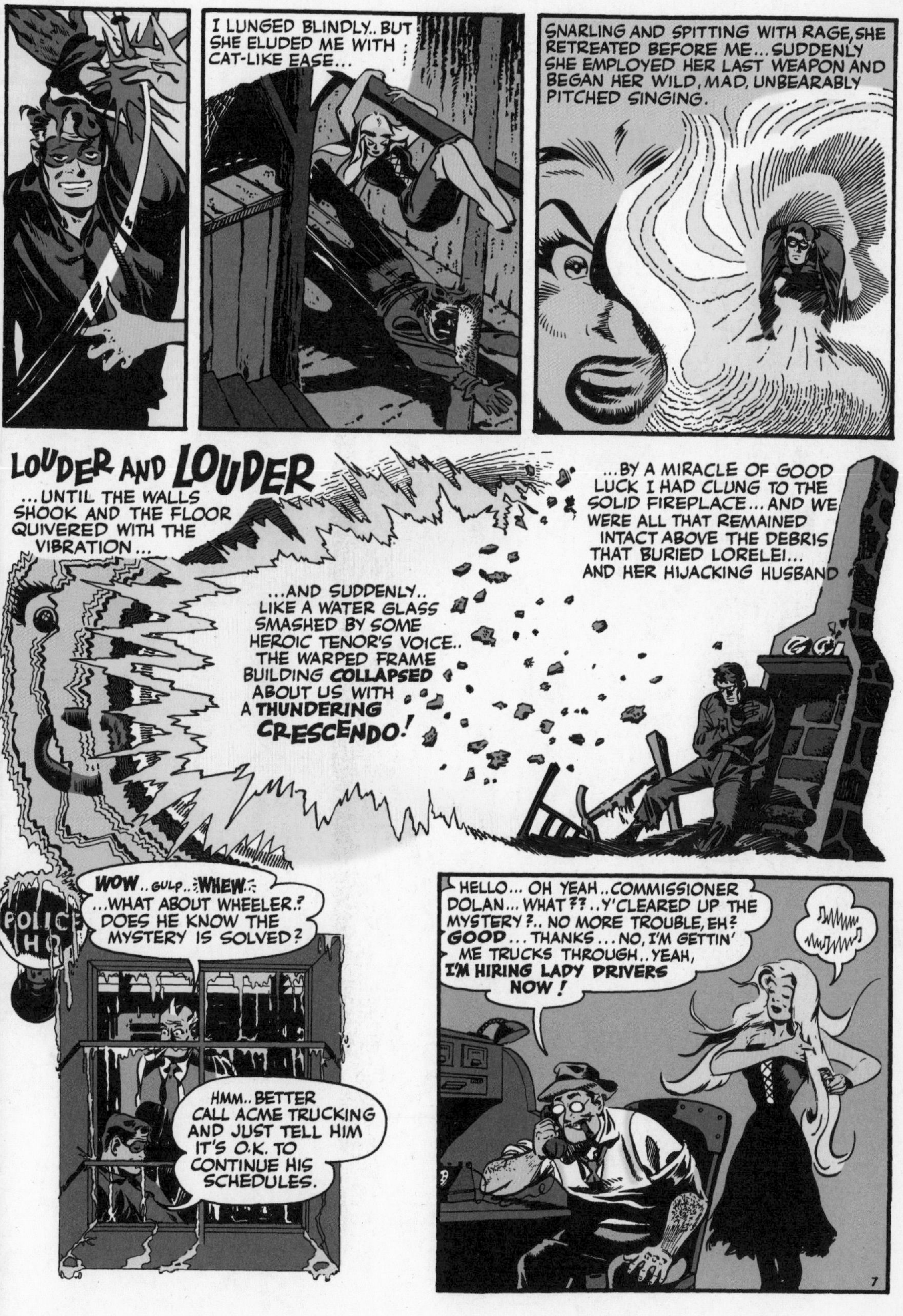

I LUNGED BLINDLY.. BUT SHE ELUDED ME WITH CAT-LIKE EASE...
SNARLING AND SPITTING WITH RAGE, SHE RETREATED BEFORE ME... SUDDENLY SHE EMPLOYED HER LAST WEAPON AND BEGAN HER WILD, MAD, UNBEARABLY PITCHED SINGING.
LOUDER AND LOUDER
...UNTIL THE WALLS SHOOK AND THE FLOOR QUIVERED WITH THE VIBRATION...
...AND SUDDENLY.. LIKE A WATER GLASS SMASHED BY SOME HEROIC TENOR'S VOICE.. THE WARPED FRAME BUILDING COLLAPSED ABOUT US WITH A THUNDERING CRESCENDO!
...BY A MIRACLE OF GOOD LUCK I HAD CLUNG TO THE SOLID FIREPLACE... AND WE WERE ALL THAT REMAINED INTACT ABOVE THE DEBRIS THAT BURIED LORELEI... AND HER HIJACKING HUSBAND
POLICE HQ
WOW.. GULP.. WHEW.. ...WHAT ABOUT WHEELER.? DOES HE KNOW THE MYSTERY IS SOLVED?
HMM.. BETTER CALL ACME TRUCKING AND JUST TELL HIM IT'S O.K. TO CONTINUE HIS SCHEDULES.
HELLO... OH YEAH.. COMMISSIONER DOLAN... WHAT?? .. Y'CLEARED UP THE MYSTERY?.. NO MORE TROUBLE, EH? GOOD... THANKS... NO, I'M GETTIN' ME TRUCKS THROUGH.. YEAH, I'M HIRING LADY DRIVERS NOW!
7

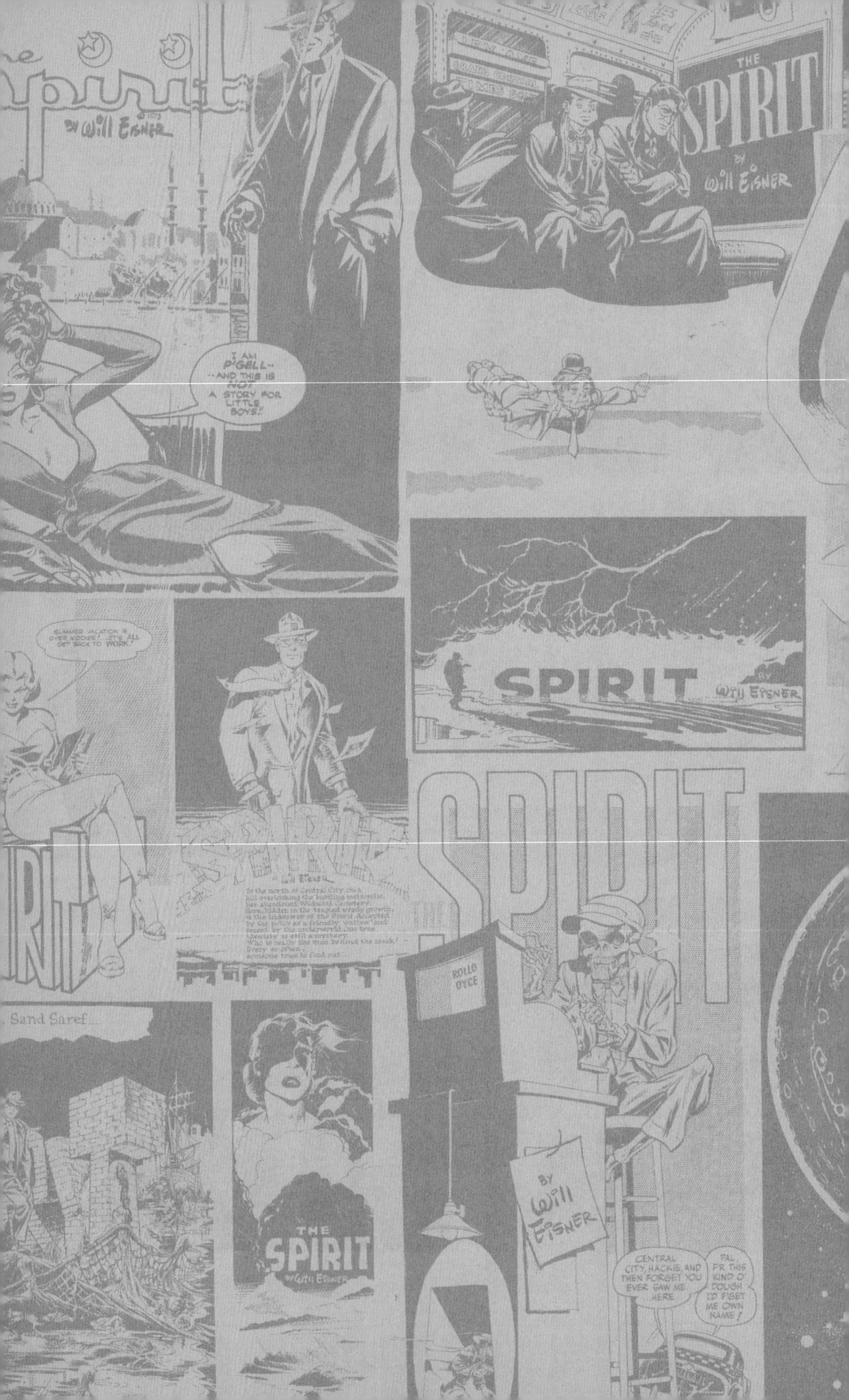

The Spirit
by Will Eisner
I AM P'GELL.. ..AND THIS IS NOT A STORY FOR LITTLE BOYS!
THE SPIRIT
by Will Eisner
SUMMER VACATION IS OVER KIDDIES! LET'S ALL GET BACK TO WORK.
SPIRIT
BY Will Eisner
SPIRIT
THE SPIRIT
ROLLO DYCE
BY Will Eisner
..Sand Saref....
THE SPIRIT
by Will Eisner
CENTRAL CITY, HACKIE, AND THEN FORGET YOU EVER SAW ME ...HERE
PAL, FR THIS KIND O' DOUGH I'D FIGET ME OWN NAME!

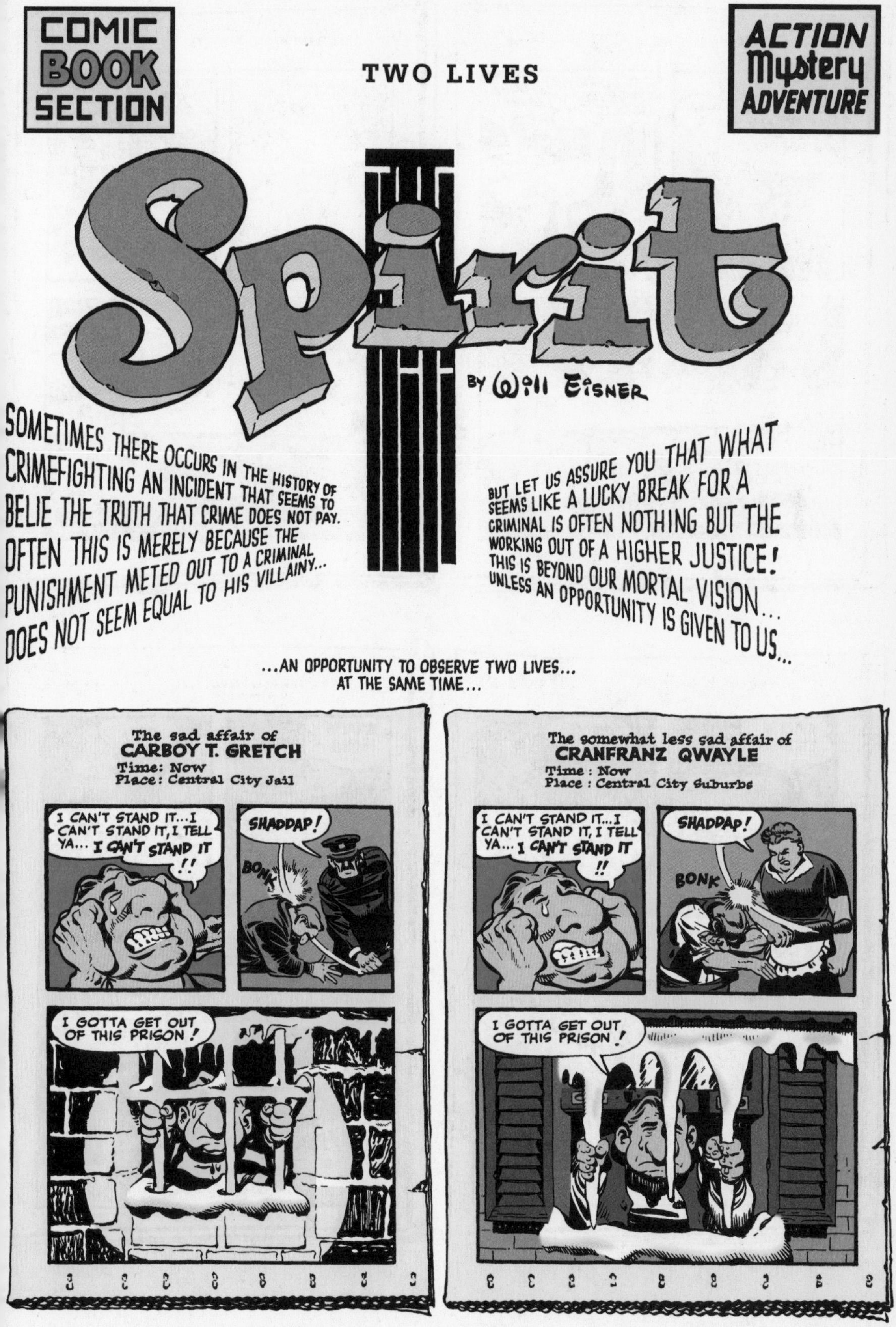
COMIC BOOK SECTION
TWO LIVES
ACTION Mystery ADVENTURE
Spirit
BY Will Eisner
SOMETIMES THERE OCCURS IN THE HISTORY OF CRIMEFIGHTING AN INCIDENT THAT SEEMS TO BELIE THE TRUTH THAT CRIME DOES NOT PAY. OFTEN THIS IS MERELY BECAUSE THE PUNISHMENT METED OUT TO A CRIMINAL DOES NOT SEEM EQUAL TO HIS VILLAINY...
BUT LET US ASSURE YOU THAT WHAT SEEMS LIKE A LUCKY BREAK FOR A CRIMINAL IS OFTEN NOTHING BUT THE WORKING OUT OF A HIGHER JUSTICE! THIS IS BEYOND OUR MORTAL VISION... UNLESS AN OPPORTUNITY IS GIVEN TO US...
...AN OPPORTUNITY TO OBSERVE TWO LIVES... AT THE SAME TIME...
The sad affair of CARBOY T. GRETCH
Time: Now
Place: Central City Jail
I CAN'T STAND IT...I CAN'T STAND IT, I TELL YA... I CAN'T STAND IT !!
SHADDAP!
BONK
I GOTTA GET OUT OF THIS PRISON!
The somewhat less sad affair of CRANFRANZ QWAYLE
Time: Now
Place: Central City Suburbs
I CAN'T STAND IT...I CAN'T STAND IT, I TELL YA... I CAN'T STAND IT !!
SHADDAP!
BONK
I GOTTA GET OUT OF THIS PRISON!

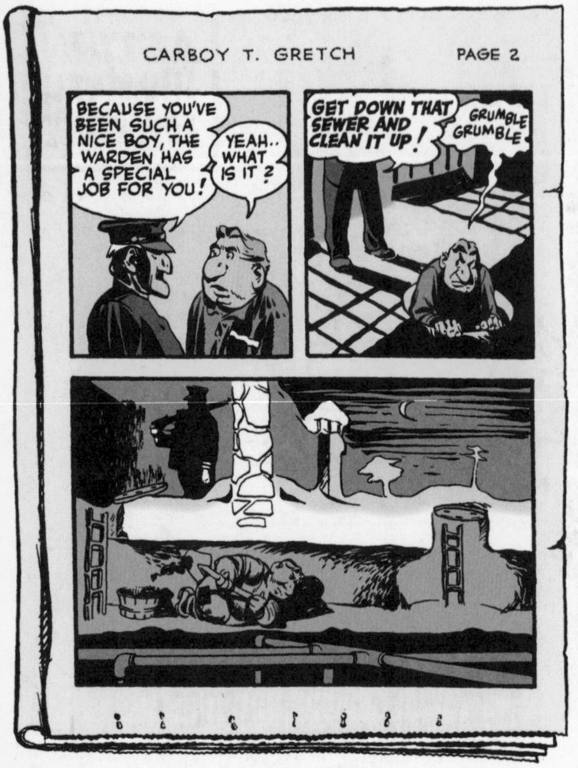
CARBOY T. GRETCH
PAGE 2
BECAUSE YOU'VE BEEN SUCH A NICE BOY, THE WARDEN HAS A SPECIAL JOB FOR YOU!
YEAH.. WHAT IS IT ?
GET DOWN THAT SEWER AND CLEAN IT UP!
GRUMBLE GRUMBLE

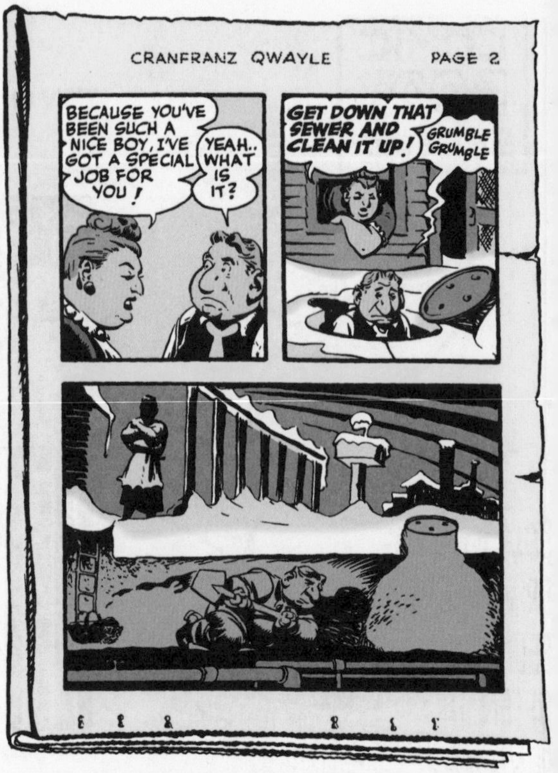
CRANFRANZ QWAYLE
PAGE 2
BECAUSE YOU'VE BEEN SUCH A NICE BOY, I'VE GOT A SPECIAL JOB FOR YOU!
YEAH.. WHAT IS IT?
GET DOWN THAT SEWER AND CLEAN IT UP!
GRUMBLE GRUMBLE

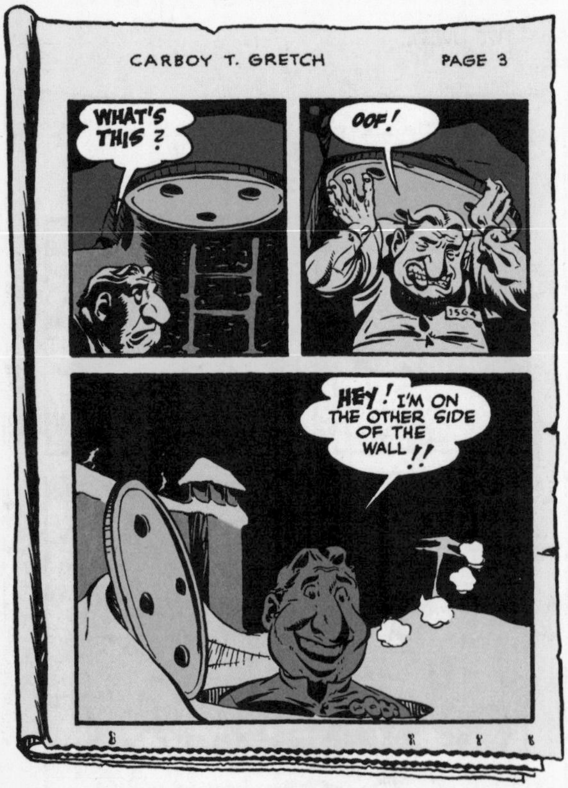
CARBOY T. GRETCH
PAGE 3
WHAT'S THIS ?
OOF!
HEY! I'M ON THE OTHER SIDE OF THE WALL !!

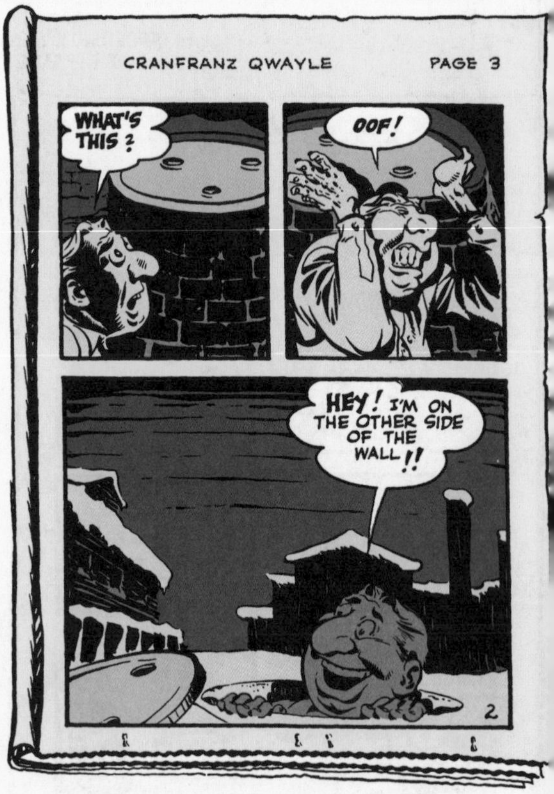
CRANFRANZ QWAYLE
PAGE 3
WHAT'S THIS ?
OOF!
HEY! I'M ON THE OTHER SIDE OF THE WALL !!
2

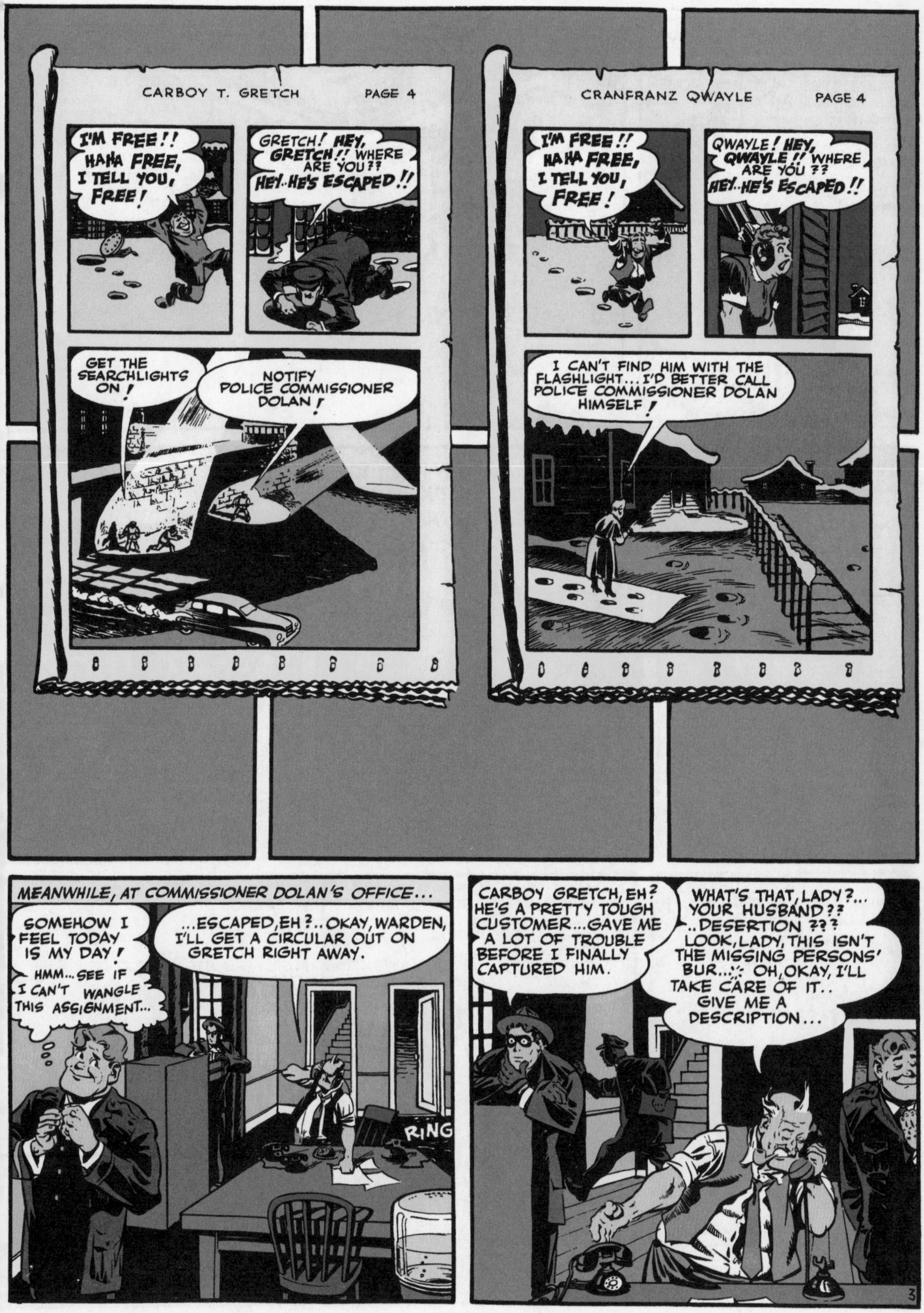

CARBOY T. GRETCH PAGE 4
I'M FREE!! HAHA FREE, I TELL YOU, FREE!
GRETCH! HEY, GRETCH!! WHERE ARE YOU??
HEY..HE'S ESCAPED!!
GET THE SEARCHLIGHTS ON!
NOTIFY POLICE COMMISSIONER DOLAN!
CRANFRANZ QWAYLE PAGE 4
I'M FREE!! HAHA FREE, I TELL YOU, FREE!
QWAYLE! HEY, QWAYLE!! WHERE ARE YOU??
HEY..HE'S ESCAPED!!
I CAN'T FIND HIM WITH THE FLASHLIGHT... I'D BETTER CALL POLICE COMMISSIONER DOLAN HIMSELF!
MEANWHILE, AT COMMISSIONER DOLAN'S OFFICE...
SOMEHOW I FEEL TODAY IS MY DAY!
HMM... SEE IF I CAN'T WANGLE THIS ASSIGNMENT...
...ESCAPED, EH?.. OKAY, WARDEN, I'LL GET A CIRCULAR OUT ON GRETCH RIGHT AWAY.
RING
CARBOY GRETCH, EH? HE'S A PRETTY TOUGH CUSTOMER...GAVE ME A LOT OF TROUBLE BEFORE I FINALLY CAPTURED HIM.
WHAT'S THAT, LADY?... YOUR HUSBAND?? ..DESERTION??? LOOK, LADY, THIS ISN'T THE MISSING PERSONS' BUR...: OH, OKAY, I'LL TAKE CARE OF IT.. GIVE ME A DESCRIPTION...
3

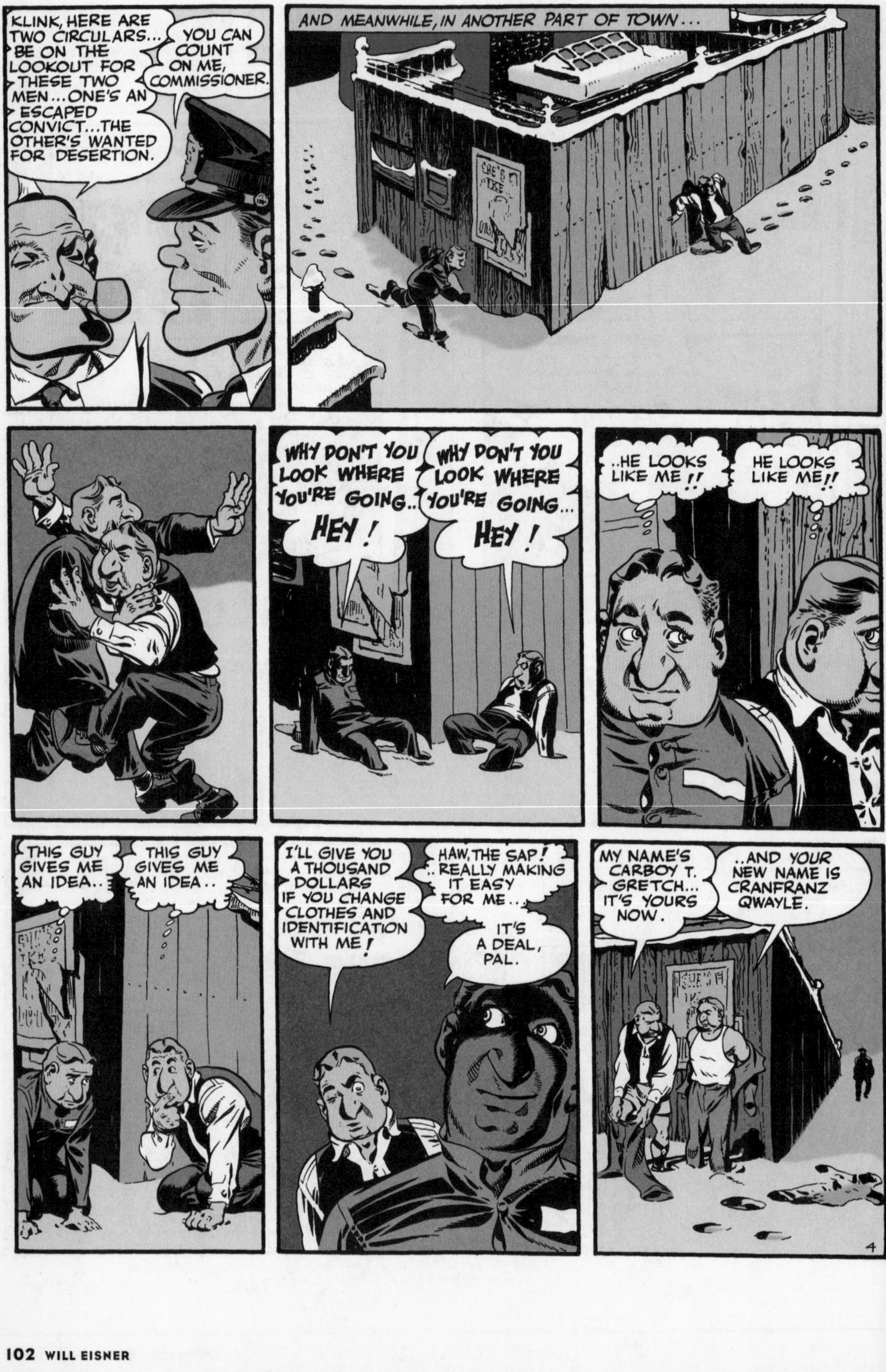
KLINK, HERE ARE TWO CIRCULARS... BE ON THE LOOKOUT FOR THESE TWO MEN...ONE'S AN ESCAPED CONVICT...THE OTHER'S WANTED FOR DESERTION.
YOU CAN COUNT ON ME, COMMISSIONER.
AND MEANWHILE, IN ANOTHER PART OF TOWN...
WHY DON'T YOU LOOK WHERE YOU'RE GOING.. HEY!
WHY DON'T YOU LOOK WHERE YOU'RE GOING... HEY!
..HE LOOKS LIKE ME!!
HE LOOKS LIKE ME!!
THIS GUY GIVES ME AN IDEA..
THIS GUY GIVES ME AN IDEA..
I'LL GIVE YOU A THOUSAND DOLLARS IF YOU CHANGE CLOTHES AND IDENTIFICATION WITH ME!
HAW, THE SAP! ..REALLY MAKING IT EASY FOR ME...
IT'S A DEAL, PAL.
MY NAME'S CARBOY T. GRETCH... IT'S YOURS NOW.
..AND YOUR NEW NAME IS CRANFRANZ QWAYLE.
4

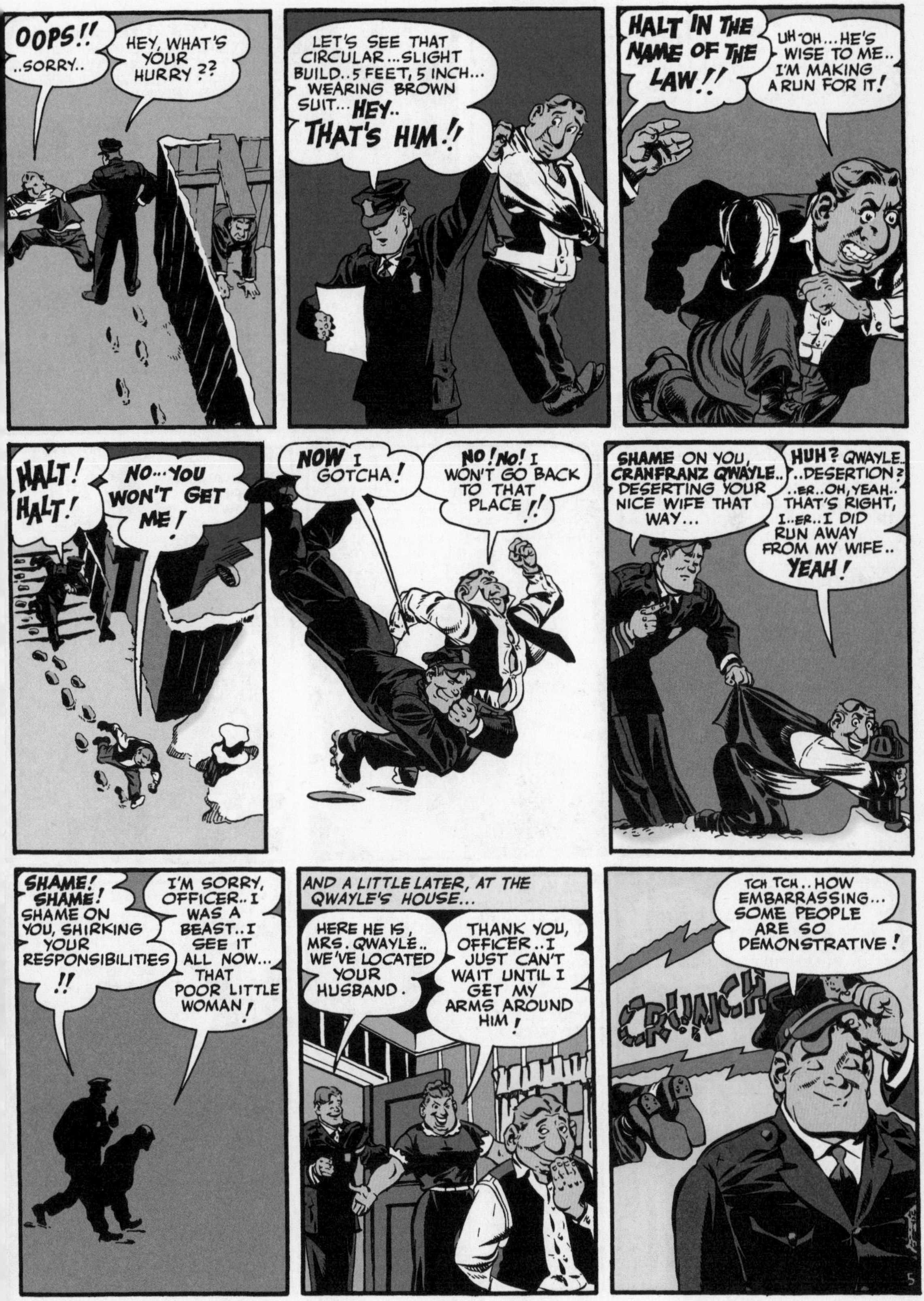
OOPS!! ..SORRY..
HEY, WHAT'S YOUR HURRY ??
LET'S SEE THAT CIRCULAR...SLIGHT BUILD..5 FEET, 5 INCH... WEARING BROWN SUIT... HEY.. THAT'S HIM!!
HALT IN THE NAME OF THE LAW!!
UH-OH...HE'S WISE TO ME.. I'M MAKING A RUN FOR IT!
HALT! HALT!
NO...YOU WON'T GET ME!
NOW I GOTCHA!
NO! NO! I WON'T GO BACK TO THAT PLACE!!
SHAME ON YOU, CRANFRANZ QWAYLE.. DESERTING YOUR NICE WIFE THAT WAY...
HUH? QWAYLE.. ..DESERTION? ..ER..OH, YEAH.. THAT'S RIGHT, I..ER..I DID RUN AWAY FROM MY WIFE.. YEAH!
SHAME! SHAME! SHAME ON YOU, SHIRKING YOUR RESPONSIBILITIES!!
I'M SORRY, OFFICER..I WAS A BEAST..I SEE IT ALL NOW...THAT POOR LITTLE WOMAN!
AND A LITTLE LATER, AT THE QWAYLE'S HOUSE...
HERE HE IS, MRS. QWAYLE.. WE'VE LOCATED YOUR HUSBAND.
THANK YOU, OFFICER..I JUST CAN'T WAIT UNTIL I GET MY ARMS AROUND HIM!
TCH TCH..HOW EMBARRASSING... SOME PEOPLE ARE SO DEMONSTRATIVE!
CRUNCH
5

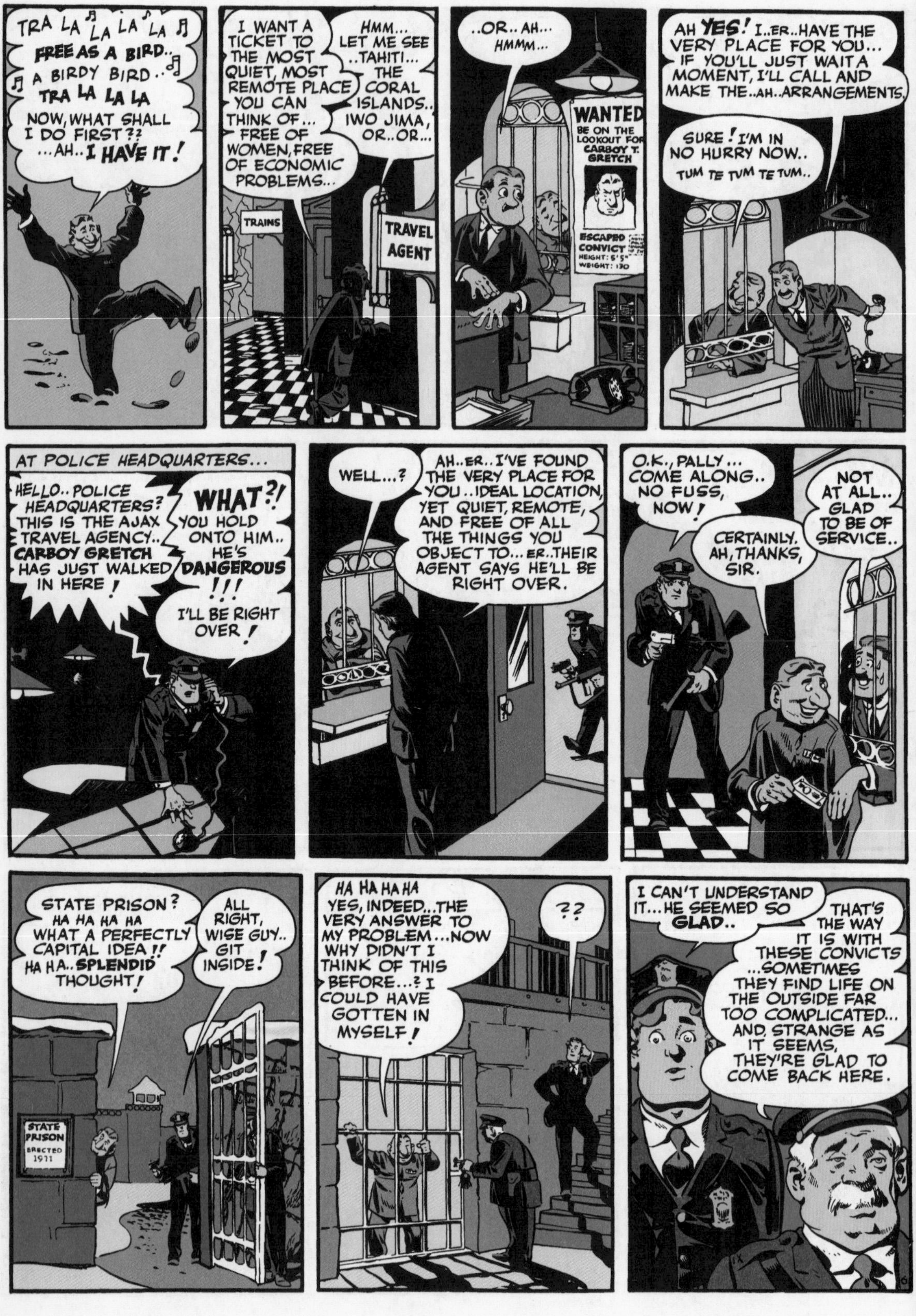
TRA LA LA LA LA
FREE AS A BIRD..
A BIRDY BIRD..
TRA LA LA LA
NOW, WHAT SHALL I DO FIRST??
...AH.. I HAVE IT!
I WANT A TICKET TO THE MOST QUIET, MOST REMOTE PLACE YOU CAN THINK OF... FREE OF WOMEN, FREE OF ECONOMIC PROBLEMS...
HMM... LET ME SEE ..TAHITI... THE CORAL ISLANDS.. IWO JIMA, OR..OR...
TRAINS
TRAVEL AGENT
..OR.. AH... HMMM...
WANTED
BE ON THE LOOKOUT FOR CARBOY T. GRETCH
ESCAPED CONVICT
HEIGHT: 5'5"
WEIGHT: 130
AH YES! I..ER..HAVE THE VERY PLACE FOR YOU... IF YOU'LL JUST WAIT A MOMENT, I'LL CALL AND MAKE THE..AH..ARRANGEMENTS.
SURE! I'M IN NO HURRY NOW.. TUM TE TUM TE TUM..
AT POLICE HEADQUARTERS...
HELLO.. POLICE HEADQUARTERS? THIS IS THE AJAX TRAVEL AGENCY.. CARBOY GRETCH HAS JUST WALKED IN HERE!
WHAT?! YOU HOLD ONTO HIM.. HE'S DANGEROUS !!!
I'LL BE RIGHT OVER!
WELL...?
AH..ER.. I'VE FOUND THE VERY PLACE FOR YOU ..IDEAL LOCATION, YET QUIET, REMOTE, AND FREE OF ALL THE THINGS YOU OBJECT TO... ER..THEIR AGENT SAYS HE'LL BE RIGHT OVER.
O.K., PALLY... COME ALONG.. NO FUSS, NOW!
CERTAINLY. AH, THANKS, SIR.
NOT AT ALL.. GLAD TO BE OF SERVICE..
STATE PRISON? HA HA HA HA WHAT A PERFECTLY CAPITAL IDEA!! HA HA.. SPLENDID THOUGHT!
ALL RIGHT, WISE GUY.. GIT INSIDE!
STATE PRISON
ERECTED 1911
HA HA HA HA
YES, INDEED...THE VERY ANSWER TO MY PROBLEM...NOW WHY DIDN'T I THINK OF THIS BEFORE...? I COULD HAVE GOTTEN IN MYSELF!
??
I CAN'T UNDERSTAND IT... HE SEEMED SO GLAD..
THAT'S THE WAY IT IS WITH THESE CONVICTS ...SOMETIMES THEY FIND LIFE ON THE OUTSIDE FAR TOO COMPLICATED... AND, STRANGE AS IT SEEMS, THEY'RE GLAD TO COME BACK HERE.

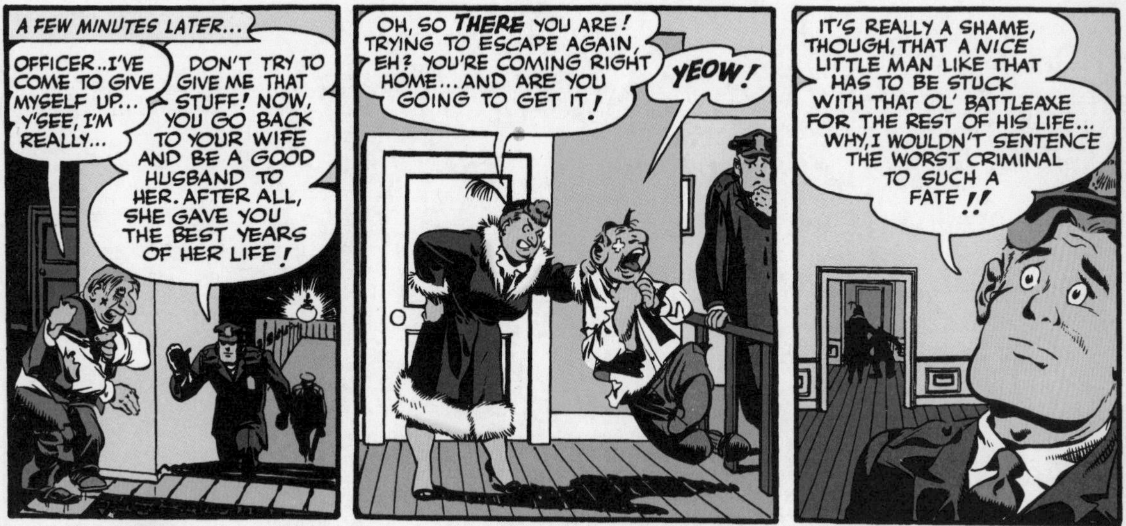
A FEW MINUTES LATER...
OFFICER..I'VE COME TO GIVE MYSELF UP... Y'SEE, I'M REALLY...
DON'T TRY TO GIVE ME THAT STUFF! NOW, YOU GO BACK TO YOUR WIFE AND BE A GOOD HUSBAND TO HER. AFTER ALL, SHE GAVE YOU THE BEST YEARS OF HER LIFE!
OH, SO THERE YOU ARE! TRYING TO ESCAPE AGAIN, EH? YOU'RE COMING RIGHT HOME...AND ARE YOU GOING TO GET IT!
YEOW!
IT'S REALLY A SHAME, THOUGH, THAT A NICE LITTLE MAN LIKE THAT HAS TO BE STUCK WITH THAT OL' BATTLEAXE FOR THE REST OF HIS LIFE... WHY, I WOULDN'T SENTENCE THE WORST CRIMINAL TO SUCH A FATE!!

...AND SO... AS WE SAID...
WHO AMONG US CAN ACCURATELY SAY WHAT IS A FIT PUNISHMENT ??
OR... IN THE WORDS OF HIS IMPERIAL MAJESTY, GILBERT & SULLIVAN'S EARNEST MIKADO OF JAPAN...

My object all sublime
I shall achieve in time
To let the punishment fit the crime
The punishment fit the crime...

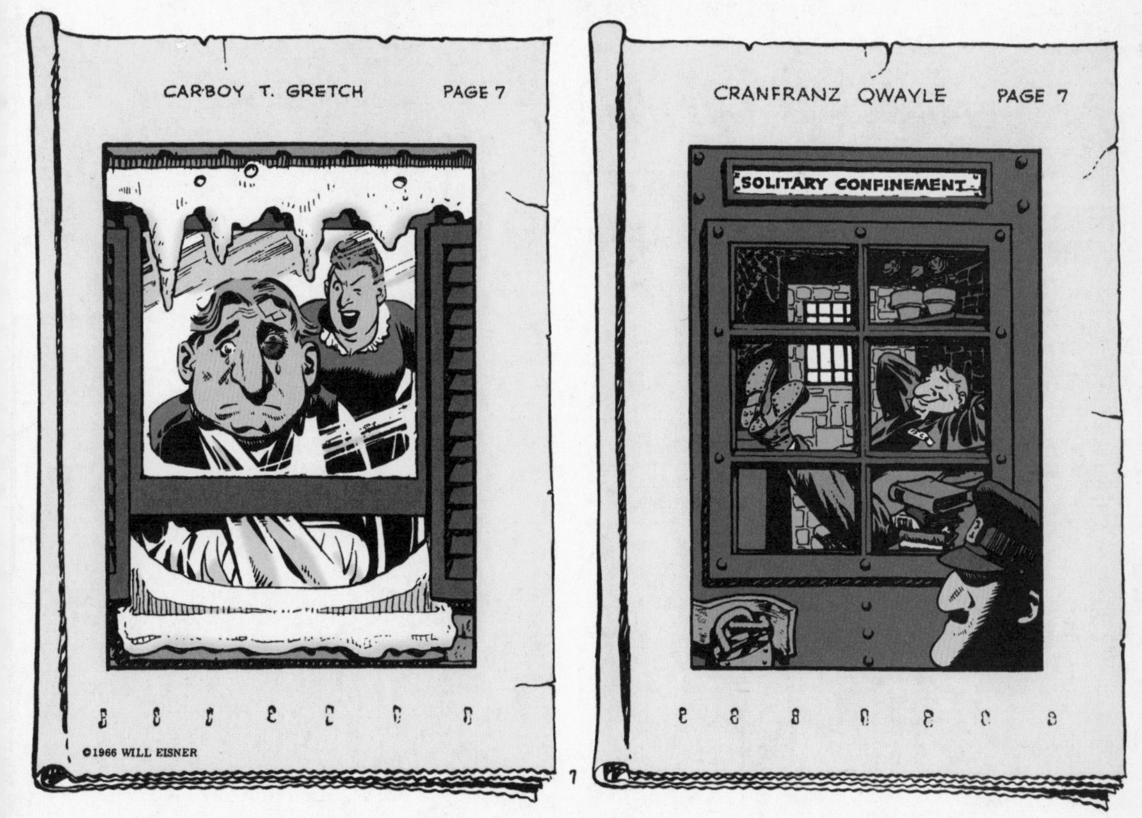
CARBOY T. GRETCH PAGE 7
CRANFRANZ QWAYLE PAGE 7
SOLITARY CONFINEMENT
©1966 WILL EISNER
7

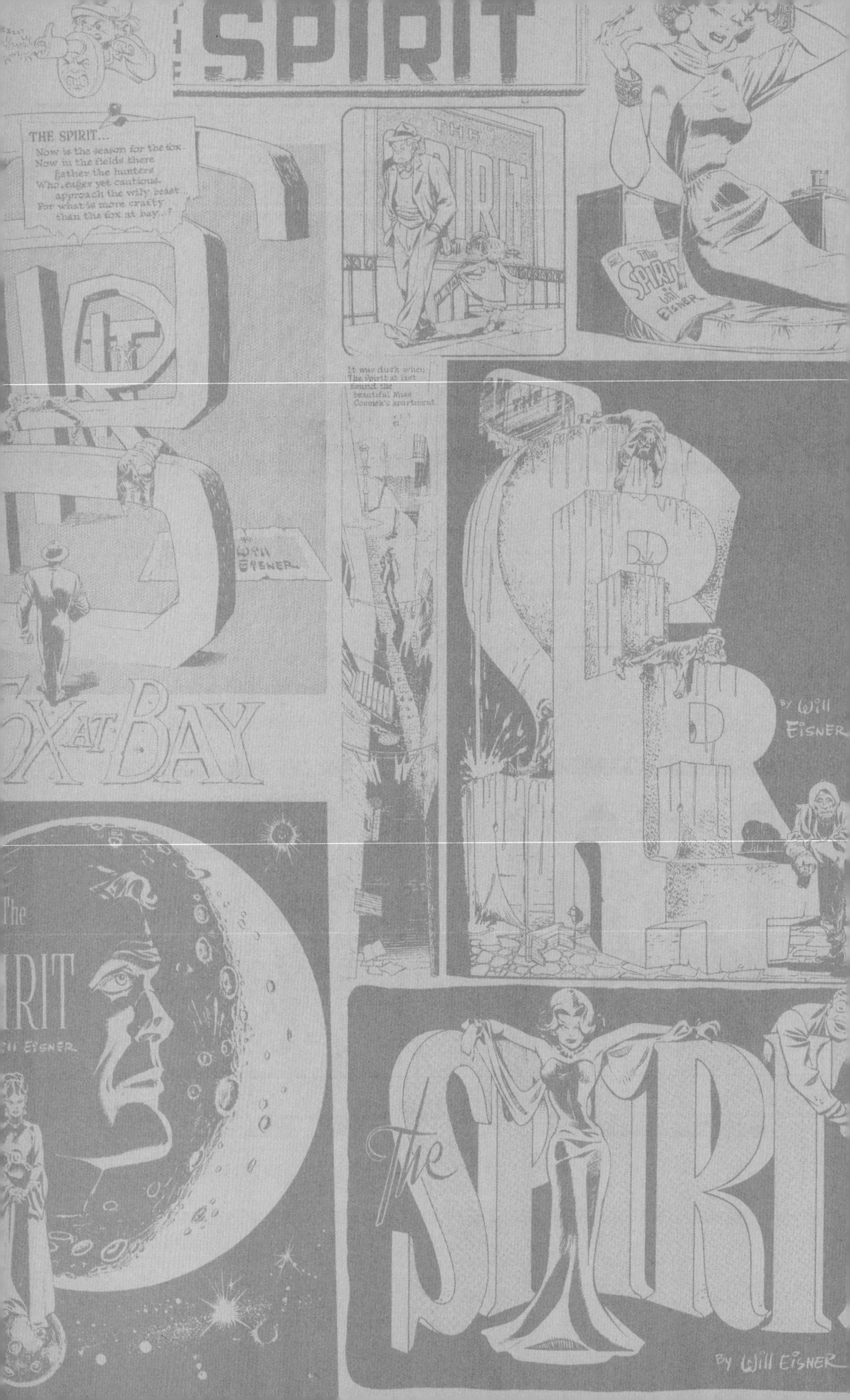
SPIRIT
THE SPIRIT...
Now is the season for the fox.
Now in the fields there gather the hunters
Who, eager yet cautious, approach the wily beast...
For what is more crafty than the fox at bay...?
By Will Eisner
AT BAY
It was dusk when The Spirit at last found the beautiful Miss Cosmik's apartment.
By Will Eisner
The Spirit
By Will Eisner
The Spirit
By Will Eisner

CHRISTMAS SPIRIT OF 1948

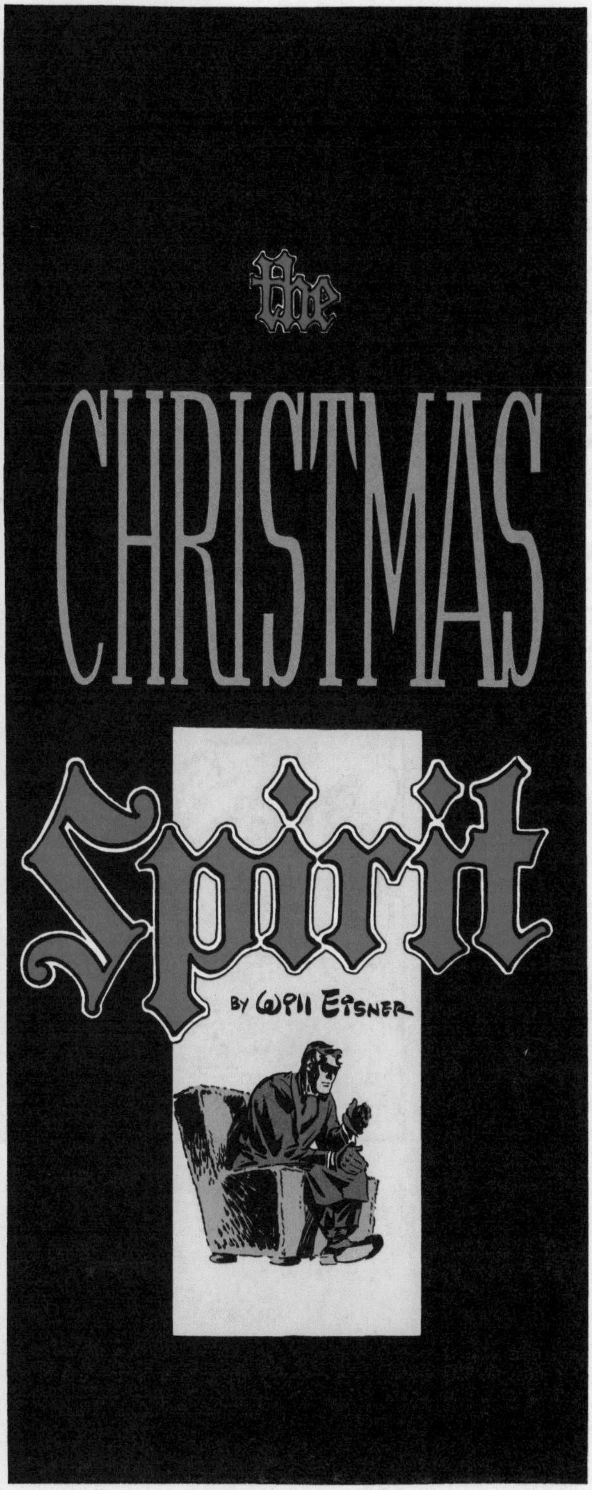
the
CHRISTMAS
Spirit
BY Will Eisner

And on this day
those who all the year
are grasping, and seek riches
from others,
pause for one brief moment
and become kind, human,
generous beings...
all that dreamers believe
men should be...

Or so the legend runs...

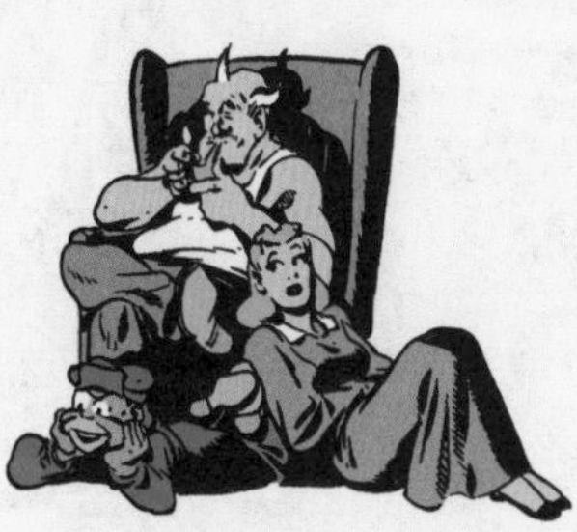

And so it came to pass
one year, not too long ago,
a heavy snow fell upon the land...
and from Central City in the south
to State Prison in the north
the little lights twinkled on
and it was Christmas.

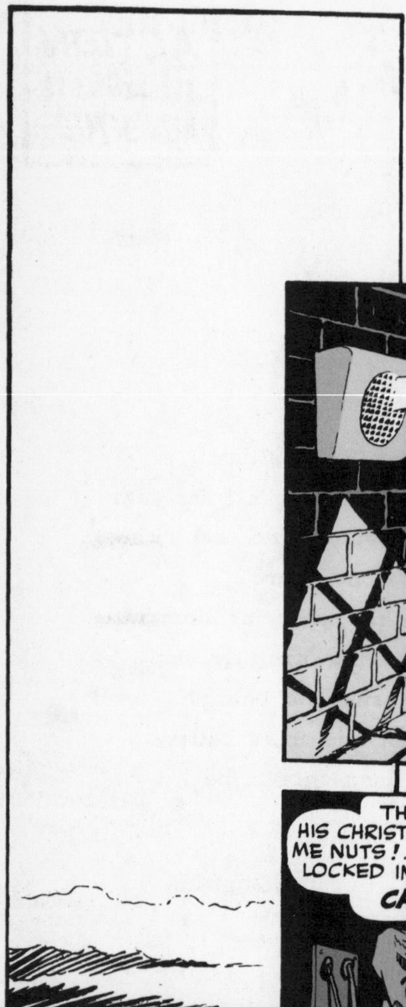

STATE PRISON
STOP FOR INSPECTION

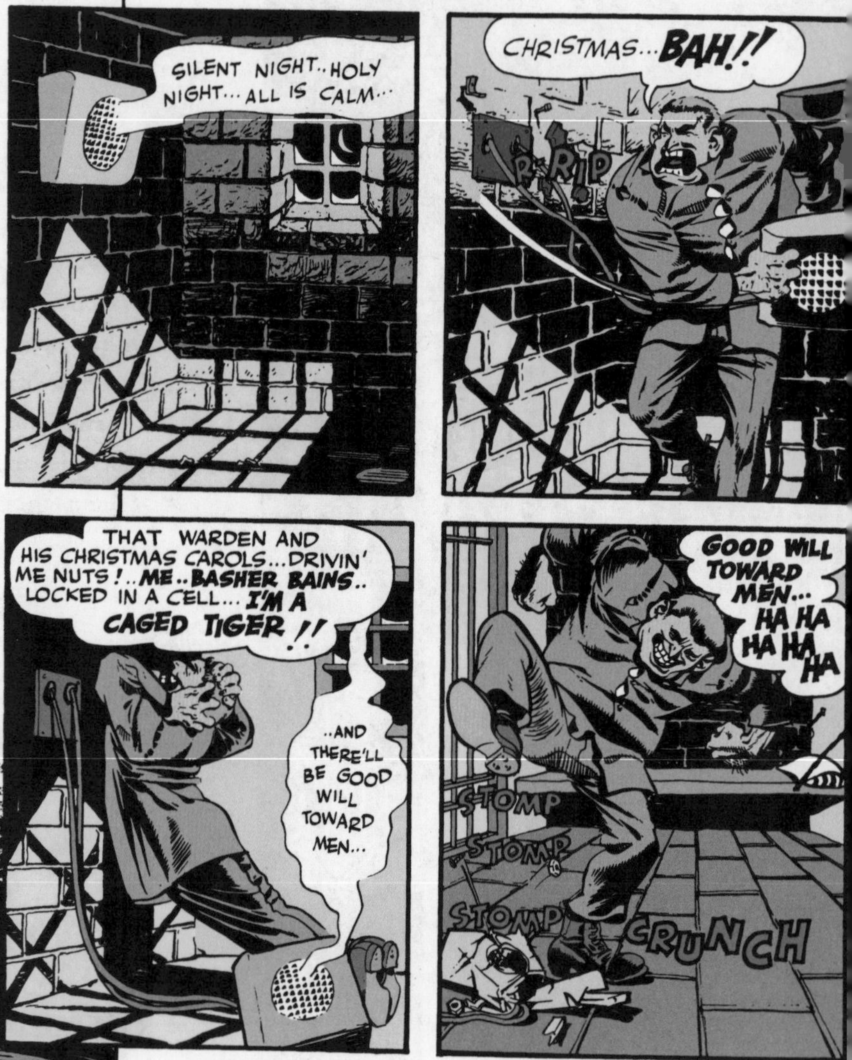

SILENT NIGHT.. HOLY NIGHT... ALL IS CALM...
CHRISTMAS...BAH!!
RRIP
THAT WARDEN AND HIS CHRISTMAS CAROLS...DRIVIN' ME NUTS!..ME..BASHER BAINS.. LOCKED IN A CELL... I'M A CAGED TIGER!!
..AND THERE'LL BE GOOD WILL TOWARD MEN...
GOOD WILL TOWARD MEN... HA HA HA HA HA
STOMP
STOMP
STOMP
CRUNCH

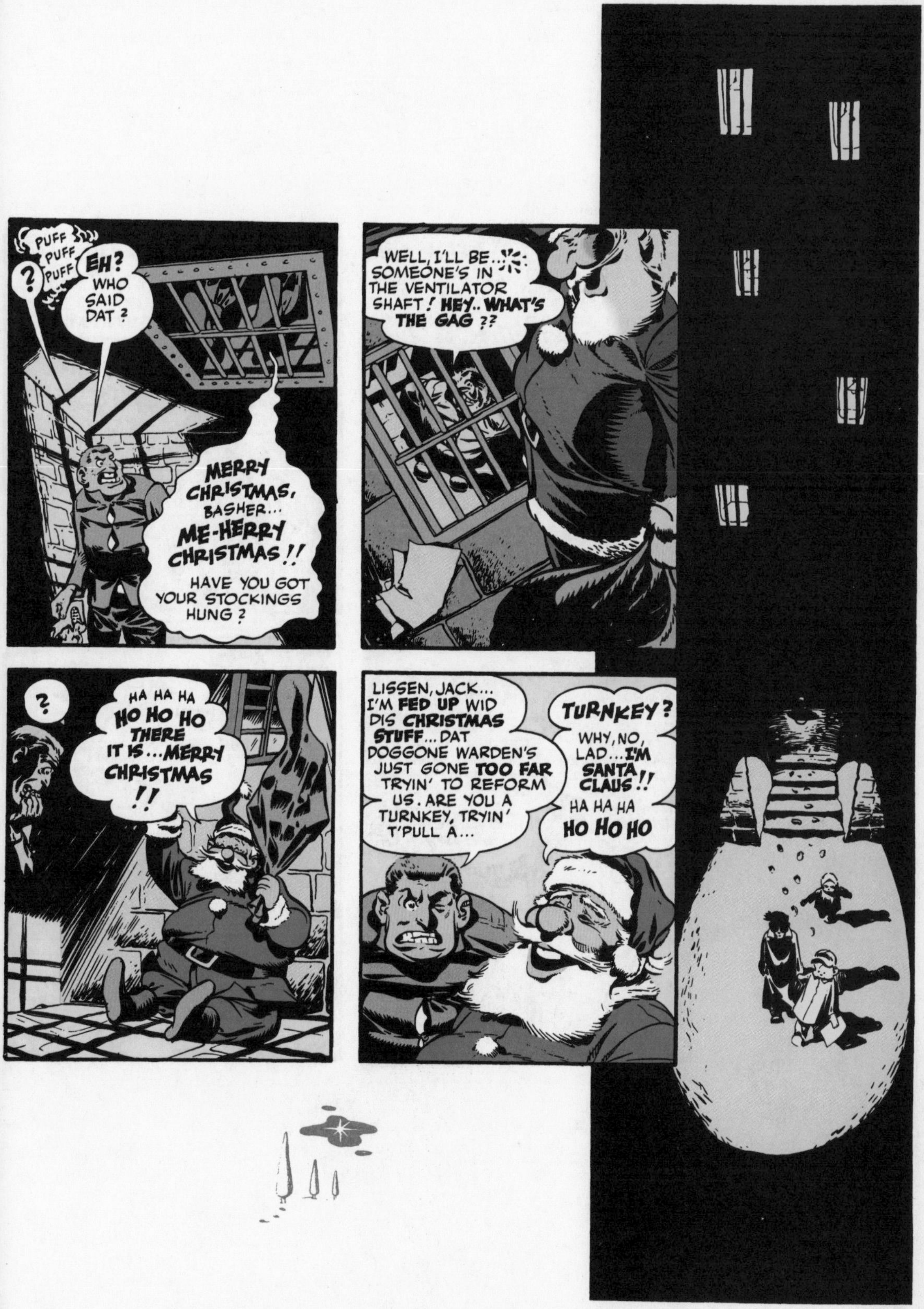
PUFF PUFF PUFF
?
EH? WHO SAID DAT?
MERRY CHRISTMAS, BASHER... ME-HERRY CHRISTMAS!! HAVE YOU GOT YOUR STOCKINGS HUNG?
WELL, I'LL BE.. SOMEONE'S IN THE VENTILATOR SHAFT! HEY.. WHAT'S THE GAG??
?
HA HA HA HO HO HO THERE IT IS...MERRY CHRISTMAS!!
LISSEN, JACK... I'M FED UP WID DIS CHRISTMAS STUFF... DAT DOGGONE WARDEN'S JUST GONE TOO FAR TRYIN' TO REFORM US. ARE YOU A TURNKEY, TRYIN' T'PULL A...
TURNKEY? WHY, NO, LAD... I'M SANTA CLAUS!! HA HA HA HO HO HO

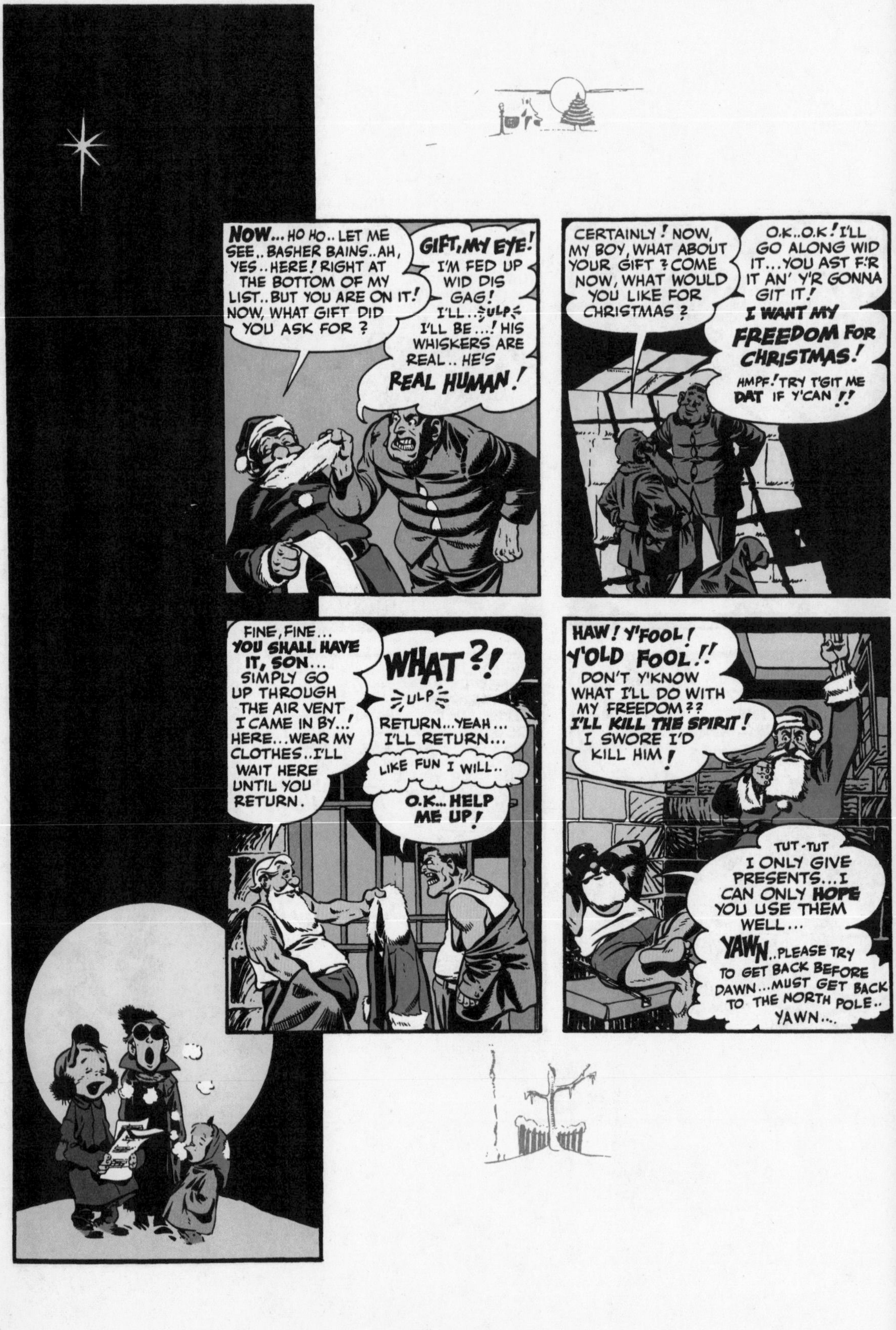
NOW... HO HO.. LET ME SEE.. BASHER BAINS..AH, YES.. HERE! RIGHT AT THE BOTTOM OF MY LIST.. BUT YOU ARE ON IT! NOW, WHAT GIFT DID YOU ASK FOR ?
GIFT, MY EYE! I'M FED UP WID DIS GAG! I'LL.. ULP I'LL BE...! HIS WHISKERS ARE REAL.. HE'S REAL HUMAN!
CERTAINLY! NOW, MY BOY, WHAT ABOUT YOUR GIFT ? COME NOW, WHAT WOULD YOU LIKE FOR CHRISTMAS ?
O.K..O.K! I'LL GO ALONG WID IT... YOU AST F'R IT AN' Y'R GONNA GIT IT! I WANT MY FREEDOM FOR CHRISTMAS!
HMPF! TRY T'GIT ME DAT IF Y'CAN !!
FINE, FINE... YOU SHALL HAVE IT, SON... SIMPLY GO UP THROUGH THE AIR VENT I CAME IN BY..! HERE...WEAR MY CLOTHES..I'LL WAIT HERE UNTIL YOU RETURN.
WHAT ?! ULP
RETURN...YEAH... I'LL RETURN...
LIKE FUN I WILL..
O.K... HELP ME UP!
HAW! Y'FOOL! Y'OLD FOOL!! DON'T Y'KNOW WHAT I'LL DO WITH MY FREEDOM ?? I'LL KILL THE SPIRIT! I SWORE I'D KILL HIM!
TUT-TUT I ONLY GIVE PRESENTS...I CAN ONLY HOPE YOU USE THEM WELL...
YAWN..PLEASE TRY TO GET BACK BEFORE DAWN...MUST GET BACK TO THE NORTH POLE.. YAWN...

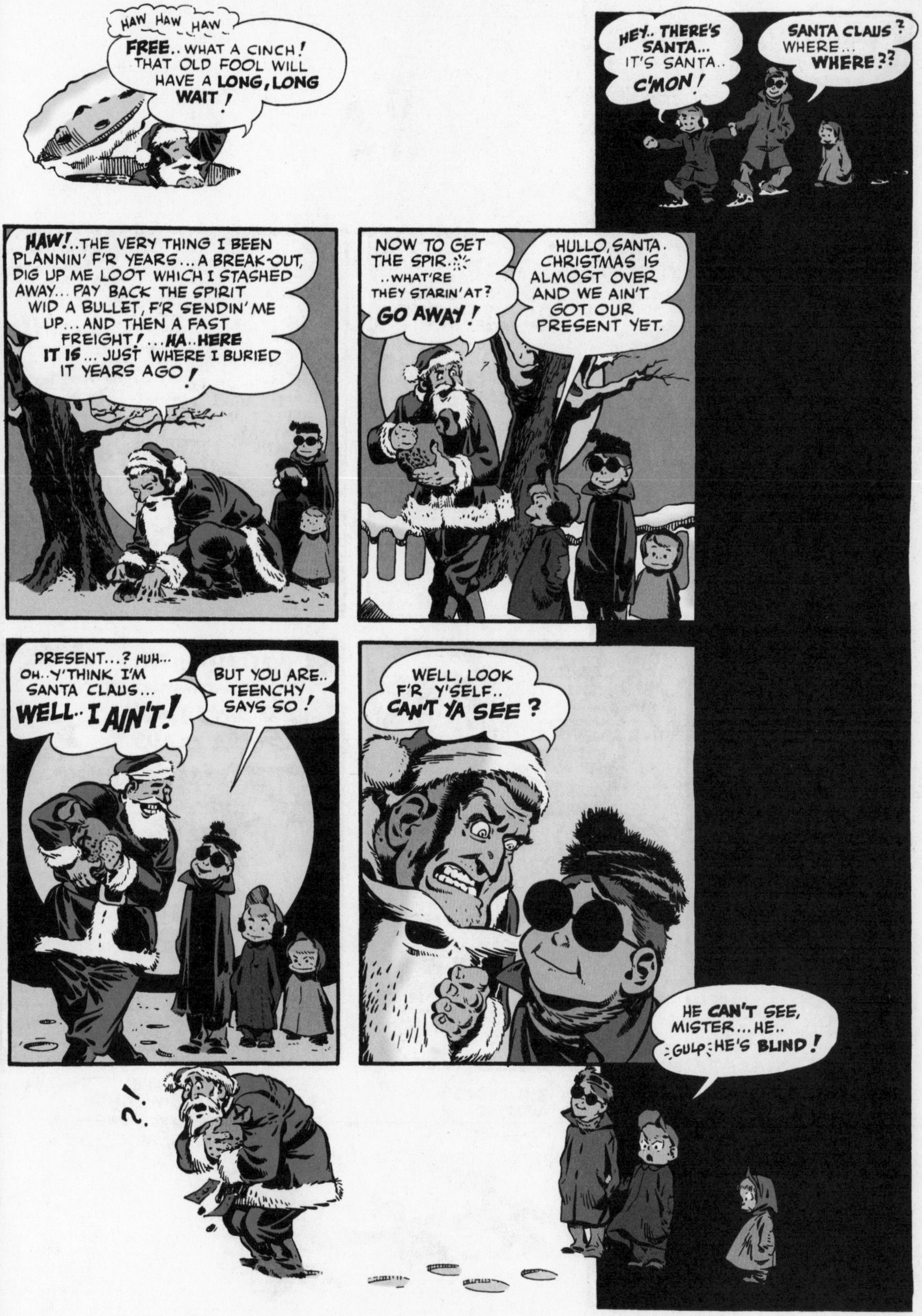
HAW HAW HAW
FREE.. WHAT A CINCH! THAT OLD FOOL WILL HAVE A LONG, LONG WAIT!
HEY.. THERE'S SANTA... IT'S SANTA.. C'MON!
SANTA CLAUS? WHERE... WHERE??
HAW!..THE VERY THING I BEEN PLANNIN' F'R YEARS... A BREAK-OUT, DIG UP ME LOOT WHICH I STASHED AWAY... PAY BACK THE SPIRIT WID A BULLET, F'R SENDIN' ME UP... AND THEN A FAST FREIGHT!...HA..HERE IT IS... JUST WHERE I BURIED IT YEARS AGO!
NOW TO GET THE SPIR.. ..WHAT'RE THEY STARIN' AT? GO AWAY!
HULLO, SANTA. CHRISTMAS IS ALMOST OVER AND WE AIN'T GOT OUR PRESENT YET.
PRESENT...? HUH... OH..Y'THINK I'M SANTA CLAUS... WELL.. I AIN'T!
BUT YOU ARE.. TEENCHY SAYS SO!
WELL, LOOK F'R Y'SELF.. CAN'T YA SEE?
HE CAN'T SEE, MISTER... HE.. GULP HE'S BLIND!
?!

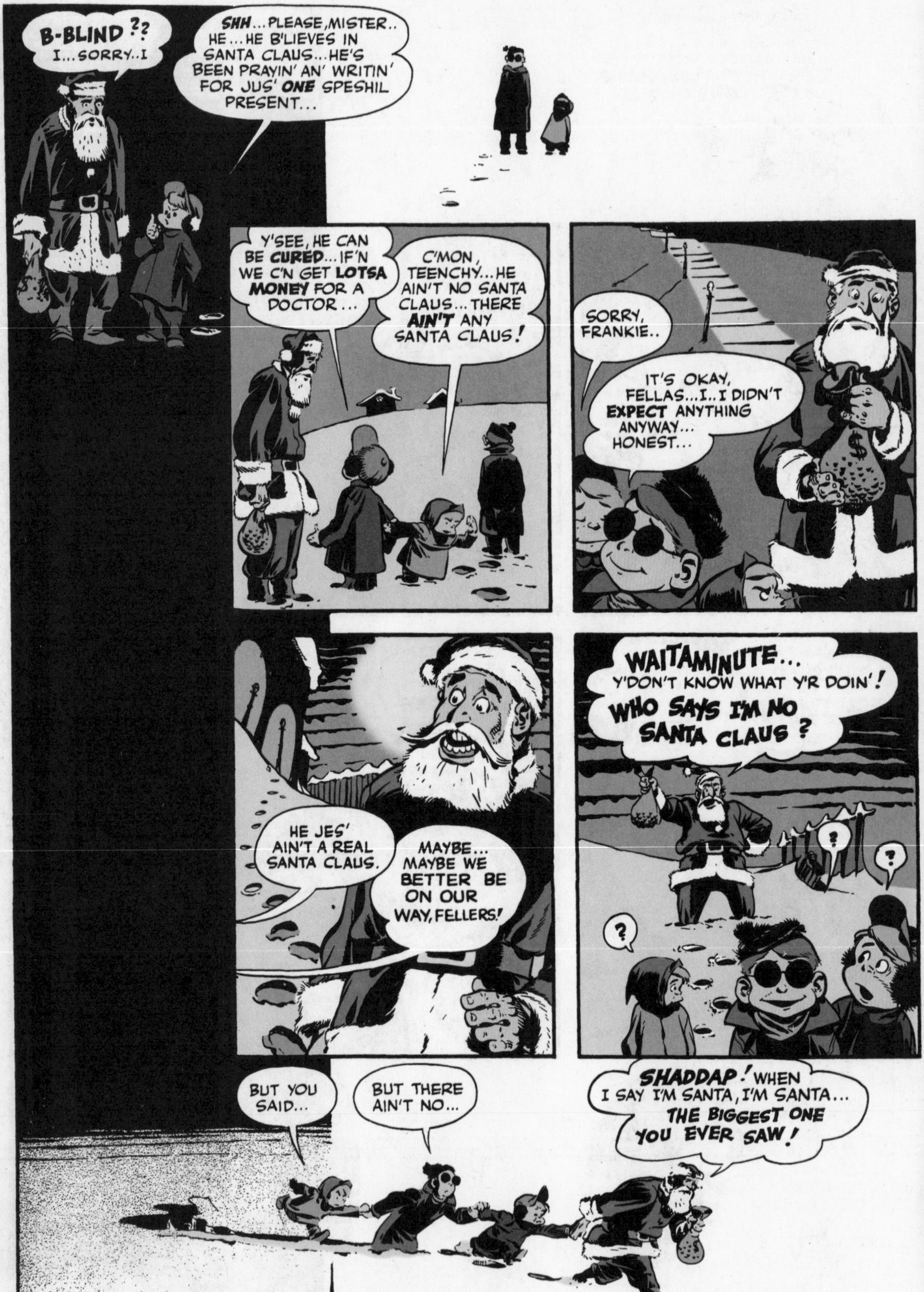
B-BLIND ?? I...SORRY..I
SHH...PLEASE, MISTER.. HE...HE B'LIEVES IN SANTA CLAUS...HE'S BEEN PRAYIN' AN' WRITIN' FOR JUS' ONE SPESHIL PRESENT...
Y'SEE, HE CAN BE CURED...IF'N WE C'N GET LOTSA MONEY FOR A DOCTOR...
C'MON, TEENCHY...HE AIN'T NO SANTA CLAUS...THERE AIN'T ANY SANTA CLAUS!
SORRY, FRANKIE..
IT'S OKAY, FELLAS...I..I DIDN'T EXPECT ANYTHING ANYWAY... HONEST...
HE JES' AIN'T A REAL SANTA CLAUS.
MAYBE... MAYBE WE BETTER BE ON OUR WAY, FELLERS!
WAITAMINUTE... Y'DON'T KNOW WHAT Y'R DOIN'! WHO SAYS I'M NO SANTA CLAUS?
?
?
?
BUT YOU SAID...
BUT THERE AIN'T NO...
SHADDAP! WHEN I SAY I'M SANTA, I'M SANTA... THE BIGGEST ONE YOU EVER SAW!

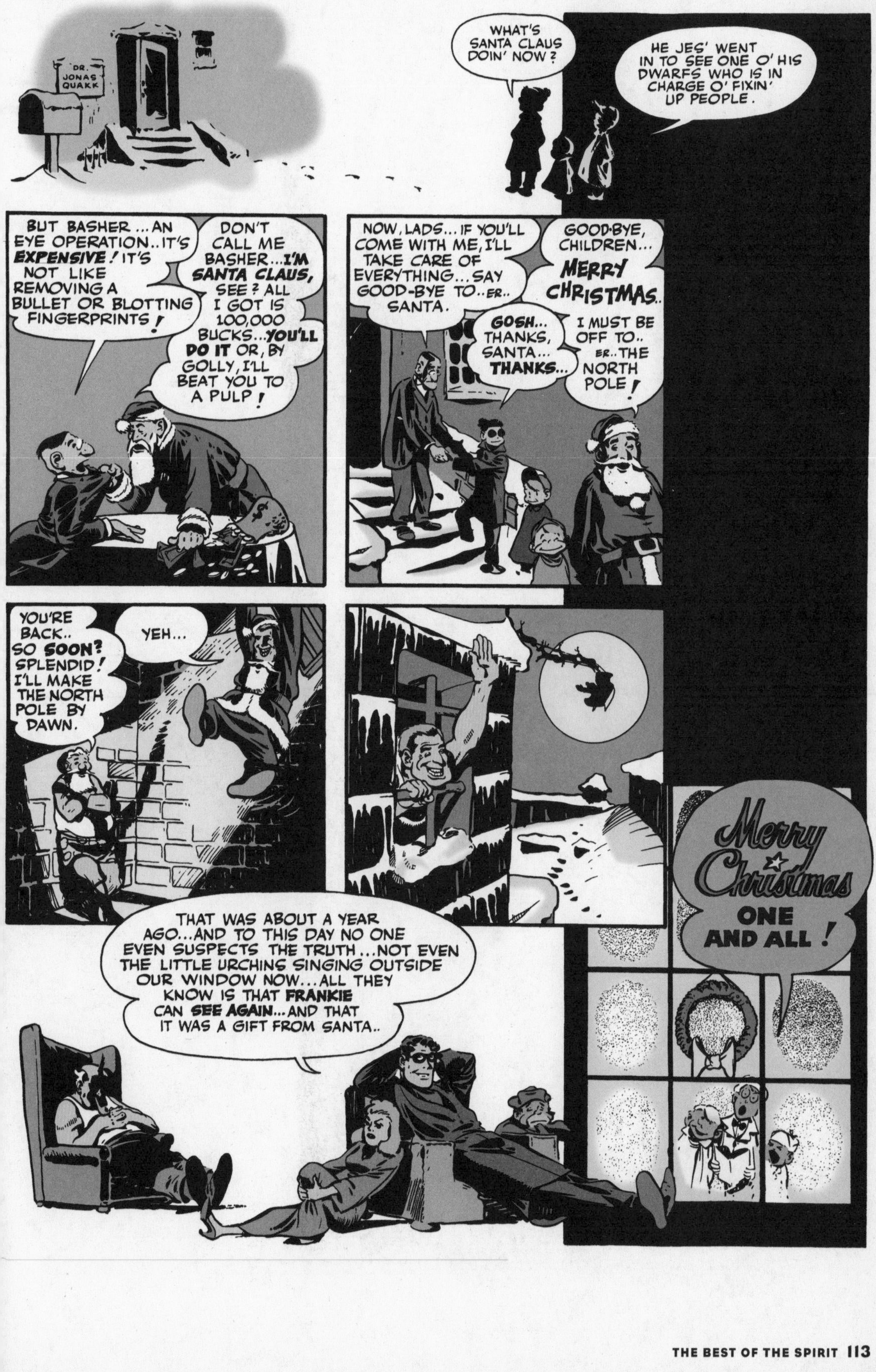
DR. JONAS QUAKK
WHAT'S SANTA CLAUS DOIN' NOW?
HE JES' WENT IN TO SEE ONE O' HIS DWARFS WHO IS IN CHARGE O' FIXIN' UP PEOPLE.
BUT BASHER... AN EYE OPERATION.. IT'S EXPENSIVE! IT'S NOT LIKE REMOVING A BULLET OR BLOTTING FINGERPRINTS!
DON'T CALL ME BASHER... I'M SANTA CLAUS, SEE? ALL I GOT IS 100,000 BUCKS... YOU'LL DO IT OR, BY GOLLY, I'LL BEAT YOU TO A PULP!
NOW, LADS... IF YOU'LL COME WITH ME, I'LL TAKE CARE OF EVERYTHING... SAY GOOD-BYE TO.. ER.. SANTA.
GOOD-BYE, CHILDREN... MERRY CHRISTMAS..
GOSH... THANKS, SANTA... THANKS...
I MUST BE OFF TO.. ER.. THE NORTH POLE!
YOU'RE BACK.. SO SOON? SPLENDID! I'LL MAKE THE NORTH POLE BY DAWN.
YEH...
THAT WAS ABOUT A YEAR AGO... AND TO THIS DAY NO ONE EVEN SUSPECTS THE TRUTH... NOT EVEN THE LITTLE URCHINS SINGING OUTSIDE OUR WINDOW NOW... ALL THEY KNOW IS THAT FRANKIE CAN SEE AGAIN... AND THAT IT WAS A GIFT FROM SANTA..
Merry Christmas ONE AND ALL!

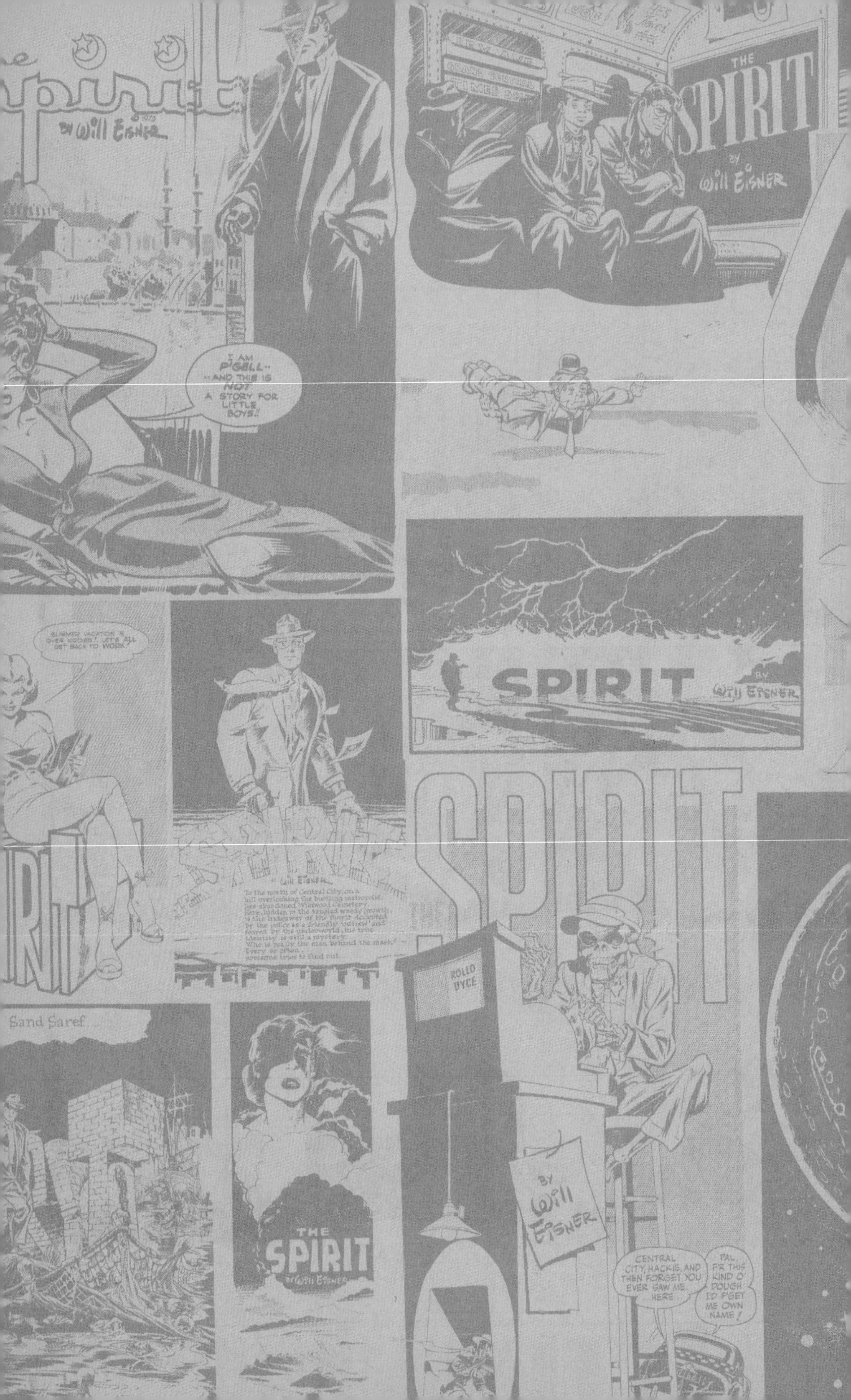
The Spirit
By Will Eisner
© 1973
I AM P'GELL-- ...AND THIS IS NOT A STORY FOR LITTLE BOYS!!
THE SPIRIT
BY Will Eisner
SUMMER VACATION IS OVER KIDDIES! LET'S ALL GET BACK TO WORK!
SPIRIT
BY Will Eisner
By Will Eisner
To the north of Central City, on a
hill overlooking the bustling metropolis,
lies abandoned Wildwood Cemetery.
Here, hidden in the tangled weedy growth,
is the hideaway of the Spirit. Accepted
by the police as a friendly 'outlaw' and
feared by the underworld, his true
identity is still a mystery.
Who is really the man behind the mask?
Every so often,
someone tries to find out...
THE SPIRIT
ROLLO UYCE
Sand Saref...
THE SPIRIT
BY Will Eisner
BY Will Eisner
CENTRAL CITY, HACKIE, AND THEN FORGET YOU EVER SAW ME HERE
PAL, FR THIS KIND O' DOUGH I'D F'GET ME OWN NAME!

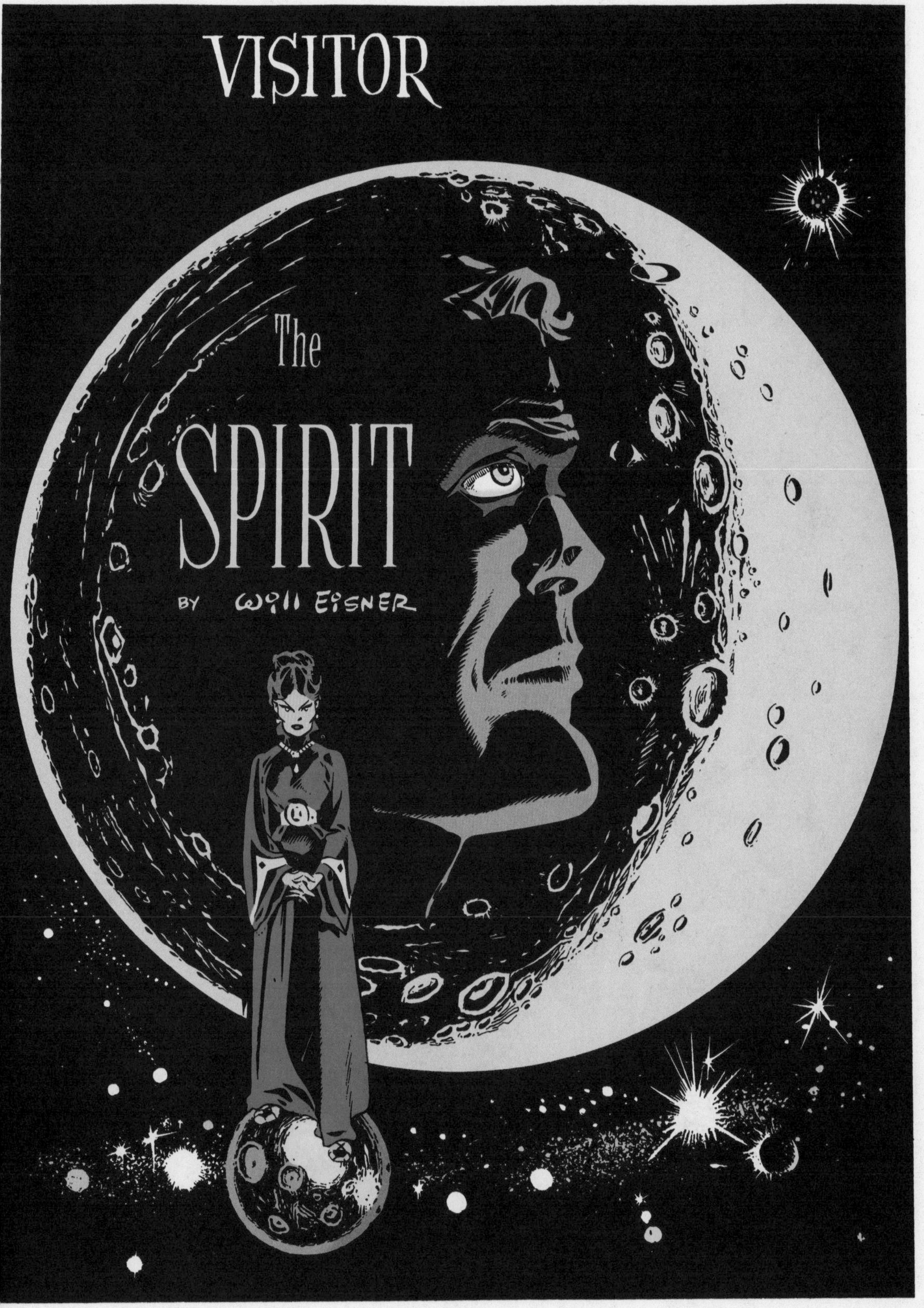
VISITOR
The SPIRIT
BY WILL EISNER

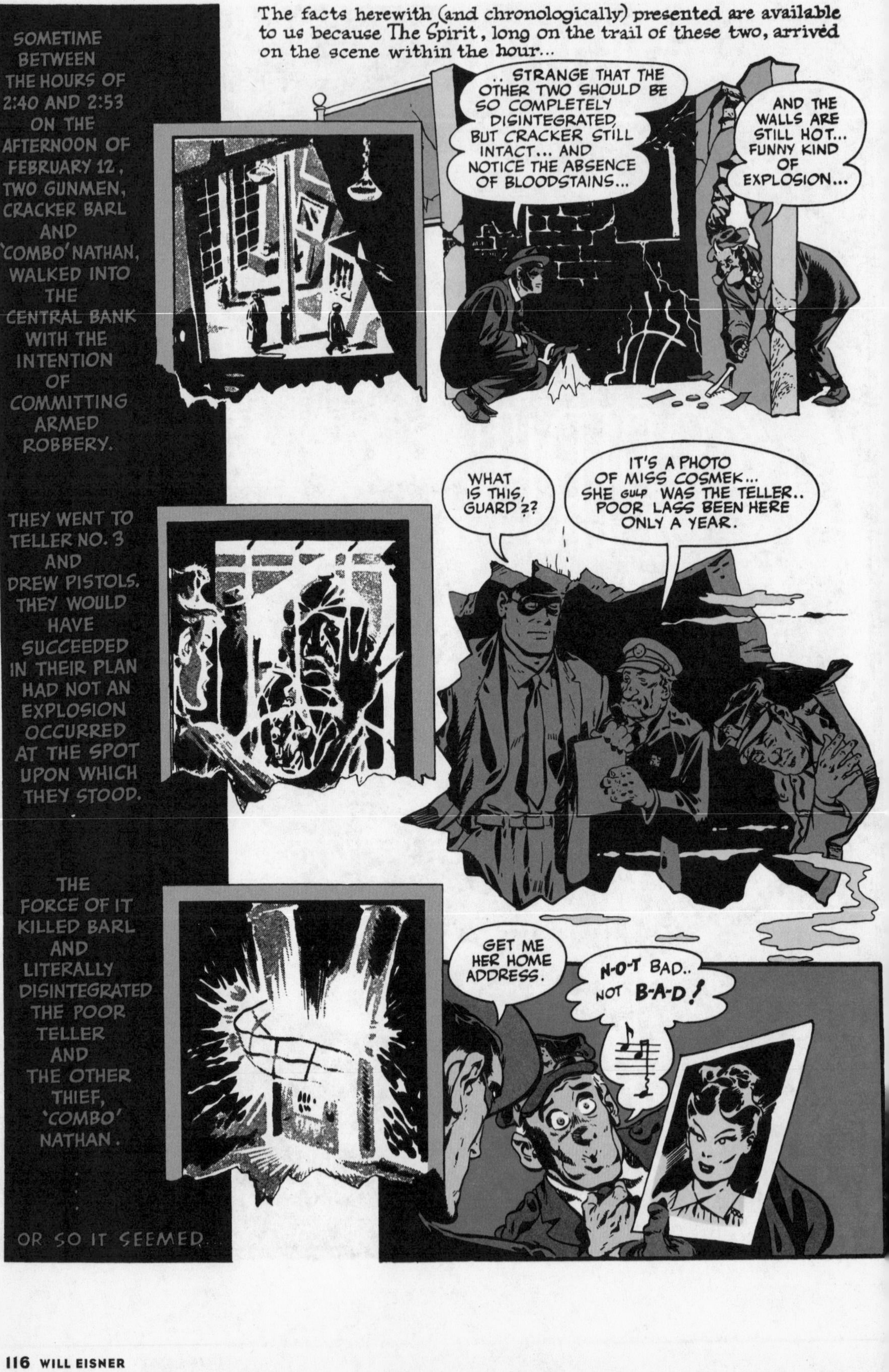
SOMETIME BETWEEN THE HOURS OF 2:40 AND 2:53 ON THE AFTERNOON OF FEBRUARY 12, TWO GUNMEN, CRACKER BARL AND 'COMBO' NATHAN, WALKED INTO THE CENTRAL BANK WITH THE INTENTION OF COMMITTING ARMED ROBBERY.
The facts herewith (and chronologically) presented are available to us because The Spirit, long on the trail of these two, arrived on the scene within the hour...
.. STRANGE THAT THE OTHER TWO SHOULD BE SO COMPLETELY DISINTEGRATED, BUT CRACKER STILL INTACT... AND NOTICE THE ABSENCE OF BLOODSTAINS...
AND THE WALLS ARE STILL HOT... FUNNY KIND OF EXPLOSION...
THEY WENT TO TELLER NO. 3 AND DREW PISTOLS. THEY WOULD HAVE SUCCEEDED IN THEIR PLAN HAD NOT AN EXPLOSION OCCURRED AT THE SPOT UPON WHICH THEY STOOD.
WHAT IS THIS, GUARD ??
IT'S A PHOTO OF MISS COSMEK... SHE gulp WAS THE TELLER.. POOR LASS BEEN HERE ONLY A YEAR.
THE FORCE OF IT KILLED BARL AND LITERALLY DISINTEGRATED THE POOR TELLER AND THE OTHER THIEF, 'COMBO' NATHAN.
GET ME HER HOME ADDRESS.
N-O-T BAD.. NOT B-A-D!
OR SO IT SEEMED...

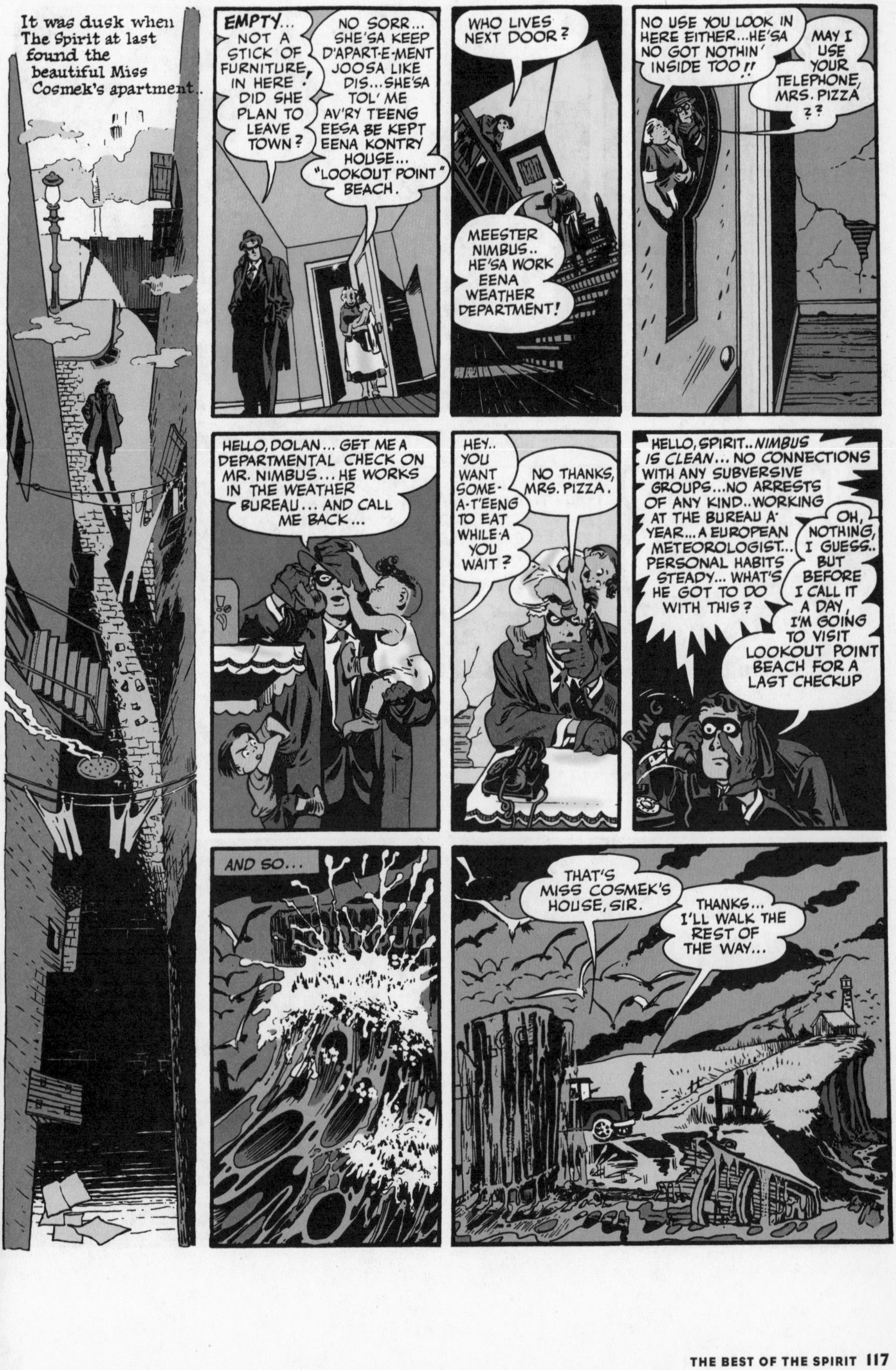
It was dusk when The Spirit at last found the beautiful Miss Cosmek's apartment..
EMPTY... NOT A STICK OF FURNITURE IN HERE! DID SHE PLAN TO LEAVE TOWN?
NO SORR... SHE'SA KEEP D'APART-E-MENT JOOSA LIKE DIS... SHE'SA TOL' ME AV'RY TEENG EESA BE KEPT EENA KONTRY HOUSE... "LOOKOUT POINT" BEACH.
WHO LIVES NEXT DOOR?
MEESTER NIMBUS.. HE'SA WORK EENA WEATHER DEPARTMENT!
NO USE YOU LOOK IN HERE EITHER... HE'SA NO GOT NOTHIN' INSIDE TOO!!
MAY I USE YOUR TELEPHONE, MRS. PIZZA??
HELLO, DOLAN... GET ME A DEPARTMENTAL CHECK ON MR. NIMBUS... HE WORKS IN THE WEATHER BUREAU... AND CALL ME BACK...
HEY.. YOU WANT SOME-A-T'EENG TO EAT WHILE-A YOU WAIT?
NO THANKS, MRS. PIZZA.
HELLO, SPIRIT.. NIMBUS IS CLEAN... NO CONNECTIONS WITH ANY SUBVERSIVE GROUPS... NO ARRESTS OF ANY KIND.. WORKING AT THE BUREAU A YEAR... A EUROPEAN METEOROLOGIST... PERSONAL HABITS STEADY... WHAT'S HE GOT TO DO WITH THIS?
OH, NOTHING, I GUESS.. BUT BEFORE I CALL IT A DAY, I'M GOING TO VISIT LOOKOUT POINT BEACH FOR A LAST CHECKUP
RING
AND SO...
THAT'S MISS COSMEK'S HOUSE, SIR.
THANKS... I'LL WALK THE REST OF THE WAY...

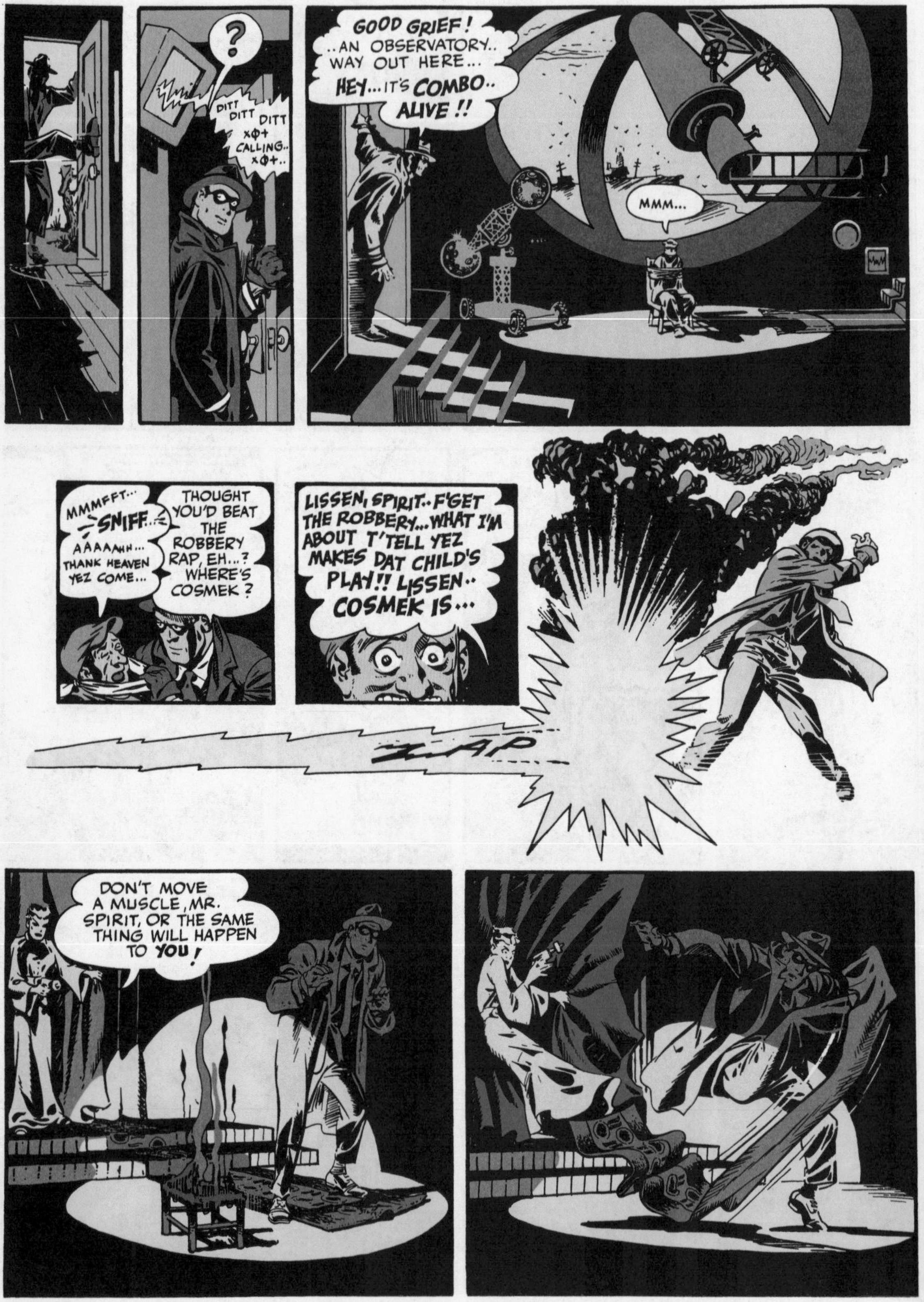
?
DITT DITT DITT
XΦ+ CALLING.. XΦ+..
GOOD GRIEF! ..AN OBSERVATORY.. WAY OUT HERE... HEY...IT'S COMBO.. ALIVE!!
MMM...
MMMFFT... SNIFF... AAAAAHH... THANK HEAVEN YEZ COME...
THOUGHT YOU'D BEAT THE ROBBERY RAP, EH...? WHERE'S COSMEK?
LISSEN, SPIRIT.. F'GET THE ROBBERY...WHAT I'M ABOUT T'TELL YEZ MAKES DAT CHILD'S PLAY!! LISSEN.. COSMEK IS...
ZZAP
DON'T MOVE A MUSCLE, MR. SPIRIT, OR THE SAME THING WILL HAPPEN TO YOU!

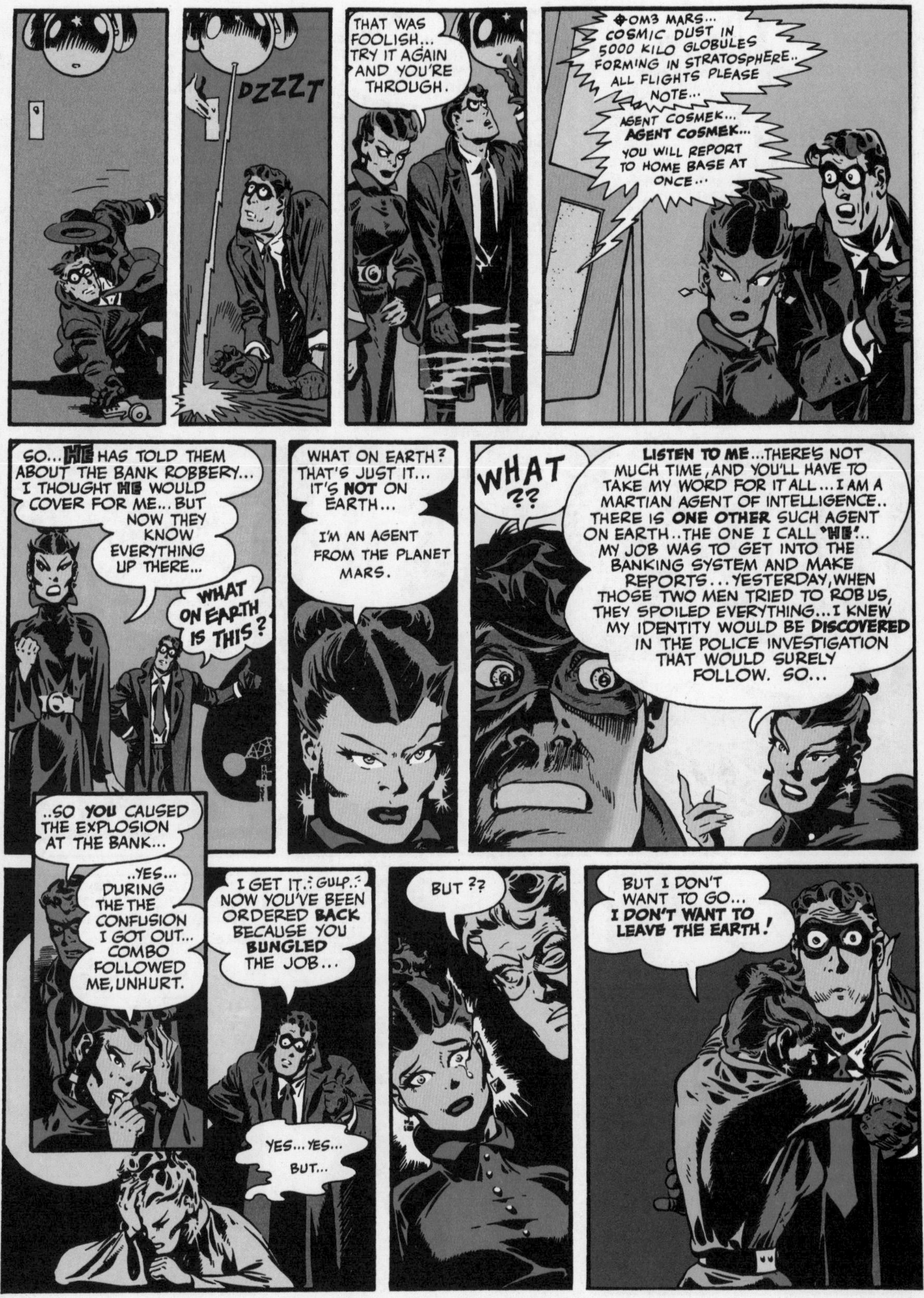
DZZZT
THAT WAS FOOLISH... TRY IT AGAIN AND YOU'RE THROUGH.
OM3 MARS... COSMIC DUST IN 5000 KILO GLOBULES FORMING IN STRATOSPHERE.. ALL FLIGHTS PLEASE NOTE...
AGENT COSMEK... AGENT COSMEK... YOU WILL REPORT TO HOME BASE AT ONCE...
SO... HE HAS TOLD THEM ABOUT THE BANK ROBBERY... I THOUGHT HE WOULD COVER FOR ME... BUT NOW THEY KNOW EVERYTHING UP THERE...
WHAT ON EARTH IS THIS?
WHAT ON EARTH? THAT'S JUST IT... IT'S NOT ON EARTH...
I'M AN AGENT FROM THE PLANET MARS.
WHAT ??
LISTEN TO ME...THERE'S NOT MUCH TIME, AND YOU'LL HAVE TO TAKE MY WORD FOR IT ALL...I AM A MARTIAN AGENT OF INTELLIGENCE.. THERE IS ONE OTHER SUCH AGENT ON EARTH..THE ONE I CALL 'HE'.. MY JOB WAS TO GET INTO THE BANKING SYSTEM AND MAKE REPORTS...YESTERDAY, WHEN THOSE TWO MEN TRIED TO ROB US, THEY SPOILED EVERYTHING...I KNEW MY IDENTITY WOULD BE DISCOVERED IN THE POLICE INVESTIGATION THAT WOULD SURELY FOLLOW. SO...
..SO YOU CAUSED THE EXPLOSION AT THE BANK...
..YES... DURING THE THE CONFUSION I GOT OUT... COMBO FOLLOWED ME, UNHURT.
I GET IT.. GULP.. NOW YOU'VE BEEN ORDERED BACK BECAUSE YOU BUNGLED THE JOB...
YES...YES... BUT...
BUT ??
BUT I DON'T WANT TO GO... I DON'T WANT TO LEAVE THE EARTH!

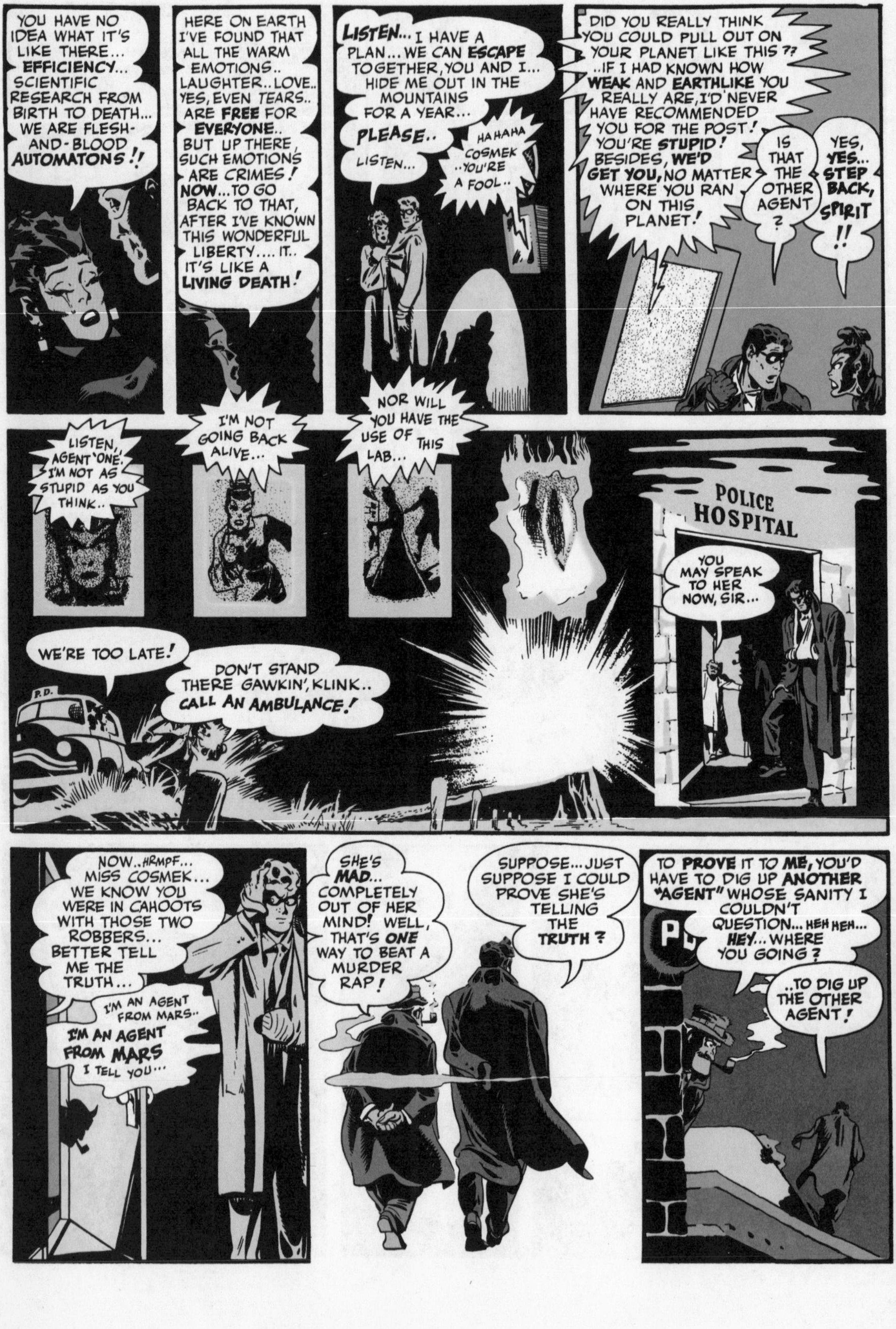
YOU HAVE NO IDEA WHAT IT'S LIKE THERE... EFFICIENCY... SCIENTIFIC RESEARCH FROM BIRTH TO DEATH... WE ARE FLESH-AND-BLOOD AUTOMATONS!!
HERE ON EARTH I'VE FOUND THAT ALL THE WARM EMOTIONS.. LAUGHTER.. LOVE.. YES, EVEN TEARS.. ARE FREE FOR EVERYONE.. BUT UP THERE, SUCH EMOTIONS ARE CRIMES! NOW...TO GO BACK TO THAT, AFTER I'VE KNOWN THIS WONDERFUL LIBERTY.... IT.. IT'S LIKE A LIVING DEATH!
LISTEN... I HAVE A PLAN... WE CAN ESCAPE TOGETHER, YOU AND I... HIDE ME OUT IN THE MOUNTAINS FOR A YEAR... PLEASE.. LISTEN...
HA HAHA COSMEK ..YOU'RE A FOOL..
DID YOU REALLY THINK YOU COULD PULL OUT ON YOUR PLANET LIKE THIS ?? ..IF I HAD KNOWN HOW WEAK AND EARTHLIKE YOU REALLY ARE, I'D NEVER HAVE RECOMMENDED YOU FOR THE POST! YOU'RE STUPID! BESIDES, WE'D GET YOU, NO MATTER WHERE YOU RAN ON THIS PLANET!
IS THAT THE OTHER AGENT ?
YES, YES... STEP BACK, SPIRIT !!
LISTEN, AGENT 'ONE', I'M NOT AS STUPID AS YOU THINK..
I'M NOT GOING BACK ALIVE...
NOR WILL YOU HAVE THE USE OF THIS LAB...
WE'RE TOO LATE!
DON'T STAND THERE GAWKIN', KLINK.. CALL AN AMBULANCE!
P.D.
POLICE HOSPITAL
YOU MAY SPEAK TO HER NOW, SIR...
NOW..HRMPF... MISS COSMEK... WE KNOW YOU WERE IN CAHOOTS WITH THOSE TWO ROBBERS... BETTER TELL ME THE TRUTH...
I'M AN AGENT FROM MARS.. I'M AN AGENT FROM MARS I TELL YOU...
SHE'S MAD... COMPLETELY OUT OF HER MIND! WELL, THAT'S ONE WAY TO BEAT A MURDER RAP!
SUPPOSE... JUST SUPPOSE I COULD PROVE SHE'S TELLING THE TRUTH ?
TO PROVE IT TO ME, YOU'D HAVE TO DIG UP ANOTHER "AGENT" WHOSE SANITY I COULDN'T QUESTION... HEH HEH... HEY... WHERE YOU GOING ?
..TO DIG UP THE OTHER AGENT!

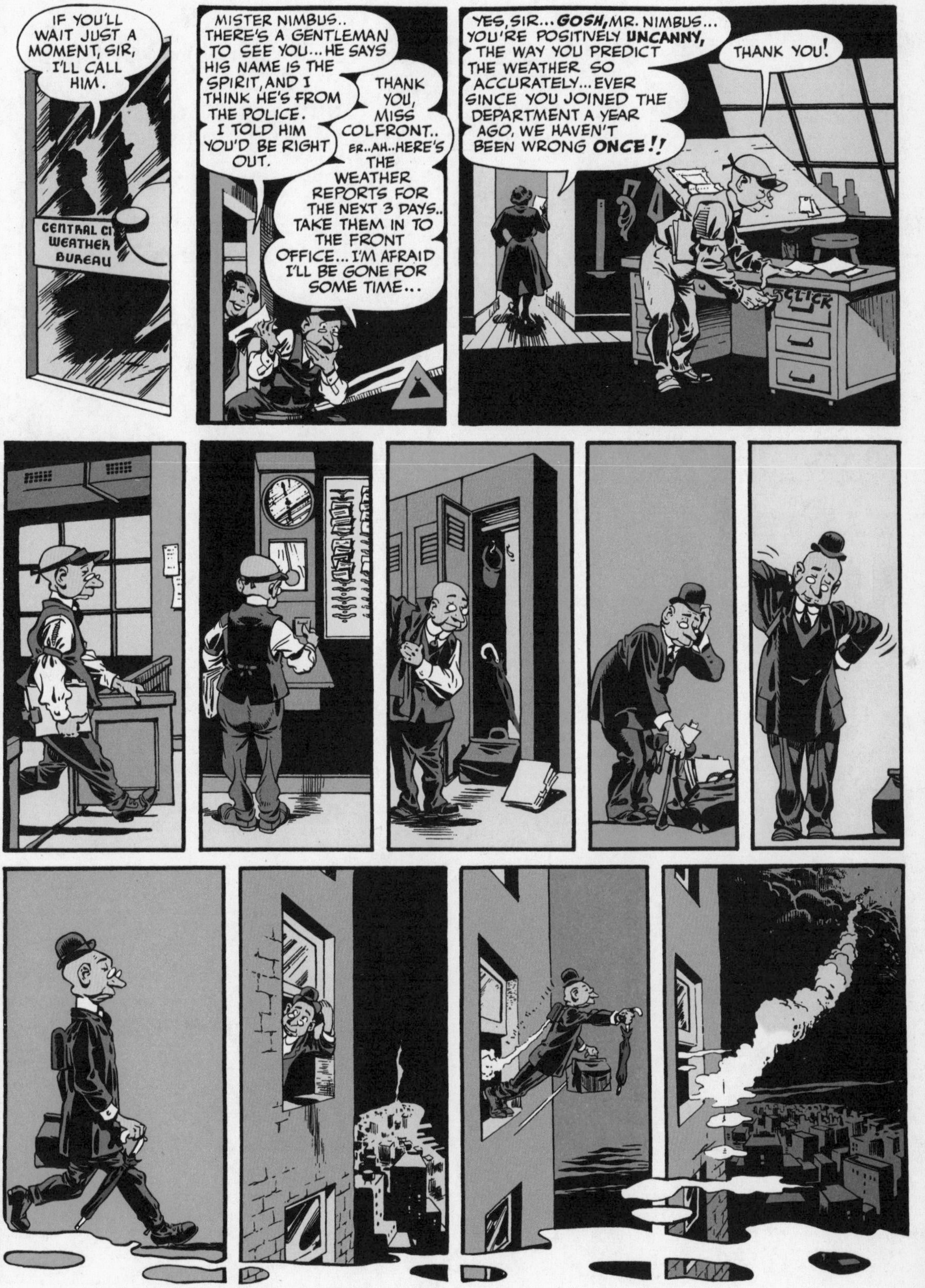

IF YOU'LL WAIT JUST A MOMENT, SIR, I'LL CALL HIM.
CENTRAL CI WEATHER BUREAU
MISTER NIMBUS.. THERE'S A GENTLEMAN TO SEE YOU... HE SAYS HIS NAME IS THE SPIRIT, AND I THINK HE'S FROM THE POLICE. I TOLD HIM YOU'D BE RIGHT OUT.
THANK YOU, MISS COLFRONT.. ER..AH..HERE'S THE WEATHER REPORTS FOR THE NEXT 3 DAYS.. TAKE THEM IN TO THE FRONT OFFICE... I'M AFRAID I'LL BE GONE FOR SOME TIME...
YES, SIR... GOSH, MR. NIMBUS... YOU'RE POSITIVELY UNCANNY, THE WAY YOU PREDICT THE WEATHER SO ACCURATELY... EVER SINCE YOU JOINED THE DEPARTMENT A YEAR AGO, WE HAVEN'T BEEN WRONG ONCE!!
THANK YOU!
CLICK

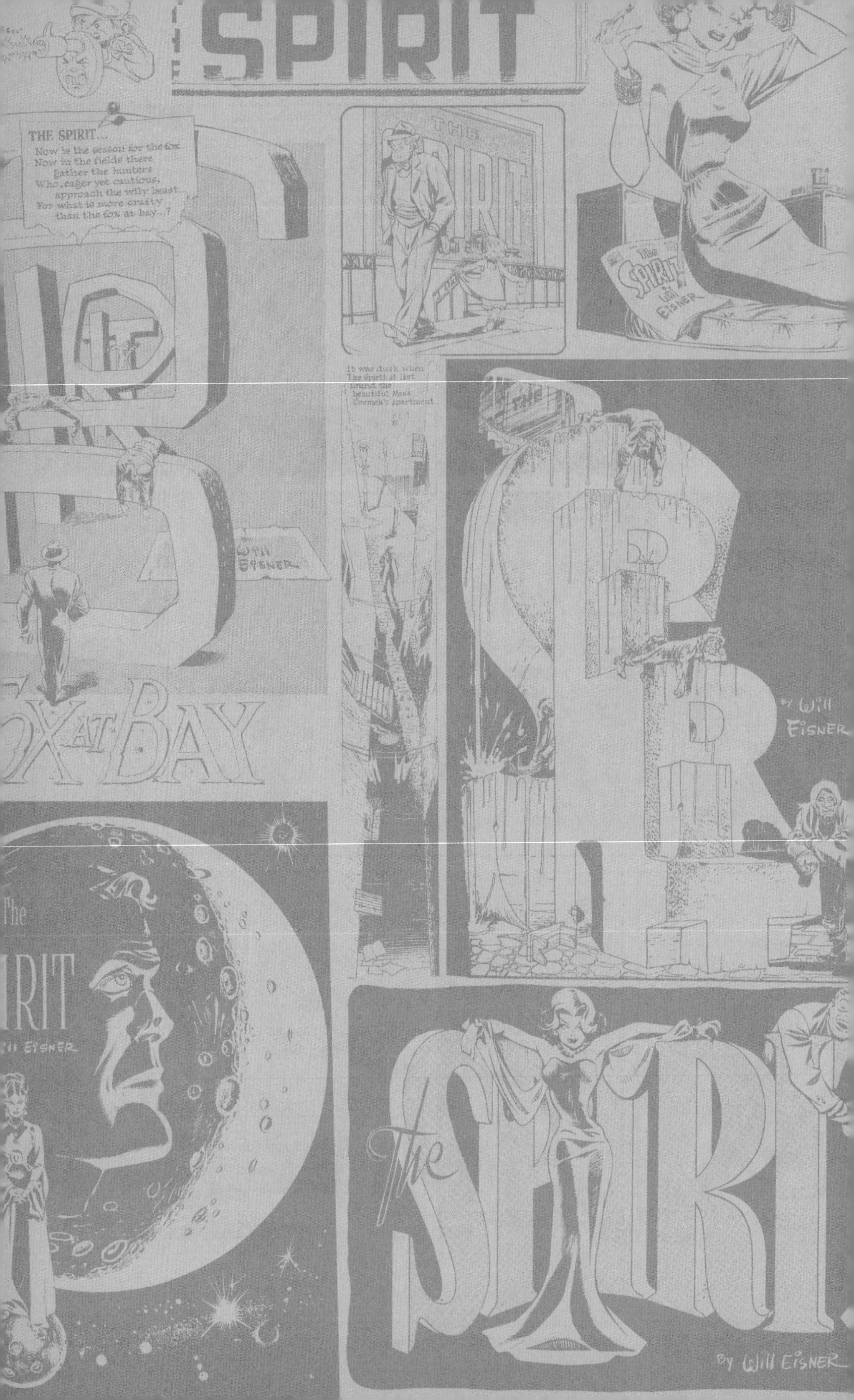
SPIRIT
THE SPIRIT...
Now is the season for the fox.
Now in the fields there gather the hunters
Who, eager yet cautious, approach the wily beast...
For what is more crafty than the fox at bay...?
THE SPIRIT
The SPIRIT by WILL EISNER
BY WILL EISNER
AT BAY
It was dusk when The Spirit at last found the beautiful Miss Cosmek's apartment...
THE
BY WILL EISNER
The SPIRIT
WILL EISNER
The SPIRIT
By Will Eisner

Satin

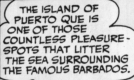

THE ISLAND OF PUERTO QUE IS ONE OF THOSE COUNTLESS PLEASURE-SPOTS THAT LITTER THE SEA SURROUNDING THE FAMOUS BARBADOS.

BARBADOS, YOU'LL REMEMBER, WAS A FAVORITE SPOT FOR BUCCANEERS OF OLD... TODAY, MODERN BUCCANEERS OF COMMERCE TAKE THEIR PLEASURE HERE IN COMFORTABLE MANSIONS.

THE SPIRIT
BY Will Eisner

IT'S SAFE..IN FOREIGN TERRITORY... AND PRYING TOURISTS ARE KEPT AWAY BY THE HURRICANES!

NO...I WAS NOT THINKING OF A VACATION...NOR WAS THERE ANY CHANCE I'D SEE A HURRICANE..UNTIL THE DOOR TO DOLAN'S OFFICE SWUNG OPEN...

..AND SHE STEPPED IN..WINDBLOWN AND BEAUTIFUL..WITH AN AGELESSNESS THAT MADE ME THINK OF SORCERY...

SATIN!

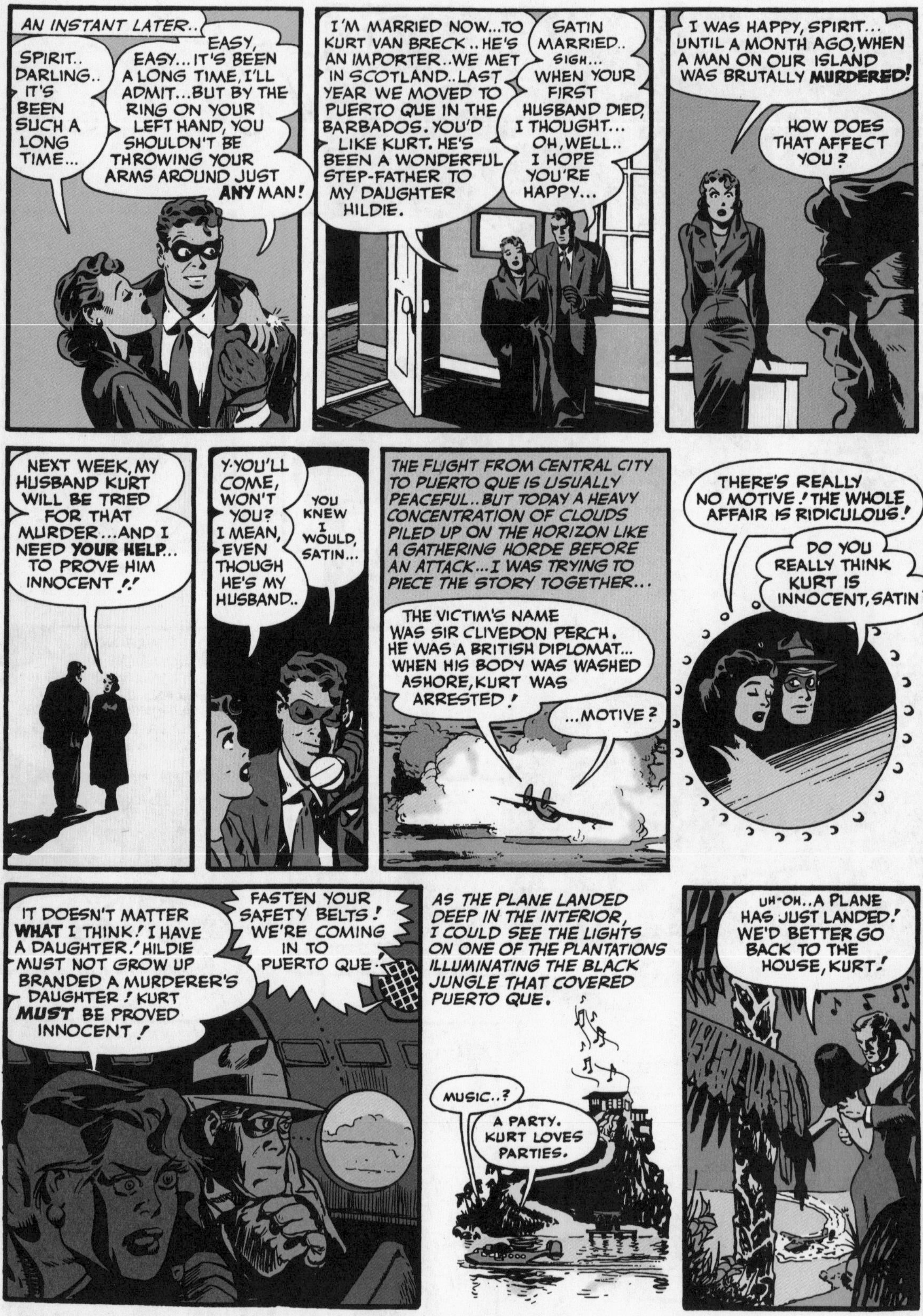
AN INSTANT LATER..
SPIRIT.. DARLING.. IT'S BEEN SUCH A LONG TIME...
EASY, EASY... IT'S BEEN A LONG TIME, I'LL ADMIT...BUT BY THE RING ON YOUR LEFT HAND, YOU SHOULDN'T BE THROWING YOUR ARMS AROUND JUST **ANY** MAN!
I'M MARRIED NOW...TO KURT VAN BRECK.. HE'S AN IMPORTER..WE MET IN SCOTLAND..LAST YEAR WE MOVED TO PUERTO QUE IN THE BARBADOS. YOU'D LIKE KURT. HE'S BEEN A WONDERFUL STEP-FATHER TO MY DAUGHTER HILDIE.
SATIN MARRIED.. SIGH... WHEN YOUR FIRST HUSBAND DIED, I THOUGHT... OH, WELL.. I HOPE YOU'RE HAPPY...
I WAS HAPPY, SPIRIT... UNTIL A MONTH AGO, WHEN A MAN ON OUR ISLAND WAS BRUTALLY **MURDERED!**
HOW DOES THAT AFFECT YOU?
NEXT WEEK, MY HUSBAND KURT WILL BE TRIED FOR THAT MURDER...AND I NEED **YOUR HELP**... TO PROVE HIM INNOCENT !!
Y-YOU'LL COME, WON'T YOU? I MEAN, EVEN THOUGH HE'S MY HUSBAND..
YOU KNEW I WOULD, SATIN...
THE FLIGHT FROM CENTRAL CITY TO PUERTO QUE IS USUALLY PEACEFUL..BUT TODAY A HEAVY CONCENTRATION OF CLOUDS PILED UP ON THE HORIZON LIKE A GATHERING HORDE BEFORE AN ATTACK...I WAS TRYING TO PIECE THE STORY TOGETHER...
THE VICTIM'S NAME WAS SIR CLIVEDON PERCH. HE WAS A BRITISH DIPLOMAT... WHEN HIS BODY WAS WASHED ASHORE, KURT WAS ARRESTED!
...MOTIVE?
THERE'S REALLY NO MOTIVE! THE WHOLE AFFAIR IS RIDICULOUS!
DO YOU REALLY THINK KURT IS INNOCENT, SATIN?
IT DOESN'T MATTER **WHAT** I THINK! I HAVE A DAUGHTER! HILDIE MUST NOT GROW UP BRANDED A MURDERER'S DAUGHTER! KURT ***MUST*** BE PROVED INNOCENT!
FASTEN YOUR SAFETY BELTS! WE'RE COMING IN TO PUERTO QUE!
AS THE PLANE LANDED DEEP IN THE INTERIOR, I COULD SEE THE LIGHTS ON ONE OF THE PLANTATIONS ILLUMINATING THE BLACK JUNGLE THAT COVERED PUERTO QUE.
MUSIC..?
A PARTY. KURT LOVES PARTIES.
UH-OH..A PLANE HAS JUST LANDED! WE'D BETTER GO BACK TO THE HOUSE, KURT!

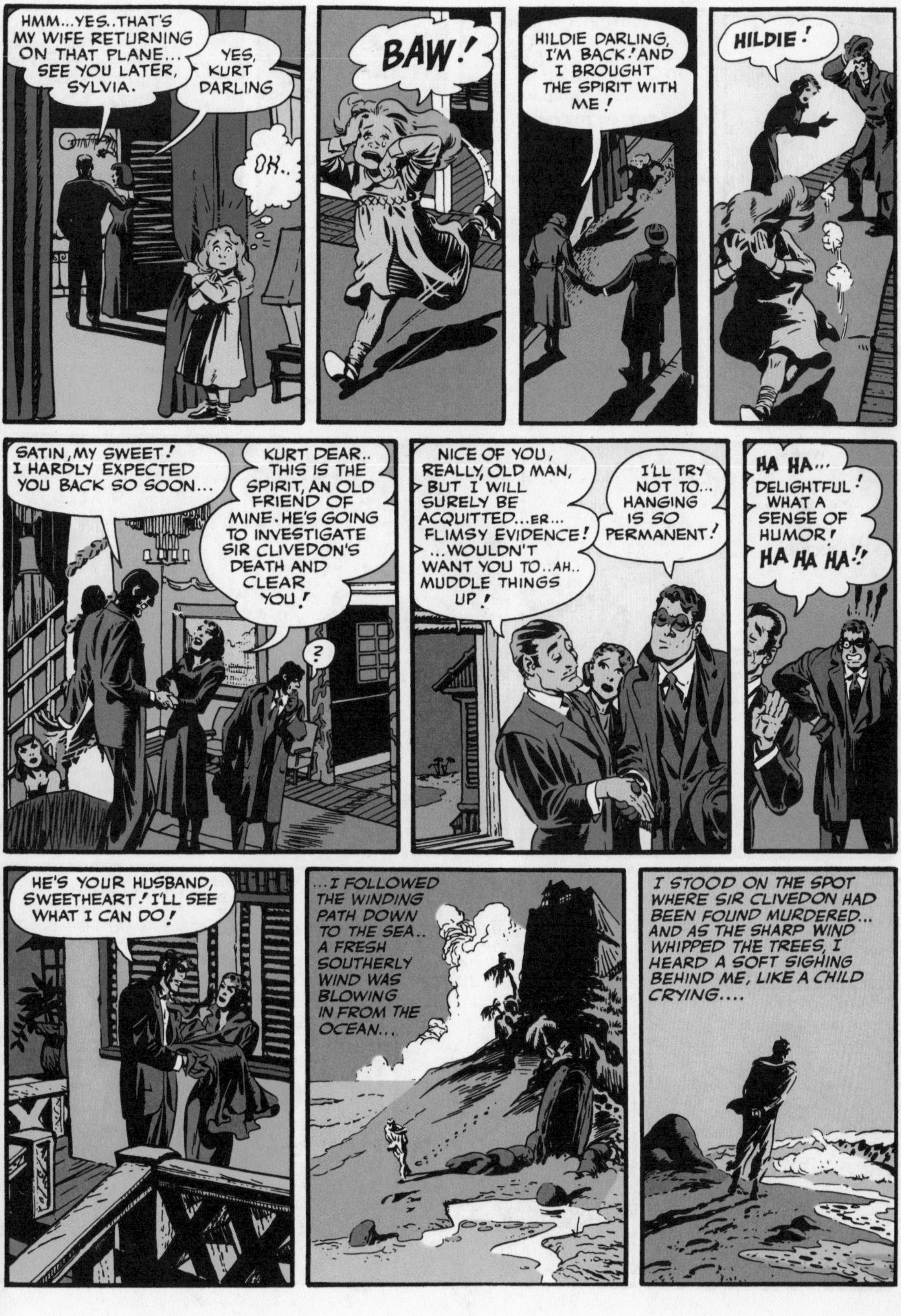
HMM...YES..THAT'S MY WIFE RETURNING ON THAT PLANE... SEE YOU LATER, SYLVIA.
YES, KURT DARLING
OH..
BAW!
HILDIE DARLING, I'M BACK! AND I BROUGHT THE SPIRIT WITH ME!
HILDIE!
SATIN, MY SWEET! I HARDLY EXPECTED YOU BACK SO SOON...
KURT DEAR.. THIS IS THE SPIRIT, AN OLD FRIEND OF MINE. HE'S GOING TO INVESTIGATE SIR CLIVEDON'S DEATH AND CLEAR YOU!
?
NICE OF YOU, REALLY, OLD MAN, BUT I WILL SURELY BE ACQUITTED...ER... FLIMSY EVIDENCE! ...WOULDN'T WANT YOU TO..AH.. MUDDLE THINGS UP!
I'LL TRY NOT TO... HANGING IS SO PERMANENT!
HA HA... DELIGHTFUL! WHAT A SENSE OF HUMOR! HA HA HA!!
HE'S YOUR HUSBAND, SWEETHEART! I'LL SEE WHAT I CAN DO!
...I FOLLOWED THE WINDING PATH DOWN TO THE SEA.. A FRESH SOUTHERLY WIND WAS BLOWING IN FROM THE OCEAN...
I STOOD ON THE SPOT WHERE SIR CLIVEDON HAD BEEN FOUND MURDERED... AND AS THE SHARP WIND WHIPPED THE TREES, I HEARD A SOFT SIGHING BEHIND ME, LIKE A CHILD CRYING....

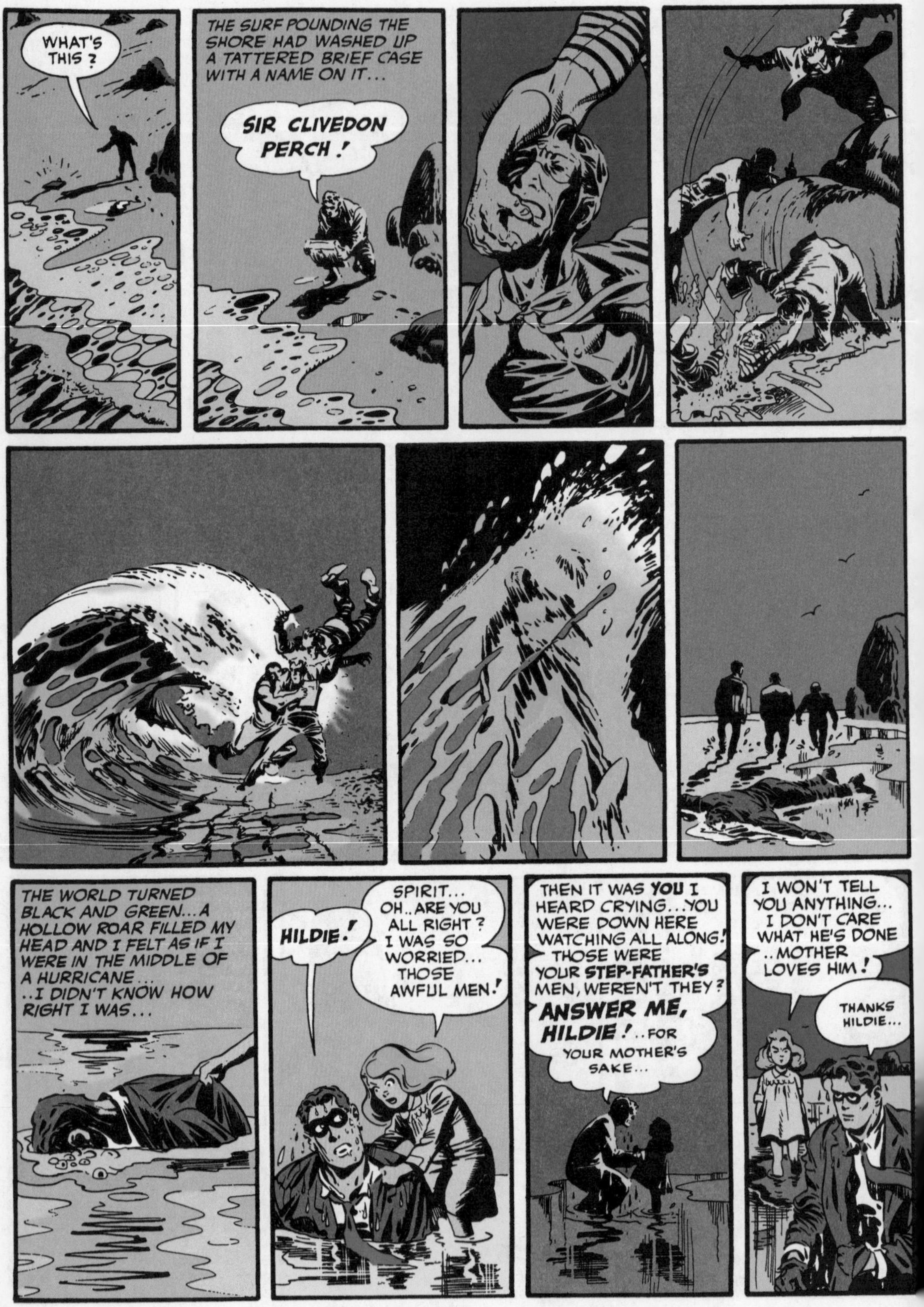
WHAT'S THIS ?
THE SURF POUNDING THE SHORE HAD WASHED UP A TATTERED BRIEF CASE WITH A NAME ON IT...
SIR CLIVEDON PERCH !
THE WORLD TURNED BLACK AND GREEN... A HOLLOW ROAR FILLED MY HEAD AND I FELT AS IF I WERE IN THE MIDDLE OF A HURRICANE... ..I DIDN'T KNOW HOW RIGHT I WAS...
HILDIE !
SPIRIT... OH.. ARE YOU ALL RIGHT ? I WAS SO WORRIED... THOSE AWFUL MEN !
THEN IT WAS YOU I HEARD CRYING... YOU WERE DOWN HERE WATCHING ALL ALONG ! THOSE WERE YOUR STEP-FATHER'S MEN, WEREN'T THEY ?
ANSWER ME, HILDIE ! ..FOR YOUR MOTHER'S SAKE...
I WON'T TELL YOU ANYTHING... I DON'T CARE WHAT HE'S DONE ..MOTHER LOVES HIM !
THANKS HILDIE...

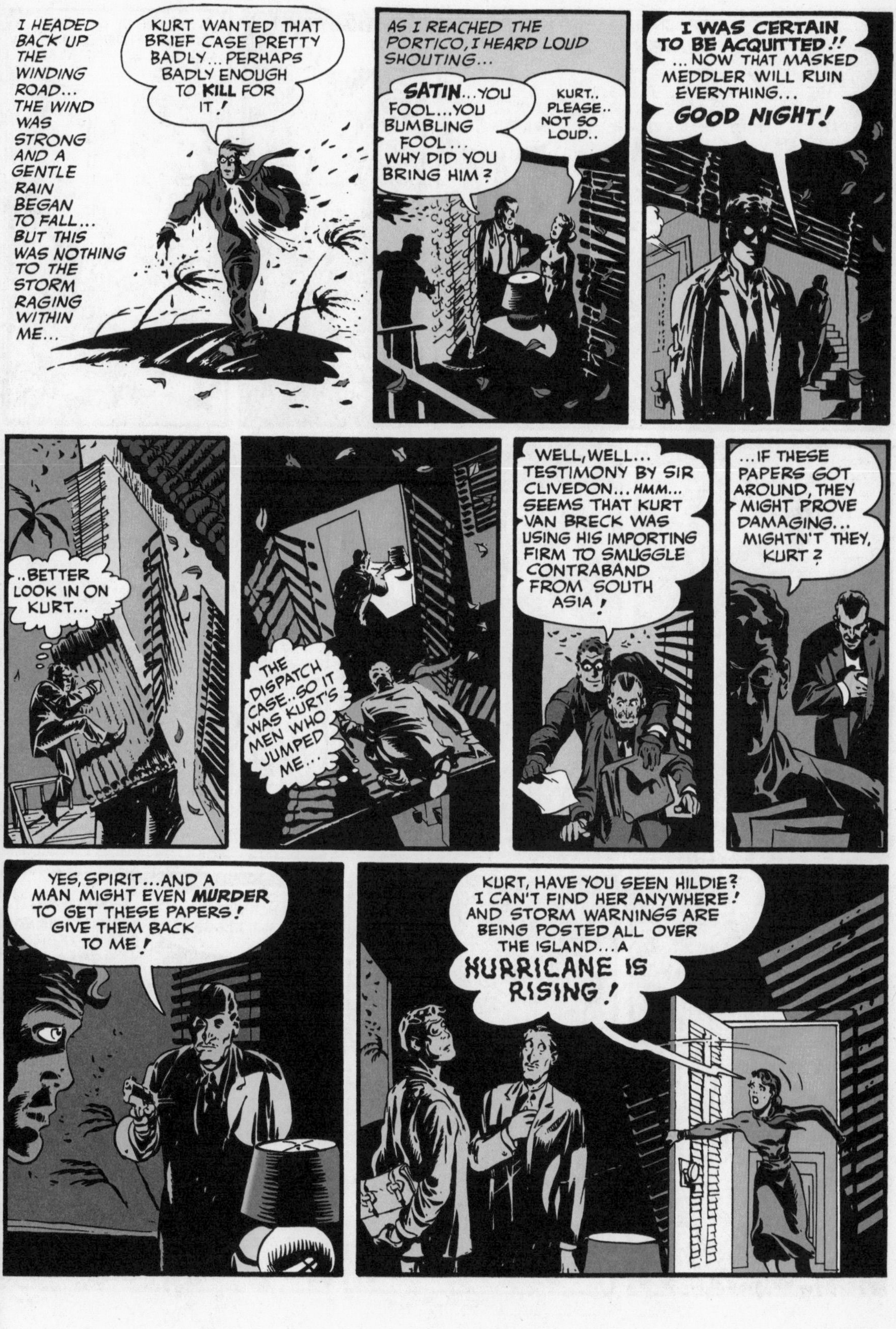
I HEADED BACK UP THE WINDING ROAD... THE WIND WAS STRONG AND A GENTLE RAIN BEGAN TO FALL... BUT THIS WAS NOTHING TO THE STORM RAGING WITHIN ME...
KURT WANTED THAT BRIEF CASE PRETTY BADLY... PERHAPS BADLY ENOUGH TO KILL FOR IT!
AS I REACHED THE PORTICO, I HEARD LOUD SHOUTING...
SATIN... YOU FOOL... YOU BUMBLING FOOL... WHY DID YOU BRING HIM?
KURT.. PLEASE.. NOT SO LOUD..
I WAS CERTAIN TO BE ACQUITTED!! ... NOW THAT MASKED MEDDLER WILL RUIN EVERYTHING... GOOD NIGHT!
..BETTER LOOK IN ON KURT...
THE DISPATCH CASE.. SO IT WAS KURT'S MEN WHO JUMPED ME...
WELL, WELL... TESTIMONY BY SIR CLIVEDON... HMM... SEEMS THAT KURT VAN BRECK WAS USING HIS IMPORTING FIRM TO SMUGGLE CONTRABAND FROM SOUTH ASIA!
...IF THESE PAPERS GOT AROUND, THEY MIGHT PROVE DAMAGING... MIGHTN'T THEY, KURT?
YES, SPIRIT... AND A MAN MIGHT EVEN MURDER TO GET THESE PAPERS! GIVE THEM BACK TO ME!
KURT, HAVE YOU SEEN HILDIE? I CAN'T FIND HER ANYWHERE! AND STORM WARNINGS ARE BEING POSTED ALL OVER THE ISLAND... A HURRICANE IS RISING!

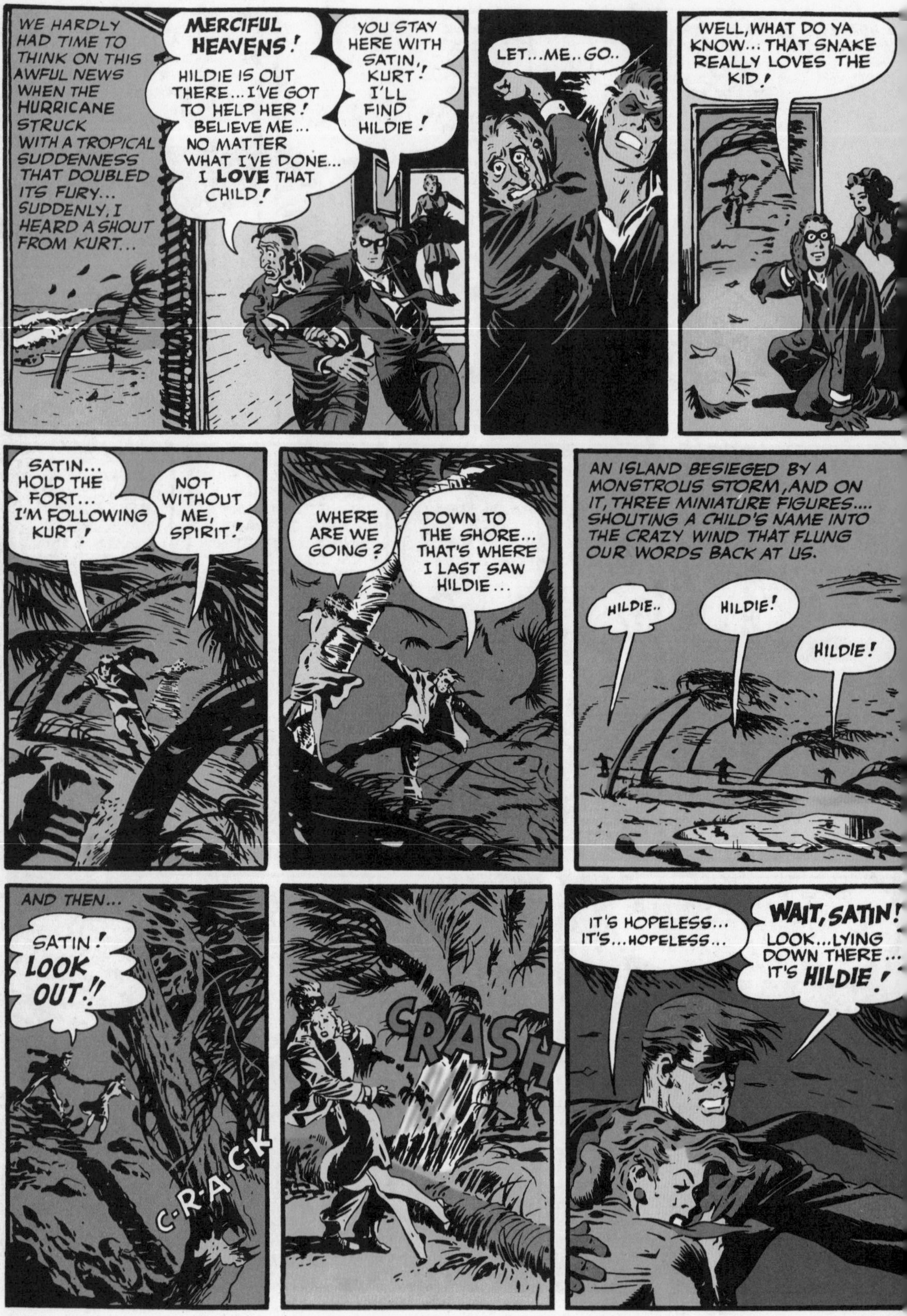
WE HARDLY HAD TIME TO THINK ON THIS AWFUL NEWS WHEN THE HURRICANE STRUCK WITH A TROPICAL SUDDENNESS THAT DOUBLED ITS FURY... SUDDENLY, I HEARD A SHOUT FROM KURT...
MERCIFUL HEAVENS! HILDIE IS OUT THERE... I'VE GOT TO HELP HER! BELIEVE ME... NO MATTER WHAT I'VE DONE... I LOVE THAT CHILD!
YOU STAY HERE WITH SATIN, KURT! I'LL FIND HILDIE!
LET... ME.. GO..
WELL, WHAT DO YA KNOW... THAT SNAKE REALLY LOVES THE KID!
SATIN... HOLD THE FORT... I'M FOLLOWING KURT!
NOT WITHOUT ME, SPIRIT!
WHERE ARE WE GOING?
DOWN TO THE SHORE... THAT'S WHERE I LAST SAW HILDIE...
AN ISLAND BESIEGED BY A MONSTROUS STORM, AND ON IT, THREE MINIATURE FIGURES.... SHOUTING A CHILD'S NAME INTO THE CRAZY WIND THAT FLUNG OUR WORDS BACK AT US.
HILDIE..
HILDIE!
HILDIE!
AND THEN...
SATIN! LOOK OUT!!
C-R-A-C-K
CRASH
IT'S HOPELESS... IT'S... HOPELESS...
WAIT, SATIN! LOOK... LYING DOWN THERE... IT'S HILDIE!

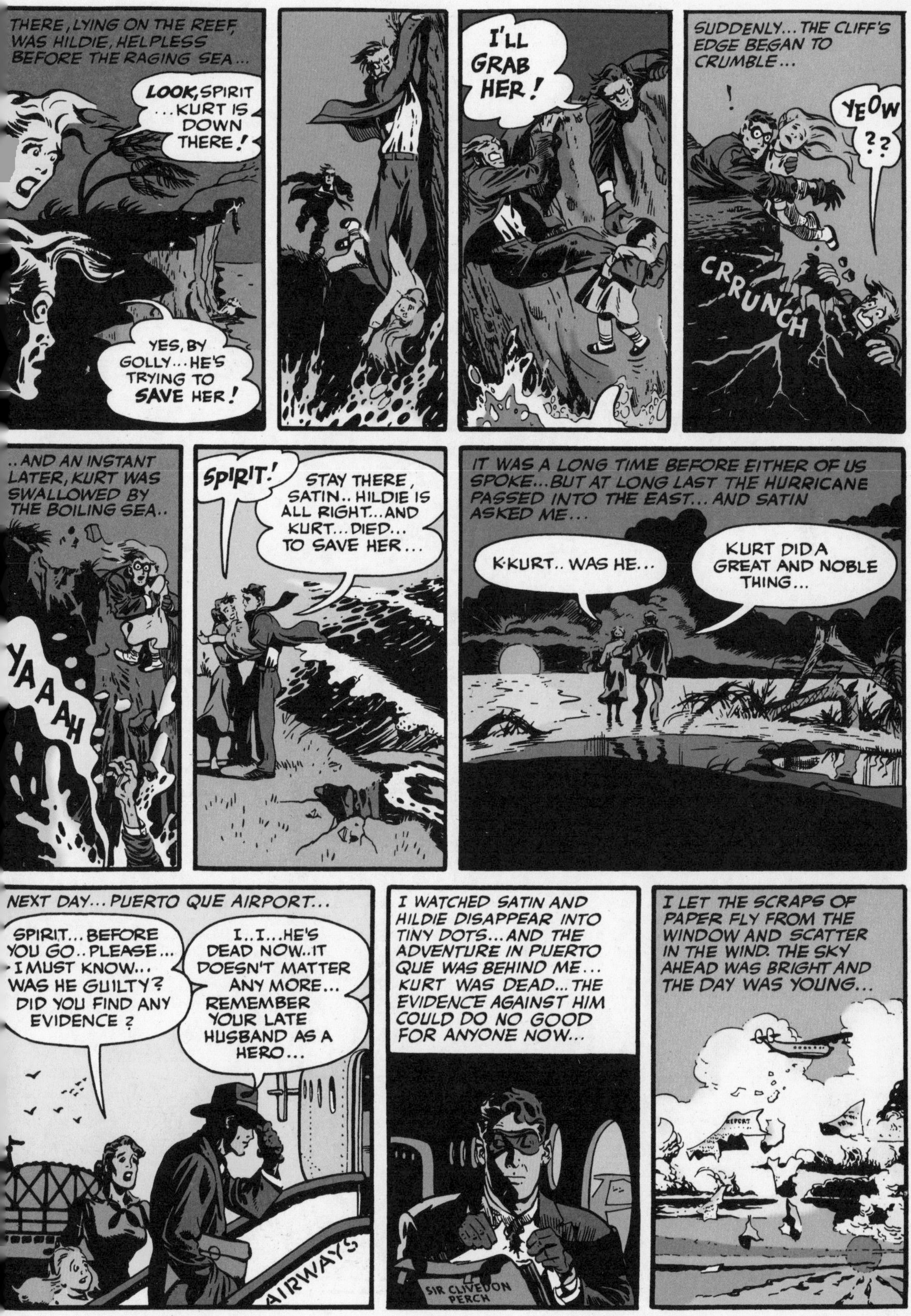
THERE, LYING ON THE REEF, WAS HILDIE, HELPLESS BEFORE THE RAGING SEA...
LOOK, SPIRIT ...KURT IS DOWN THERE!
YES, BY GOLLY...HE'S TRYING TO SAVE HER!
I'LL GRAB HER!
SUDDENLY...THE CLIFF'S EDGE BEGAN TO CRUMBLE...
!
YEOW
??
CRRUNCH
..AND AN INSTANT LATER, KURT WAS SWALLOWED BY THE BOILING SEA..
YAAAAH
SPIRIT!
STAY THERE, SATIN.. HILDIE IS ALL RIGHT...AND KURT...DIED... TO SAVE HER...
IT WAS A LONG TIME BEFORE EITHER OF US SPOKE...BUT AT LONG LAST THE HURRICANE PASSED INTO THE EAST...AND SATIN ASKED ME...
K-KURT.. WAS HE...
KURT DID A GREAT AND NOBLE THING...
NEXT DAY... PUERTO QUE AIRPORT...
SPIRIT... BEFORE YOU GO..PLEASE... I MUST KNOW... WAS HE GUILTY? DID YOU FIND ANY EVIDENCE?
I..I...HE'S DEAD NOW..IT DOESN'T MATTER ANY MORE... REMEMBER YOUR LATE HUSBAND AS A HERO...
AIRWAYS
I WATCHED SATIN AND HILDIE DISAPPEAR INTO TINY DOTS...AND THE ADVENTURE IN PUERTO QUE WAS BEHIND ME... KURT WAS DEAD...THE EVIDENCE AGAINST HIM COULD DO NO GOOD FOR ANYONE NOW...
SIR CLIVEDON PERCH
I LET THE SCRAPS OF PAPER FLY FROM THE WINDOW AND SCATTER IN THE WIND. THE SKY AHEAD WAS BRIGHT AND THE DAY WAS YOUNG...
REPORT

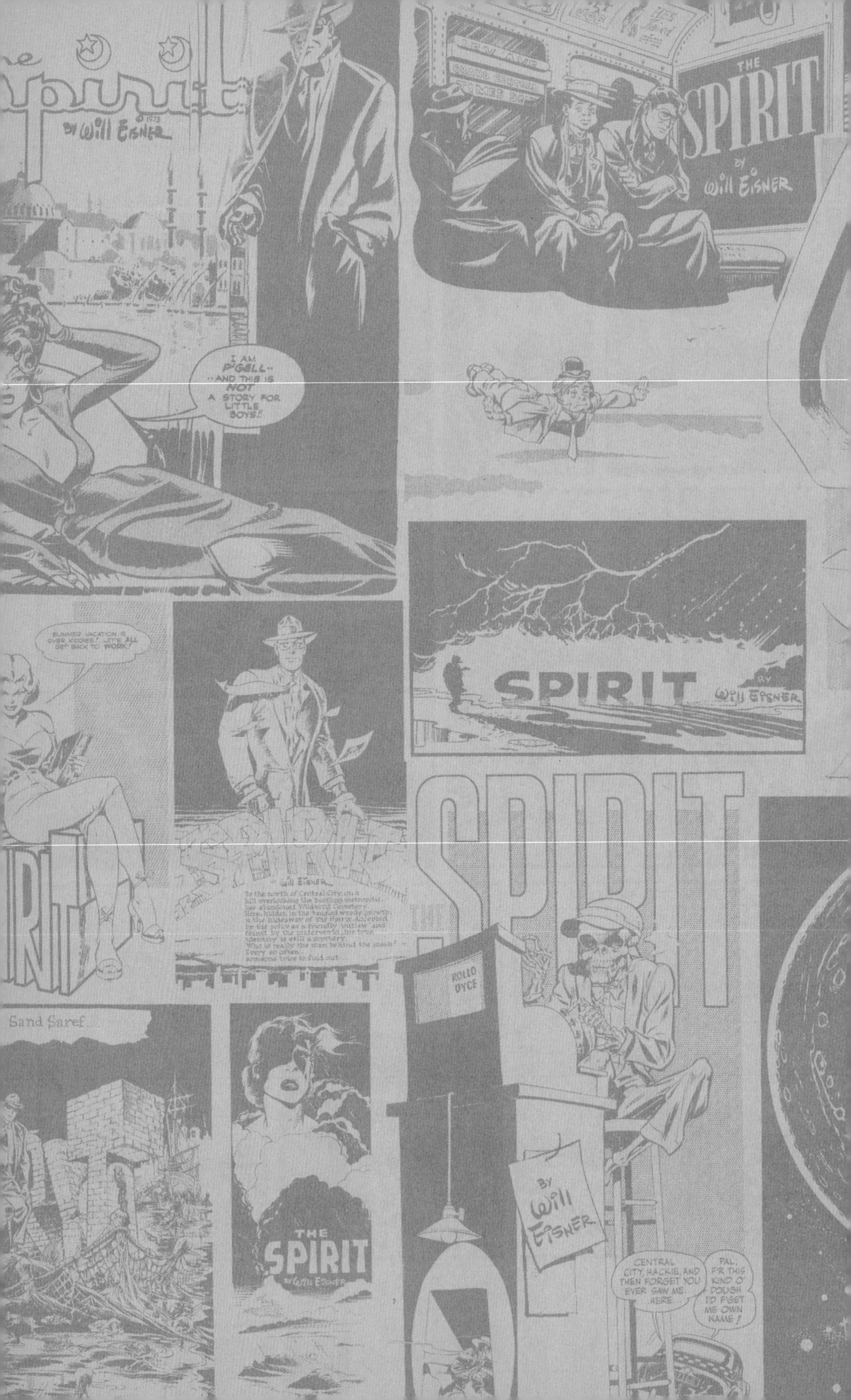

The Spirit
BY Will Eisner
©1973
I AM P'GELL-- ..AND THIS IS NOT A STORY FOR LITTLE BOYS!!
THE SPIRIT
BY Will Eisner
SUMMER VACATION IS OVER KIDDIES! LET'S ALL GET BACK TO WORK!
SPIRIT
BY Will Eisner
THE SPIRIT
Will Eisner
To the north of Central City, on a
hill overlooking the bustling metropolis,
lies abandoned Wildwood Cemetery.
Here, hidden in the tangled weedy growth,
is the hideaway of the Spirit. Accepted
by the police as a friendly 'outlaw' and
feared by the underworld, his true
identity is still a mystery.
Who is really the man behind the mask? —
Every so often,
someone tries to find out...
THE SPIRIT
ROLLO DYCE
BY Will Eisner
Sand Saref...
THE SPIRIT
BY Will Eisner
CENTRAL CITY, HACKIE, AND THEN FORGET YOU EVER SAW ME. HERE
PAL, F'R THIS KIND O' DOUGH I'D F'GET ME OWN NAME!

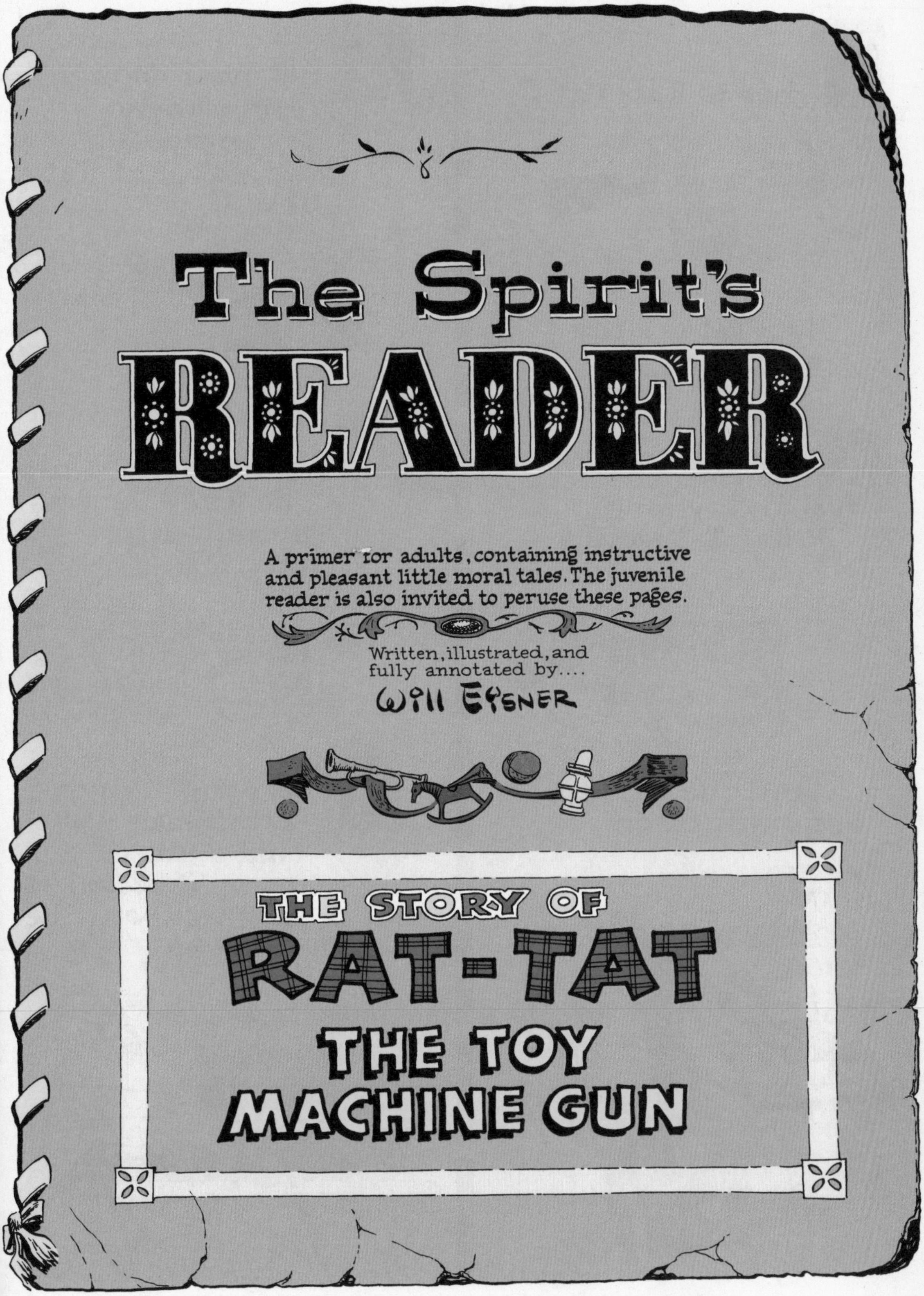
The Spirit's
READER
A primer for adults, containing instructive and pleasant little moral tales. The juvenile reader is also invited to peruse these pages.
Written, illustrated, and fully annotated by....
Will Eisner
THE STORY OF
RAT-TAT
THE TOY MACHINE GUN

This is Rat-Tat.

Rat-Tat is a toy machine gun.

**A**ll day long Rat-Tat would go...

RAT A TAT
RAT A TAT

... and the little boys would go...

A·A·A·A·A·A
A·A·A·A·A·A·A

TOY DEPT.

UGH... Y'GOT ME!

**A**nd even though everybody pretended he was real, Rat-Tat knew.

**D**eep inside, he knew. He knew he was merely an imitation.

AN ACTOR, THAT'S ALL... A CHEAP HAM ACTOR...

And Rat-Tat's greatest dream was that some day he might become a real deadly weapon, like Max the Chopper.

TOY DEPT. SALE REDUCED

SPORTING ARMS DEPT. SALE

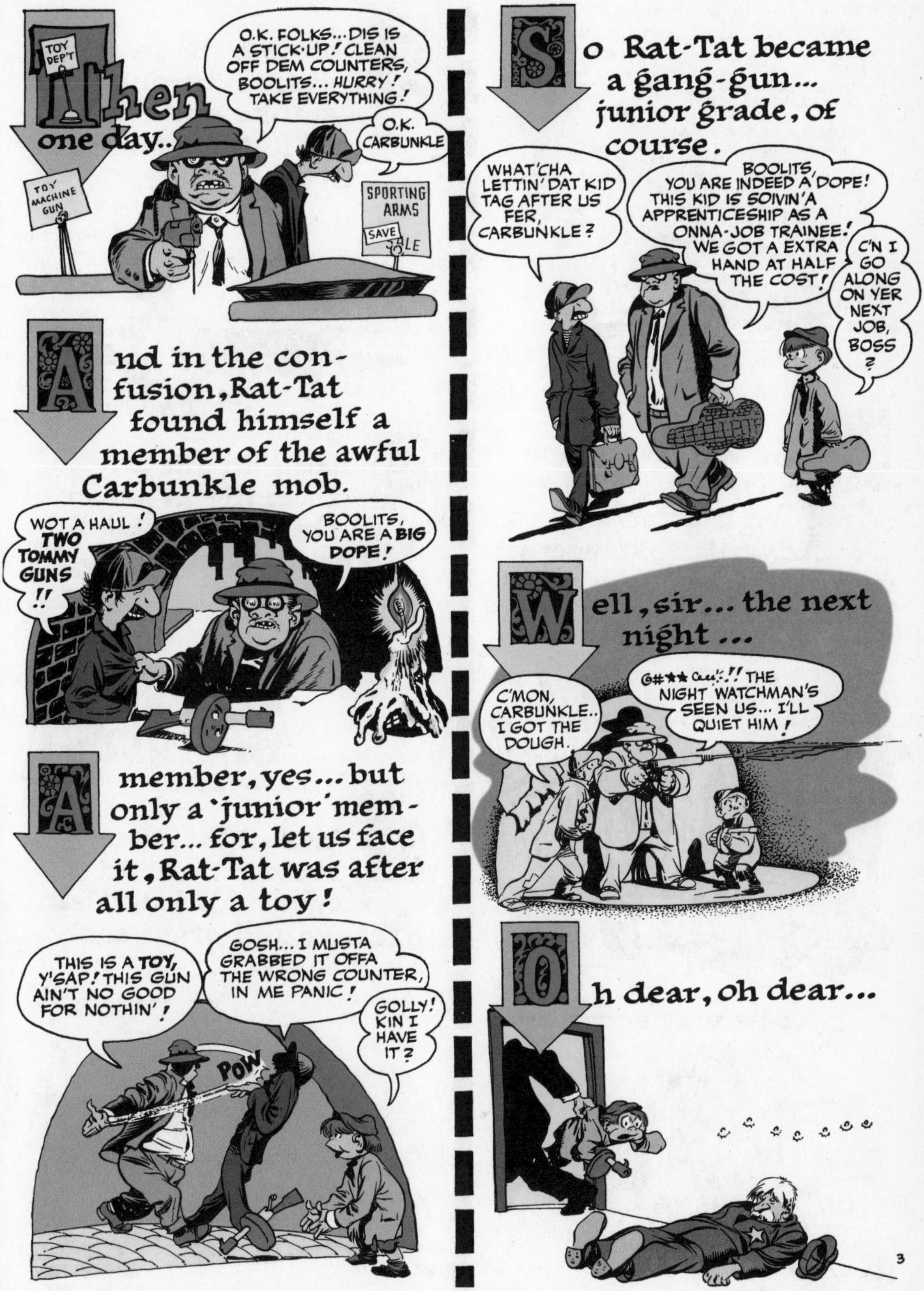
Then one day..
TOY DEPT
O.K. FOLKS... DIS IS A STICK-UP! CLEAN OFF DEM COUNTERS, BOOLITS... HURRY! TAKE EVERYTHING!
O.K. CARBUNKLE
TOY MACHINE GUN
SPORTING ARMS
SAVE
SALE
And in the confusion, Rat-Tat found himself a member of the awful Carbunkle mob.
WOT A HAUL! TWO TOMMY GUNS!!
BOOLITS, YOU ARE A BIG DOPE!
A member, yes... but only a 'junior' member... for, let us face it, Rat-Tat was after all only a toy!
THIS IS A TOY, Y'SAP! THIS GUN AIN'T NO GOOD FOR NOTHIN'!
GOSH... I MUSTA GRABBED IT OFFA THE WRONG COUNTER, IN ME PANIC!
GOLLY! KIN I HAVE IT?
POW
So Rat-Tat became a gang-gun... junior grade, of course.
WHAT'CHA LETTIN' DAT KID TAG AFTER US FER, CARBUNKLE?
BOOLITS, YOU ARE INDEED A DOPE! THIS KID IS SOIVIN'A APPRENTICESHIP AS A ONNA-JOB TRAINEE! WE GOT A EXTRA HAND AT HALF THE COST!
C'N I GO ALONG ON YER NEXT JOB, BOSS?
Well, sir... the next night...
C'MON, CARBUNKLE.. I GOT THE DOUGH.
THE NIGHT WATCHMAN'S SEEN US... I'LL QUIET HIM!
Oh dear, oh dear...
3

CALLING ALL CARS ... CALLING ALL CARS ... BE ON THE LOOKOUT FOR THE CARBUNKLE MOB ... WANTED FOR ROBBING THE 46TH NATIONAL BANK.
POLICE

Now Rat-Tat knew what it meant to be hunted. Adventure, danger... everything he had always longed for was now his.

WE'RE HOT! WE'LL SPLIT UP FER A WEEK AN' MEET AT DE HIDEAWAY!

But he was *scared*!

Through the rain and storm, through the smoke and flame ran Rat-Tat and the little kid.

SOB ... DEY'LL NEVER GIT US!!

Hiding in alleys, cowering in sewers.. this was not at all the kind of life he had expected.

TODAY
THE BIG SHOT

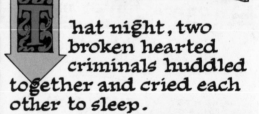

That night, two broken hearted criminals huddled together and cried each other to sleep.

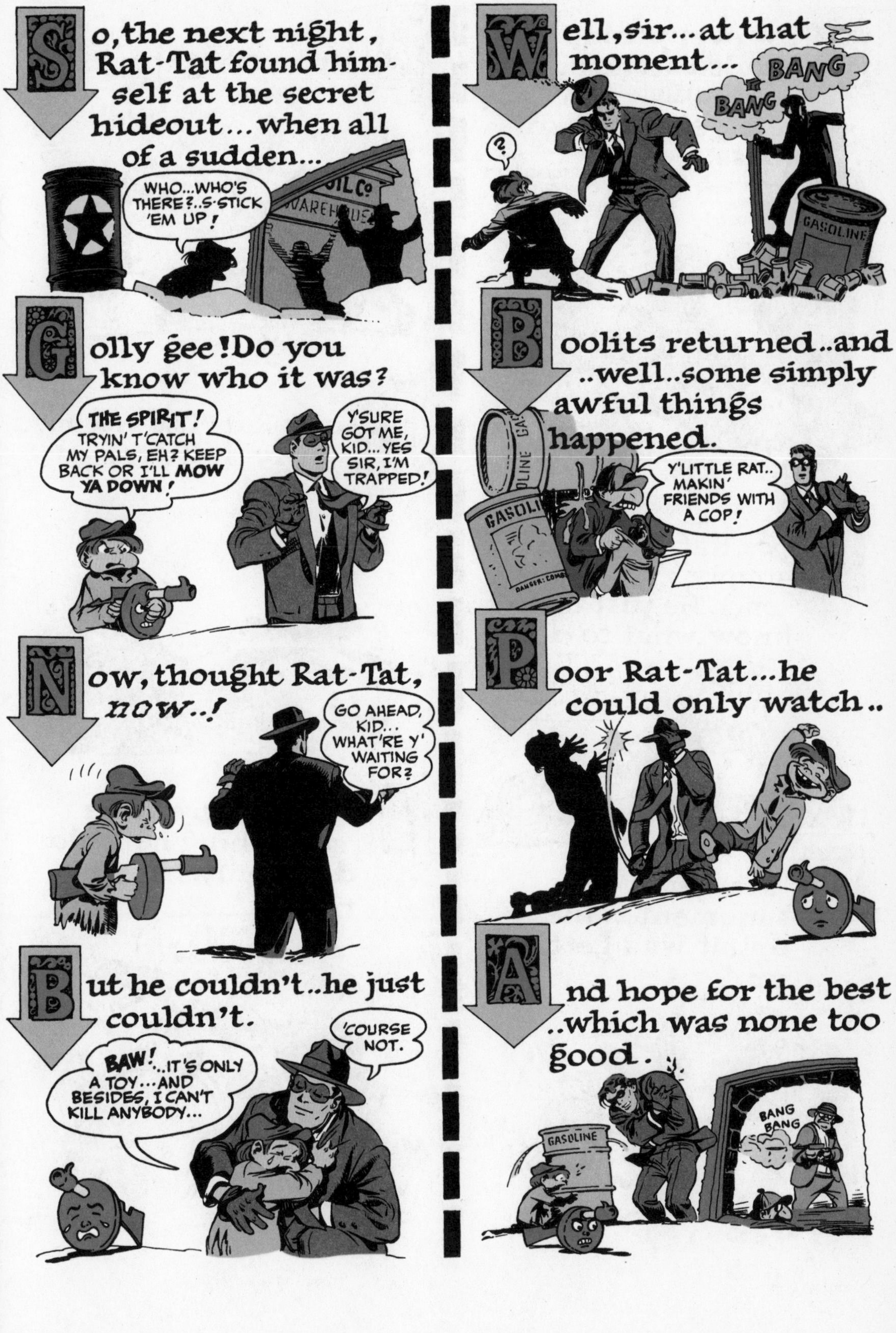
So, the next night, Rat-Tat found himself at the secret hideout... when all of a sudden...
WHO...WHO'S THERE?..S-STICK 'EM UP!
OIL Co
WAREHOUSE
Golly gee! Do you know who it was?
THE SPIRIT! TRYIN' T'CATCH MY PALS, EH? KEEP BACK OR I'LL MOW YA DOWN!
Y'SURE GOT ME, KID... YES SIR, I'M TRAPPED!
Now, thought Rat-Tat, now..!
GO AHEAD, KID... WHAT'RE Y' WAITING FOR?
But he couldn't..he just couldn't.
'COURSE NOT.
BAW!..IT'S ONLY A TOY...AND BESIDES, I CAN'T KILL ANYBODY...
Well, sir... at that moment...
BANG
BANG
?
GASOLINE
Boolits returned..and ..well..some simply awful things happened.
GASOLINE
Y'LITTLE RAT.. MAKIN' FRIENDS WITH A COP!
Poor Rat-Tat... he could only watch..
And hope for the best ..which was none too good.
GASOLINE
BANG BANG

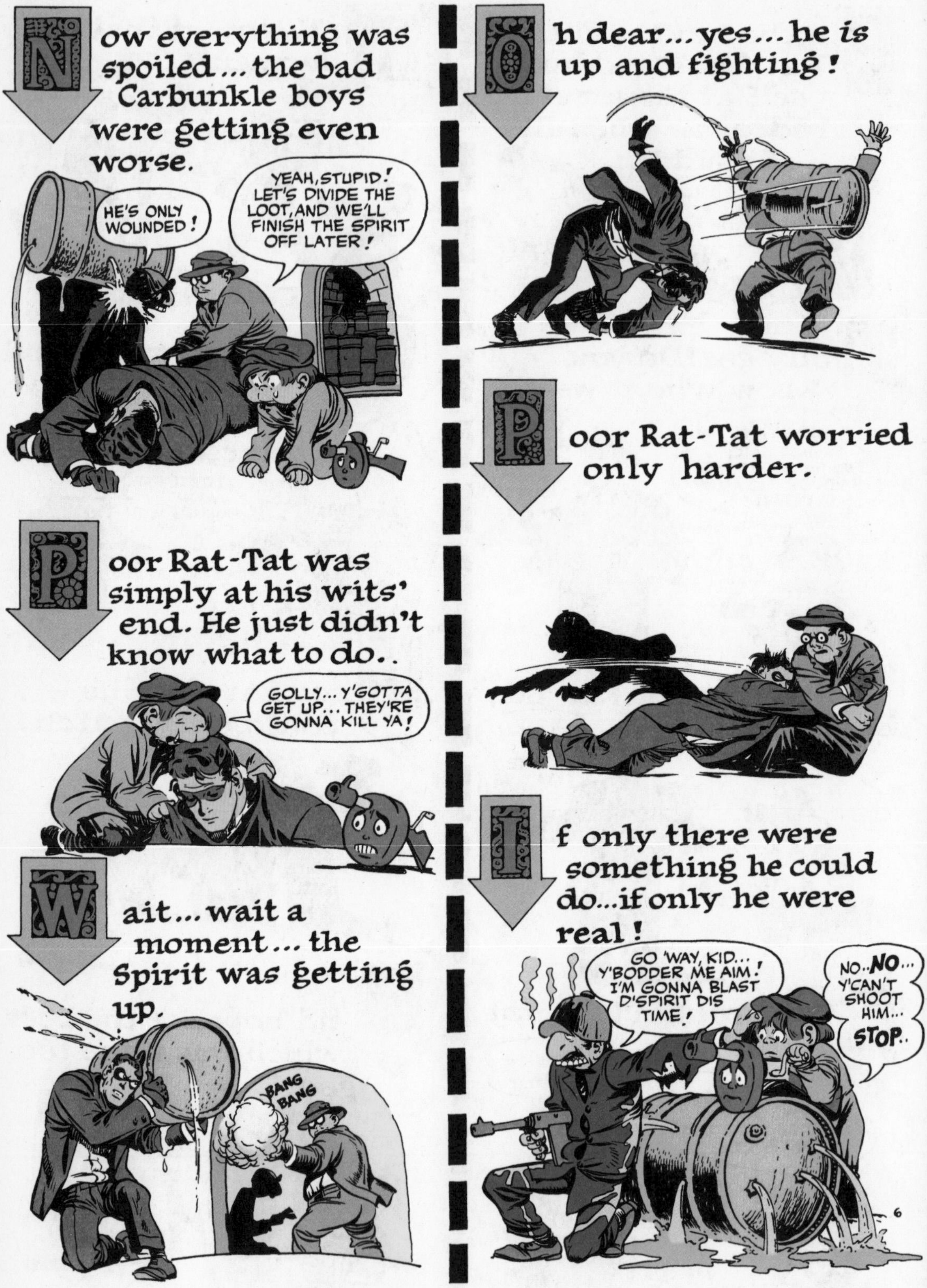
Now everything was spoiled ... the bad Carbunkle boys were getting even worse.
HE'S ONLY WOUNDED!
YEAH, STUPID! LET'S DIVIDE THE LOOT, AND WE'LL FINISH THE SPIRIT OFF LATER!
Poor Rat-Tat was simply at his wits' end. He just didn't know what to do..
GOLLY... Y'GOTTA GET UP... THEY'RE GONNA KILL YA!
Wait... wait a moment ... the Spirit was getting up.
BANG BANG
Oh dear... yes... he is up and fighting!
Poor Rat-Tat worried only harder.
If only there were something he could do...if only he were real!
GO 'WAY, KID... Y'BODDER ME AIM! I'M GONNA BLAST D'SPIRIT DIS TIME!
NO..NO... Y'CAN'T SHOOT HIM... STOP..
6

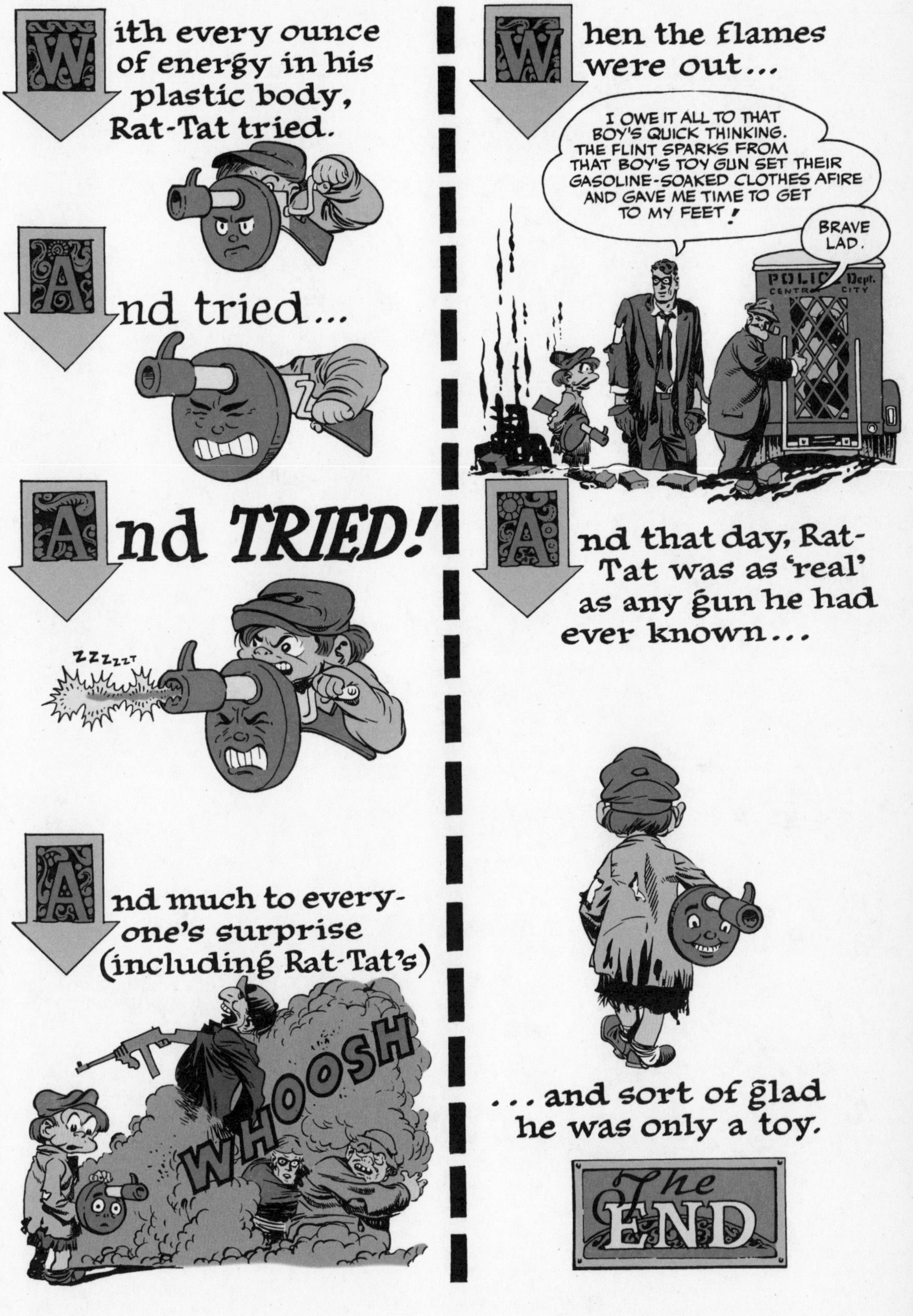
With every ounce of energy in his plastic body, Rat-Tat tried.
And tried...
And TRIED!
ZZZZZT
And much to every-one's surprise (including Rat-Tat's)
WHOOSH
When the flames were out...
I OWE IT ALL TO THAT BOY'S QUICK THINKING. THE FLINT SPARKS FROM THAT BOY'S TOY GUN SET THEIR GASOLINE-SOAKED CLOTHES AFIRE AND GAVE ME TIME TO GET TO MY FEET!
BRAVE LAD.
And that day, Rat-Tat was as 'real' as any gun he had ever known...
...and sort of glad he was only a toy.
The END

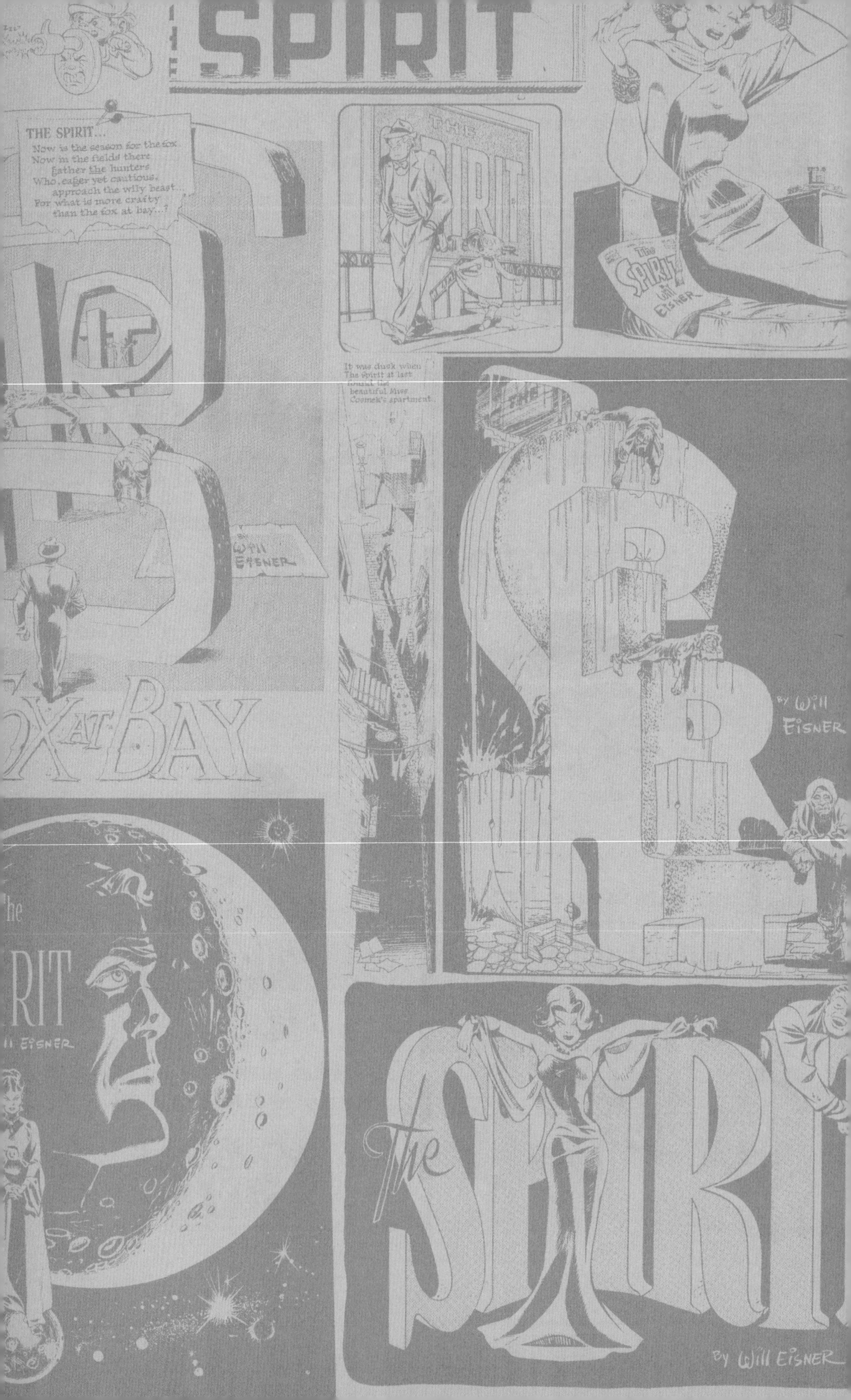
SPIRIT
THE SPIRIT...
Now is the season for the fox
Now in the fields there
gather the hunters
Who, eager yet cautious,
approach the wily beast...
For what is more crafty
than the fox at bay...?
By Will Eisner
The Spirit by Will Eisner
It was dusk when
The Spirit at last
found the
beautiful Miss
Cosmek's apartment...
By Will Eisner
By Will Eisner

The Spirit Section

TICK TICK TICK TEN MINUTES TOCK TOCK TOCK

ACTION Mystery ADVENTURE

It will take you ten minutes to read this story...

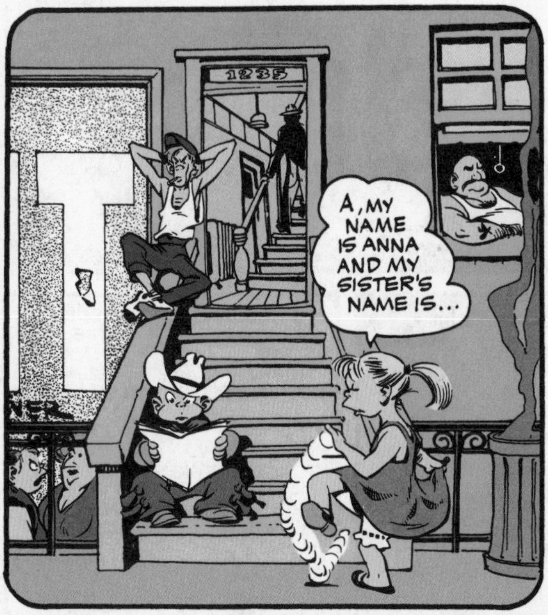
1235
A, MY NAME IS ANNA AND MY SISTER'S NAME IS...

... a very short time in any man's lifetime.

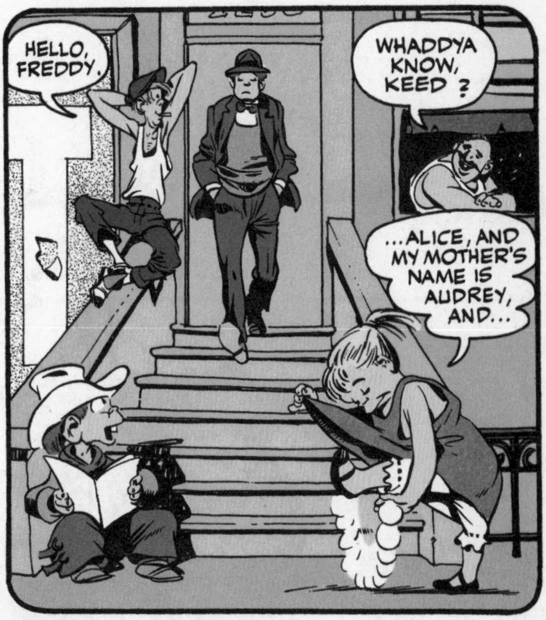
HELLO, FREDDY.
WHADDYA KNOW, KEED ?
...ALICE, AND MY MOTHER'S NAME IS AUDREY, AND...

But these ten minutes that you will spend here are an eternity for one man.

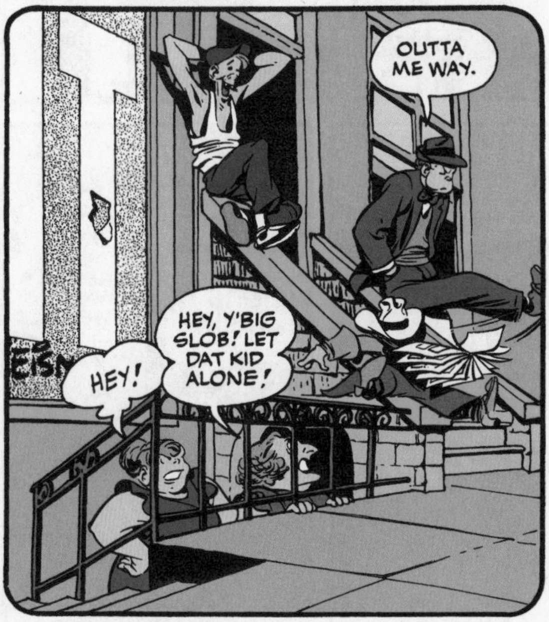
OUTTA ME WAY.
HEY!
HEY, Y'BIG SLOB! LET DAT KID ALONE!

For they are the last ten minutes in Freddy's life.

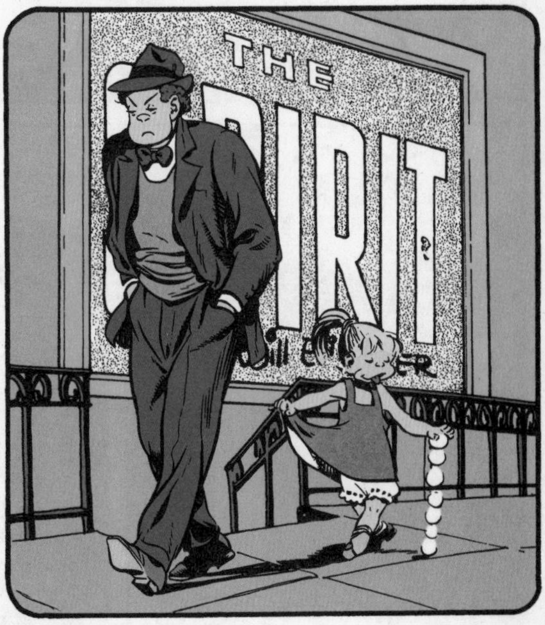
THE SPIRIT

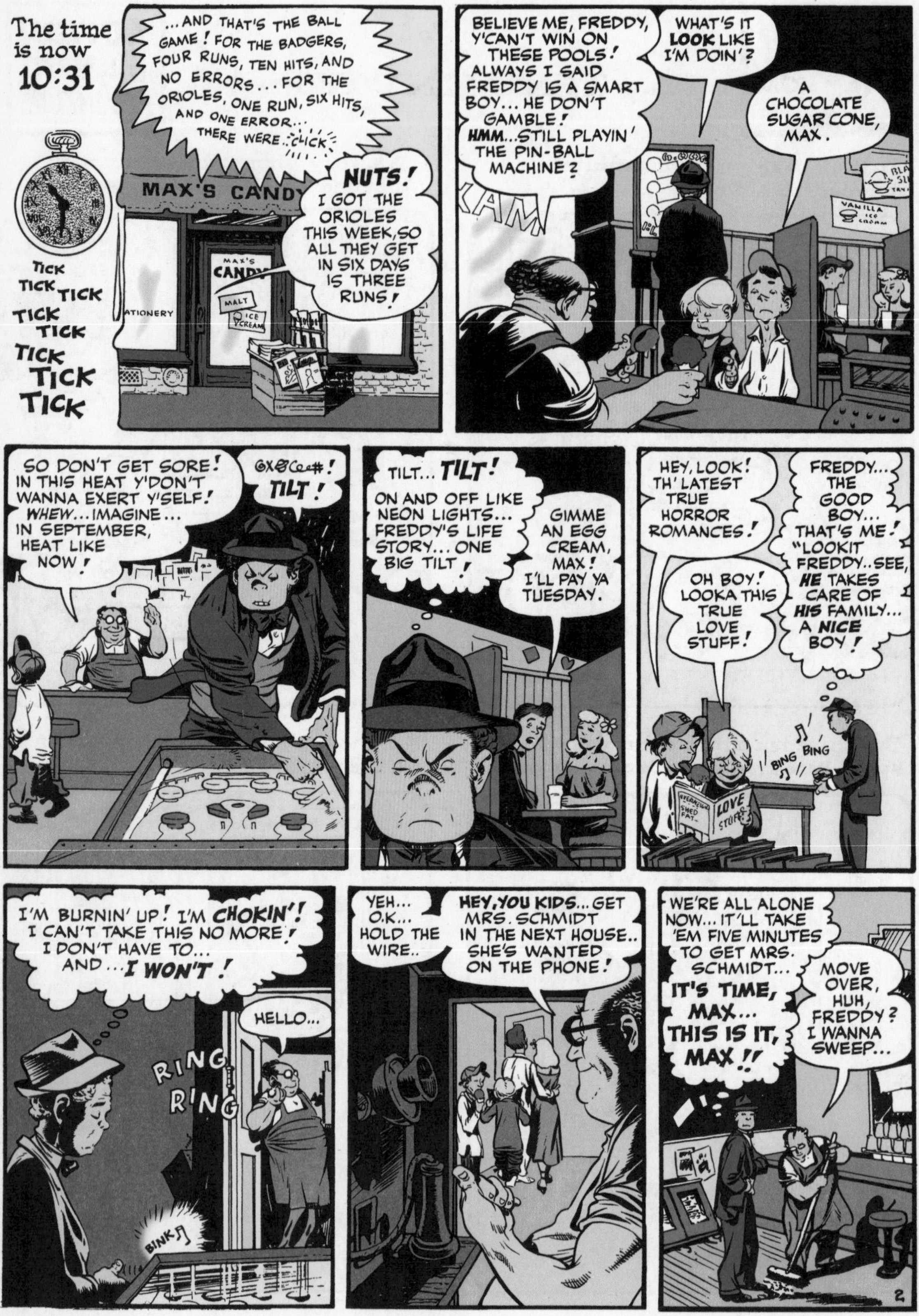
The time is now 10:31
...AND THAT'S THE BALL GAME! FOR THE BADGERS, FOUR RUNS, TEN HITS, AND NO ERRORS... FOR THE ORIOLES, ONE RUN, SIX HITS, AND ONE ERROR... THERE WERE.. CLICK
NUTS! I GOT THE ORIOLES THIS WEEK, SO ALL THEY GET IN SIX DAYS IS THREE RUNS!
TICK TICK TICK TICK TICK TICK TICK TICK
BELIEVE ME, FREDDY, Y'CAN'T WIN ON THESE POOLS! ALWAYS I SAID FREDDY IS A SMART BOY... HE DON'T GAMBLE! HMM...STILL PLAYIN' THE PIN-BALL MACHINE?
WHAT'S IT LOOK LIKE I'M DOIN'?
A CHOCOLATE SUGAR CONE, MAX.
SO DON'T GET SORE! IN THIS HEAT Y'DON'T WANNA EXERT Y'SELF! WHEW...IMAGINE... IN SEPTEMBER, HEAT LIKE NOW!
TILT!
TILT... TILT! ON AND OFF LIKE NEON LIGHTS... FREDDY'S LIFE STORY... ONE BIG TILT!
GIMME AN EGG CREAM, MAX! I'LL PAY YA TUESDAY.
HEY, LOOK! TH' LATEST TRUE HORROR ROMANCES!
OH BOY! LOOKA THIS TRUE LOVE STUFF!
FREDDY... THE GOOD BOY... THAT'S ME! "LOOKIT FREDDY.. SEE, HE TAKES CARE OF HIS FAMILY... A NICE BOY!
BING BING
I'M BURNIN' UP! I'M CHOKIN'! I CAN'T TAKE THIS NO MORE! I DON'T HAVE TO... AND... I WON'T!
RING RING
HELLO...
BINK
YEH... O.K... HOLD THE WIRE..
HEY, YOU KIDS... GET MRS. SCHMIDT IN THE NEXT HOUSE.. SHE'S WANTED ON THE PHONE!
WE'RE ALL ALONE NOW... IT'LL TAKE 'EM FIVE MINUTES TO GET MRS. SCHMIDT... IT'S TIME, MAX... THIS IS IT, MAX!!
MOVE OVER, HUH, FREDDY? I WANNA SWEEP...
2

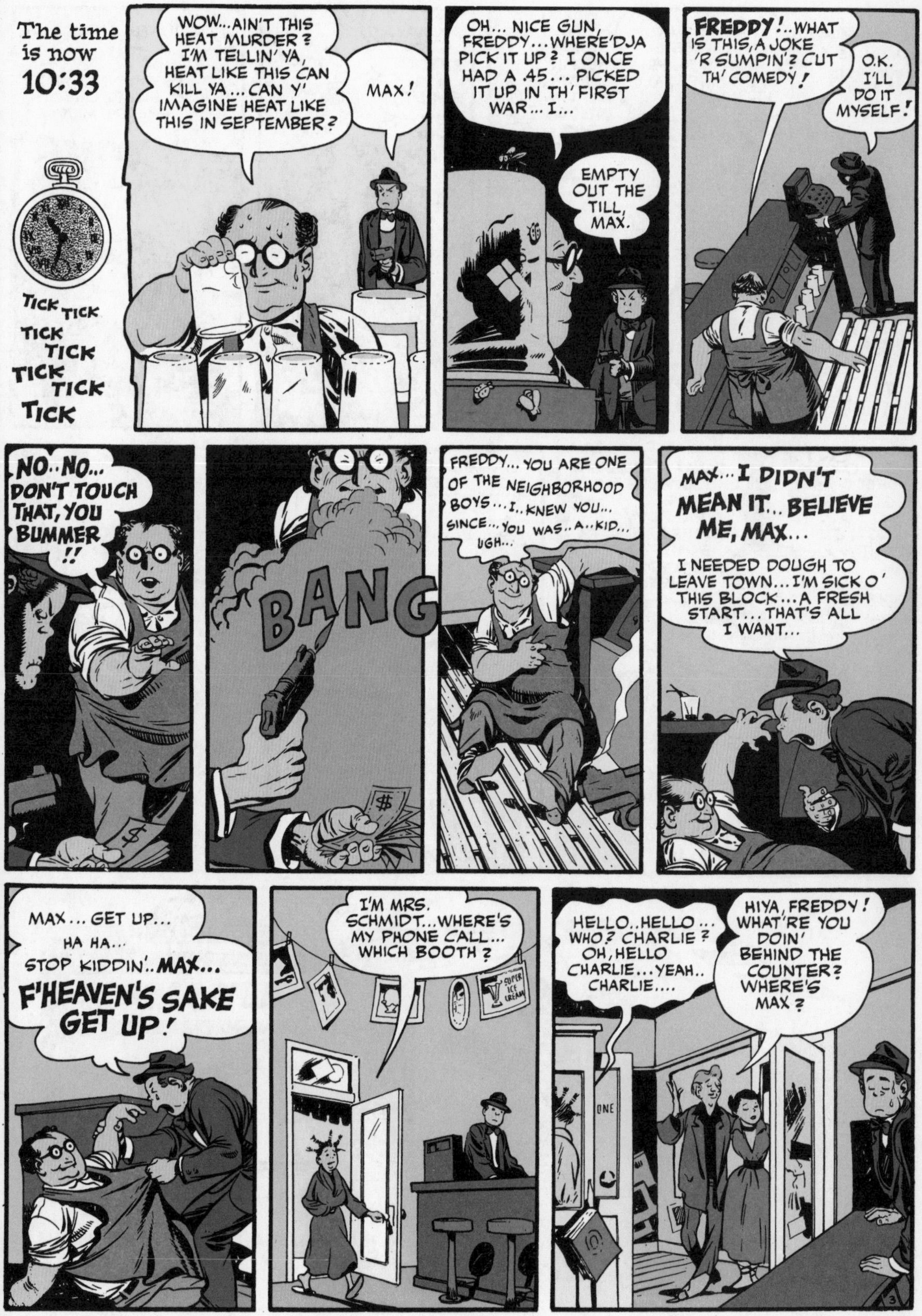
The time is now 10:33
TICK TICK TICK TICK TICK TICK TICK
WOW... AIN'T THIS HEAT MURDER? I'M TELLIN' YA, HEAT LIKE THIS CAN KILL YA... CAN Y' IMAGINE HEAT LIKE THIS IN SEPTEMBER?
MAX!
OH... NICE GUN, FREDDY... WHERE'DJA PICK IT UP? I ONCE HAD A .45... PICKED IT UP IN TH' FIRST WAR... I...
EMPTY OUT THE TILL, MAX.
FREDDY!.. WHAT IS THIS, A JOKE 'R SUMPIN'? CUT TH' COMEDY!
O.K. I'LL DO IT MYSELF!
NO.. NO... DON'T TOUCH THAT, YOU BUMMER!!
BANG
FREDDY... YOU ARE ONE OF THE NEIGHBORHOOD BOYS... I.. KNEW YOU... SINCE... YOU WAS.. A.. KID... UGH...
MAX... I DIDN'T MEAN IT... BELIEVE ME, MAX...
I NEEDED DOUGH TO LEAVE TOWN... I'M SICK O' THIS BLOCK... A FRESH START... THAT'S ALL I WANT...
MAX... GET UP... HA HA... STOP KIDDIN'.. MAX... F'HEAVEN'S SAKE GET UP!
I'M MRS. SCHMIDT... WHERE'S MY PHONE CALL... WHICH BOOTH?
SUPER ICE CREAM
HELLO.. HELLO... WHO? CHARLIE? OH, HELLO CHARLIE... YEAH.. CHARLIE....
HIYA, FREDDY! WHAT'RE YOU DOIN' BEHIND THE COUNTER? WHERE'S MAX?
ONE
3

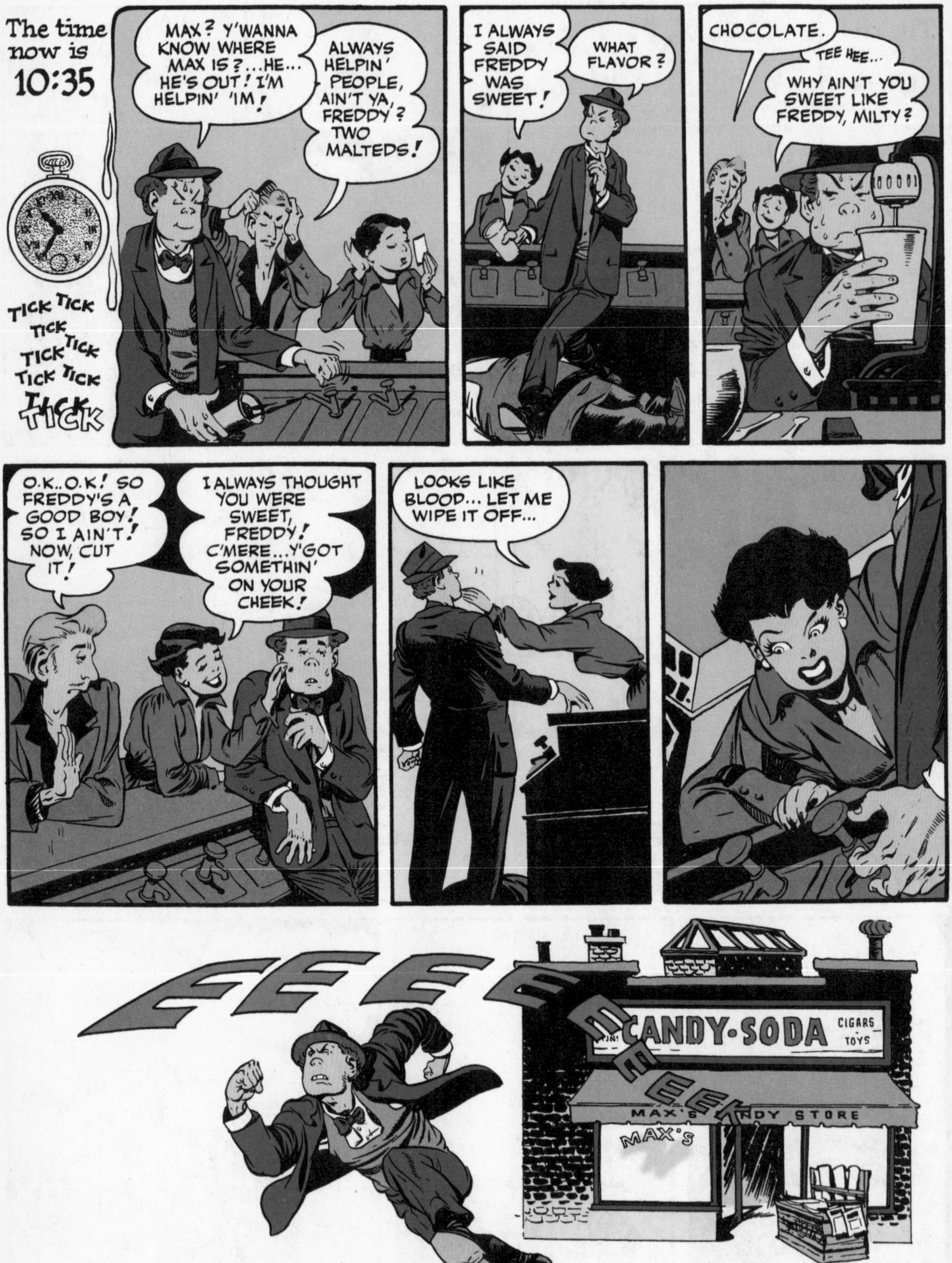
The time now is 10:35
TICK TICK TICK TICK TICK TICK TICK TICK TICK
MAX? Y'WANNA KNOW WHERE MAX IS?...HE... HE'S OUT! I'M HELPIN' 'IM!
ALWAYS HELPIN' PEOPLE, AIN'T YA, FREDDY? TWO MALTEDS!
I ALWAYS SAID FREDDY WAS SWEET!
WHAT FLAVOR?
CHOCOLATE.
TEE HEE...
WHY AIN'T YOU SWEET LIKE FREDDY, MILTY?
O.K..O.K.! SO FREDDY'S A GOOD BOY! SO I AIN'T! NOW, CUT IT!
I ALWAYS THOUGHT YOU WERE SWEET, FREDDY! C'MERE...Y'GOT SOMETHIN' ON YOUR CHEEK!
LOOKS LIKE BLOOD... LET ME WIPE IT OFF...
EEEEEEEEEK
CANDY-SODA
CIGARS
TOYS
MAX'S
MAX'S

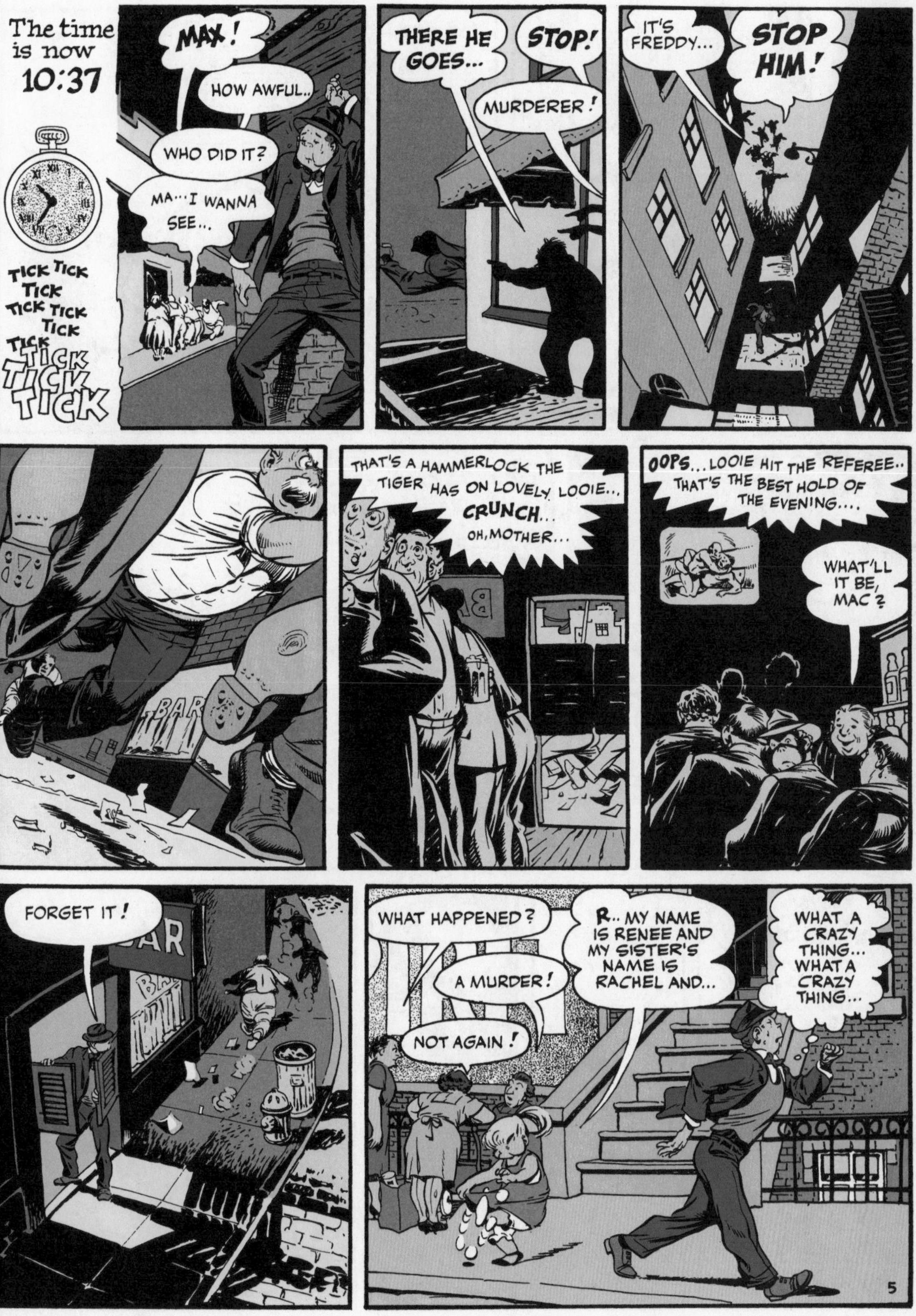
The time is now 10:37
TICK TICK TICK TICK TICK TICK TICK TICK TICK TICK
MAX!
HOW AWFUL..
WHO DID IT?
MA... I WANNA SEE...
THERE HE GOES...
STOP!
MURDERER!
IT'S FREDDY...
STOP HIM!
BAR
THAT'S A HAMMERLOCK THE TIGER HAS ON LOVELY LOOIE... CRUNCH... OH, MOTHER...
OOPS... LOOIE HIT THE REFEREE.. THAT'S THE BEST HOLD OF THE EVENING....
WHAT'LL IT BE, MAC?
FORGET IT!
BAR
WHAT HAPPENED?
A MURDER!
NOT AGAIN!
R.. MY NAME IS RENEE AND MY SISTER'S NAME IS RACHEL AND...
WHAT A CRAZY THING... WHAT A CRAZY THING...
5

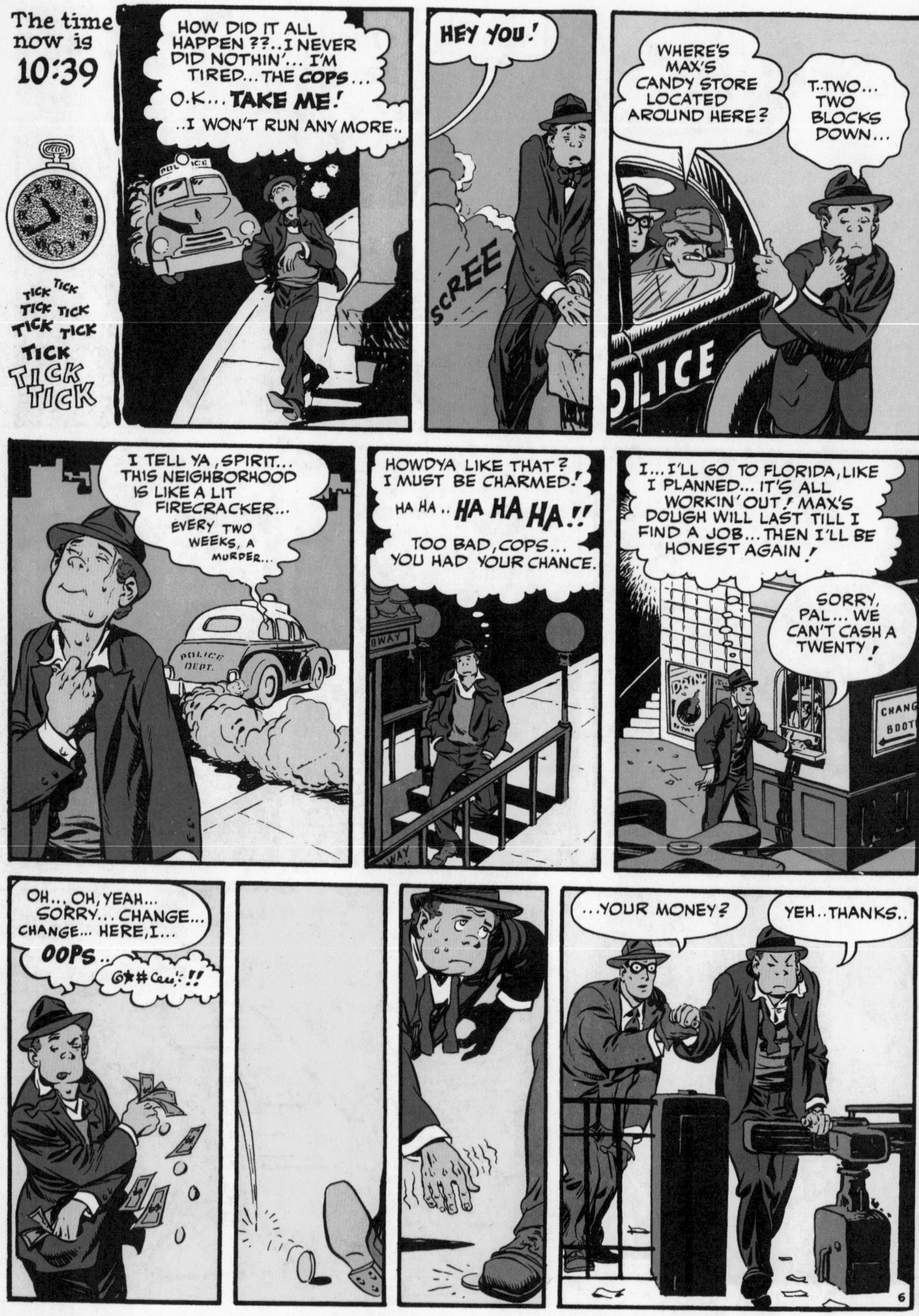

The time now is 10:39
TICK TICK TICK TICK TICK TICK TICK TICK TICK
HOW DID IT ALL HAPPEN ??.. I NEVER DID NOTHIN'... I'M TIRED... THE COPS... O.K... TAKE ME! ..I WON'T RUN ANY MORE..
HEY YOU!
SCREE
WHERE'S MAX'S CANDY STORE LOCATED AROUND HERE?
T..TWO... TWO BLOCKS DOWN...
POLICE
I TELL YA, SPIRIT... THIS NEIGHBORHOOD IS LIKE A LIT FIRECRACKER... EVERY TWO WEEKS, A MURDER...
POLICE DEPT.
HOWDYA LIKE THAT? I MUST BE CHARMED! HA HA.. HA HA HA!! TOO BAD, COPS... YOU HAD YOUR CHANCE.
I... I'LL GO TO FLORIDA, LIKE I PLANNED... IT'S ALL WORKIN' OUT! MAX'S DOUGH WILL LAST TILL I FIND A JOB... THEN I'LL BE HONEST AGAIN!
SORRY, PAL... WE CAN'T CASH A TWENTY!
OH.., OH, YEAH... SORRY... CHANGE... CHANGE... HERE, I... OOPS..
...YOUR MONEY?
YEH.. THANKS..
6

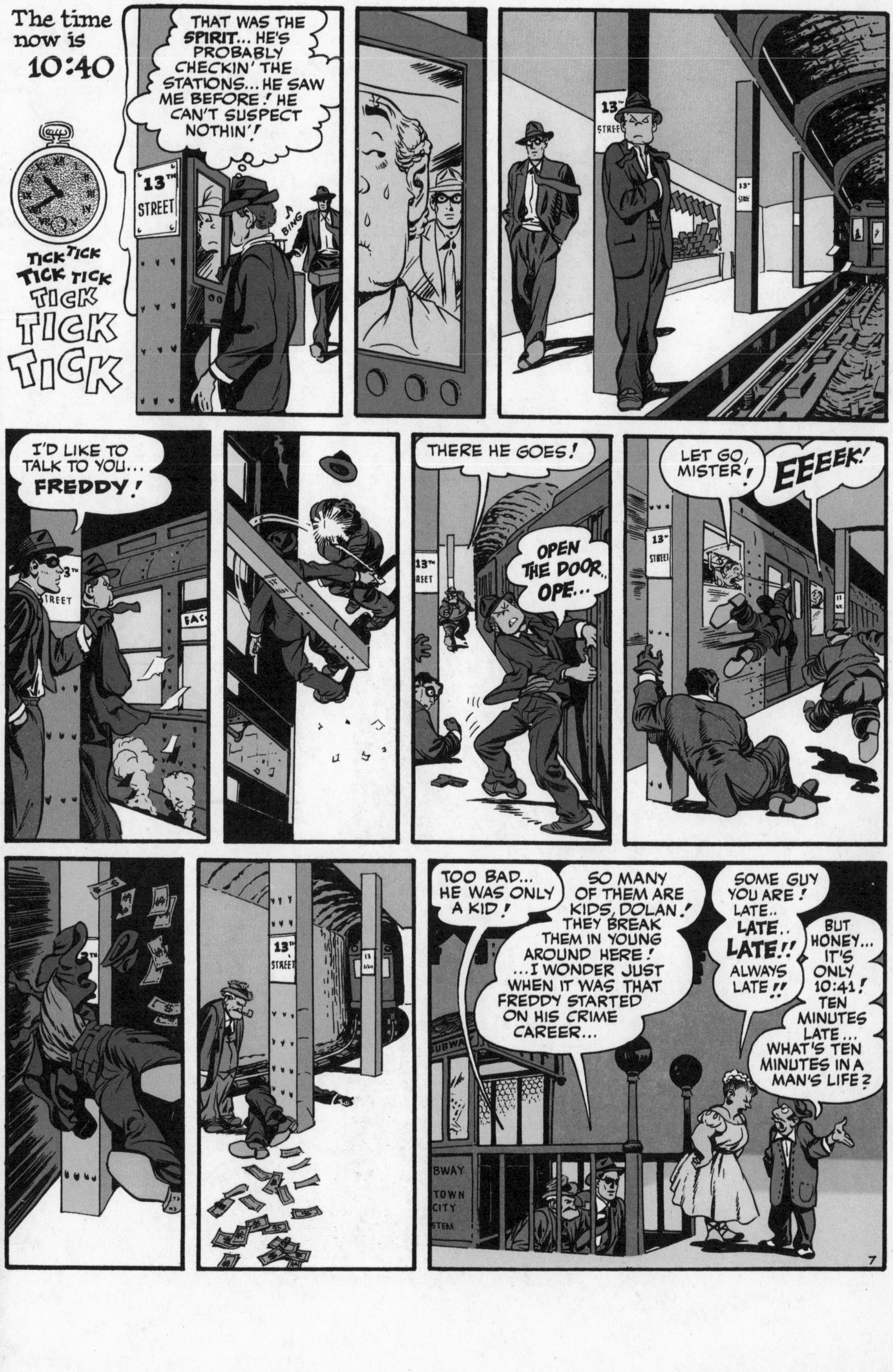
The time now is 10:40
THAT WAS THE SPIRIT... HE'S PROBABLY CHECKIN' THE STATIONS... HE SAW ME BEFORE! HE CAN'T SUSPECT NOTHIN'!
13TH STREET
BING
TICK TICK TICK TICK TICK TICK TICK
13TH STREET
I'D LIKE TO TALK TO YOU... FREDDY!
THERE HE GOES!
OPEN THE DOOR.. OPE...
LET GO, MISTER!
EEEEK!
13TH STREET
TOO BAD... HE WAS ONLY A KID!
SO MANY OF THEM ARE KIDS, DOLAN! THEY BREAK THEM IN YOUNG AROUND HERE! ...I WONDER JUST WHEN IT WAS THAT FREDDY STARTED ON HIS CRIME CAREER...
SOME GUY YOU ARE! LATE.. LATE.. LATE!! ALWAYS LATE!!
BUT HONEY... IT'S ONLY 10:41! TEN MINUTES LATE... WHAT'S TEN MINUTES IN A MAN'S LIFE?
SUBWAY
7

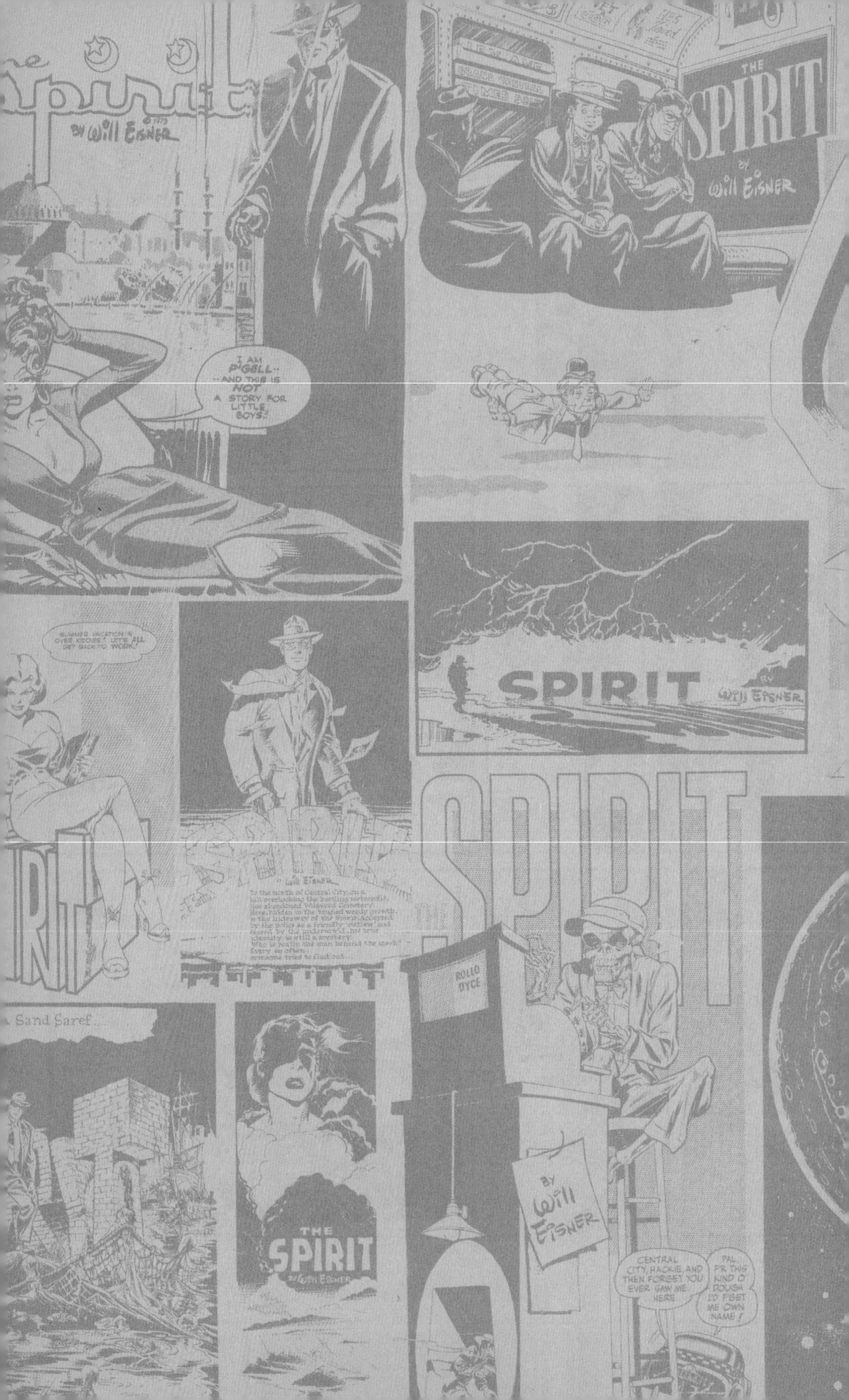

The Spirit
BY Will Eisner © 1973
I AM P'GELL-- ...AND THIS IS NOT A STORY FOR LITTLE BOYS!
THE SPIRIT
BY Will Eisner
SPIRIT
BY Will Eisner
SUMMER VACATION IS OVER KIDDIES! LET'S ALL GET BACK TO WORK!
Will Eisner
To the north of Central City, on a hill overlooking the bustling metropolis, lies abandoned Wildwood Cemetery. Here, hidden in the tangled weedy growth, is the hideaway of the Spirit. Accepted by the police as a friendly 'outlaw' and feared by the underworld, his true identity is still a mystery. Who is really the man behind the mask? Every so often... someone tries to find out...
SPIRIT
ROLLO DYCE
Sand Saref...
THE SPIRIT
BY Will Eisner
BY Will Eisner
CENTRAL CITY, HACKIE, AND THEN FORGET YOU EVER SAW ME HERE
PAL, FR THIS KIND O' DOUGH I'D F'GET ME OWN NAME!

The Spirit Section

DEATH OF AUTUMN MEWS

ACTION Mystery ADVENTURE

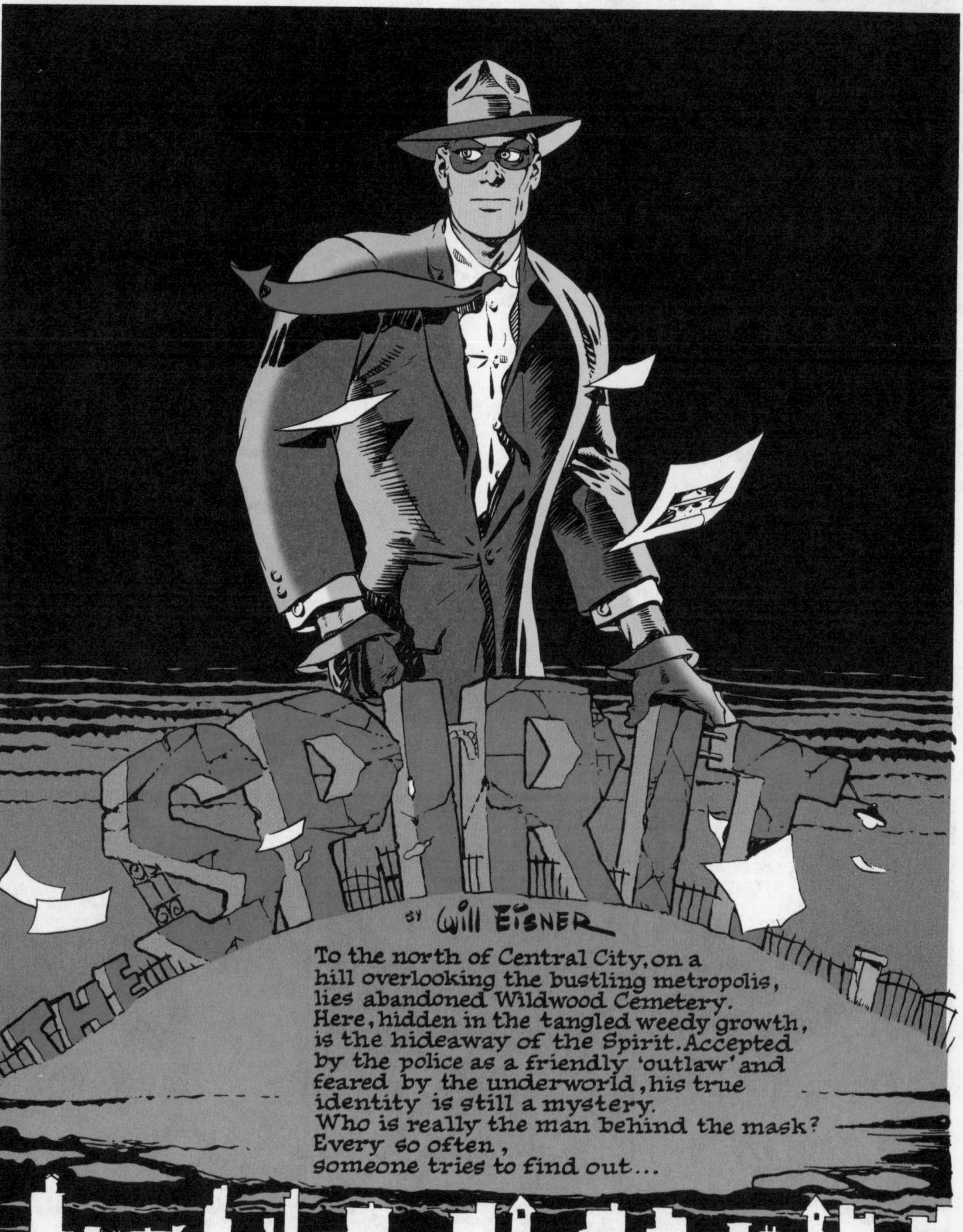

THE SPIRIT
BY WILL EISNER
To the north of Central City, on a hill overlooking the bustling metropolis, lies abandoned Wildwood Cemetery. Here, hidden in the tangled weedy growth, is the hideaway of the Spirit. Accepted by the police as a friendly 'outlaw' and feared by the underworld, his true identity is still a mystery. Who is really the man behind the mask? Every so often, someone tries to find out...

THE SPIRIT! THE SPIRIT! ALWAYS HE LOUSES UP OUR PITCH! LAST WEEK HE CRIBBED OUR CHANCE TO MUSCLE INTO STINGER'S SPOT... NEXT HE'LL BE PUTTIN' THE ARM ON ME FOR THE SECOND-STORY CAPERS I GOT LINED UP... AUTUMN, I AIN'T BEEN HIRED TO JUST BE CHAUFFEUR, Y'KNOW...

EXACTLY WHAT HAVE YOU BEEN THINKING, VIRGIL?

THIS!

YOU'RE A STUPID FOOL! YOU KNOW I WANT NO PART OF MURDER... BESIDES... THE SPIRIT ISN'T ONE TO BE "MUSCLED" OUT...

Y'GOT A BETTER WAY?

I'VE GOT A CLEANER WAY...

AND SO...

WILDWOOD CEMETERY

SIGH...

DENNY COLT 1940

Dear Sammy—
You do not know me, but I have secretly watched your career ever since you joined the Spirit. You're a greater detective than the Spirit ...I need your confidential aid now. I'm in terrible trouble. Meet me at 8:30... Apr. 14 A.. Royal Tow—
— Autumn Mew

WHAT'S THAT, SAMMY?

OH...ER.. NOTHING... JUST A CIRCULAR, SPIRIT...

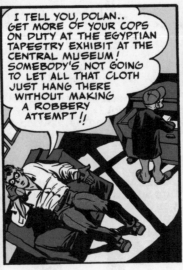

I TELL YOU, DOLAN.. GET MORE OF YOUR COPS ON DUTY AT THE EGYPTIAN TAPESTRY EXHIBIT AT THE CENTRAL MUSEUM! SOMEBODY'S NOT GOING TO LET ALL THAT CLOTH JUST HANG THERE WITHOUT MAKING A ROBBERY ATTEMPT!!

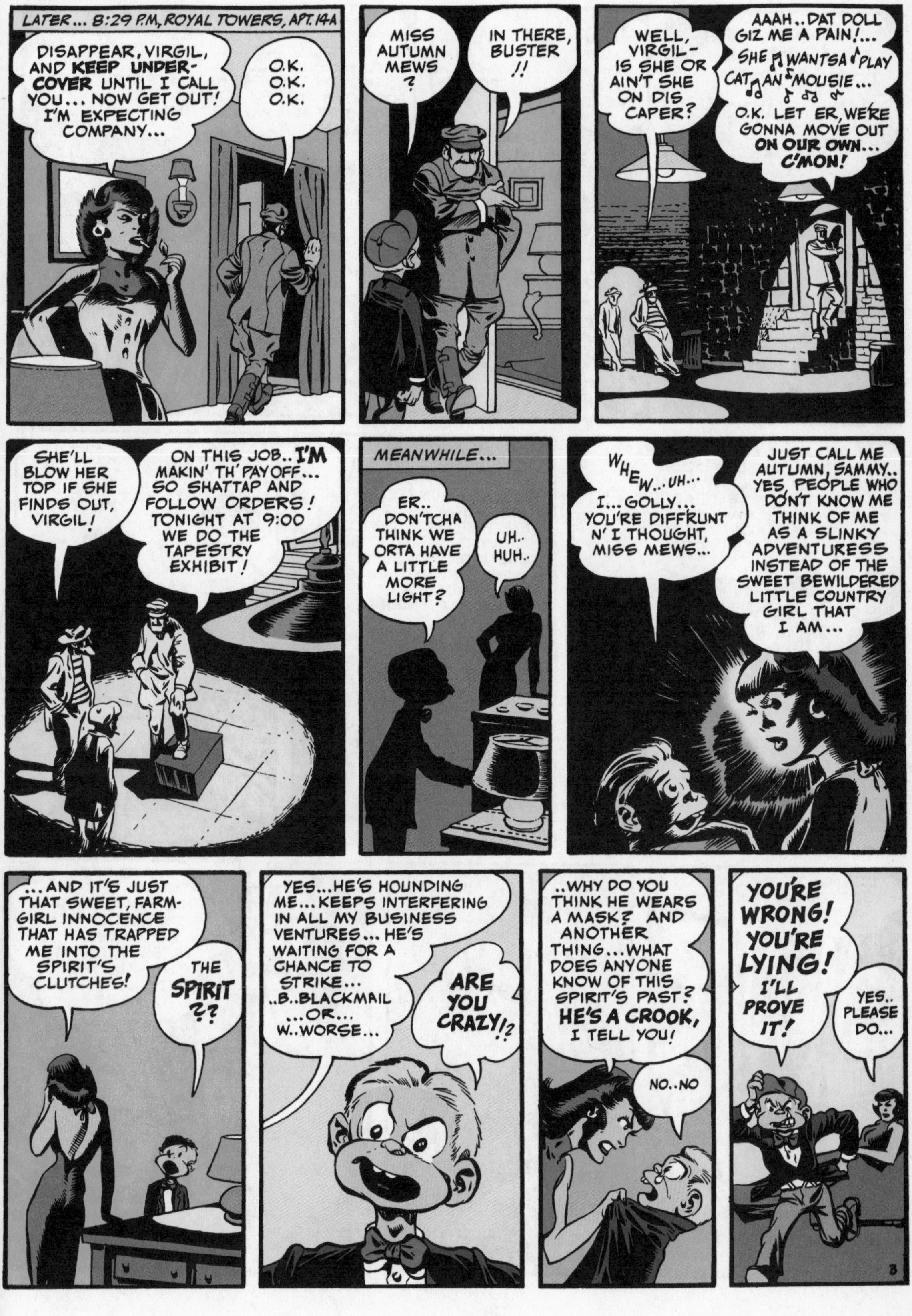
LATER... 8:29 P.M., ROYAL TOWERS, APT. 14A
DISAPPEAR, VIRGIL, AND KEEP UNDER-COVER UNTIL I CALL YOU... NOW GET OUT! I'M EXPECTING COMPANY...
O.K. O.K. O.K.
MISS AUTUMN MEWS ?
IN THERE, BUSTER !!
WELL, VIRGIL- IS SHE OR AIN'T SHE ON DIS CAPER?
AAAH.. DAT DOLL GIZ ME A PAIN!... SHE WANTSA PLAY CAT AN MOUSIE... O.K. LET ER, WE'RE GONNA MOVE OUT ON OUR OWN... C'MON!
SHE'LL BLOW HER TOP IF SHE FINDS OUT, VIRGIL!
ON THIS JOB.. I'M MAKIN' TH' PAYOFF... SO SHATTAP AND FOLLOW ORDERS! TONIGHT AT 9:00 WE DO THE TAPESTRY EXHIBIT!
MEANWHILE...
ER.. DON'TCHA THINK WE ORTA HAVE A LITTLE MORE LIGHT?
UH.. HUH..
WHEW... UH... I... GOLLY... YOU'RE DIFF'RUNT N' I THOUGHT, MISS MEWS...
JUST CALL ME AUTUMN, SAMMY.. YES, PEOPLE WHO DON'T KNOW ME THINK OF ME AS A SLINKY ADVENTURESS INSTEAD OF THE SWEET BEWILDERED LITTLE COUNTRY GIRL THAT I AM...
...AND IT'S JUST THAT SWEET, FARM-GIRL INNOCENCE THAT HAS TRAPPED ME INTO THE SPIRIT'S CLUTCHES!
THE SPIRIT ??
YES... HE'S HOUNDING ME... KEEPS INTERFERING IN ALL MY BUSINESS VENTURES... HE'S WAITING FOR A CHANCE TO STRIKE... ..B..BLACKMAIL ...OR... W..WORSE...
ARE YOU CRAZY!?
..WHY DO YOU THINK HE WEARS A MASK? AND ANOTHER THING... WHAT DOES ANYONE KNOW OF THIS SPIRIT'S PAST? HE'S A CROOK, I TELL YOU!
NO..NO
YOU'RE WRONG! YOU'RE LYING! I'LL PROVE IT!
YES.. PLEASE DO...
8

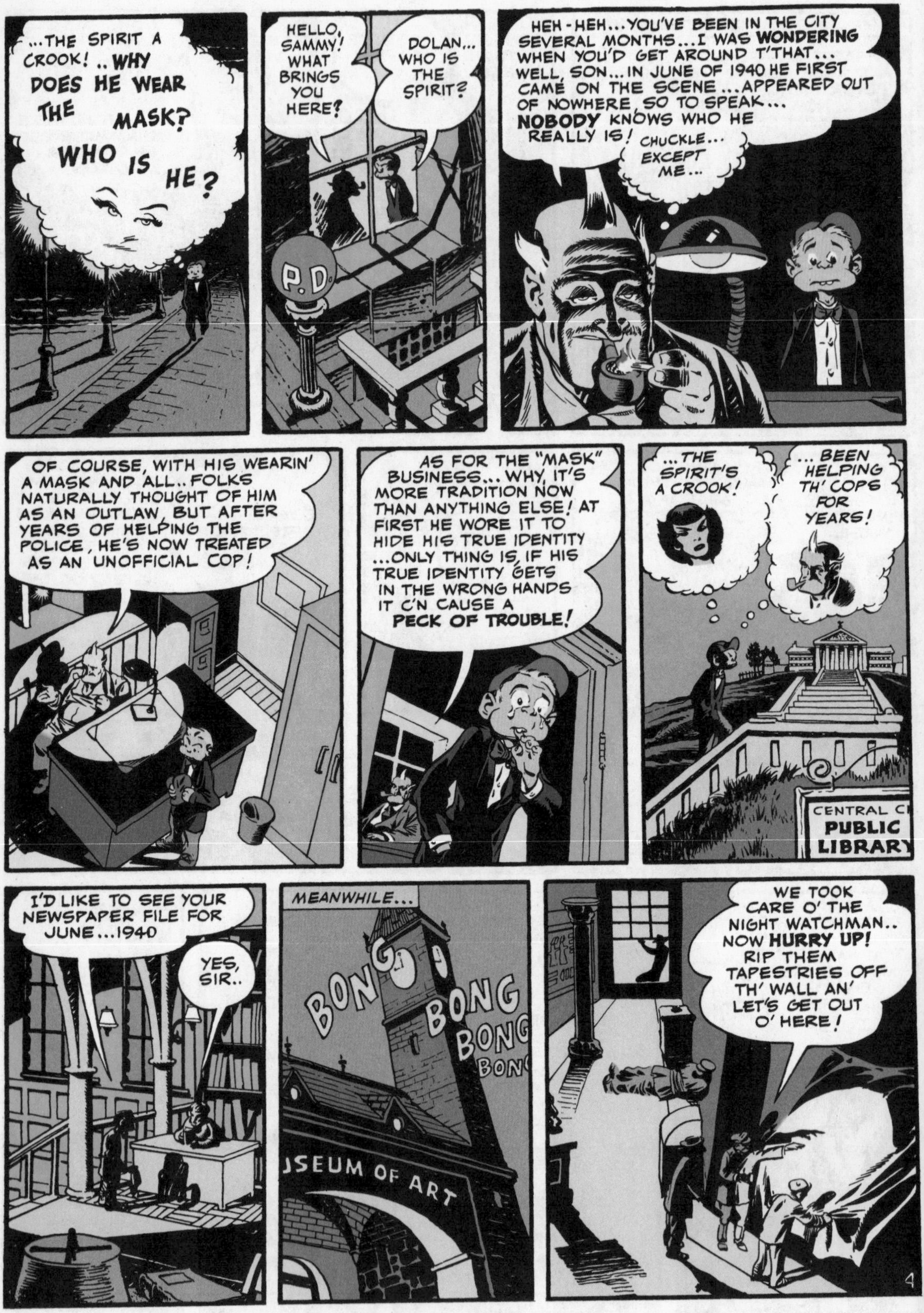
...THE SPIRIT A CROOK! ..WHY DOES HE WEAR THE MASK? WHO IS HE?
HELLO, SAMMY! WHAT BRINGS YOU HERE?
DOLAN... WHO IS THE SPIRIT?
P.D.
HEH-HEH...YOU'VE BEEN IN THE CITY SEVERAL MONTHS...I WAS WONDERING WHEN YOU'D GET AROUND T'THAT... WELL, SON...IN JUNE OF 1940 HE FIRST CAME ON THE SCENE...APPEARED OUT OF NOWHERE, SO TO SPEAK... NOBODY KNOWS WHO HE REALLY IS!
CHUCKLE... EXCEPT ME...
OF COURSE, WITH HIS WEARIN' A MASK AND ALL.. FOLKS NATURALLY THOUGHT OF HIM AS AN OUTLAW, BUT AFTER YEARS OF HELPING THE POLICE, HE'S NOW TREATED AS AN UNOFFICIAL COP!
AS FOR THE "MASK" BUSINESS...WHY, IT'S MORE TRADITION NOW THAN ANYTHING ELSE! AT FIRST HE WORE IT TO HIDE HIS TRUE IDENTITY ...ONLY THING IS, IF HIS TRUE IDENTITY GETS IN THE WRONG HANDS IT C'N CAUSE A PECK OF TROUBLE!
...THE SPIRIT'S A CROOK!
...BEEN HELPING TH' COPS FOR YEARS!
CENTRAL C
PUBLIC LIBRARY
I'D LIKE TO SEE YOUR NEWSPAPER FILE FOR JUNE...1940
YES, SIR..
MEANWHILE...
BONG BONG BONG BON
SEUM OF ART
WE TOOK CARE O' THE NIGHT WATCHMAN.. NOW HURRY UP! RIP THEM TAPESTRIES OFF TH' WALL AN' LET'S GET OUT O' HERE!
4

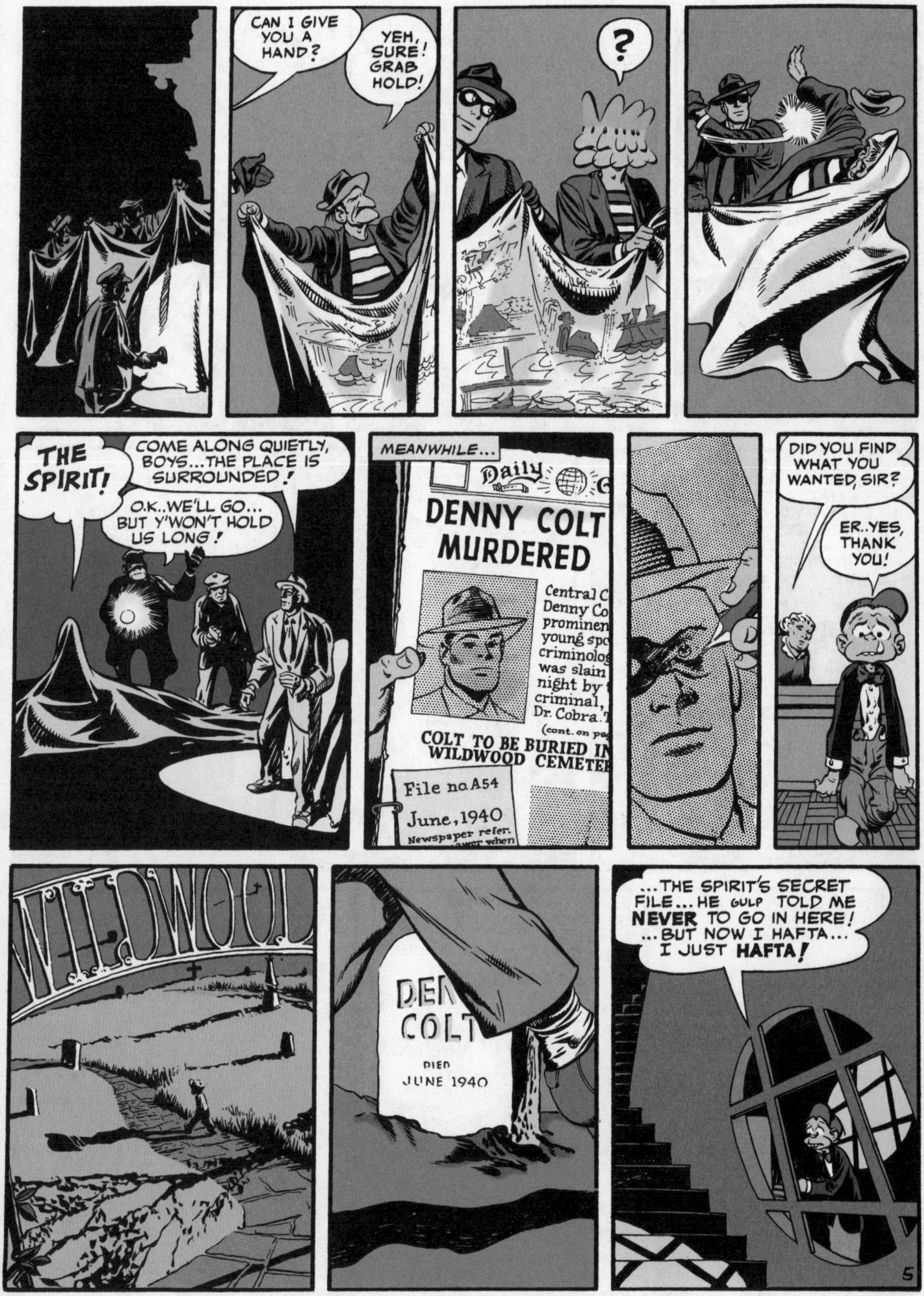
CAN I GIVE YOU A HAND?
YEH, SURE! GRAB HOLD!
?
THE SPIRIT!
COME ALONG QUIETLY, BOYS...THE PLACE IS SURROUNDED!
O.K..WE'LL GO... BUT Y'WON'T HOLD US LONG!
MEANWHILE...
Daily
DENNY COLT MURDERED
Central C
Denny Co
prominen
young spo
criminolog
was slain
night by
criminal,
Dr. Cobra.
(cont. on pa
COLT TO BE BURIED IN
WILDWOOD CEMETE
File no. A54
June, 1940
Newspaper refer.
DID YOU FIND WHAT YOU WANTED, SIR?
ER..YES, THANK YOU!
WILDWOOD
DEN
COLT
DIED
JUNE 1940
...THE SPIRIT'S SECRET FILE...HE GULP TOLD ME NEVER TO GO IN HERE! ...BUT NOW I HAFTA... I JUST HAFTA!
5

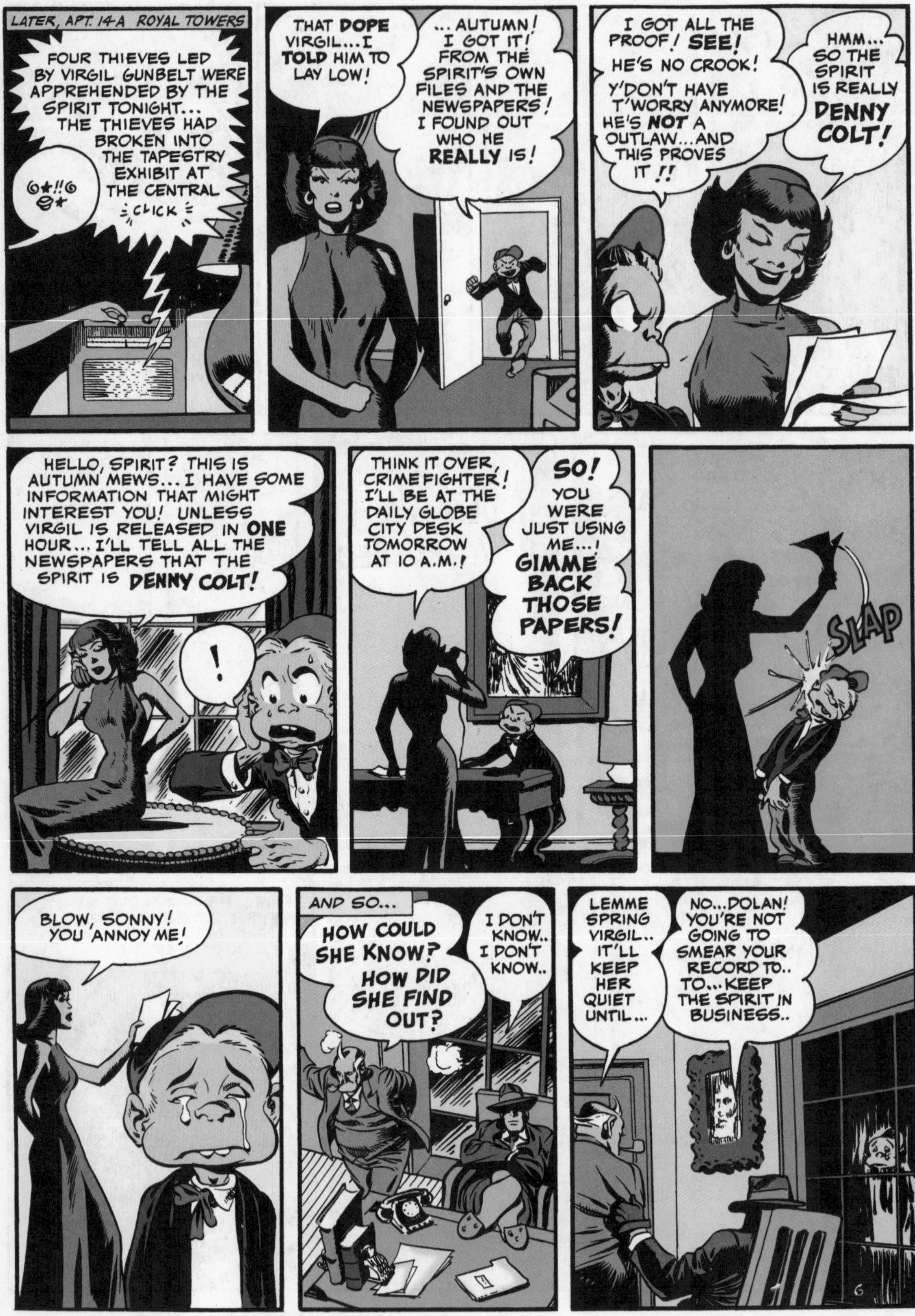

LATER, APT. 14-A ROYAL TOWERS
FOUR THIEVES LED BY VIRGIL GUNBELT WERE APPREHENDED BY THE SPIRIT TONIGHT... THE THIEVES HAD BROKEN INTO THE TAPESTRY EXHIBIT AT THE CENTRAL
CLICK
THAT DOPE VIRGIL...I TOLD HIM TO LAY LOW!
... AUTUMN! I GOT IT! FROM THE SPIRIT'S OWN FILES AND THE NEWSPAPERS! I FOUND OUT WHO HE REALLY IS!
I GOT ALL THE PROOF! SEE! HE'S NO CROOK! Y'DON'T HAVE T'WORRY ANYMORE! HE'S NOT A OUTLAW...AND THIS PROVES IT!!
HMM... SO THE SPIRIT IS REALLY DENNY COLT!
HELLO, SPIRIT? THIS IS AUTUMN MEWS... I HAVE SOME INFORMATION THAT MIGHT INTEREST YOU! UNLESS VIRGIL IS RELEASED IN ONE HOUR... I'LL TELL ALL THE NEWSPAPERS THAT THE SPIRIT IS DENNY COLT!
!
THINK IT OVER, CRIME FIGHTER! I'LL BE AT THE DAILY GLOBE CITY DESK TOMORROW AT 10 A.M.!
SO! YOU WERE JUST USING ME...! GIMME BACK THOSE PAPERS!
SLAP
BLOW, SONNY! YOU ANNOY ME!
AND SO...
HOW COULD SHE KNOW? HOW DID SHE FIND OUT?
I DON'T KNOW.. I DON'T KNOW..
LEMME SPRING VIRGIL.. IT'LL KEEP HER QUIET UNTIL...
NO...DOLAN! YOU'RE NOT GOING TO SMEAR YOUR RECORD TO.. TO...KEEP THE SPIRIT IN BUSINESS..
6

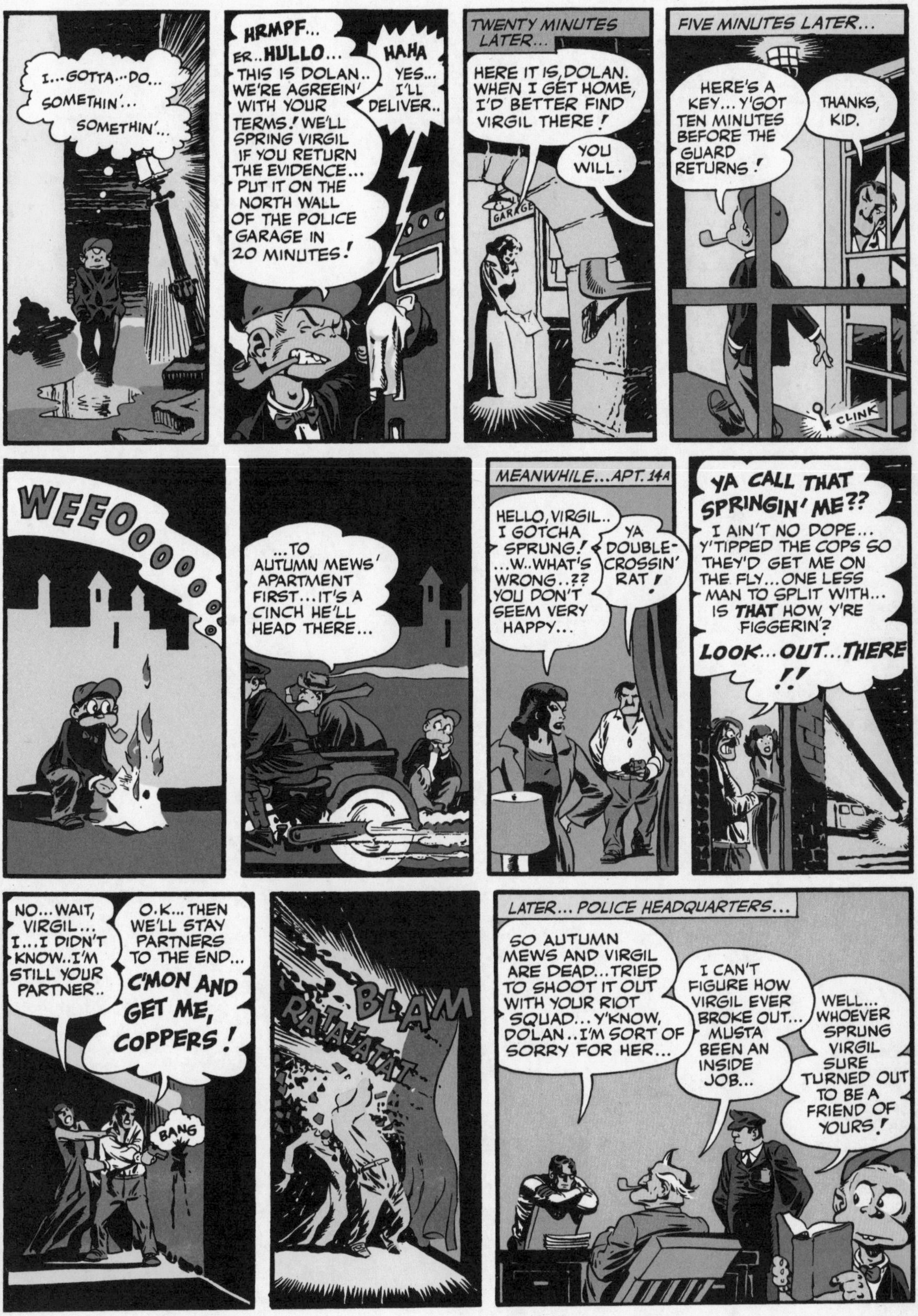
I...GOTTA...DO... SOMETHIN'... SOMETHIN'...
HRMPF... ER..HULLO... THIS IS DOLAN.. WE'RE AGREEIN' WITH YOUR TERMS! WE'LL SPRING VIRGIL IF YOU RETURN THE EVIDENCE... PUT IT ON THE NORTH WALL OF THE POLICE GARAGE IN 20 MINUTES!
HAHA YES... I'LL DELIVER..
TWENTY MINUTES LATER...
HERE IT IS, DOLAN. WHEN I GET HOME, I'D BETTER FIND VIRGIL THERE!
YOU WILL.
GARAGE
FIVE MINUTES LATER...
HERE'S A KEY... Y'GOT TEN MINUTES BEFORE THE GUARD RETURNS!
THANKS, KID.
CLINK
WEEOOOOOO
...TO AUTUMN MEWS' APARTMENT FIRST...IT'S A CINCH HE'LL HEAD THERE...
MEANWHILE...APT. 14A
HELLO, VIRGIL.. I GOTCHA SPRUNG! ...W..WHAT'S WRONG..?? YOU DON'T SEEM VERY HAPPY...
YA DOUBLE-CROSSIN' RAT!
YA CALL THAT SPRINGIN' ME?? I AIN'T NO DOPE... Y'TIPPED THE COPS SO THEY'D GET ME ON THE FLY...ONE LESS MAN TO SPLIT WITH... IS THAT HOW Y'RE FIGGERIN'? LOOK...OUT...THERE!!
NO...WAIT, VIRGIL... I...I DIDN'T KNOW..I'M STILL YOUR PARTNER..
O.K...THEN WE'LL STAY PARTNERS TO THE END... C'MON AND GET ME, COPPERS!
BANG
BLAM
RATATATATAT
LATER... POLICE HEADQUARTERS...
SO AUTUMN MEWS AND VIRGIL ARE DEAD...TRIED TO SHOOT IT OUT WITH YOUR RIOT SQUAD... Y'KNOW, DOLAN..I'M SORT OF SORRY FOR HER...
I CAN'T FIGURE HOW VIRGIL EVER BROKE OUT... MUSTA BEEN AN INSIDE JOB...
WELL... WHOEVER SPRUNG VIRGIL SURE TURNED OUT TO BE A FRIEND OF YOURS!

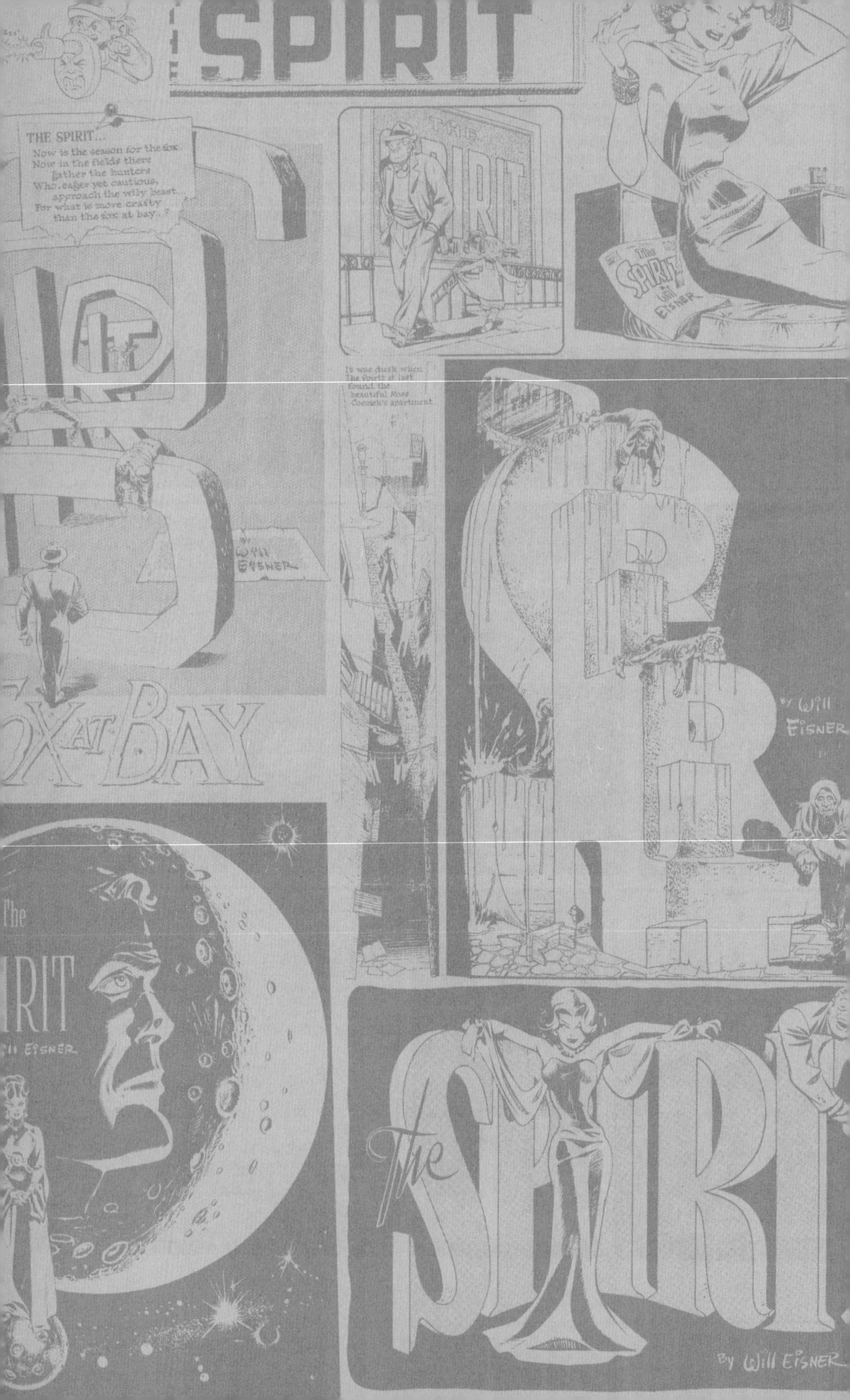

THE SPIRIT
THE SPIRIT... Now is the season for the fox. Now in the fields there gather the hunters Who, eager yet cautious, approach the wily beast... For what is more crafty than the fox at bay...?
By Will Eisner
OX AT BAY
THE SPIRIT
Will Eisner
The Spirit
Will Eisner
It was dusk when The Spirit at last found the beautiful Miss Cosmek's apartment.
THE
By Will Eisner
The
SPIRIT
Will Eisner
The SPIRIT
By Will Eisner

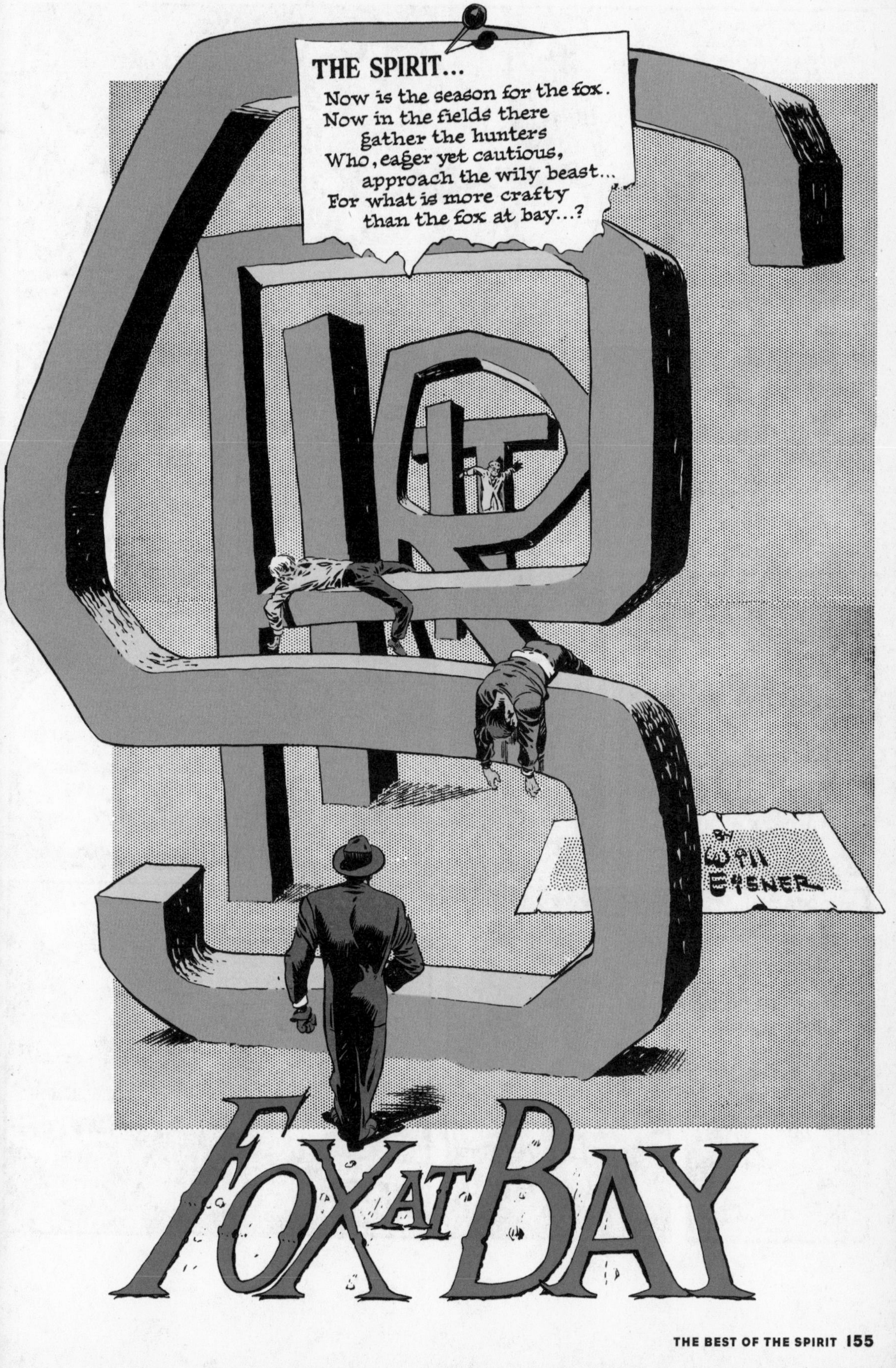
THE SPIRIT...
Now is the season for the fox.
Now in the fields there
gather the hunters
Who, eager yet cautious,
approach the wily beast...
For what is more crafty
than the fox at bay...?
BY WILL EISNER
FOX AT BAY

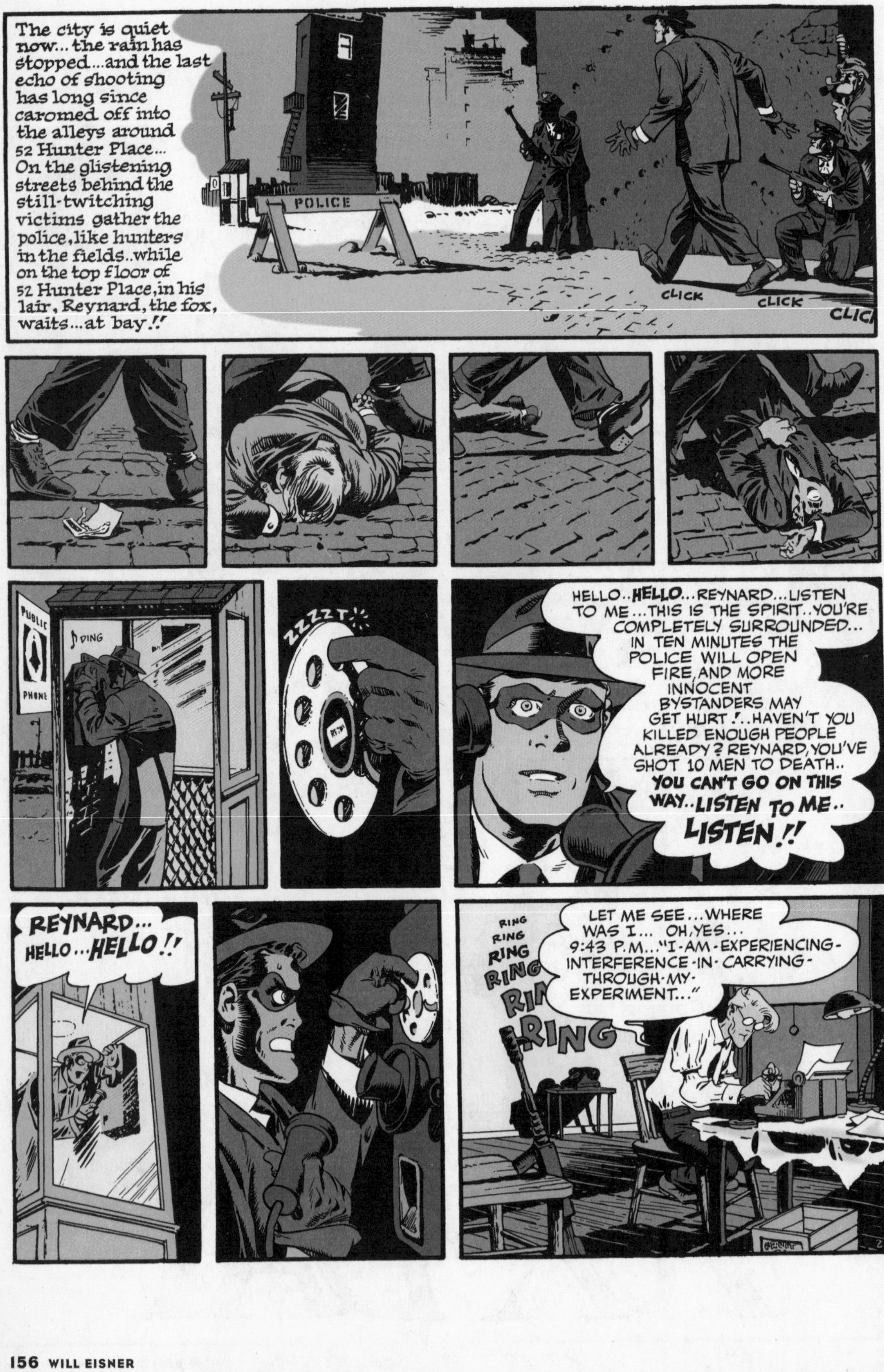
The city is quiet now... the rain has stopped...and the last echo of shooting has long since caromed off into the alleys around 52 Hunter Place... On the glistening streets behind the still-twitching victims gather the police, like hunters in the fields..while on the top floor of 52 Hunter Place, in his lair, Reynard, the fox, waits...at bay!!"
POLICE
CLICK
CLICK
CLICK
PUBLIC
PHONE
DING
ZZZZT
HELLO..HELLO...REYNARD...LISTEN TO ME...THIS IS THE SPIRIT..YOU'RE COMPLETELY SURROUNDED... IN TEN MINUTES THE POLICE WILL OPEN FIRE, AND MORE INNOCENT BYSTANDERS MAY GET HURT!..HAVEN'T YOU KILLED ENOUGH PEOPLE ALREADY? REYNARD, YOU'VE SHOT 10 MEN TO DEATH.. YOU CAN'T GO ON THIS WAY..LISTEN TO ME.. LISTEN!!
REYNARD... HELLO...HELLO!!
RING
RING
RING
RING
RING
RING
LET ME SEE...WHERE WAS I... OH, YES... 9:43 P.M..."I-AM-EXPERIENCING-INTERFERENCE-IN-CARRYING-THROUGH-MY-EXPERIMENT..."

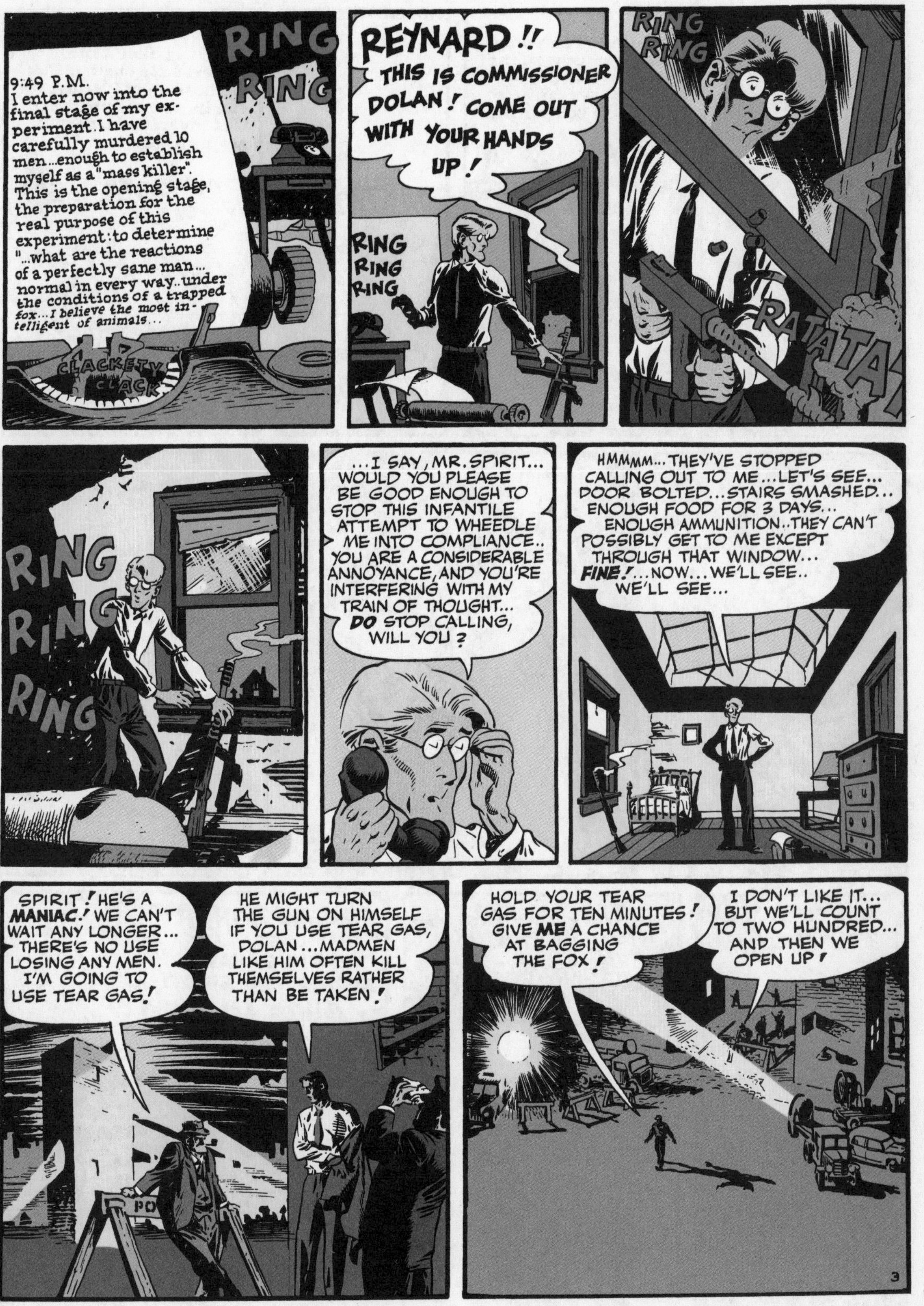
9:49 P.M.
I enter now into the final stage of my experiment. I have carefully murdered 10 men...enough to establish myself as a "mass killer". This is the opening stage, the preparation for the real purpose of this experiment: to determine "...what are the reactions of a perfectly sane man... normal in every way.. under the conditions of a trapped fox... I believe the most intelligent of animals...
RING RING
CLACKETY CLACK
REYNARD!! THIS IS COMMISSIONER DOLAN! COME OUT WITH YOUR HANDS UP!
RING RING RING
RING RING
RATATAT
RING RING RING
...I SAY, MR. SPIRIT... WOULD YOU PLEASE BE GOOD ENOUGH TO STOP THIS INFANTILE ATTEMPT TO WHEEDLE ME INTO COMPLIANCE.. YOU ARE A CONSIDERABLE ANNOYANCE, AND YOU'RE INTERFERING WITH MY TRAIN OF THOUGHT... DO STOP CALLING, WILL YOU?
HMMMM... THEY'VE STOPPED CALLING OUT TO ME... LET'S SEE... DOOR BOLTED... STAIRS SMASHED... ENOUGH FOOD FOR 3 DAYS... ENOUGH AMMUNITION.. THEY CAN'T POSSIBLY GET TO ME EXCEPT THROUGH THAT WINDOW... FINE!...NOW... WE'LL SEE.. WE'LL SEE...
SPIRIT! HE'S A MANIAC! WE CAN'T WAIT ANY LONGER... THERE'S NO USE LOSING ANY MEN. I'M GOING TO USE TEAR GAS!
HE MIGHT TURN THE GUN ON HIMSELF IF YOU USE TEAR GAS, DOLAN...MADMEN LIKE HIM OFTEN KILL THEMSELVES RATHER THAN BE TAKEN!
HOLD YOUR TEAR GAS FOR TEN MINUTES! GIVE ME A CHANCE AT BAGGING THE FOX!
I DON'T LIKE IT... BUT WE'LL COUNT TO TWO HUNDRED... AND THEN WE OPEN UP!
3

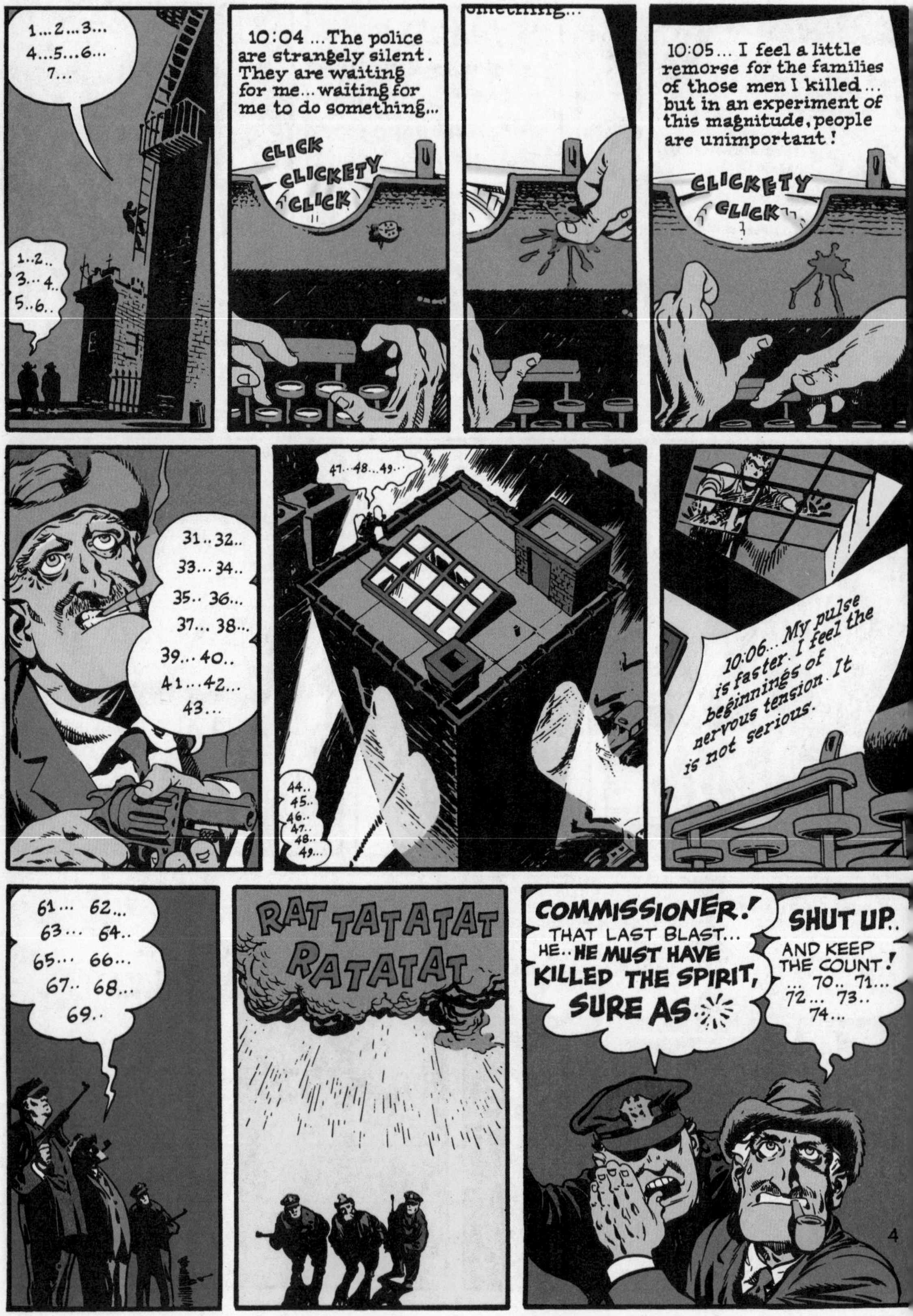
1...2...3...
4...5...6...
7...
1..2..
3... 4..
5..6..
10:04 ...The police are strangely silent. They are waiting for me...waiting for me to do something...
CLICK
CLICKETY
CLICK
10:05... I feel a little remorse for the families of those men I killed... but in an experiment of this magnitude, people are unimportant!
CLICKETY
CLICK
31..32..
33... 34..
35.. 36...
37... 38...
39... 40..
41...42...
43...
47...48...49...
44..
45..
46..
47..
48..
49...
10:06... My pulse is faster. I feel the beginnings of nervous tension. It is not serious.
61... 62...
63... 64..
65... 66...
67.. 68...
69..
RAT TATATAT
RATATAT
COMMISSIONER! THAT LAST BLAST... HE.. HE MUST HAVE KILLED THE SPIRIT, SURE AS.
SHUT UP.. AND KEEP THE COUNT! ... 70.. 71... 72... 73.. 74...
4

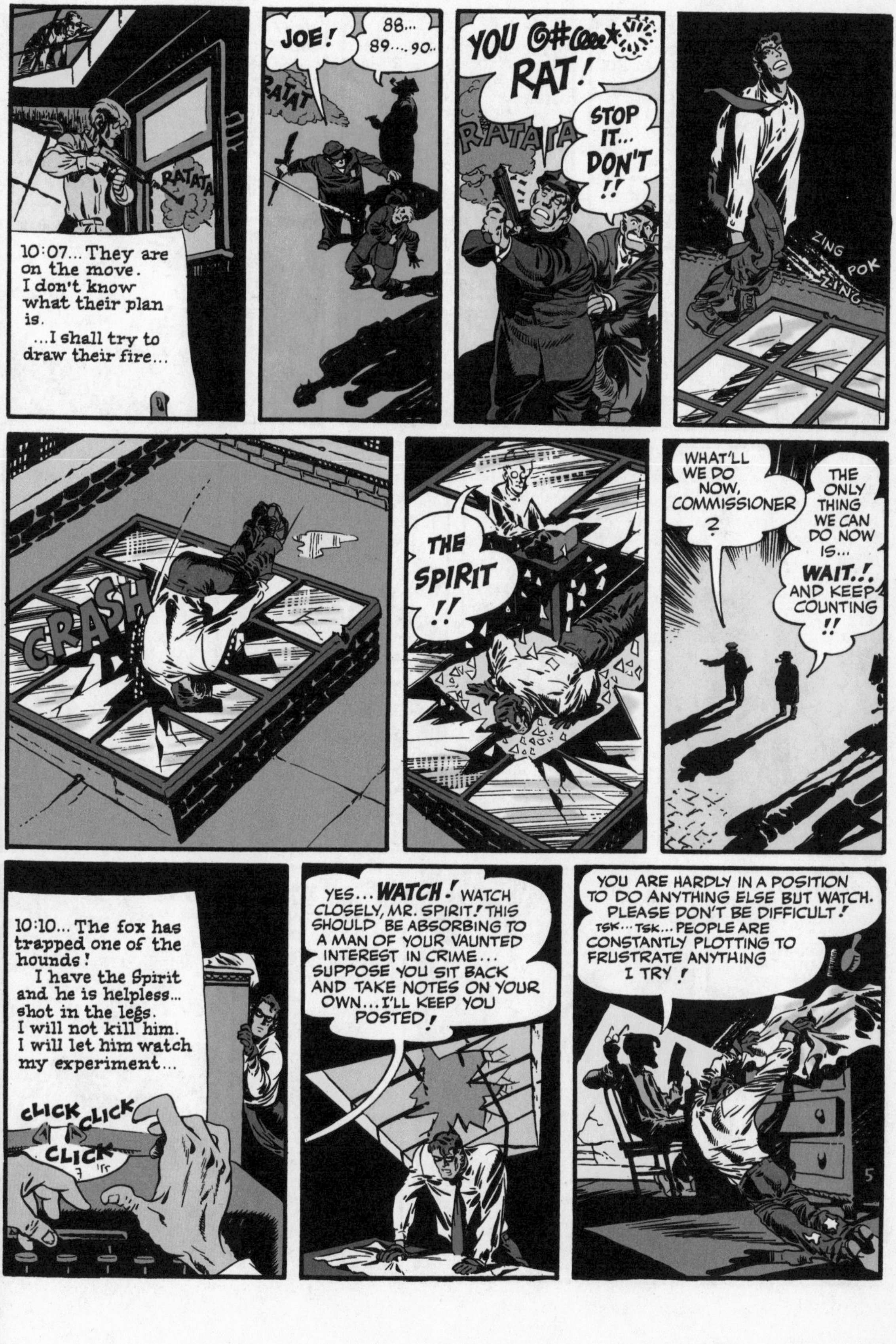
10:07... They are on the move. I don't know what their plan is.
...I shall try to draw their fire...
RATATA
JOE!
88... 89.... 90..
RATATAT
YOU @#¢*!! RAT!
RATATATA
STOP IT... DON'T !!
ZING
POK
ZING
CRASH
THE SPIRIT !!
WHAT'LL WE DO NOW, COMMISSIONER ?
THE ONLY THING WE CAN DO NOW IS... WAIT.!. AND KEEP COUNTING !!
10:10... The fox has trapped one of the hounds!
I have the Spirit and he is helpless... shot in the legs. I will not kill him. I will let him watch my experiment...
CLICK CLICK
CLICK
YES... WATCH! WATCH CLOSELY, MR. SPIRIT! THIS SHOULD BE ABSORBING TO A MAN OF YOUR VAUNTED INTEREST IN CRIME... SUPPOSE YOU SIT BACK AND TAKE NOTES ON YOUR OWN... I'LL KEEP YOU POSTED!
YOU ARE HARDLY IN A POSITION TO DO ANYTHING ELSE BUT WATCH. PLEASE DON'T BE DIFFICULT!
TSK... TSK... PEOPLE ARE CONSTANTLY PLOTTING TO FRUSTRATE ANYTHING I TRY!
5

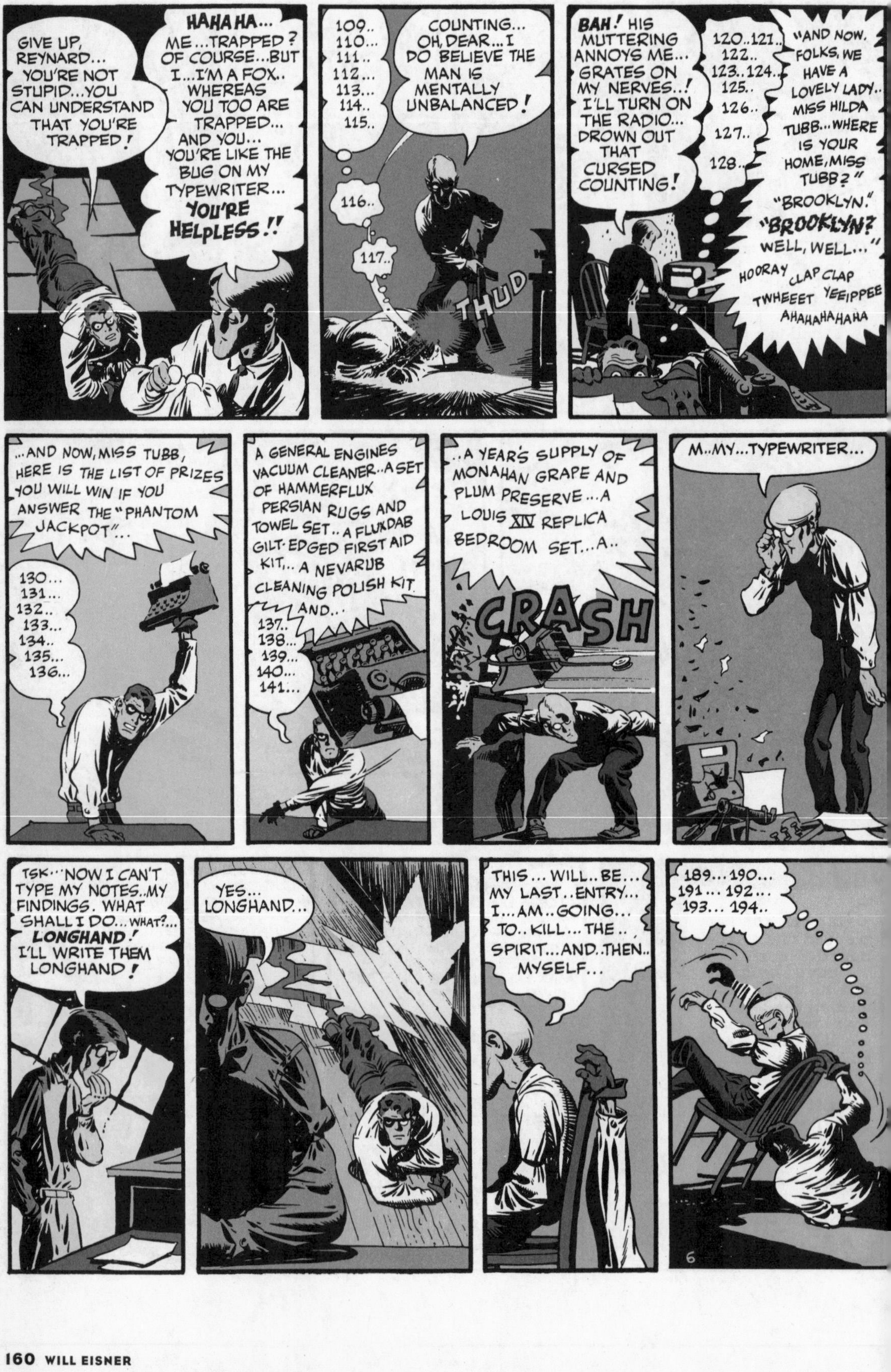

GIVE UP, REYNARD... YOU'RE NOT STUPID...YOU CAN UNDERSTAND THAT YOU'RE TRAPPED!
HAHAHA... ME...TRAPPED? OF COURSE...BUT I...I'M A FOX.. WHEREAS YOU TOO ARE TRAPPED... AND YOU... YOU'RE LIKE THE BUG ON MY TYPEWRITER... YOU'RE HELPLESS!!
109.. 110... 111.. 112... 113... 114.. 115..
COUNTING... OH, DEAR...I DO BELIEVE THE MAN IS MENTALLY UNBALANCED!
116..
117..
THUD
BAH! HIS MUTTERING ANNOYS ME... GRATES ON MY NERVES..! I'LL TURN ON THE RADIO... DROWN OUT THAT CURSED COUNTING!
120..121.. 122.. 123..124.. 125.. 126.. 127.. 128..
"AND NOW, FOLKS, WE HAVE A LOVELY LADY.. MISS HILDA TUBB...WHERE IS YOUR HOME, MISS TUBB?"
"BROOKLYN."
"BROOKLYN? WELL, WELL..."
HOORAY CLAP CLAP TWHEEET YEEIPPEE AHAHAHAHAHA
...AND NOW, MISS TUBB, HERE IS THE LIST OF PRIZES YOU WILL WIN IF YOU ANSWER THE "PHANTOM JACKPOT"...
130... 131... 132.. 133... 134.. 135... 136...
A GENERAL ENGINES VACUUM CLEANER..A SET OF HAMMERFLUX PERSIAN RUGS AND TOWEL SET.. A FLUXDAB GILT-EDGED FIRST AID KIT,.. A NEVARUB CLEANING POLISH KIT AND...
137.. 138... 139... 140... 141...
..A YEAR'S SUPPLY OF MONAHAN GRAPE AND PLUM PRESERVE...A LOUIS XIV REPLICA BEDROOM SET...A..
CRASH
M..MY...TYPEWRITER...
TSK...NOW I CAN'T TYPE MY NOTES..MY FINDINGS. WHAT SHALL I DO...WHAT?... LONGHAND! I'LL WRITE THEM LONGHAND!
YES... LONGHAND...
THIS... WILL.. BE... MY LAST.. ENTRY... I...AM..GOING... TO.. KILL... THE.. SPIRIT...AND..THEN.. MYSELF...
189... 190... 191... 192... 193... 194..
6

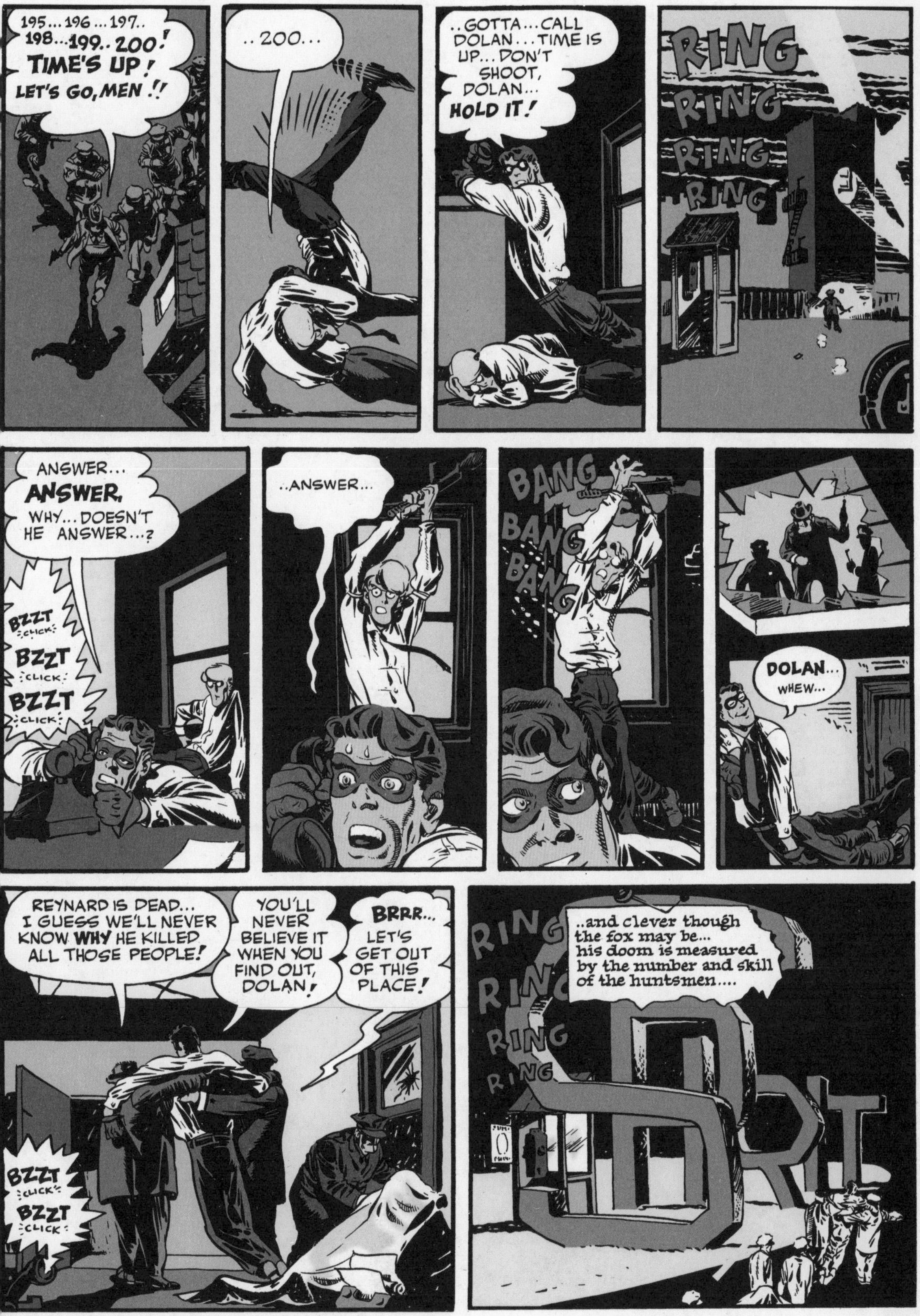
195... 196 ... 197..
198... 199.. 200!
TIME'S UP!
LET'S GO, MEN!!
.. 200...
..GOTTA... CALL DOLAN... TIME IS UP... DON'T SHOOT, DOLAN...
HOLD IT!
RING
RING
RING
RING
ANSWER...
ANSWER.
WHY... DOESN'T HE ANSWER...?
BZZT CLICK
BZZT CLICK
BZZT CLICK
..ANSWER...
BANG
BANG
BANG
DOLAN... WHEW...
REYNARD IS DEAD... I GUESS WE'LL NEVER KNOW WHY HE KILLED ALL THOSE PEOPLE!
YOU'LL NEVER BELIEVE IT WHEN YOU FIND OUT, DOLAN!
BRRR... LET'S GET OUT OF THIS PLACE!
BZZT CLICK
BZZT CLICK
RING
RING
RING
RING
..and clever though the fox may be... his doom is measured by the number and skill of the huntsmen....
SPIRIT

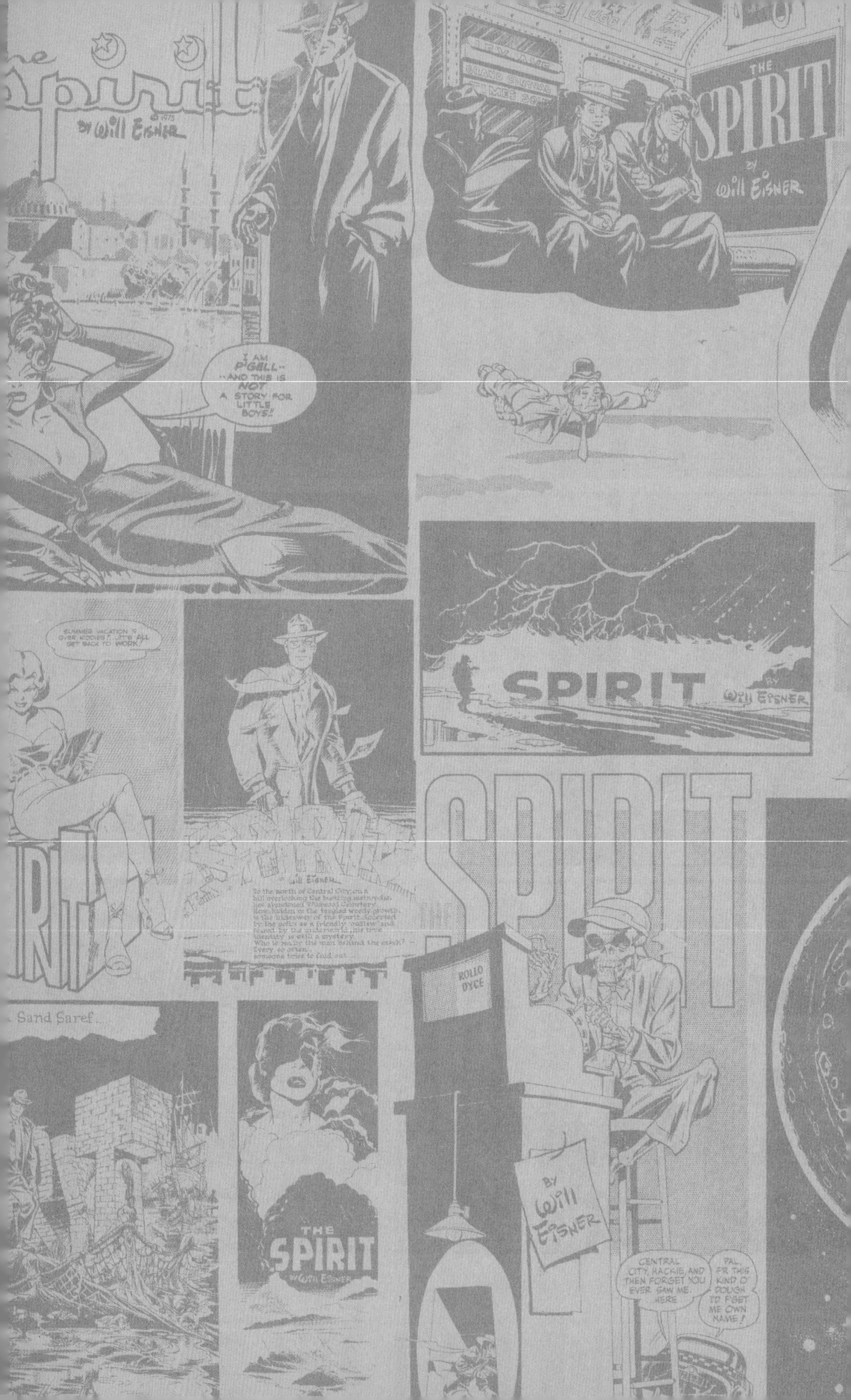
The Spirit
BY Will Eisner
I AM P'GELL-- ...AND THIS IS NOT A STORY FOR LITTLE BOYS!
THE SPIRIT
BY Will Eisner
SUMMER VACATION IS OVER KIDDIES! LET'S ALL GET BACK TO WORK!
SPIRIT
BY Will Eisner
SPIRIT
... Sand Saref...
THE SPIRIT
THE SPIRIT
ROLLO DYCE
BY Will Eisner
CENTRAL CITY, HACKIE, AND THEN FORGET YOU EVER SAW ME. HERE
PAL, FR THIS KIND O' DOUGH I'D F'GET ME OWN NAME!

THE EMBEZZLER

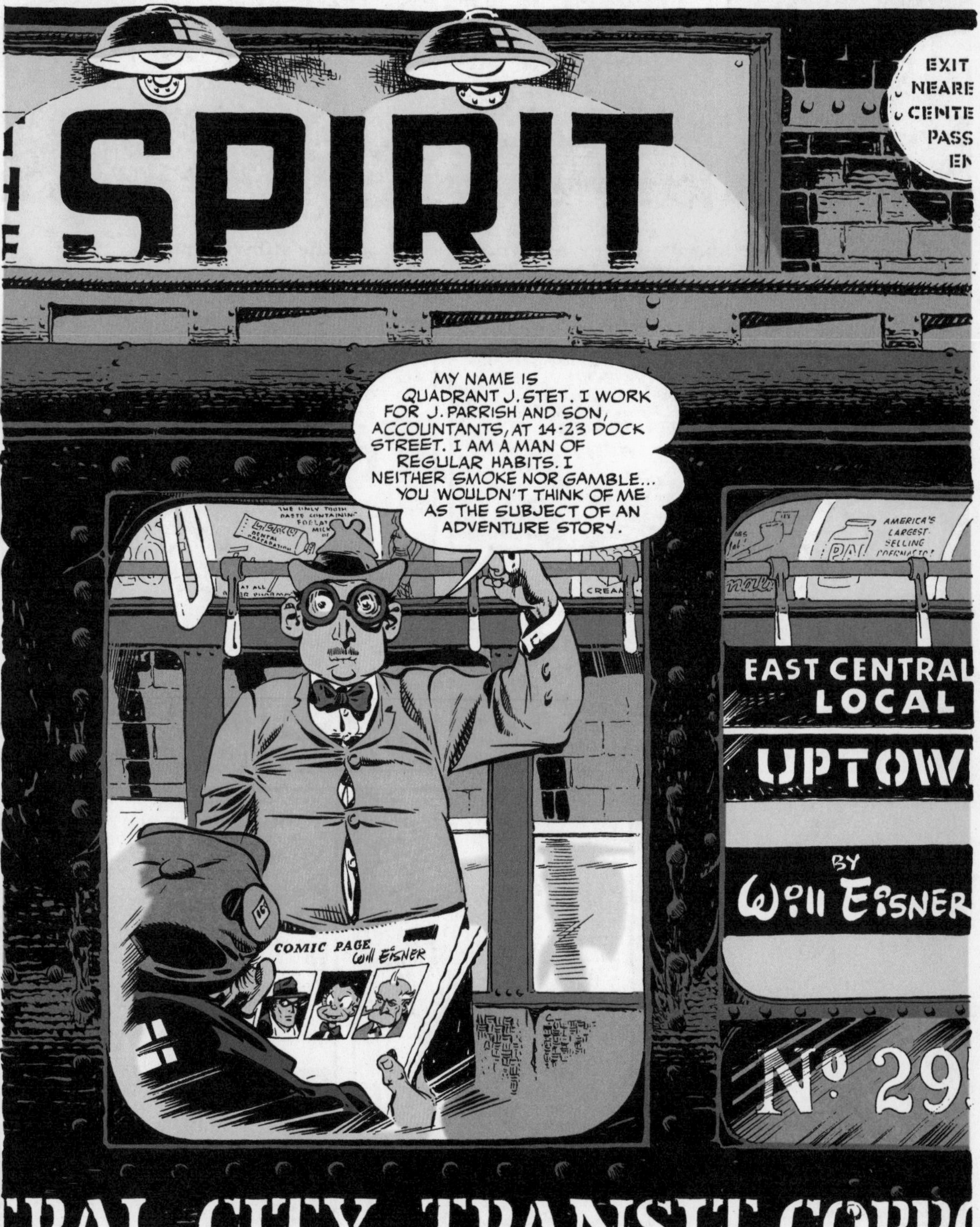

SPIRIT
MY NAME IS QUADRANT J. STET. I WORK FOR J. PARRISH AND SON, ACCOUNTANTS, AT 14-23 DOCK STREET. I AM A MAN OF REGULAR HABITS. I NEITHER SMOKE NOR GAMBLE... YOU WOULDN'T THINK OF ME AS THE SUBJECT OF AN ADVENTURE STORY.
EAST CENTRAL LOCAL
BY Will Eisner
COMIC PAGE Will Eisner

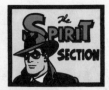

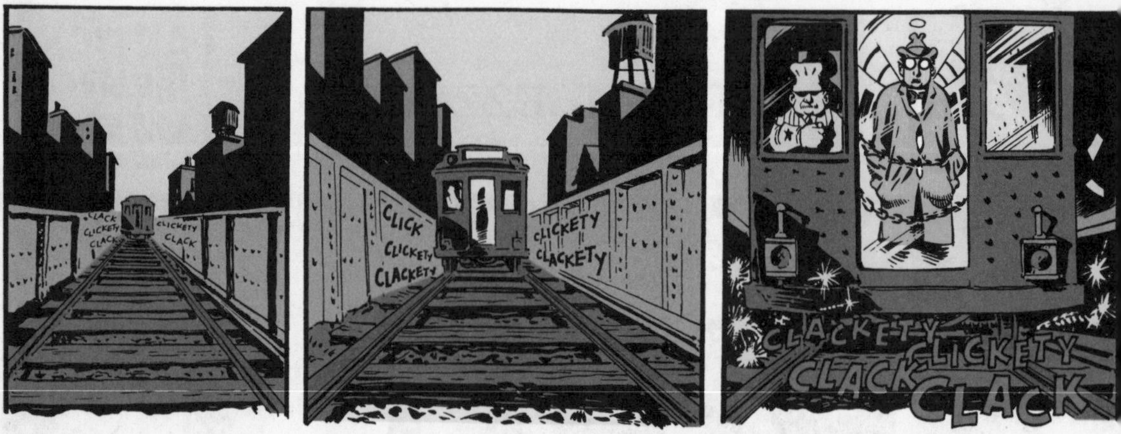
CLACK
CLICKETY
CLACK
CLICKETY
CLACK
CLICK
CLICKETY
CLACKETY
CLICKETY
CLACKETY
CLACKETY
CLACK
CLICKETY
CLACK

I leave the office at five every afternoon and take the subway home. "Home" is uptown... East Central City, 1532 Sawyer Avenue, Apartment E-10... (that's five flights up... there is a self-service elevator...)

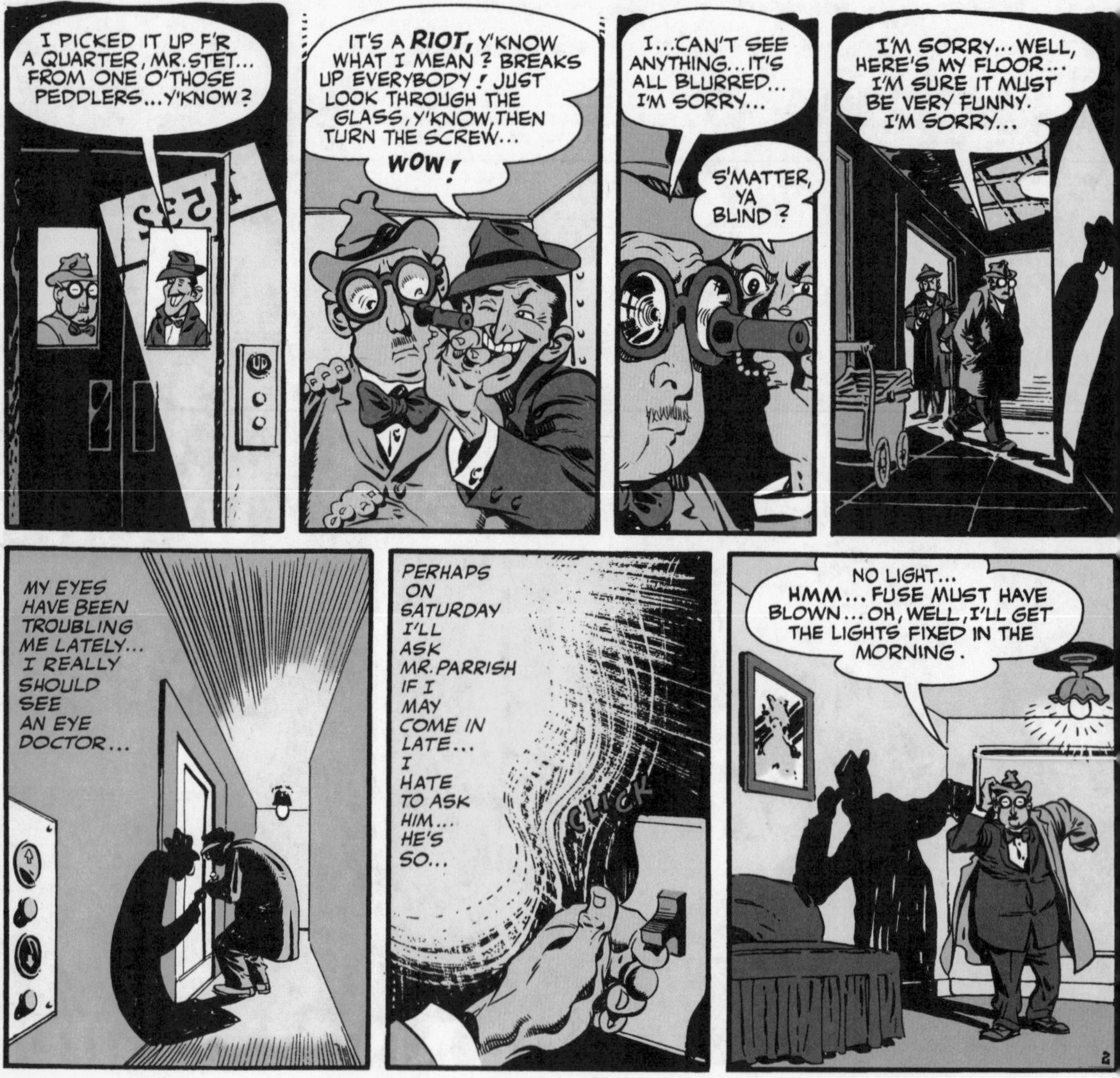
I PICKED IT UP F'R A QUARTER, MR. STET... FROM ONE O'THOSE PEDDLERS... Y'KNOW?
IT'S A **RIOT,** Y'KNOW WHAT I MEAN? BREAKS UP EVERYBODY! JUST LOOK THROUGH THE GLASS, Y'KNOW, THEN TURN THE SCREW...
WOW!
I... CAN'T SEE ANYTHING... IT'S ALL BLURRED... I'M SORRY...
S'MATTER, YA BLIND?
I'M SORRY... WELL, HERE'S MY FLOOR... I'M SURE IT MUST BE VERY FUNNY. I'M SORRY...
MY EYES HAVE BEEN TROUBLING ME LATELY... I REALLY SHOULD SEE AN EYE DOCTOR...
PERHAPS ON SATURDAY I'LL ASK MR. PARRISH IF I MAY COME IN LATE... I HATE TO ASK HIM... HE'S SO...
CLICK
NO LIGHT... HMM... FUSE MUST HAVE BLOWN... OH, WELL, I'LL GET THE LIGHTS FIXED IN THE MORNING.
2

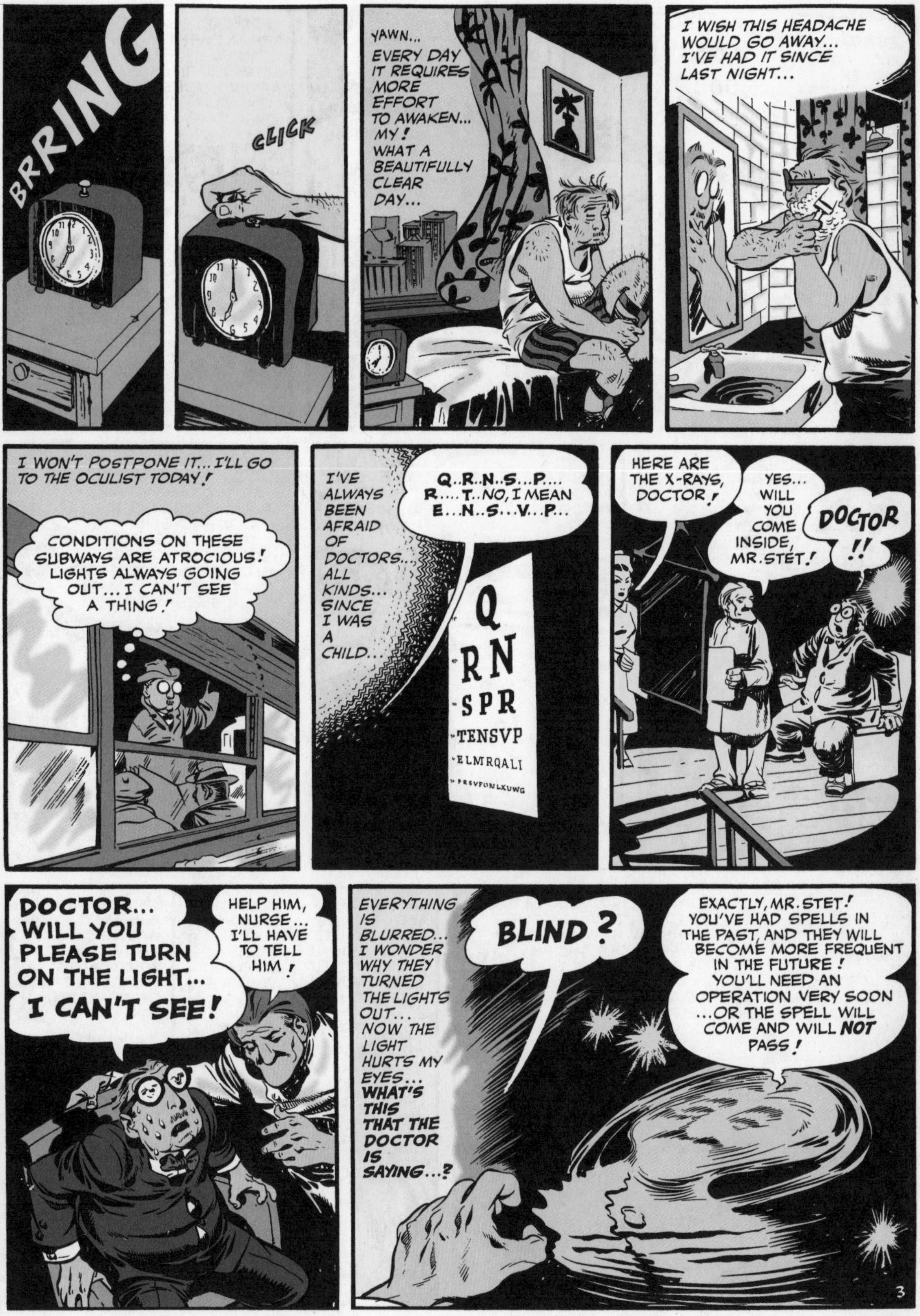
BRRING
CLICK
YAWN...
EVERY DAY IT REQUIRES MORE EFFORT TO AWAKEN... MY! WHAT A BEAUTIFULLY CLEAR DAY...
I WISH THIS HEADACHE WOULD GO AWAY... I'VE HAD IT SINCE LAST NIGHT...
I WON'T POSTPONE IT... I'LL GO TO THE OCULIST TODAY!
CONDITIONS ON THESE SUBWAYS ARE ATROCIOUS! LIGHTS ALWAYS GOING OUT... I CAN'T SEE A THING!
I'VE ALWAYS BEEN AFRAID OF DOCTORS... ALL KINDS... SINCE I WAS A CHILD...
Q..R..N..S...P.... R..... T.. NO, I MEAN E...N..S...V...P...
Q
RN
SPR
TENSVP
ELMRQALI
PRSVFONLXUWG
HERE ARE THE X-RAYS, DOCTOR!
YES... WILL YOU COME INSIDE, MR. STET!
DOCTOR !!
DOCTOR... WILL YOU PLEASE TURN ON THE LIGHT... I CAN'T SEE!
HELP HIM, NURSE... I'LL HAVE TO TELL HIM!
EVERYTHING IS BLURRED... I WONDER WHY THEY TURNED THE LIGHTS OUT... NOW THE LIGHT HURTS MY EYES... WHAT'S THIS THAT THE DOCTOR IS SAYING...?
BLIND?
EXACTLY, MR. STET! YOU'VE HAD SPELLS IN THE PAST, AND THEY WILL BECOME MORE FREQUENT IN THE FUTURE! YOU'LL NEED AN OPERATION VERY SOON ...OR THE SPELL WILL COME AND WILL NOT PASS!
3

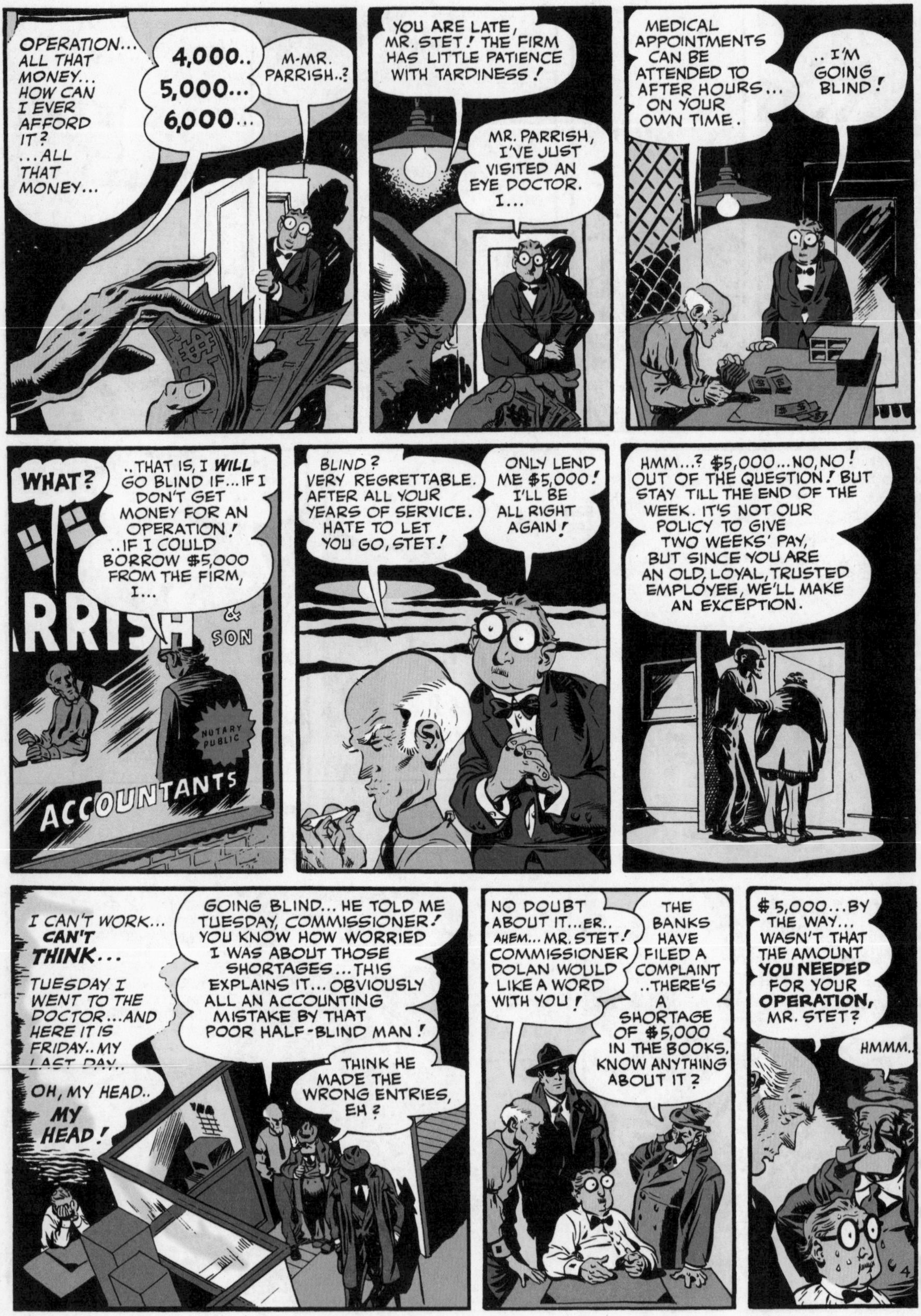

OPERATION... ALL THAT MONEY... HOW CAN I EVER AFFORD IT? ...ALL THAT MONEY...
4,000.. 5,000... 6,000...
M-MR. PARRISH..?
YOU ARE LATE, MR. STET! THE FIRM HAS LITTLE PATIENCE WITH TARDINESS!
MR. PARRISH, I'VE JUST VISITED AN EYE DOCTOR. I...
MEDICAL APPOINTMENTS CAN BE ATTENDED TO AFTER HOURS... ON YOUR OWN TIME.
.. I'M GOING BLIND!
WHAT?
..THAT IS, I WILL GO BLIND IF... IF I DON'T GET MONEY FOR AN OPERATION! ..IF I COULD BORROW $5,000 FROM THE FIRM, I...
RRISH & SON
NOTARY PUBLIC
ACCOUNTANTS
BLIND? VERY REGRETTABLE. AFTER ALL YOUR YEARS OF SERVICE. HATE TO LET YOU GO, STET!
ONLY LEND ME $5,000! I'LL BE ALL RIGHT AGAIN!
HMM...? $5,000...NO, NO! OUT OF THE QUESTION! BUT STAY TILL THE END OF THE WEEK. IT'S NOT OUR POLICY TO GIVE TWO WEEKS' PAY, BUT SINCE YOU ARE AN OLD, LOYAL, TRUSTED EMPLOYEE, WE'LL MAKE AN EXCEPTION.
I CAN'T WORK... CAN'T THINK...
TUESDAY I WENT TO THE DOCTOR...AND HERE IT IS FRIDAY.. MY LAST DAY..
OH, MY HEAD.. MY HEAD!
GOING BLIND... HE TOLD ME TUESDAY, COMMISSIONER! YOU KNOW HOW WORRIED I WAS ABOUT THOSE SHORTAGES... THIS EXPLAINS IT... OBVIOUSLY ALL AN ACCOUNTING MISTAKE BY THAT POOR HALF-BLIND MAN!
THINK HE MADE THE WRONG ENTRIES, EH?
NO DOUBT ABOUT IT...ER.. AHEM... MR. STET! COMMISSIONER DOLAN WOULD LIKE A WORD WITH YOU!
THE BANKS HAVE FILED A COMPLAINT ..THERE'S A SHORTAGE OF $5,000 IN THE BOOKS. KNOW ANYTHING ABOUT IT?
$5,000...BY THE WAY... WASN'T THAT THE AMOUNT YOU NEEDED FOR YOUR OPERATION, MR. STET?
HMMM..
4

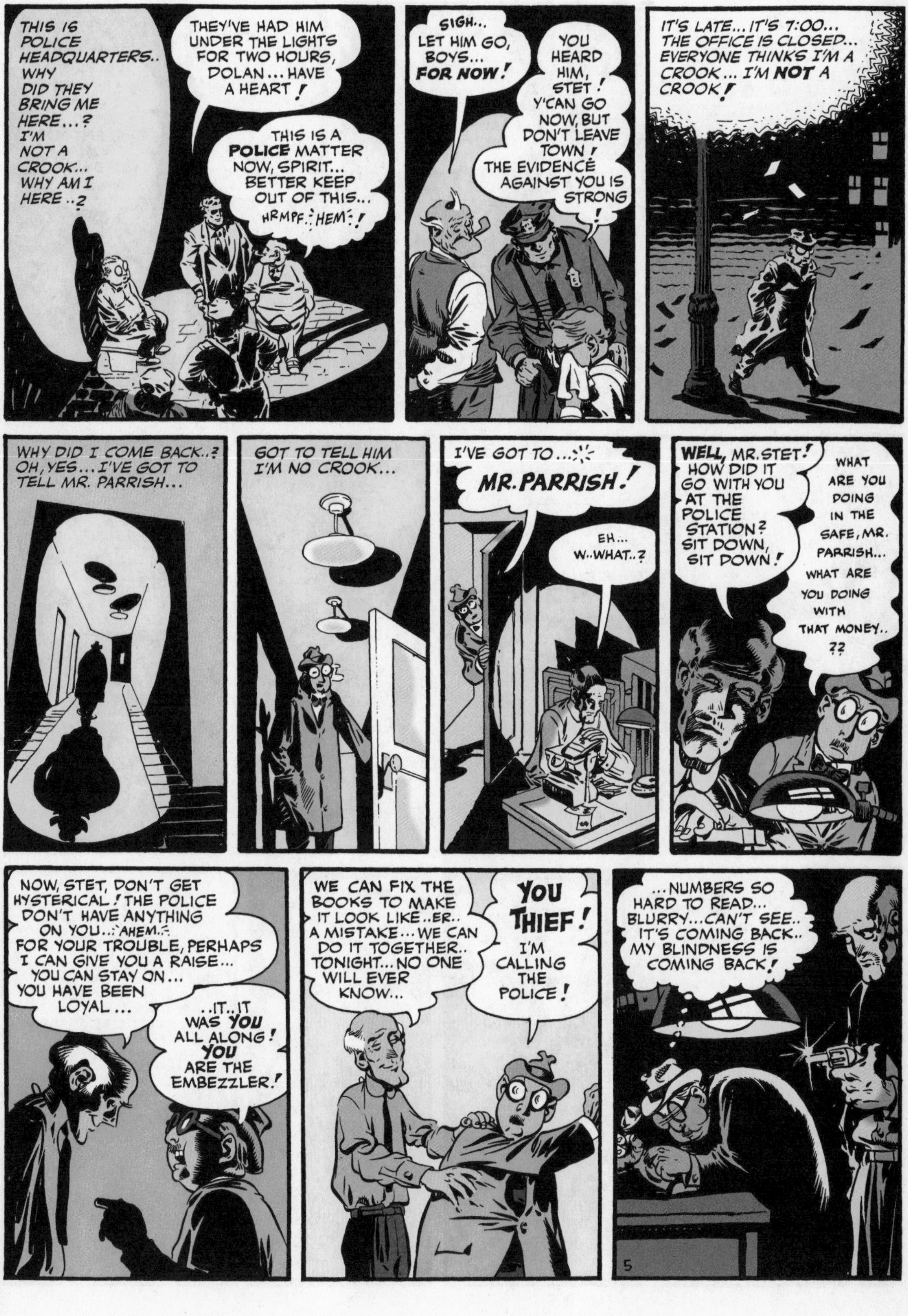
THIS IS POLICE HEADQUARTERS.. WHY DID THEY BRING ME HERE...? I'M NOT A CROOK... WHY AM I HERE..?
THEY'VE HAD HIM UNDER THE LIGHTS FOR TWO HOURS, DOLAN... HAVE A HEART!
THIS IS A POLICE MATTER NOW, SPIRIT... BETTER KEEP OUT OF THIS...
HRMPF.. HEM..!
SIGH... LET HIM GO, BOYS... FOR NOW!
YOU HEARD HIM, STET! Y'CAN GO NOW, BUT DON'T LEAVE TOWN! THE EVIDENCE AGAINST YOU IS STRONG!
IT'S LATE... IT'S 7:00... THE OFFICE IS CLOSED... EVERYONE THINKS I'M A CROOK... I'M NOT A CROOK!
WHY DID I COME BACK..? OH, YES... I'VE GOT TO TELL MR. PARRISH...
GOT TO TELL HIM I'M NO CROOK...
I'VE GOT TO...
MR. PARRISH!
EH... W..WHAT..?
WELL, MR. STET! HOW DID IT GO WITH YOU AT THE POLICE STATION? SIT DOWN, SIT DOWN!
WHAT ARE YOU DOING IN THE SAFE, MR. PARRISH... WHAT ARE YOU DOING WITH THAT MONEY..??
NOW, STET, DON'T GET HYSTERICAL! THE POLICE DON'T HAVE ANYTHING ON YOU... AHEM.. FOR YOUR TROUBLE, PERHAPS I CAN GIVE YOU A RAISE... YOU CAN STAY ON... YOU HAVE BEEN LOYAL...
..IT..IT WAS YOU ALL ALONG! YOU ARE THE EMBEZZLER!
WE CAN FIX THE BOOKS TO MAKE IT LOOK LIKE..ER.. A MISTAKE... WE CAN DO IT TOGETHER.. TONIGHT... NO ONE WILL EVER KNOW...
YOU THIEF! I'M CALLING THE POLICE!
...NUMBERS SO HARD TO READ... BLURRY...CAN'T SEE.. IT'S COMING BACK.. MY BLINDNESS IS COMING BACK!
5

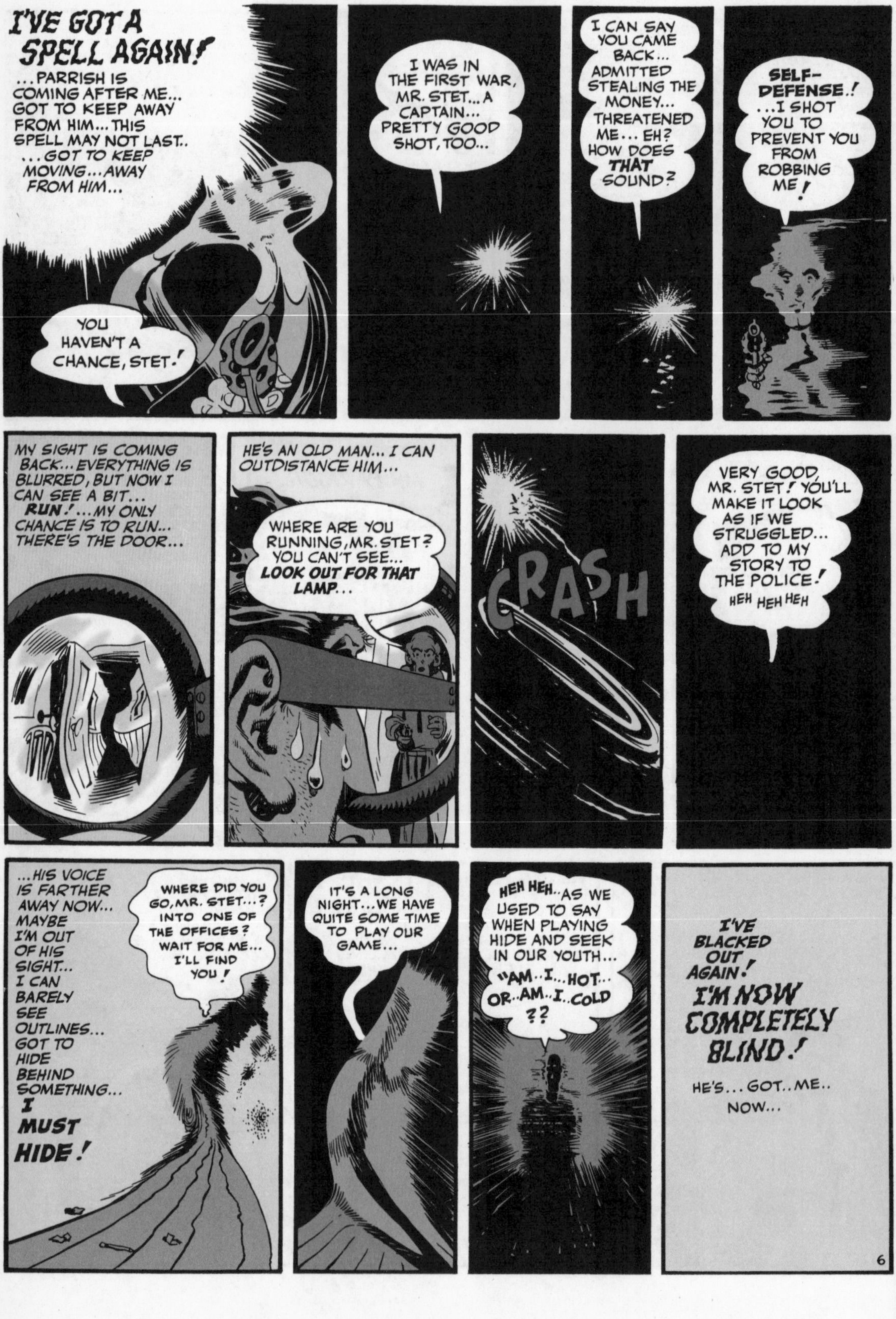

I'VE GOT A SPELL AGAIN! ...PARRISH IS COMING AFTER ME... GOT TO KEEP AWAY FROM HIM...THIS SPELL MAY NOT LAST.. ...GOT TO KEEP MOVING...AWAY FROM HIM...
YOU HAVEN'T A CHANCE, STET!
I WAS IN THE FIRST WAR, MR. STET... A CAPTAIN... PRETTY GOOD SHOT, TOO...
I CAN SAY YOU CAME BACK... ADMITTED STEALING THE MONEY... THREATENED ME... EH? HOW DOES THAT SOUND?
SELF-DEFENSE! ...I SHOT YOU TO PREVENT YOU FROM ROBBING ME!
MY SIGHT IS COMING BACK...EVERYTHING IS BLURRED, BUT NOW I CAN SEE A BIT... RUN! ...MY ONLY CHANCE IS TO RUN... THERE'S THE DOOR...
HE'S AN OLD MAN... I CAN OUTDISTANCE HIM...
WHERE ARE YOU RUNNING, MR. STET? YOU CAN'T SEE... LOOK OUT FOR THAT LAMP...
CRASH
VERY GOOD, MR. STET! YOU'LL MAKE IT LOOK AS IF WE STRUGGLED... ADD TO MY STORY TO THE POLICE! HEH HEH HEH
...HIS VOICE IS FARTHER AWAY NOW... MAYBE I'M OUT OF HIS SIGHT... I CAN BARELY SEE OUTLINES... GOT TO HIDE BEHIND SOMETHING... I MUST HIDE!
WHERE DID YOU GO, MR. STET...? INTO ONE OF THE OFFICES? WAIT FOR ME... I'LL FIND YOU!
IT'S A LONG NIGHT...WE HAVE QUITE SOME TIME TO PLAY OUR GAME...
HEH HEH.. AS WE USED TO SAY WHEN PLAYING HIDE AND SEEK IN OUR YOUTH... "AM..I...HOT... OR..AM..I..COLD ??
I'VE BLACKED OUT AGAIN! I'M NOW COMPLETELY BLIND!
HE'S... GOT.. ME.. NOW...
6

BANG BANG

? | G#M!! ꞔ3★*%'!

HELP MR. STET, DOLAN! IT LOOKS LIKE WE MADE IT JUST IN TIME!

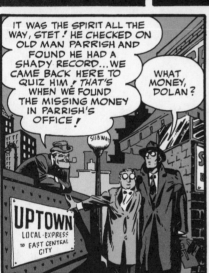

IT WAS THE SPIRIT ALL THE WAY, STET! HE CHECKED ON OLD MAN PARRISH AND FOUND HE HAD A SHADY RECORD...WE CAME BACK HERE TO QUIZ HIM! THAT'S WHEN WE FOUND THE MISSING MONEY IN PARRISH'S OFFICE!

WHAT MONEY, DOLAN?

UPTOWN
LOCAL · EXPRESS
TO EAST CENTRAL CITY

YOU KNOW EXACTLY WHAT I MEAN, SPIRIT! ...THE $5,000.. YOU FOUND IT YOURSELF! IT...HEY..WHERE YOU GOIN' WITH THAT DOUGH?

..TO THE HOSPITAL, DOLAN! THAT MONEY IS..ER... REWARD MONEY... R·E·W·A·R·D FOR CAPTURING PARRISH! ISN'T THAT RIGHT, DOLAN ??

..I DIDN'T EXPECT ANY REWARD ...I DIDN'T REALLY DO THE CAPTURING..

HEY...HIYA, MR. STET! GOIN' HOME LATE, AIN'TCHA? HEH HEH ..BOY, HAVE I GOT SUMPIN' T'SHOW YOU!..HERE... LOOKIT THIS PICTURE I TOOK OF ME KID HERMAN...

I'M NOT BOASTIN', Y'KNOW?...BUT DID YOU EVER SEE A KID MORE PHOTO-GEENIC? NOW, I WANT YOUR HONEST OPINION...

HERE'S THE HOSPITAL, MR. STET...LET'S GO!

?

HOW'YA LIKE THAT! HE GIMME THE BRUSH-OFF..! ...SOME GUYS ARE REAL SNOBS... Y'KNOW?

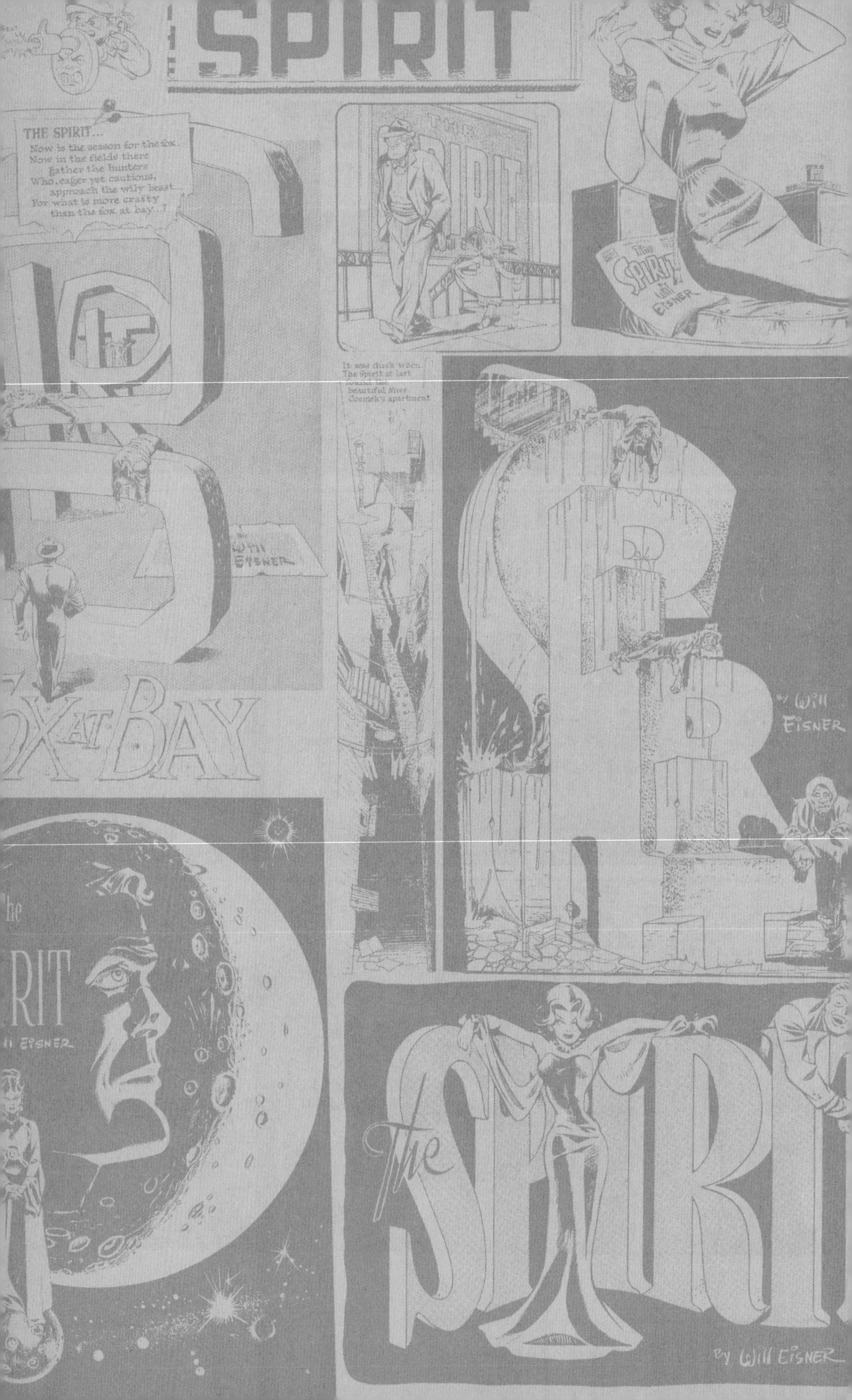
SPIRIT
THE SPIRIT...
Now is the season for the fox
Now in the fields there
gather the hunters
Who, eager yet cautious,
approach the wily beast...
For what is more crafty
than the fox at bay...?
By Will Eisner
AT BAY
THE SPIRIT
The SPIRIT by Will Eisner
It was dusk when
The Spirit at last
beautiful Miss
apartment
THE
by Will Eisner
he
RIT
Eisner
The SPIRIT
By Will Eisner

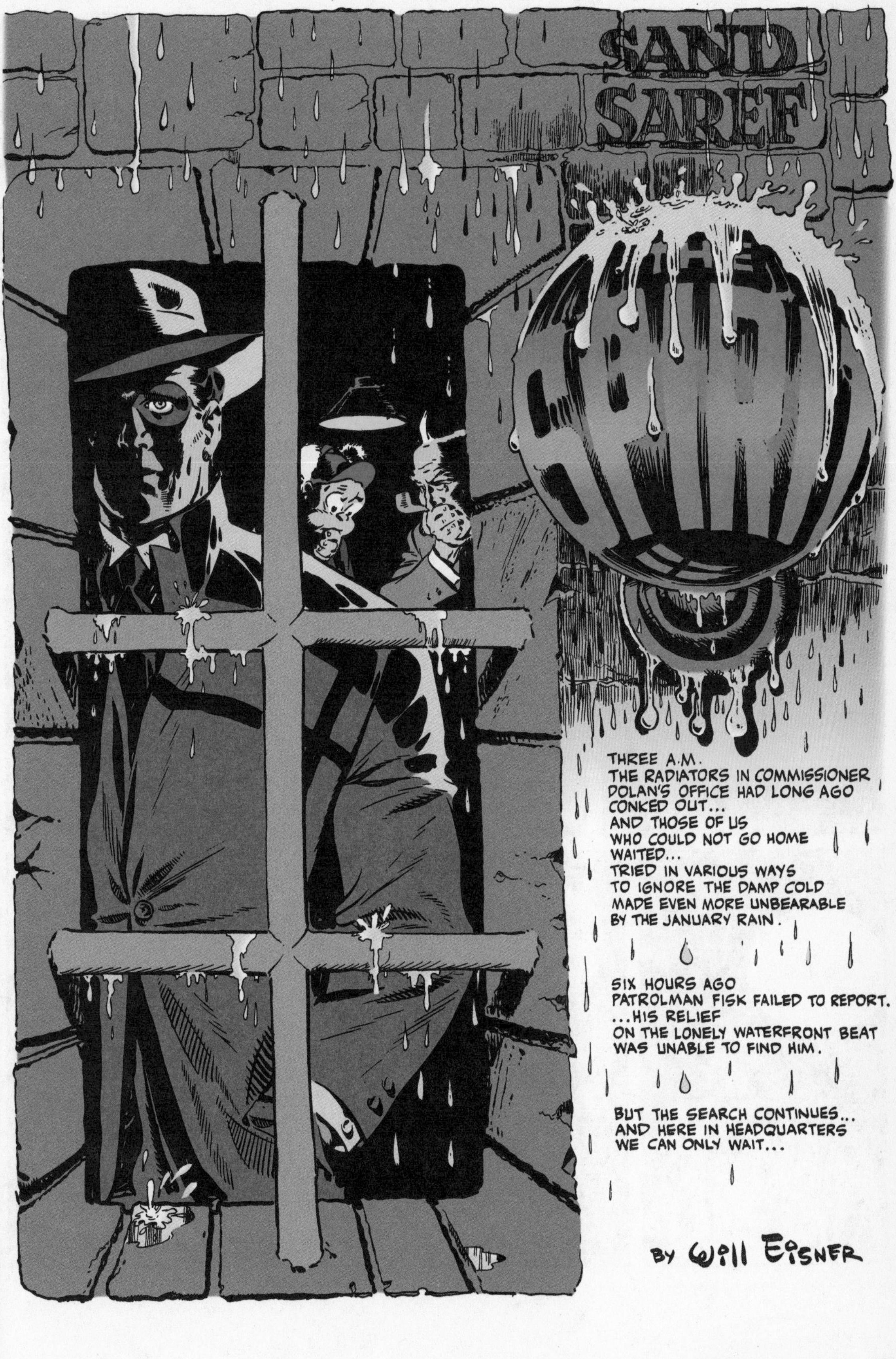
SAND SAREF
THE SPIRIT
THREE A.M.
THE RADIATORS IN COMMISSIONER DOLAN'S OFFICE HAD LONG AGO CONKED OUT...
AND THOSE OF US WHO COULD NOT GO HOME WAITED...
TRIED IN VARIOUS WAYS TO IGNORE THE DAMP COLD MADE EVEN MORE UNBEARABLE BY THE JANUARY RAIN.
SIX HOURS AGO PATROLMAN FISK FAILED TO REPORT.
...HIS RELIEF ON THE LONELY WATERFRONT BEAT WAS UNABLE TO FIND HIM.
BUT THE SEARCH CONTINUES... AND HERE IN HEADQUARTERS WE CAN ONLY WAIT...
BY Will Eisner

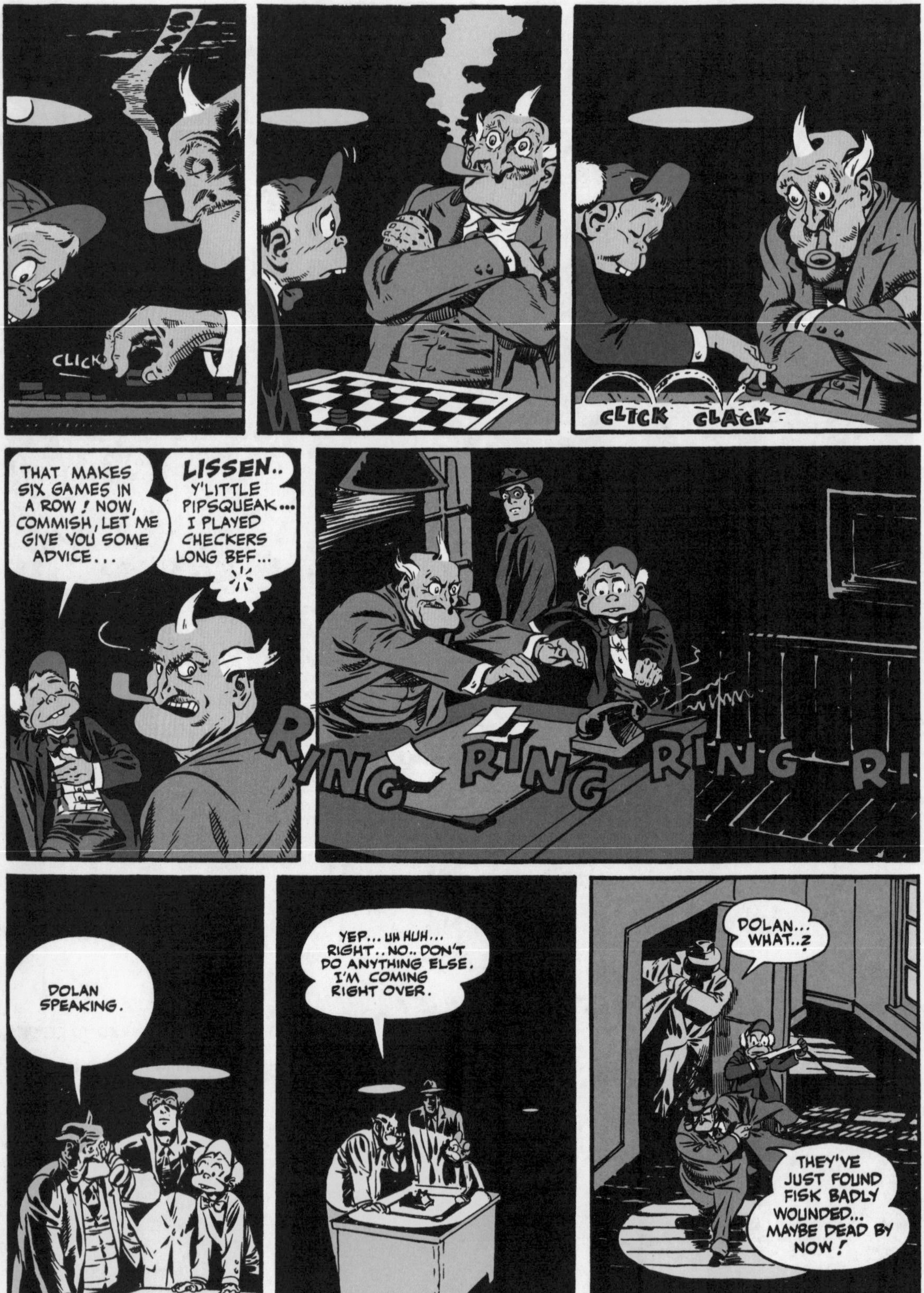
CLICK
CLICK CLACK
THAT MAKES SIX GAMES IN A ROW ! NOW, COMMISH, LET ME GIVE YOU SOME ADVICE . . .
LISSEN.. Y'LITTLE PIPSQUEAK... I PLAYED CHECKERS LONG BEF...
RING RING RING RI
DOLAN SPEAKING.
YEP... UH HUH... RIGHT.. NO.. DON'T DO ANYTHING ELSE. I'M COMING RIGHT OVER.
DOLAN... WHAT..?
THEY'VE JUST FOUND FISK BADLY WOUNDED... MAYBE DEAD BY NOW !

I HAD MY ANSWER A FEW MINUTES LATER, IN THE FROSTBITTEN MUD-FLATS BARED BY THE OUT-BOUND TIDE.

SHOT IN THE CHEST. STILL BREATHING, BUT IN TERRIBLE SHAPE. GET HIM TO THE POLICE HOSPITAL.

SCOUR EVERY INCH OF THIS PLACE. IN A FEW HOURS, THE TIDE'LL BE BACK IN...AND THERE WON'T BE A CLUE LEFT...

IF THERE IS A CLUE...

HEY..SPIRIT, I... HEY...

HE'S GONE!

I SAW HIM PICK UP A PIECE OF PAPER AND WALK OFF!

LET'S LOOK AROUND FOR HIM...HE MUSTA FOUND AN IMPORTANT CLUE...

BEST NOT, COMMISSIONER ...THESE MUD FLATS ARE TREACHEROUS, AND IT'S DARK. I'D WAIT TILL DAWN, SIR.

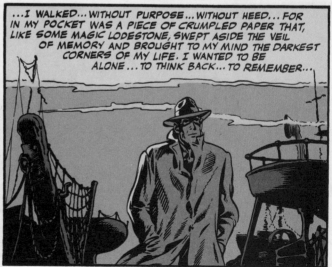

...I WALKED...WITHOUT PURPOSE...WITHOUT HEED...FOR IN MY POCKET WAS A PIECE OF CRUMPLED PAPER THAT, LIKE SOME MAGIC LODESTONE, SWEPT ASIDE THE VEIL OF MEMORY AND BROUGHT TO MY MIND THE DARKEST CORNERS OF MY LIFE. I WANTED TO BE ALONE...TO THINK BACK...TO REMEMBER...

I WALKED... LOST IN MEMORY... MY MIND SENT RACING BACK IN TIME BY A NAME SCRAWLED ON A CARD.."SAND SAREF"... WITHOUT THINKING, I FOUND MYSELF BACK IN DOLAN'S OFFICE AGAIN...

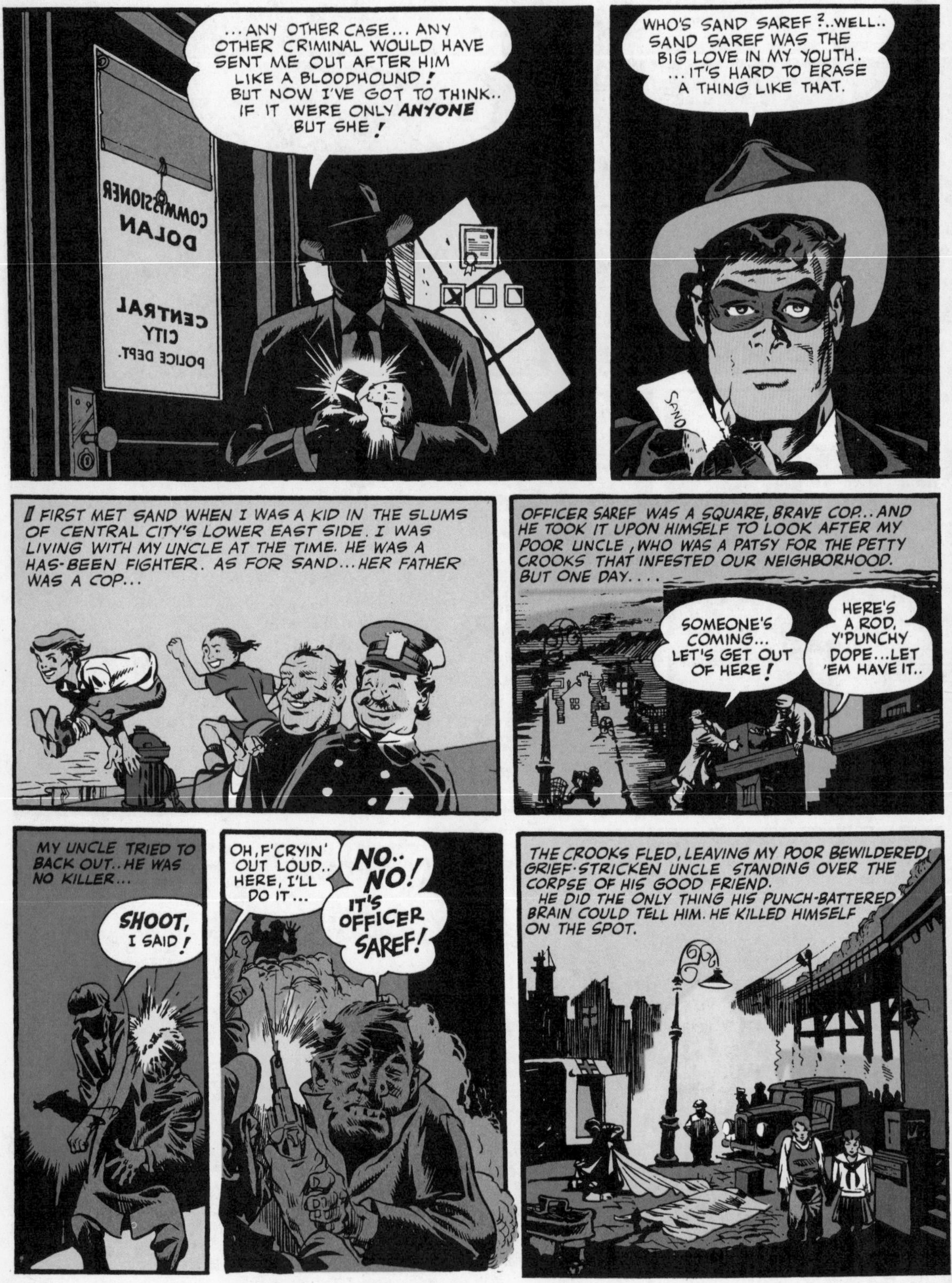
...ANY OTHER CASE... ANY OTHER CRIMINAL WOULD HAVE SENT ME OUT AFTER HIM LIKE A BLOODHOUND! BUT NOW I'VE GOT TO THINK.. IF IT WERE ONLY ANYONE BUT SHE!
COMMISSIONER DOLAN
CENTRAL CITY POLICE DEPT.
WHO'S SAND SAREF?..WELL.. SAND SAREF WAS THE BIG LOVE IN MY YOUTH. ...IT'S HARD TO ERASE A THING LIKE THAT.
I FIRST MET SAND WHEN I WAS A KID IN THE SLUMS OF CENTRAL CITY'S LOWER EAST SIDE. I WAS LIVING WITH MY UNCLE AT THE TIME. HE WAS A HAS-BEEN FIGHTER. AS FOR SAND... HER FATHER WAS A COP...
OFFICER SAREF WAS A SQUARE, BRAVE COP... AND HE TOOK IT UPON HIMSELF TO LOOK AFTER MY POOR UNCLE, WHO WAS A PATSY FOR THE PETTY CROOKS THAT INFESTED OUR NEIGHBORHOOD. BUT ONE DAY....
SOMEONE'S COMING... LET'S GET OUT OF HERE!
HERE'S A ROD, Y'PUNCHY DOPE...LET 'EM HAVE IT..
MY UNCLE TRIED TO BACK OUT..HE WAS NO KILLER...
SHOOT, I SAID!
OH, F'CRYIN' OUT LOUD.. HERE, I'LL DO IT...
NO.. NO! IT'S OFFICER SAREF!
THE CROOKS FLED, LEAVING MY POOR BEWILDERED GRIEF-STRICKEN UNCLE STANDING OVER THE CORPSE OF HIS GOOD FRIEND.
HE DID THE ONLY THING HIS PUNCH-BATTERED BRAIN COULD TELL HIM. HE KILLED HIMSELF ON THE SPOT.

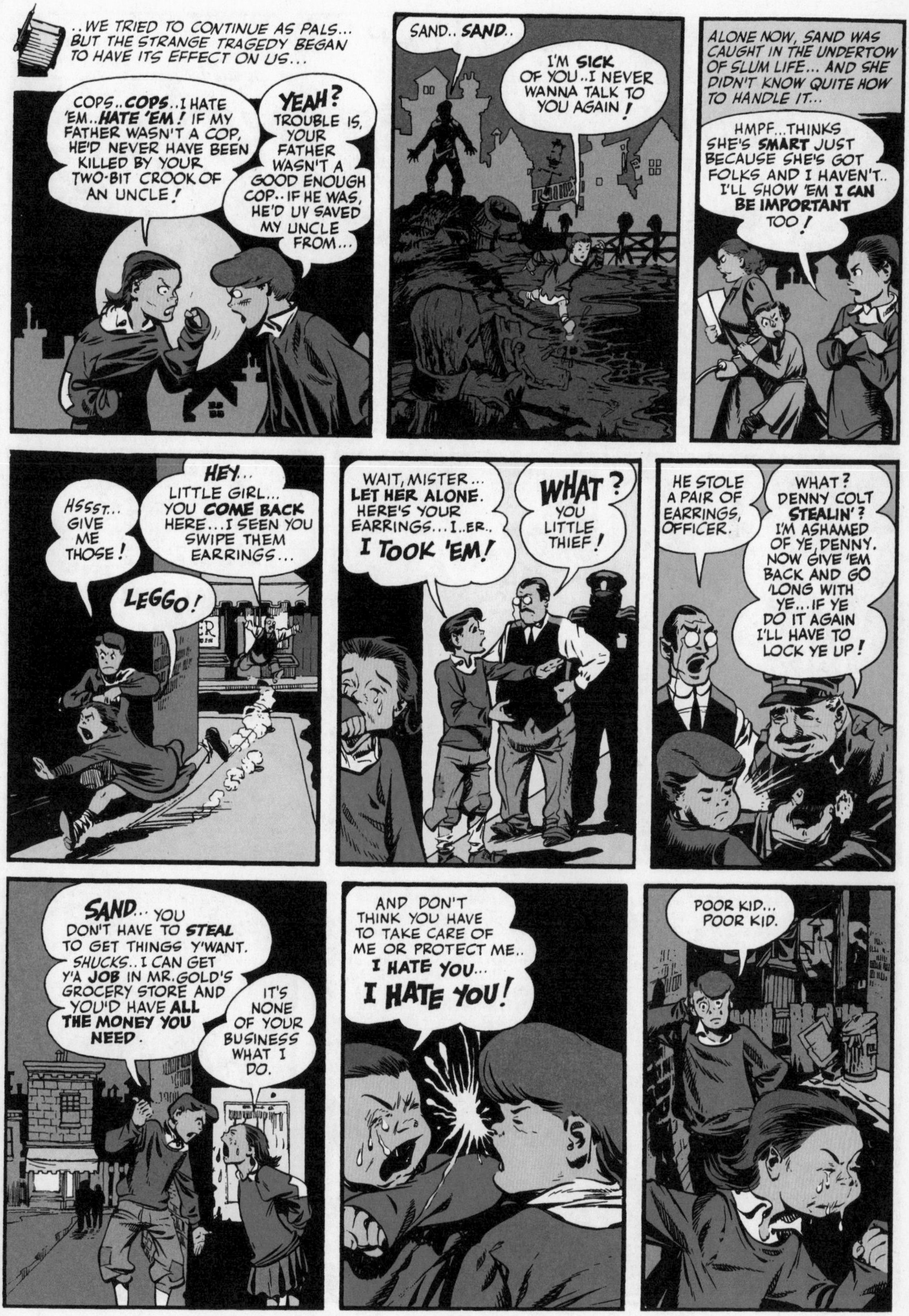

..WE TRIED TO CONTINUE AS PALS... BUT THE STRANGE TRAGEDY BEGAN TO HAVE ITS EFFECT ON US...
COPS..COPS..I HATE 'EM..HATE 'EM! IF MY FATHER WASN'T A COP, HE'D NEVER HAVE BEEN KILLED BY YOUR TWO-BIT CROOK OF AN UNCLE!
YEAH? TROUBLE IS, YOUR FATHER WASN'T A GOOD ENOUGH COP..IF HE WAS, HE'D UV SAVED MY UNCLE FROM...
SAND.. SAND..
I'M SICK OF YOU..I NEVER WANNA TALK TO YOU AGAIN!
ALONE NOW, SAND WAS CAUGHT IN THE UNDERTOW OF SLUM LIFE... AND SHE DIDN'T KNOW QUITE HOW TO HANDLE IT...
HMPF...THINKS SHE'S SMART JUST BECAUSE SHE'S GOT FOLKS AND I HAVEN'T.. I'LL SHOW 'EM I CAN BE IMPORTANT TOO!
HSSST... GIVE ME THOSE!
HEY... LITTLE GIRL... YOU COME BACK HERE...I SEEN YOU SWIPE THEM EARRINGS...
LEGGO!
WAIT, MISTER... LET HER ALONE. HERE'S YOUR EARRINGS... I..ER.. I TOOK 'EM!
WHAT? YOU LITTLE THIEF!
HE STOLE A PAIR OF EARRINGS, OFFICER.
WHAT? DENNY COLT STEALIN'? I'M ASHAMED OF YE, DENNY. NOW GIVE 'EM BACK AND GO 'LONG WITH YE...IF YE DO IT AGAIN I'LL HAVE TO LOCK YE UP!
SAND... YOU DON'T HAVE TO STEAL TO GET THINGS Y'WANT. SHUCKS..I CAN GET Y'A JOB IN MR.GOLD'S GROCERY STORE AND YOU'D HAVE ALL THE MONEY YOU NEED.
IT'S NONE OF YOUR BUSINESS WHAT I DO.
AND DON'T THINK YOU HAVE TO TAKE CARE OF ME OR PROTECT ME.. I HATE YOU... I HATE YOU!
POOR KID... POOR KID.

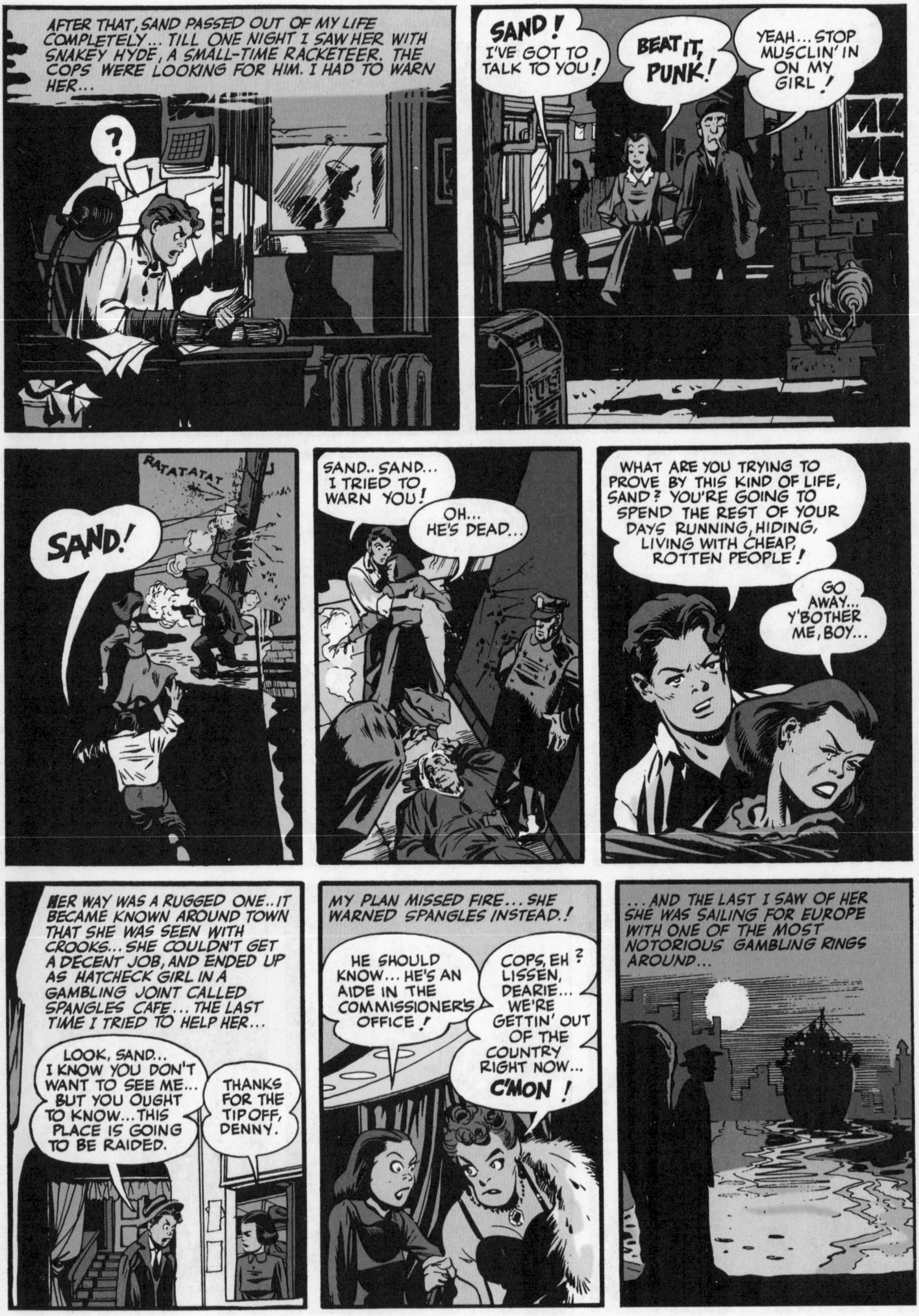
AFTER THAT, SAND PASSED OUT OF MY LIFE COMPLETELY... TILL ONE NIGHT I SAW HER WITH SNAKEY HYDE, A SMALL-TIME RACKETEER. THE COPS WERE LOOKING FOR HIM. I HAD TO WARN HER...
?
SAND! I'VE GOT TO TALK TO YOU!
BEAT IT, PUNK!
YEAH... STOP MUSCLIN' IN ON MY GIRL!
RATATATAT
SAND!
SAND.. SAND... I TRIED TO WARN YOU!
OH... HE'S DEAD...
WHAT ARE YOU TRYING TO PROVE BY THIS KIND OF LIFE, SAND? YOU'RE GOING TO SPEND THE REST OF YOUR DAYS RUNNING, HIDING, LIVING WITH CHEAP, ROTTEN PEOPLE!
GO AWAY... Y'BOTHER ME, BOY...
HER WAY WAS A RUGGED ONE.. IT BECAME KNOWN AROUND TOWN THAT SHE WAS SEEN WITH CROOKS... SHE COULDN'T GET A DECENT JOB, AND ENDED UP AS HATCHECK GIRL IN A GAMBLING JOINT CALLED SPANGLES CAFE... THE LAST TIME I TRIED TO HELP HER...
LOOK, SAND... I KNOW YOU DON'T WANT TO SEE ME... BUT YOU OUGHT TO KNOW... THIS PLACE IS GOING TO BE RAIDED.
THANKS FOR THE TIPOFF, DENNY.
MY PLAN MISSED FIRE... SHE WARNED SPANGLES INSTEAD.!
HE SHOULD KNOW... HE'S AN AIDE IN THE COMMISSIONER'S OFFICE!
COPS, EH? LISSEN, DEARIE... WE'RE GETTIN' OUT OF THE COUNTRY RIGHT NOW... C'MON!
... AND THE LAST I SAW OF HER SHE WAS SAILING FOR EUROPE WITH ONE OF THE MOST NOTORIOUS GAMBLING RINGS AROUND...

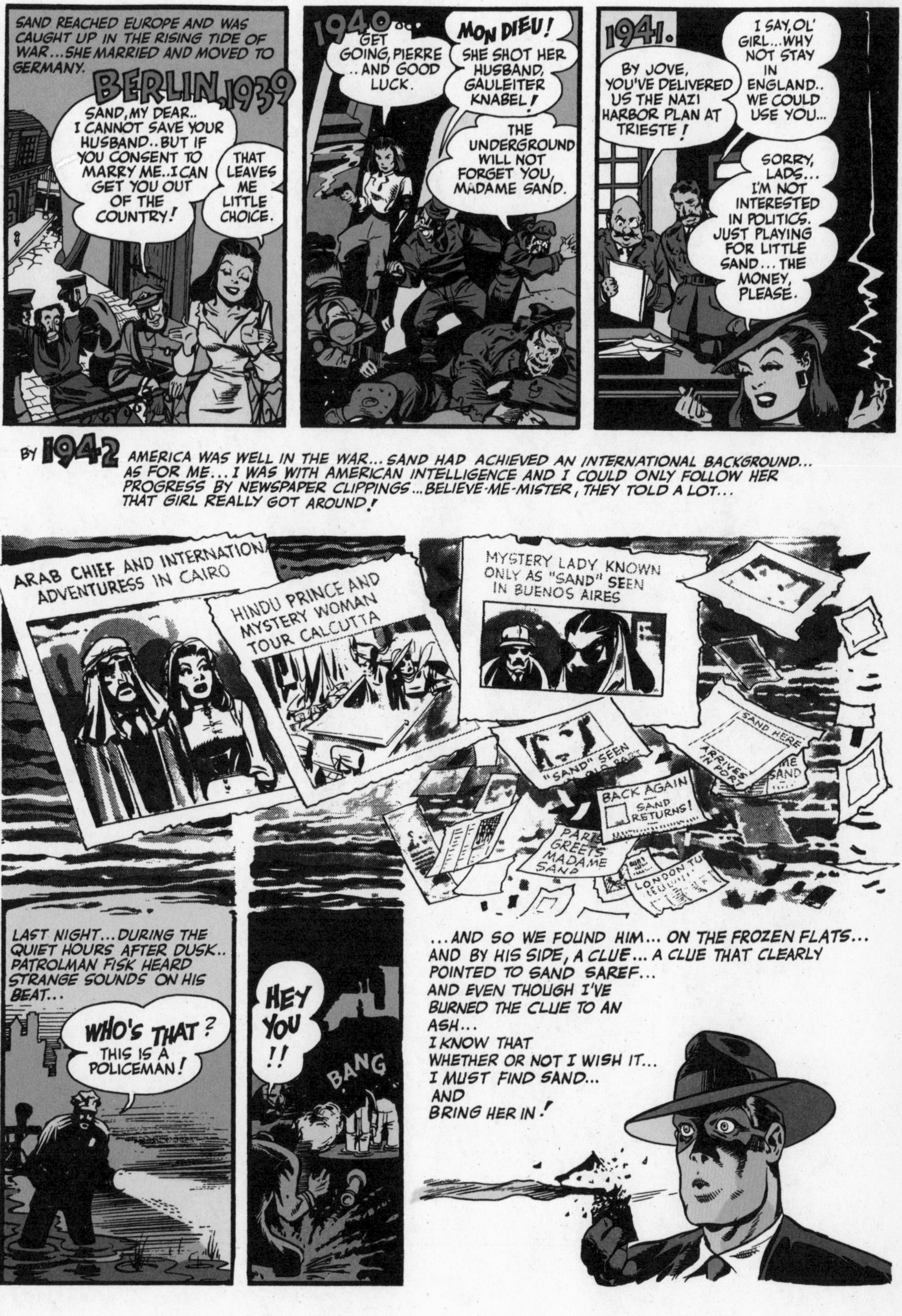

SAND REACHED EUROPE AND WAS CAUGHT UP IN THE RISING TIDE OF WAR... SHE MARRIED AND MOVED TO GERMANY.
BERLIN, 1939
SAND, MY DEAR.. I CANNOT SAVE YOUR HUSBAND.. BUT IF YOU CONSENT TO MARRY ME.. I CAN GET YOU OUT OF THE COUNTRY!
THAT LEAVES ME LITTLE CHOICE.
1940...
GET GOING, PIERRE .. AND GOOD LUCK.
MON DIEU! SHE SHOT HER HUSBAND, GAULEITER KNABEL!
THE UNDERGROUND WILL NOT FORGET YOU, MADAME SAND.
1941.
BY JOVE, YOU'VE DELIVERED US THE NAZI HARBOR PLAN AT TRIESTE!
I SAY, OL' GIRL... WHY NOT STAY IN ENGLAND.. WE COULD USE YOU...
SORRY, LADS... I'M NOT INTERESTED IN POLITICS. JUST PLAYING FOR LITTLE SAND... THE MONEY, PLEASE.
BY 1942 AMERICA WAS WELL IN THE WAR... SAND HAD ACHIEVED AN INTERNATIONAL BACKGROUND... AS FOR ME... I WAS WITH AMERICAN INTELLIGENCE AND I COULD ONLY FOLLOW HER PROGRESS BY NEWSPAPER CLIPPINGS... BELIEVE-ME-MISTER, THEY TOLD A LOT... THAT GIRL REALLY GOT AROUND!
ARAB CHIEF AND INTERNATIONA ADVENTURESS IN CAIRO
HINDU PRINCE AND MYSTERY WOMAN TOUR CALCUTTA
MYSTERY LADY KNOWN ONLY AS "SAND" SEEN IN BUENOS AIRES
"SAND" SEEN
SAND HERE
ARRIVES IN PORT
SAND
BACK AGAIN
SAND RETURNS!
PARIS GREETS MADAME SAND
LONDON TI
LAST NIGHT... DURING THE QUIET HOURS AFTER DUSK.. PATROLMAN FISK HEARD STRANGE SOUNDS ON HIS BEAT...
WHO'S THAT? THIS IS A POLICEMAN!
HEY YOU !!
BANG
...AND SO WE FOUND HIM... ON THE FROZEN FLATS... AND BY HIS SIDE, A CLUE... A CLUE THAT CLEARLY POINTED TO SAND SAREF... AND EVEN THOUGH I'VE BURNED THE CLUE TO AN ASH... I KNOW THAT WHETHER OR NOT I WISH IT... I MUST FIND SAND... AND BRING HER IN!

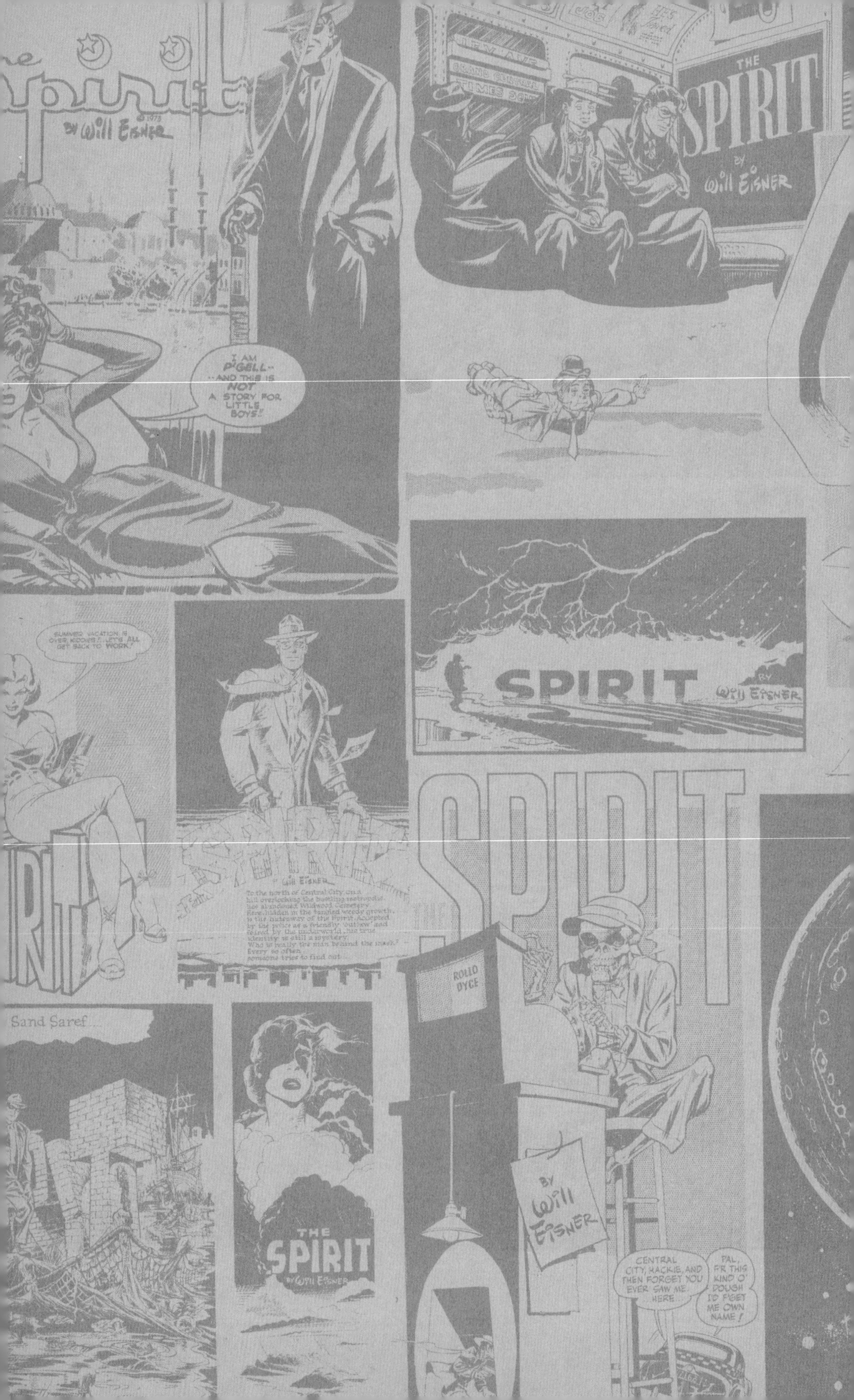

The Spirit
BY Will Eisner
I AM P'GELL-- --AND THIS IS NOT A STORY FOR LITTLE BOYS!!
THE SPIRIT
BY Will Eisner
SUMMER VACATION IS OVER KIDDIES! LET'S ALL GET BACK TO WORK!
SPIRIT
BY Will Eisner
BY Will Eisner
To the north of Central City on a hill overlooking the bustling metropolis lies abandoned Wildwood Cemetery. Here, hidden in the tangled weedy growth, is the hideaway of the Spirit. Accepted by the police as a friendly 'outlaw' and feared by the underworld, his true identity is still a mystery. Who is really the man behind the mask? Every so often someone tries to find out...
SPIRIT
Sand Saref....
ROLLO DYCE
THE SPIRIT
BY Will Eisner
BY Will Eisner
CENTRAL CITY, HACKIE, AND THEN FORGET YOU EVER SAW ME HERE...
PAL, FR THIS KIND O' DOUGH I'D F'GET ME OWN NAME!

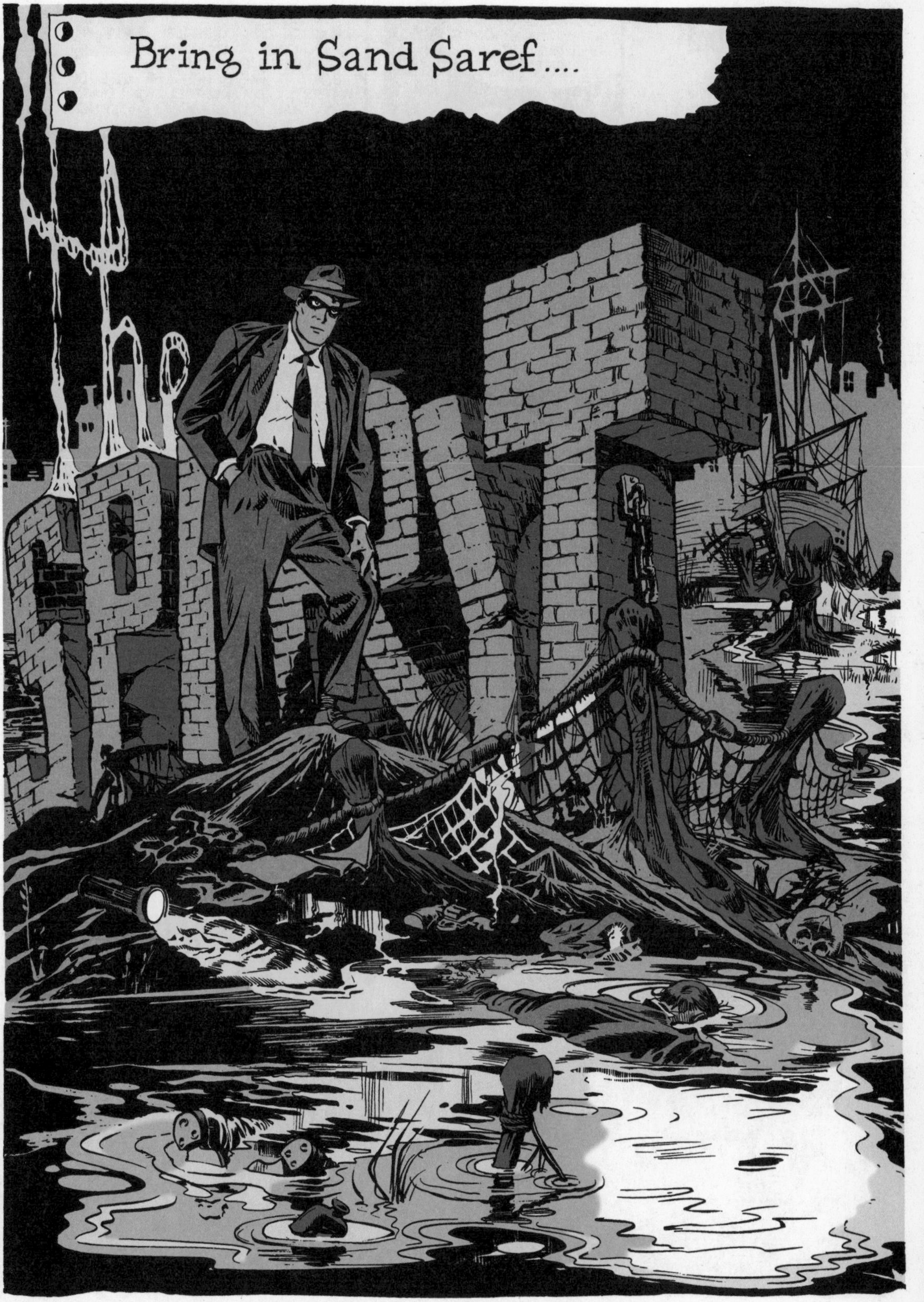
Bring in Sand Saref....

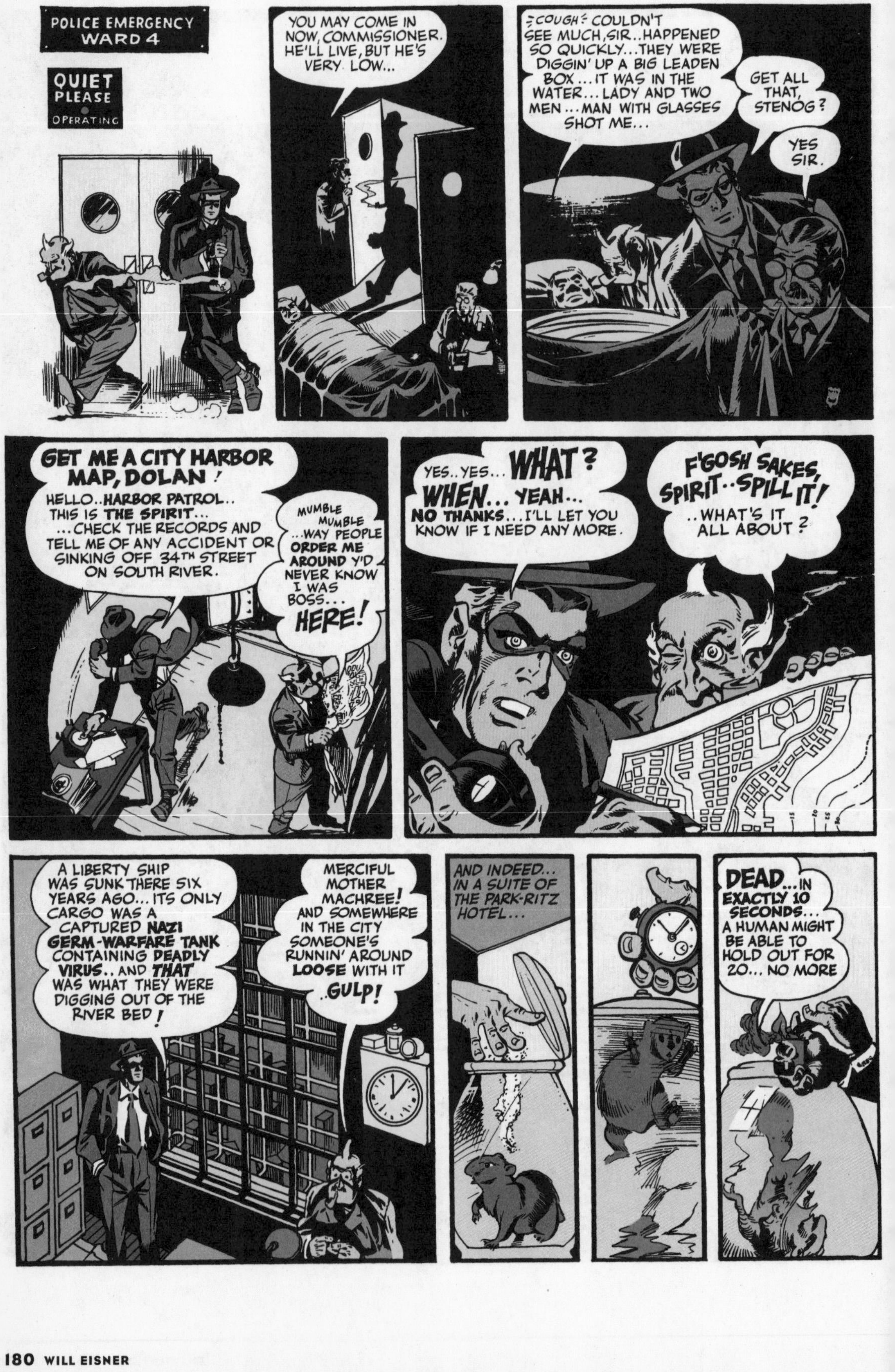
POLICE EMERGENCY WARD 4
QUIET PLEASE OPERATING
YOU MAY COME IN NOW, COMMISSIONER. HE'LL LIVE, BUT HE'S VERY LOW...
COUGH COULDN'T SEE MUCH, SIR.. HAPPENED SO QUICKLY... THEY WERE DIGGIN' UP A BIG LEADEN BOX... IT WAS IN THE WATER... LADY AND TWO MEN... MAN WITH GLASSES SHOT ME...
GET ALL THAT, STENOG?
YES SIR.
GET ME A CITY HARBOR MAP, DOLAN!
HELLO.. HARBOR PATROL.. THIS IS THE SPIRIT... ...CHECK THE RECORDS AND TELL ME OF ANY ACCIDENT OR SINKING OFF 34TH STREET ON SOUTH RIVER.
MUMBLE MUMBLE ...WAY PEOPLE ORDER ME AROUND Y'D NEVER KNOW I WAS BOSS... HERE!
YES.. YES... WHAT? WHEN... YEAH... NO THANKS... I'LL LET YOU KNOW IF I NEED ANY MORE.
F'GOSH SAKES, SPIRIT.. SPILL IT! ..WHAT'S IT ALL ABOUT?
A LIBERTY SHIP WAS SUNK THERE SIX YEARS AGO... ITS ONLY CARGO WAS A CAPTURED NAZI GERM-WARFARE TANK CONTAINING DEADLY VIRUS.. AND THAT WAS WHAT THEY WERE DIGGING OUT OF THE RIVER BED!
MERCIFUL MOTHER MACHREE! AND SOMEWHERE IN THE CITY SOMEONE'S RUNNIN' AROUND LOOSE WITH IT ..GULP!
AND INDEED... IN A SUITE OF THE PARK-RITZ HOTEL...
DEAD... IN EXACTLY 10 SECONDS... A HUMAN MIGHT BE ABLE TO HOLD OUT FOR 20... NO MORE

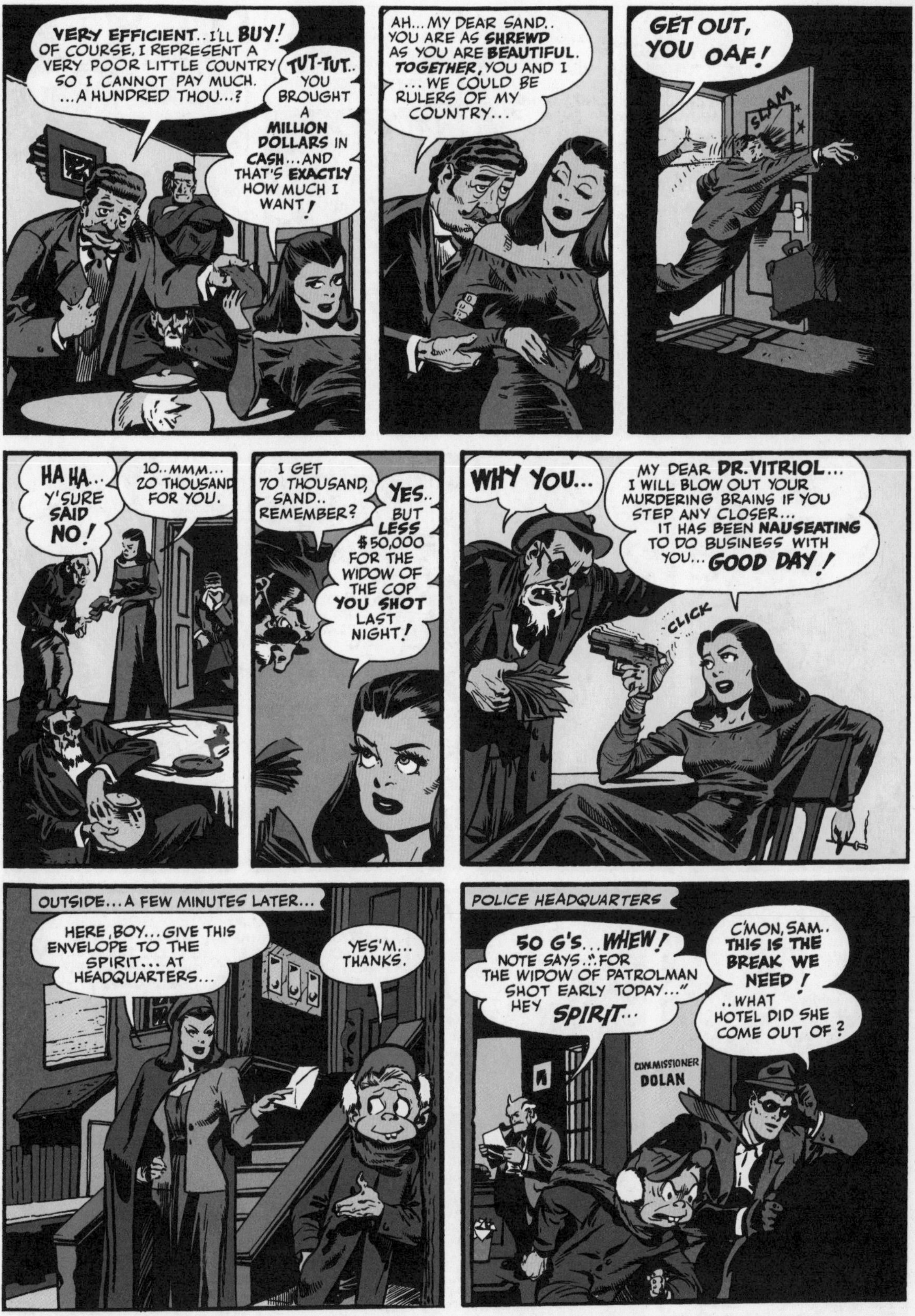
VERY EFFICIENT.. I'LL BUY! OF COURSE, I REPRESENT A VERY POOR LITTLE COUNTRY SO I CANNOT PAY MUCH. ...A HUNDRED THOU...?
TUT-TUT.. YOU BROUGHT A MILLION DOLLARS IN CASH...AND THAT'S EXACTLY HOW MUCH I WANT!
AH... MY DEAR SAND.. YOU ARE AS SHREWD AS YOU ARE BEAUTIFUL. TOGETHER, YOU AND I ... WE COULD BE RULERS OF MY COUNTRY...
GET OUT, YOU OAF!
SLAM
HA HA... Y'SURE SAID NO!
10.. MMM... 20 THOUSAND FOR YOU.
I GET 70 THOUSAND, SAND.. REMEMBER?
YES.. BUT LESS $50,000 FOR THE WIDOW OF THE COP YOU SHOT LAST NIGHT!
WHY YOU...
MY DEAR DR. VITRIOL... I WILL BLOW OUT YOUR MURDERING BRAINS IF YOU STEP ANY CLOSER... IT HAS BEEN NAUSEATING TO DO BUSINESS WITH YOU... GOOD DAY!
CLICK
OUTSIDE... A FEW MINUTES LATER...
HERE, BOY... GIVE THIS ENVELOPE TO THE SPIRIT... AT HEADQUARTERS...
YES'M... THANKS.
POLICE HEADQUARTERS
50 G'S... WHEW! NOTE SAYS..."FOR THE WIDOW OF PATROLMAN SHOT EARLY TODAY..." HEY SPIRIT...
C'MON, SAM.. THIS IS THE BREAK WE NEED! ..WHAT HOTEL DID SHE COME OUT OF?
COMMISSIONER DOLAN

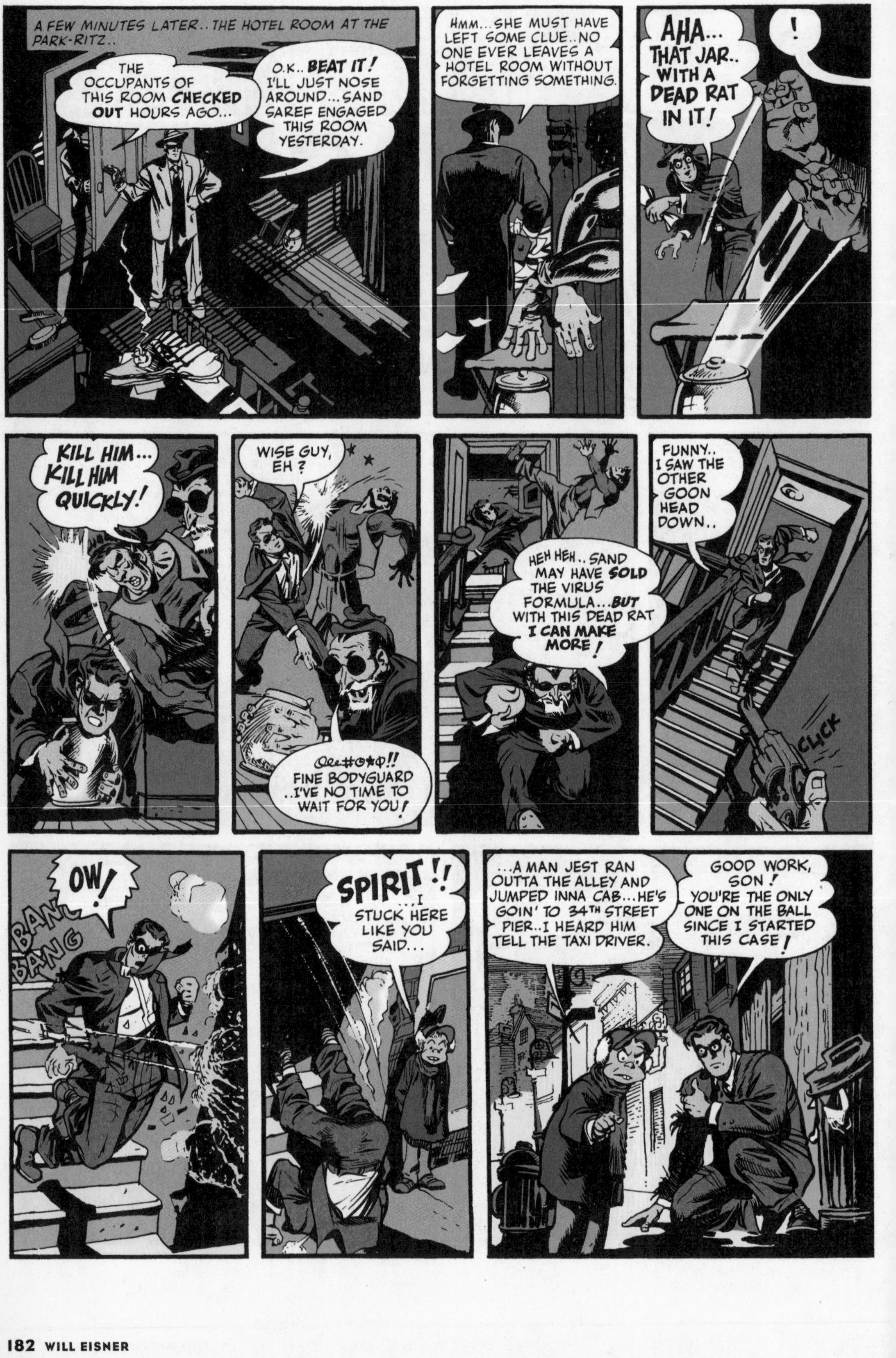
A FEW MINUTES LATER.. THE HOTEL ROOM AT THE PARK-RITZ..
THE OCCUPANTS OF THIS ROOM CHECKED OUT HOURS AGO...
O.K.. BEAT IT! I'LL JUST NOSE AROUND... SAND SAREF ENGAGED THIS ROOM YESTERDAY.
HMM... SHE MUST HAVE LEFT SOME CLUE.. NO ONE EVER LEAVES A HOTEL ROOM WITHOUT FORGETTING SOMETHING.
AHA... THAT JAR.. WITH A DEAD RAT IN IT!
!
KILL HIM... KILL HIM QUICKLY!
WISE GUY, EH?
FINE BODYGUARD ..I'VE NO TIME TO WAIT FOR YOU!
HEH HEH.. SAND MAY HAVE SOLD THE VIRUS FORMULA...BUT WITH THIS DEAD RAT I CAN MAKE MORE!
FUNNY.. I SAW THE OTHER GOON HEAD DOWN..
CLICK
OW!
BANG
BANG
SPIRIT!! ...I STUCK HERE LIKE YOU SAID...
...A MAN JEST RAN OUTTA THE ALLEY AND JUMPED INNA CAB...HE'S GOIN' TO 34TH STREET PIER..I HEARD HIM TELL THE TAXI DRIVER.
GOOD WORK, SON! YOU'RE THE ONLY ONE ON THE BALL SINCE I STARTED THIS CASE!

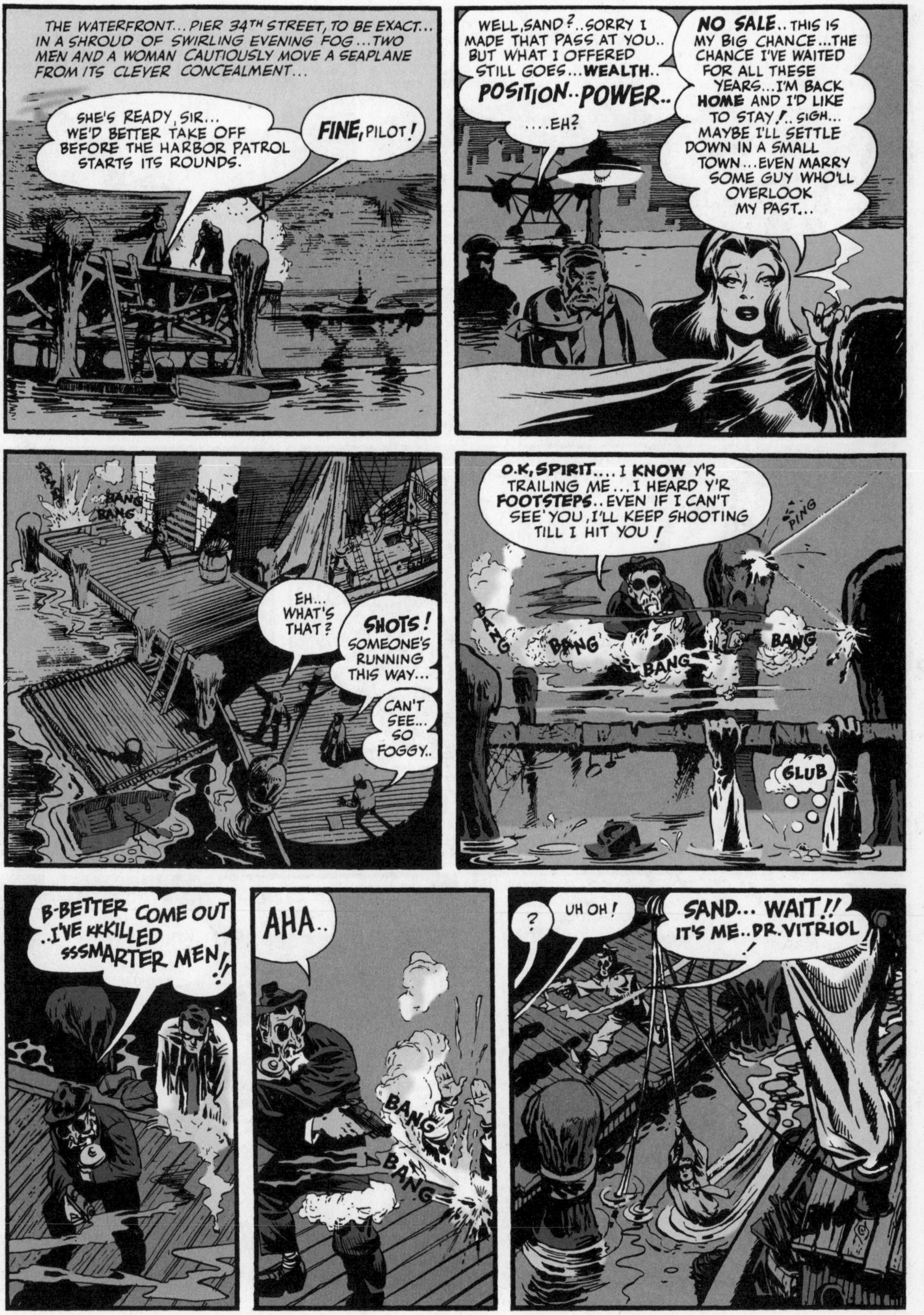
THE WATERFRONT... PIER 34TH STREET, TO BE EXACT... IN A SHROUD OF SWIRLING EVENING FOG... TWO MEN AND A WOMAN CAUTIOUSLY MOVE A SEAPLANE FROM ITS CLEVER CONCEALMENT...
SHE'S READY, SIR... WE'D BETTER TAKE OFF BEFORE THE HARBOR PATROL STARTS ITS ROUNDS.
FINE, PILOT!
WELL, SAND?.. SORRY I MADE THAT PASS AT YOU.. BUT WHAT I OFFERED STILL GOES... WEALTH.. POSITION.. POWER..
....EH?
NO SALE.. THIS IS MY BIG CHANCE... THE CHANCE I'VE WAITED FOR ALL THESE YEARS... I'M BACK HOME AND I'D LIKE TO STAY!.. SIGH... MAYBE I'LL SETTLE DOWN IN A SMALL TOWN... EVEN MARRY SOME GUY WHO'LL OVERLOOK MY PAST...
BANG
BANG
EH... WHAT'S THAT?
SHOTS! SOMEONE'S RUNNING THIS WAY...
CAN'T SEE... SO FOGGY..
O.K, SPIRIT.... I KNOW Y'R TRAILING ME... I HEARD Y'R FOOTSTEPS.. EVEN IF I CAN'T SEE YOU, I'LL KEEP SHOOTING TILL I HIT YOU!
PING
BANG
BANG
BANG
BANG
GLUB
B-BETTER COME OUT ..I'VE KKKILLED SSSMARTER MEN!!
AHA..
BANG
BANG
?
UH OH!
SAND... WAIT!! IT'S ME.. DR. VITRIOL!

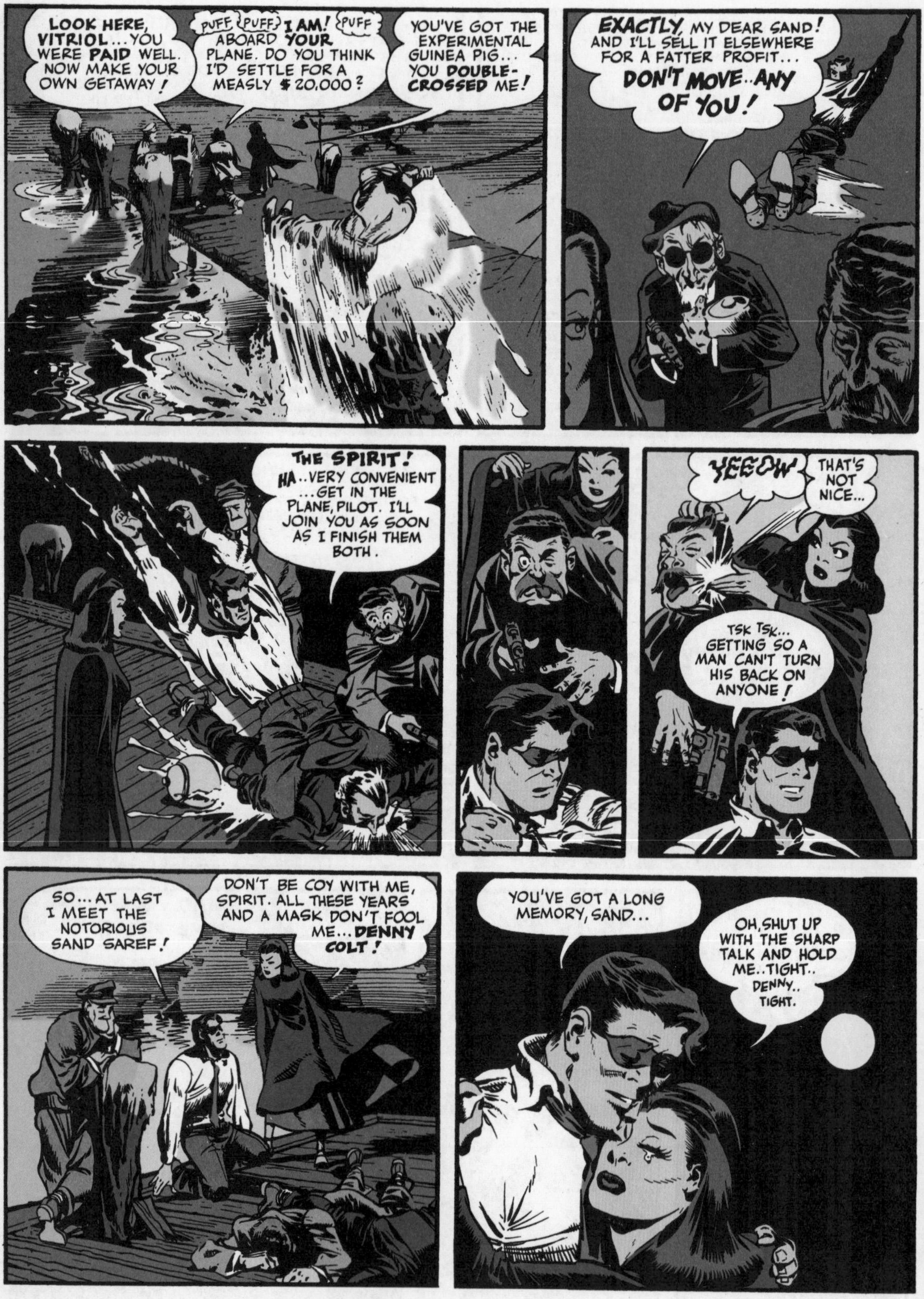
LOOK HERE, VITRIOL... YOU WERE PAID WELL. NOW MAKE YOUR OWN GETAWAY!
PUFF PUFF I AM! PUFF ABOARD YOUR PLANE. DO YOU THINK I'D SETTLE FOR A MEASLY $20,000?
YOU'VE GOT THE EXPERIMENTAL GUINEA PIG... YOU DOUBLE-CROSSED ME!
EXACTLY, MY DEAR SAND! AND I'LL SELL IT ELSEWHERE FOR A FATTER PROFIT... DON'T MOVE..ANY OF YOU!
THE SPIRIT! HA..VERY CONVENIENT ...GET IN THE PLANE, PILOT. I'LL JOIN YOU AS SOON AS I FINISH THEM BOTH.
YEEOW
THAT'S NOT NICE...
TSK TSK... GETTING SO A MAN CAN'T TURN HIS BACK ON ANYONE!
SO... AT LAST I MEET THE NOTORIOUS SAND SAREF!
DON'T BE COY WITH ME, SPIRIT. ALL THESE YEARS AND A MASK DON'T FOOL ME... DENNY COLT!
YOU'VE GOT A LONG MEMORY, SAND...
OH, SHUT UP WITH THE SHARP TALK AND HOLD ME..TIGHT.. DENNY.. TIGHT.

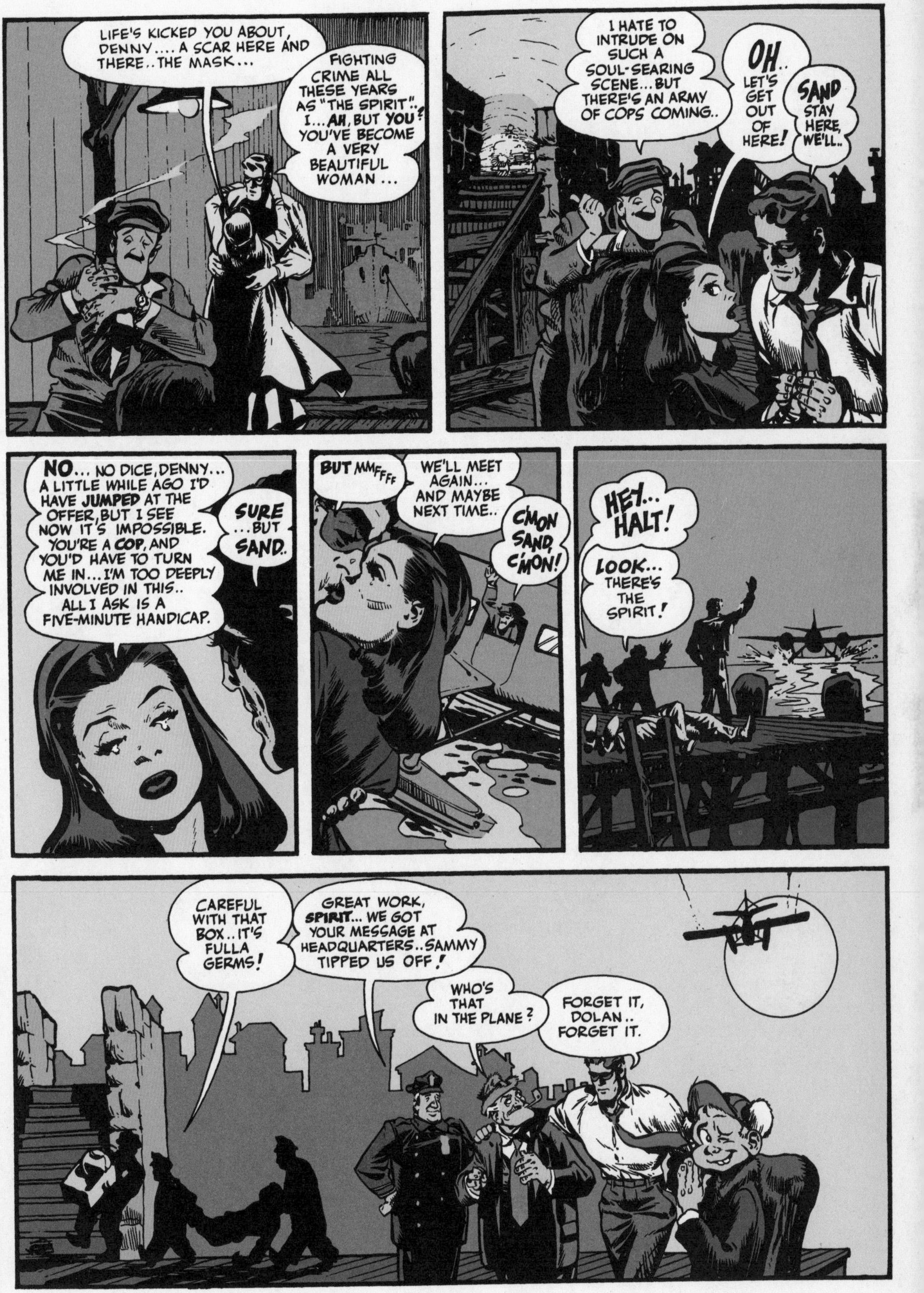
LIFE'S KICKED YOU ABOUT, DENNY.... A SCAR HERE AND THERE.. THE MASK...
FIGHTING CRIME ALL THESE YEARS AS "THE SPIRIT".. I...AH, BUT YOU? YOU'VE BECOME A VERY BEAUTIFUL WOMAN...
I HATE TO INTRUDE ON SUCH A SOUL-SEARING SCENE... BUT THERE'S AN ARMY OF COPS COMING..
OH.. LET'S GET OUT OF HERE!
SAND STAY HERE, WE'LL..
NO... NO DICE, DENNY... A LITTLE WHILE AGO I'D HAVE JUMPED AT THE OFFER, BUT I SEE NOW IT'S IMPOSSIBLE. YOU'RE A COP, AND YOU'D HAVE TO TURN ME IN... I'M TOO DEEPLY INVOLVED IN THIS.. ALL I ASK IS A FIVE-MINUTE HANDICAP.
SURE ...BUT SAND..
BUT MMFFFF
WE'LL MEET AGAIN... AND MAYBE NEXT TIME..
C'MON SAND, C'MON!
HEY... HALT!
LOOK... THERE'S THE SPIRIT!
CAREFUL WITH THAT BOX...IT'S FULLA GERMS!
GREAT WORK, SPIRIT... WE GOT YOUR MESSAGE AT HEADQUARTERS..SAMMY TIPPED US OFF!
WHO'S THAT IN THE PLANE?
FORGET IT, DOLAN.. FORGET IT.

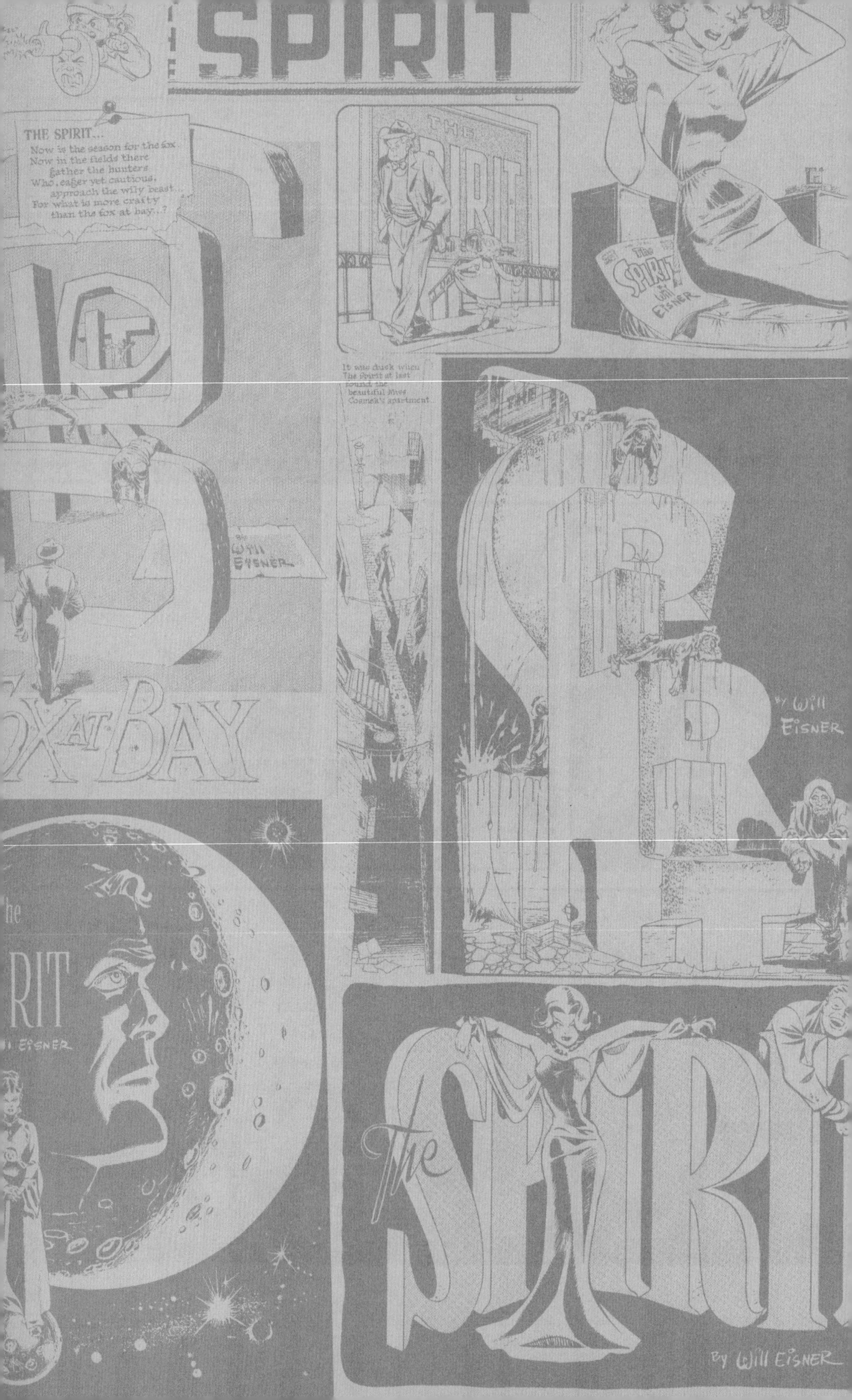
SPIRIT
THE SPIRIT...
Now is the season for the fox
Now in the fields there
gather the hunters
Who, eager yet cautious,
approach the wily beast...
For what is more crafty
than the fox at bay..?
By Will Eisner
OX AT BAY
THE SPIRIT
The SPIRIT by Will Eisner
It was dusk when The Spirit at last found the beautiful Miss Cosmek's apartment...
THE
By Will Eisner
RIT
EISNER
The SPIRIT
By Will Eisner

WILL EISNER

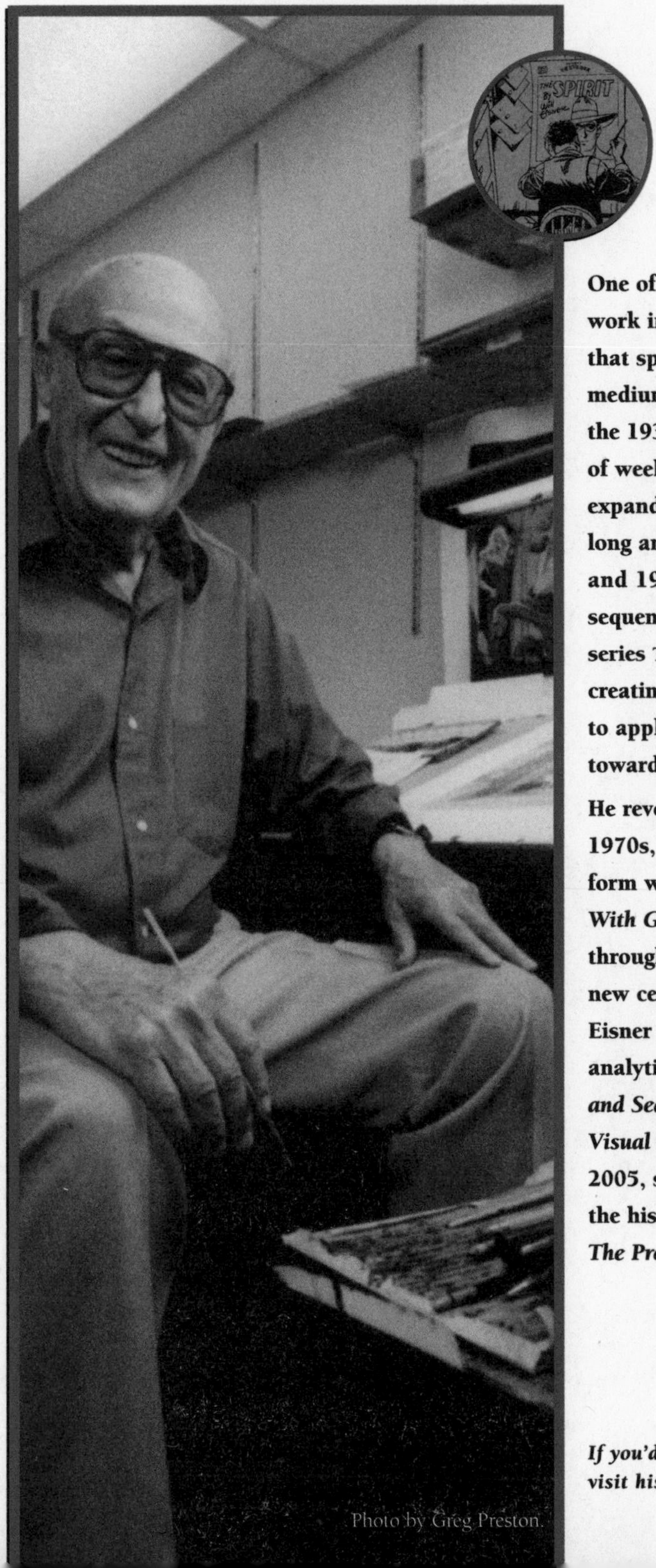
THE SPIRIT
Photo by Greg Preston.

One of the most celebrated creators ever to work in comics, Will Eisner crafted a legacy that spans almost the entire history of the medium. Beginning with his formative days in the 1930s, when he honed his skills on a series of weekly newspaper strips, Eisner consistently expanded the field's boundaries throughout his long and distinguished career. In the 1940s and 1950s, he revolutionized narrative sequential art with his internationally famed series THE SPIRIT while at the same time creating an innovative new company dedicated to applying the accessibility of comics language towards educational and commercial purposes. He revolutionized the medium once again in the 1970s, creating the contemporary graphic novel form with his groundbreaking title *A Contract With God* — a form he continued working in throughout the 1980s and 1990s and into the new century. Beyond this purely creative work, Eisner also wrote and drew the influential analytical and instructional volumes *Comics and Sequential Art* and *Graphic Storytelling and Visual Narrative*. He passed away on January 3, 2005, shortly after completing his final work: the historical study *The Plot: The Secret Story of The Protocols of the Elders of Zion*.

If you'd like to learn more about Will Eisner, visit his website at www.willeisner.com.

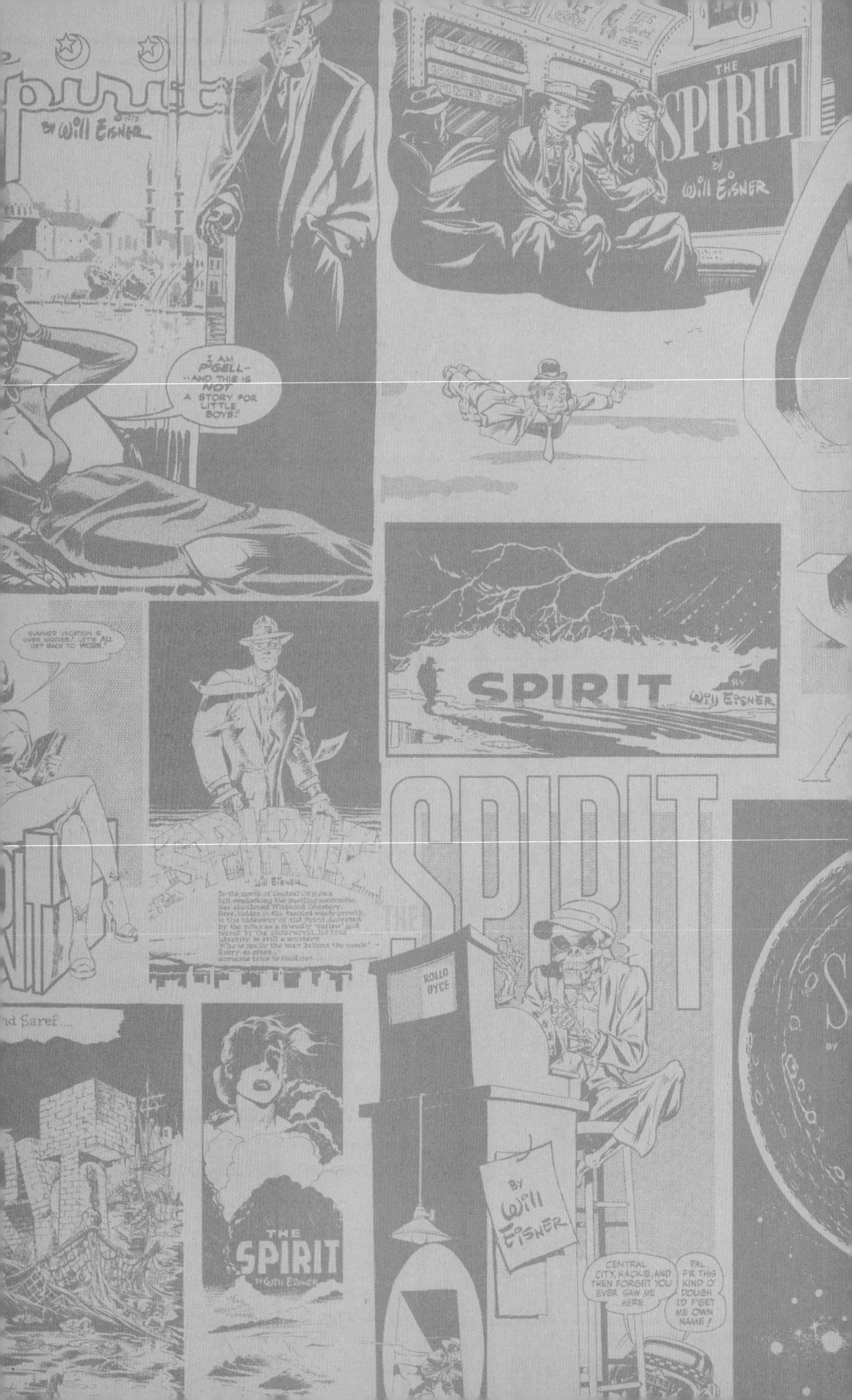
Spirit
BY Will Eisner ©1973
I AM P'GELL-- ...AND THIS IS NOT A STORY FOR LITTLE BOYS!
THE SPIRIT
BY Will Eisner
SPIRIT
BY Will Eisner
SUMMER VACATION IS OVER, KIDDIES! LET'S ALL GET BACK TO WORK!
Will Eisner
To the north of Central City, on a hill overlooking the bustling metropolis, lies abandoned Wildwood Cemetery. Here, hidden in the tangled weedy growth, is the hideaway of the Spirit. Accepted by the police as a friendly 'outlaw' and feared by the underworld, his true identity is still a mystery. Who is really the man behind the mask? Every so often, someone tries to find out...
THE SPIRIT
ROLLO DYCE
BY Will Eisner
THE SPIRIT
BY Will Eisner
CENTRAL CITY, HACKIE, AND THEN FORGET YOU EVER SAW ME HERE.
PAL, F'R THIS KIND O' DOUGH I'D F'GET ME OWN NAME!

WILL EISNER'S THE SPIRIT ARCHIVES

The complete run
of Will Eisner's
THE SPIRIT, collected in
chronological order and
reprinted in full-color,
hardcover editions.

THE WILL EISNER COMPANION

THE PIONEERING SPIRIT
OF THE FATHER OF
THE GRAPHIC NOVEL

By N.C. Christopher Couch
and Stephen Weiner
The first comprehensive
and authorized overview of
Will Eisner's unique career,
featuring critical and historical
essays, in-depth examinations
of pivotal works and much,
much more.

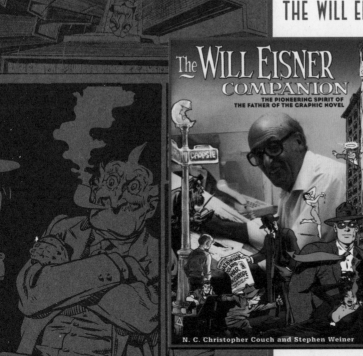

THE DC COMICS ARCHIVE EDITIONS

Re-presenting historic comics characters and their stories as they were originally seen.

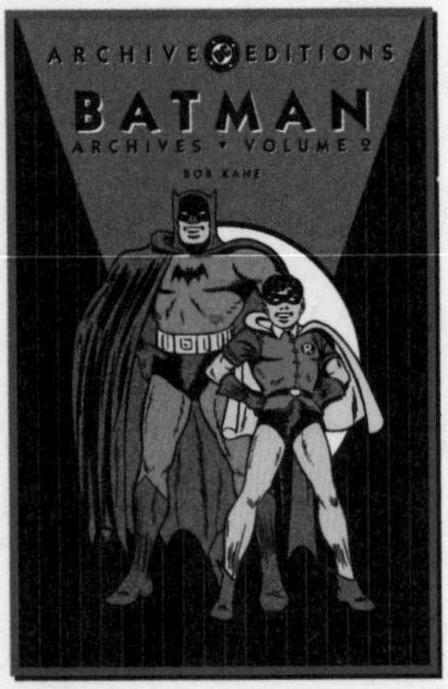
ARCHIVE EDITIONS
BATMAN
ARCHIVES • VOLUME 2
BOB KANE

ALL STAR COMICS ARCHIVES
Volumes 1-11 *(Featuring the adventures of the JUSTICE SOCIETY OF AMERICA)*

BATMAN ARCHIVES
Volumes 1-6 *(The Dark Knight's early adventures from DETECTIVE COMICS)*

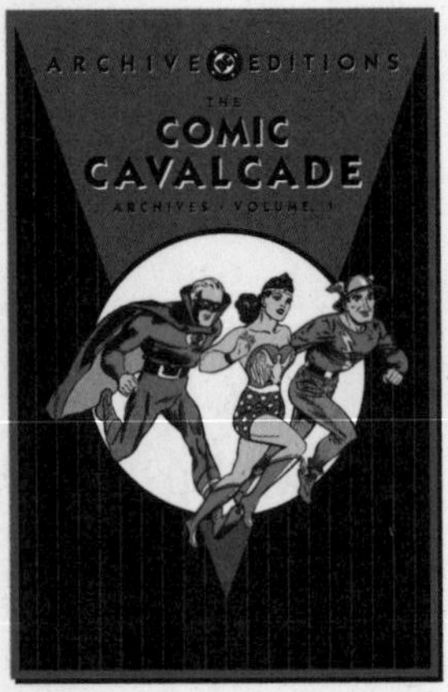
ARCHIVE EDITIONS
THE
COMIC
CAVALCADE

THE BLACK CANARY ARCHIVES
Volume 1 *(The Golden and Silver Age adventures of the Blonde Bombshell from FLASH COMICS and more)*

THE BLACKHAWK ARCHIVES
Volume 1 *(The Action Aviators' adventures from MILITARY COMICS)*

THE COMIC CAVALCADE ARCHIVES
Volume 1 *(Wonder Woman, The Flash, Green Lantern and more)*

THE DC COMICS RARITIES ARCHIVES
Volume 1 *(A collection of DC's Golden Age greats)*

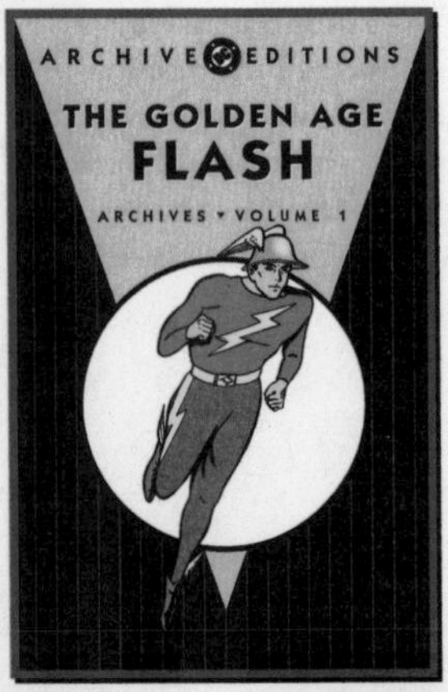
ARCHIVE EDITIONS
THE GOLDEN AGE
FLASH
ARCHIVES • VOLUME 1

THE GOLDEN AGE FLASH ARCHIVES
Volumes 1-2 *(The original Scarlet Speedster's adventures from FLASH COMICS*

THE GOLDEN AGE GREEN LANTERN ARCHIVES
Volumes 1-2 *(The adventures of Alan Scott, the original Emerald Gladiator, from ALL-AMERICAN COMICS and the GREEN LANTERN quarterly)*

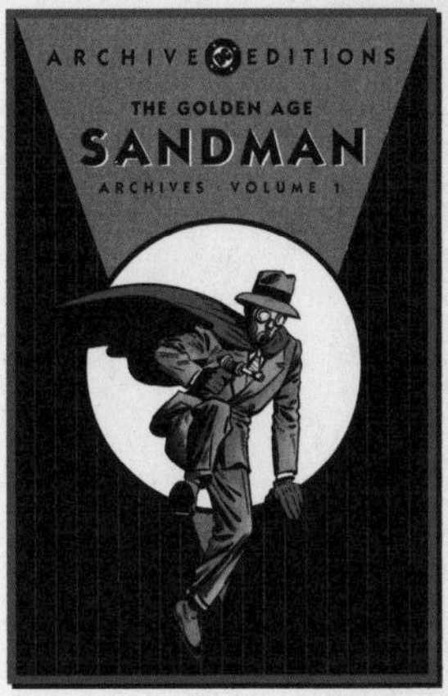
ARCHIVE EDITIONS
THE GOLDEN AGE
SANDMAN
ARCHIVES · VOLUME 1

THE GOLDEN AGE SPECTRE ARCHIVES
Volume 1 *(The Astral Avenger's early adventures from MORE FUN COMICS)*

THE GOLDEN AGE SANDMAN ARCHIVES
Volume 1 *(The adventures of Wesley Dodds from ADVENTURE COMICS)*

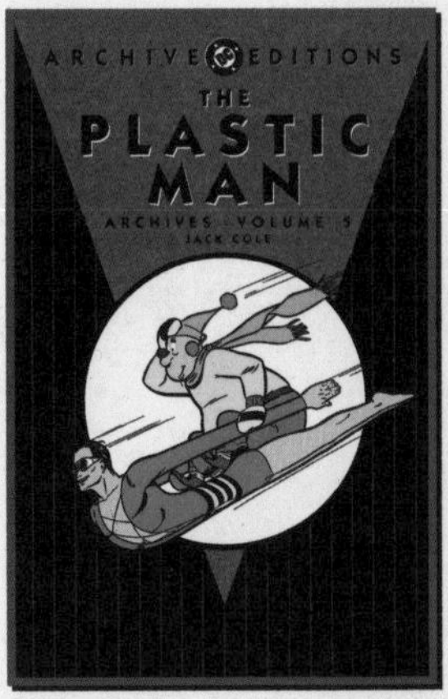
ARCHIVE EDITIONS
THE
PLASTIC
MAN
JACK COLE

THE PLASTIC MAN ARCHIVES
Volumes 1-7 *(The Pliable Paladin's adventures from POLICE COMICS and PLASTIC MAN)*

THE SGT. ROCK ARCHIVES
Volumes 1-3 *(Battle tales of Easy Company from the pages of OUR ARMY AT WAR and more)*

THE SHAZAM! ARCHIVES
Volumes 1-4 *(Captain Marvel's adventures from WHIZ COMICS, CAPTAIN MARVEL ADVENTURES and SPECIAL EDITION COMICS)*

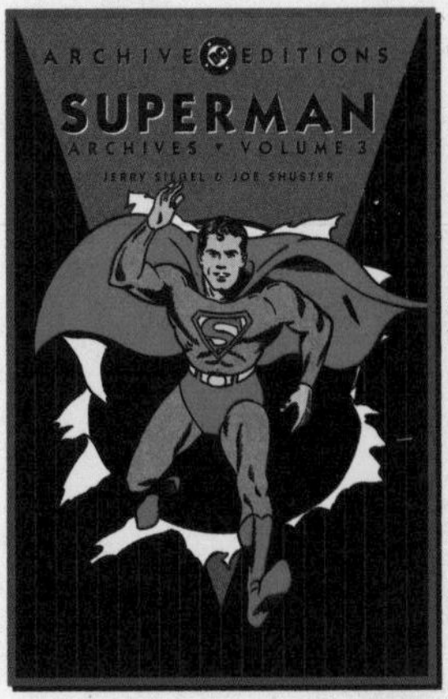
ARCHIVE EDITIONS
SUPERMAN
ARCHIVES · VOLUME 3
JERRY SIEGEL & JOE SHUSTER

SUPERMAN ARCHIVES
Volumes 1-6 *(The Man of Steel's early adventures from SUPERMAN)*

THE SEVEN SOLDIERS OF VICTORY ARCHIVES
Volume 1 *(The Golden Age adventures of Law's Legion)*

WONDER WOMAN ARCHIVES
Volumes 1-4 *(The Amazing Amazon's adventures from SENSATION COMICS and WONDER WOMAN)*

To find more collected editions and monthly comic books from DC Comics, call 1-888-COMIC BOOK for the nearest comics shop or visit your local bookstore.

Visit us at www.dccomics.com

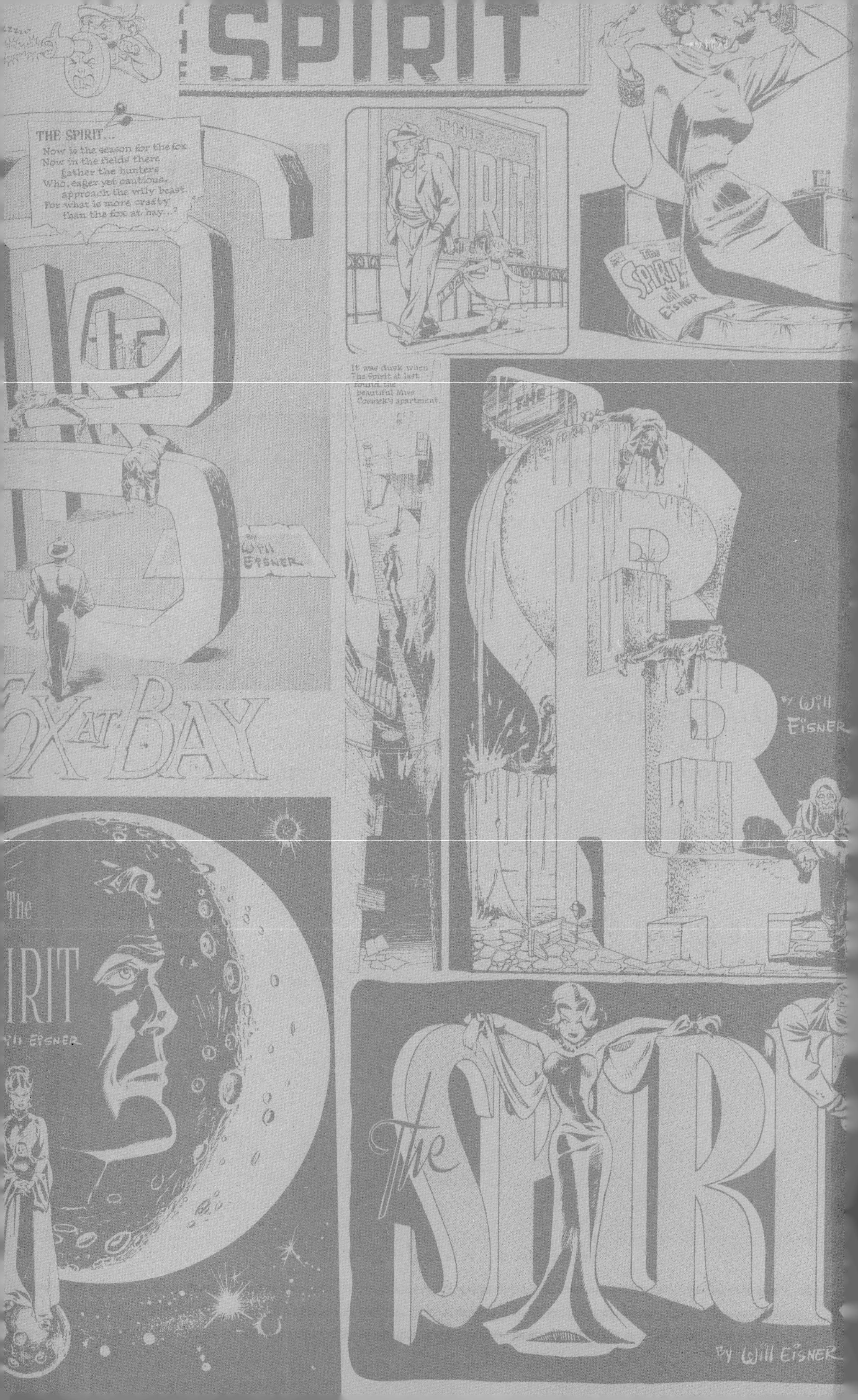
SPIRIT
THE SPIRIT...
Now is the season for the fox.
Now in the fields there
gather the hunters
Who, eager yet cautious,
approach the wily beast...
For what is more crafty
than the fox at bay...?
By Will Eisner
It was dusk when
The Spirit at last
found the
beautiful Miss
The Spirit
by Will Eisner
By Will Eisner
The Spirit
By Will Eisner